99. 62 (set) Batfield 5-67 (Huffon)

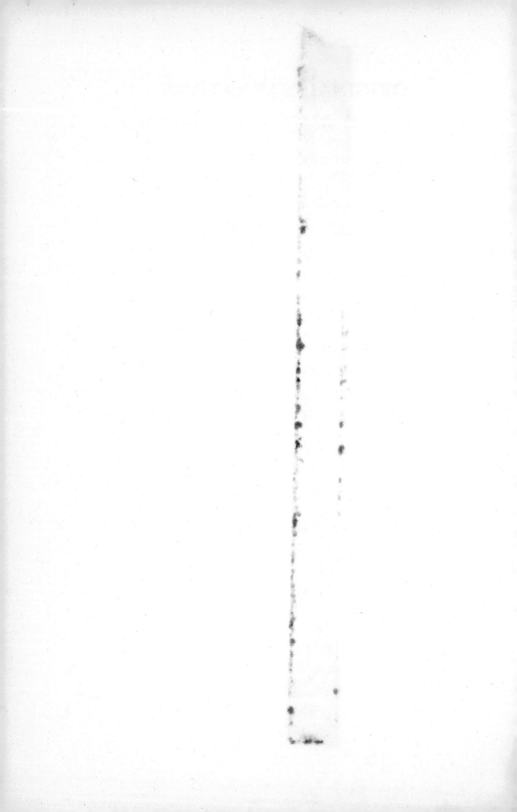

ORIGINAL NARRATIVES
OF EARLY AMERICAN HISTORY

REPRODUCED UNDER THE AUSPICES OF THE
AMERICAN HISTORICAL ASSOCIATION

GENERAL EDITOR, J. FRANKLIN JAMESON, PH.D., LL.D., LITT.D.

DIRECTOR OF THE DEPARTMENT OF HISTORICAL RESEARCH IN THE
CARNEGIE INSTITUTION OF WASHINGTON

ORIGINAL NARRATIVES
OF EARLY AMERICAN HISTORY

No. 12

SPANISH EXPLORATION
IN THE SOUTHWEST
1542—1706

EDITED BY

HERBERT EUGENE BOLTON, Ph.D.

LATE PROFESSOR OF AMERICAN HISTORY, UNIVERSITY OF CALIFORNIA

New York

BARNES & NOBLE, INC.

CONTENTS

SPANISH EXPLORATION IN THE SOUTHWEST

Edited by Herbert Eugene Bolton

CONTENTS

CONTENTS

viii CONTENTS

CONTENTS

ix

PREFACE

THIS volume is logically the successor in the series of Original Narratives to the one edited by Hodge and Lewis under the title of *Spanish Explorers in the Southern United States*, 1528–1543. In one important respect the present volume differs from the series in general. The other volumes consist mainly of reproductions of documents which have hitherto appeared in English; but of this volume approximately only one-third of the documents have hitherto been published in English; about one-third have been published in Spanish only; while nearly one-third have never been published hitherto in any language. Of the five documents in the collection which formerly have been published in English, three have been retranslated for this work.

In the selection of the documents it was decided to illustrate with some fullness the cardinal episodes in the history of the region and period covered, rather than to treat more lightly a larger number of topics. This procedure has left the history of seventeenth-century New Mexico almost a blank after its founding by Oñate. The brief historical introductions are designed to increase the interest and intelligibility of the documents by giving a connected view of the development of the whole northern frontier of New Spain during the period covered, as well as to furnish the necessary biographical and bibliographical data.

Of the translations here reprinted, that of Massanet's *Carta* is by Professor Lilia M. Casís, of the University of Texas; and that of De León's *Itinerary* of 1689 is by Miss Elizabeth Howard West, formerly state archivist of Texas. The remaining documents were translated for this work by the editor, assisted by Mrs. Beatrice Quijada Cornish, Mrs. Edith C. Galbraith, Mrs. Anne Hughes Kean, and Miss Elizabeth Howard West. For the final form of the translations the editor is in each case responsible. Thanks are due to Reverend Father Thomas Lantry O'Neill, C. S. P., of Newman Hall, Berkeley, California, and to Reverend Father Zephyrin Engelhardt, O. F. M., of Santa Barbara, California, for assistance in the rendering of expressions relating to matters of Catholic doctrine and Church practices.

H. E. BOLTON.

INTRODUCTION

WITH the discovery of the South Sea by Balboa the Spaniards began to make their way northwest along the Pacific coast. By 1543 the entire coast line had been run from Panamá to Oregon, not to mention the discoveries on the western shores of South America. In conducting these voyages along the seaboard of the northern continent the leading part was played by Hernando Cortés, but the work was brought to a culmination, in the exploration of the California coast, by the viceroy Mendoza.

Cortés had scarcely made himself master of the central valley of Mexico before he sent his lieutenants in all directions to follow up reports and rumors of other rich provinces. In 1521 Olid subdued Michoacán, lying to the westward, and in the following year a shipyard was established at Zacatula, on the South Sea, as a base for maritime exploration. Other maritime bases were soon provided at Tehuantepec and Navidad, as well as farther south on the coast of Central America. Among the leading motives for coastwise exploration were rumors of rich districts such as the Amazon Island and the Seven Cities to the northward, and a belief in the existence, in the same direction, of a strait leading from the Atlantic to the Pacific.[1]

[1] Interest in the Amazon Island is illustrated by Cortés's instructions given at Colima in 1524 to his relative, Francisco Cortés, whom he orders to continue exploration, "because I am informed that down the coast which borders the said villa there are many provinces thickly inhabited by people and containing, it is believed, great riches, and that in these parts of it there is one which is inhabited by women, with no men, who procreate in the way which the ancient histories ascribe to the Amazons, and because by learning the truth regarding this and whatever else there is on said coast, God our Lord and their Majesties will be greatly served" (Pacheco and Cárdenas, *Documentos Inéditos*, XXVI. 153).

Interest in the strait is illustrated by a letter of Cortés to the Emperor, written in October, 1524. It states, "I saw that nothing more remained for me to do but to learn the secret of the coast which is yet to be explored between the Rio Pánuco and Florida . . . and thence the coast of the said Florida northward to Bacallaos [Newfoundland]; for it is deemed certain that on that coast there is a strait which passes to the South Sea; and if it should be found, according to a certain map which I have of the region of the archipelago discovered by Magellan by order of your Highness, it seems that it would come out very near there; and if it should please God that the said strait be found there, the voyage from the spice region to your kingdom would be very easy and very short, so much so that it would be less by two-thirds than by the route now followed, and that without any risk to the vessels coming and going, because they would always come and go through your dominions, so that in case of necessity they could be repaired without danger wherever they might wish to enter port."[1]

Misfortunes caused delay in the enterprise of exploration on the South Sea, but in 1527 Saavedra was sent up the coast and reached Santiago. In 1531 conquests by land were extended to Culiacán by Guzmán, who was led north by rumors of the Amazon Island and of the Seven Cities. After several years of interruption, Cortés again pushed north by water. Hurtado de Mendoza, sent by the conqueror in 1532, reached Rio Fuerte. In the following year Jiménez discovered the Peninsula of California. In 1535 Cortés himself led a colony to Puerto de la Paz, but within a few months the enterprise was abandoned.

Renewed interest in northward exploration was aroused by the reports given by Cabeza de Vaca, who reached Culiacán in 1536, after six years of wandering across the continent.

[1] Quoted in Bancroft. *North Mexican States*, I. 5, foot-note.

In 1539 Friar Marcos, sent by Mendoza by land, reached what he called the Seven Cities of Cíbola (Zuñi). His reports caused new enthusiasm, and Mendoza, Cortés, and Pedro de Alvarado all prepared to win honors in further exploration. Cortés in 1539 sent Ulloa northward with three vessels. He ascended to the head of the Gulf, sailed round the extremity of the Peninsula, and reached Cabo del Engaño, in latitude 29° 56′. This voyage made known the peninsular character of California. Mendoza in 1540 sent out the Coronado expedition, in the course of which Alarcón explored the lower Colorado River, Cárdenas discovered the Grand Canyon, and Coronado marched northeastward as far as central Kansas. Alvarado prepared a fleet and formed a partnership with Mendoza for northern discovery, but was killed in 1541 in the Mixton War. His death left the fleet in the hands of Mendoza, who in 1542 sent a part of it across the Pacific to the Philippines under Villalobos, and the rest up the California coast under Cabrillo, in the hope of finding the northern strait, and thereby a new route to Europe. It is the diary of the last-mentioned expedition which is given hereinafter.

Of Juan Rodríguez Cabrillo, commander of the expedition, little is known except that he was a Portuguese by birth and a skilled mariner.[1] There are indications that he had been with Cortés in the conquest of Mexico, and later with Alvarado.[2] For the expedition the *San Salvador*, flagship, and the *Victoria*, a *fragata* or frigate, were equipped. As chief pilot went Bartolomé Ferrelo (Ferrer, Ferrel); as pilot Bartolomé Fernández; and as masters, Antonio Carrera and S. Remo. Concerning Ferrelo, who became commander after the death of Cabrillo, little is known except that he was a native of the Levant. Of the outfit Davidson writes: "The vessels were

[1] "Persona muy platica en las cosas de la Mar" (Herrera, *Historia General*, dec. VII., lib. V., cap. III., p. 89).
[2] Bancroft, *North Mexican States*, I. 133; Lowery, *Spanish Settlements*, I. 340.

smaller than any of our coasting schooners. They were poorly built and very badly outfitted. Their anchors and ironwork were carried by men from the Gulf of Mexico to the Pacific; they were manned by conscripts and natives; were badly provisioned, and the crews subject to that deadly scourge of the sea, scurvy."[1]

The start was made on June 27, 1542, from Puerto de Navidad, a port twenty miles above Manzanillo, in latitude 19° 13'. The vessels returned to the same point on April 14, 1543, nine and one-half months later, having explored the entire Pacific coast to latitude $42\frac{1}{2}°$, all that part of the voyage above Cabo del Engaño being in unknown waters.

On July 3 Cabrillo reached the southern extremity of the Peninsula, and on the 19th Magdalena Bay, called in the diary Puerto de San Pedro. On August 5 he anchored at Cerros Island, near the northern limits of Ulloa's exploration. On August 21 he discovered Port San Quentín. Going ashore next day, he took formal possession of the country in the name of the king and viceroy, in honor of which ceremony the harbor was named Puerto de la Posesión. The Indians here made signs which were understood to mean that they had seen Spaniards before—men with beards, dogs, and Spanish weapons—and that they were now five days inland. To communicate with these men, if perchance the report were true, Cabrillo left a letter to be delivered by the Indians. In all probability the report was genuine, and referred to Coronado's party, which was now in the interior.

On September 28 Cabrillo discovered "a port enclosed and very good, to which they gave the name of San Miguel." It was the beautiful San Diego Bay. Here again they were told by the natives of Spaniards in the interior. While at this

---

[1] Geographical Society of the Pacific, *Transactions and Proceedings*, second ser., IV. (1907) 13.

place a storm arose, the first they had encountered, but the harbor was so good that no damage was done.

Continuing up the coast, they discovered and named Santa Catalina and San Clemente Islands, which they called San Salvador and La Victoria, in honor of the vessels. Santa Monica Bay they called Bahía de los Fumos. Reaching San Buenaventura (Pueblo de las Canoas) on October 10, Cabrillo again went ashore and took formal possession of the country. Here once more they heard of white men in the interior, and at a venture despatched to them a letter.

Leaving San Buenaventura on the 13th, they sailed west through the Santa Barbara channel, anchoring at Rincón, at the Carpintería, above Point Goleta, at Cañada del Refugio, and at Gaviota Pass, and on October 18 reached Point Concepción, at the western extremity of the channel. As they passed they noted Santa Cruz and Santa Rosa Islands to their left, but, supposing them to be only one, named them La Isla de San Lucas.

At Point Concepción their real difficulties began. Encountering a strong northwest wind, they stood off from the shore and distinguished San Miguel and Santa Rosa Islands, to which they now gave the plural name of Las Islas de San Lucas. Making port at Cuyler's Harbor on San Miguel Island, they took formal possession, calling it Isla de la Posesión. While here Cabrillo suffered a fall and a broken arm. Rounding Point Concepción in an attempt to continue north, they encountered another storm and returned to the Indian town of Cicacut, or Pueblo de las Sardinas, at Gaviota Pass.

Weighing anchor again on November 6, they succeeded in rounding Point Concepción, and sailed up the coast in sight of Santa Lucía Mountain. Standing out to sea in a heavy southwester shortly before reaching Point Pinos, which they sighted, they did not make land again till November 14, having passed and missed the Bay of Monterey, Point Año Nuevo,

Half Moon Bay, the Golden Gate, and Drake's Bay. On the way up the vessels became separated in the storm. Fair weather returning, the flagship stood in toward the coast in search of her consort, and on November 14 sighted land near Northwest Cape (Cabo de Pinos), in latitude 38° 31′, near Fort Ross. Next day the two vessels were reunited.

Turning south, driven now by a storm from the opposite direction, on November 16 they discovered Drake's Bay, in latitude 38°, calling it Bahía de los Pinos. Running rapidly southward, again missing the Golden Gate, but noting on the way the Gulf of the Farallones, the Santa Cruz Mountains (Las Sierras Nevadas) and Black Mountain (Cabo de Nieve), on the night of the 18th they were opposite Point Pinos. On the 23d they put in again at Cuyler's Harbor (Puerto de la Posesión) on San Miguel Island. Since they had found no shelter after leaving Northwest Cape, above Point Pinos, and had missed Monterey Bay, it is inferred that they could not have run very near the coast on the return voyage.

On San Miguel Island, which the natives called Ciqui-muymu, Cabrillo's party spent the winter from November 23 to January 19, two months of almost continuous storms. On January 3 Cabrillo died, as a result of his fall while on the same island before. In his honor the place was named Isla de Juan Rodríguez.

The command now fell to Ferrelo, who made another attempt at northward exploration. Weighing anchor on January 19, 1543, to go to the mainland for supplies, he was driven by a storm among the islands for eight days, after which he returned to the port on San Miguel Island.

On January 29, before heading north, Ferrelo went to Santa Rosa Island to recover some anchors which he had left at that place in the storm. Remaining there till February 12, on that day he went to Cicacut (Gaviota Pass), whence he returned to Santa Cruz Island for greater security. Starting out again on Sunday the 18th, he sailed southwest, standing out to sea five days. At the end of that time, and after running about one hundred leagues, he stood in again, in an endeavor to reach Northwest Cape (Cabo de Pinos), the northwestern limit of Cabrillo's voyage.

On the morning of the 25th, after having been driven in a storm for three days, he saw the object of his search. Toward night Punta de Arena was sighted, in latitude 38° 57'. Running before the wind all night, next morning he was opposite King's Peak (Cabo de Fortunas), in latitude 40°. He continued before the wind during the 27th, but at night it veered toward the west and he ran south in a high sea, with lowered sail. At daybreak of the 28th the wind shifted to the southwest again, and Ferrelo once more ran north. That day he observed latitude 43°, which Davidson corrects to 41½°. Scudding again before the storm that night, next day, March 1, he reached his farthest north. Ferrelo gives the latitude 44°, which Davidson corrects to 42½°, placing the limit of the voyage about at Rogue River, Oregon.[1]

In the afternoon of the 28th a heavy rain-storm from the north occurred and the return voyage began. On March 3 they passed Point Arena and Northwest Cape. On the night of the 4th the vessels separated, and were not reunited till they reached Cerros Island, three weeks later.

On the 5th the flagship was off San Miguel Island, but could not put into port because of a storm; accordingly it sought shelter on Santa Cruz Island. From here it crossed over on the 8th to San Buenaventura, in search of the consort, but returned on the 9th. On the 11th it reached San Diego Bay, where it waited six days for the other vessel. Setting sail on the 17th, it reached Todos Santos Bay on the

---

[1] Davidson thinks they did not see land above Punta de Arena (Geographical Society of the Pacific, *Transactions and Proceedings*, second ser., IV. 16). In this he is borne out by the diary.

18th, Puerto de San Quentín on the 19th, and Cerros Island on the 24th. Here, on the 26th, it was joined by the *fragata*. The latter vessel had passed by San Miguel Island in the storm on the night of the 4th or the 5th, and had taken shelter at Santa Rosa Island.

Leaving Cerros Island together on April 2, on April 14 the two vessels put into Puerto de Navidad, whence they had set out in the previous June.

Regarding Cabrillo's voyage as a feat of navigation under difficulties, the following quotation from Navarrete is apt:

Those who know the coast which Cabrillo discovered and explored, the kind of vessels in which he undertook the expedition, the rigorous season during which he pursued his voyage in those intemperate climes, and the state of the science of navigation at that period, cannot help admiring a courage and intrepidity which, though common among sea-faring Spaniards of that time, cannot be appreciated in our day, when the navigator is fairly dazzled by the assistance furnished him through the wonderful progress of the arts and sciences, rendering his operations easier and supplying him with advantages which, as they were lacking to the early discoverers, make their courage and perseverance as portentous as their discoveries. Perhaps it is failure to realize these considerations, added to ignorance of our history, which has led some foreign writers to belittle the merit of Cabrillo.

The source of most of what is known of the Cabrillo expedition is the diary hereinafter published, although Herrera and Navarrete give a few slight additions from other sources.[1] The authorship of the diary is not known with certainty. It has been attributed to Ferrelo and also to Juan Paez,[2] with whom the weight of the evidence seems to be.

[1] Antonio Herrera, *Historia General de los Hechos de los Castellanos en las Islas y Tierra Firme del Mar Oceano*, decada setima (Madrid, 1728), lib. V., caps. III., IV., pp. 89–91; Martín Fernández Navarrete, *Relacion del Viage hecho por las Goletas Sutil y Mexicana* (Madrid, 1802), Introducción, pp. xxix.–xxxv. It is clear from Herrera's language in places that he used the Paez diary.

[2] Lowery, I. 340, note; Bancroft, *History of California*, I. 69, note; Henshaw in Wheeler, *Report upon United States Geographical Surveys*, vol. VII., p. 294.

The diary was published in Spanish in 1857 by Buckingham Smith in his *Colección de Varios Documentos para la Historia de la Florida y Tierras Adyacentes* (London), pp. 173–189, from an unsigned contemporary manuscript in the Archivo General de Indias at Seville, among the papers transferred from Simancas, *legajo* 9 of Descripciones y Poblaciones. Another Spanish version was printed in 1870 by Pacheco and Cárdenas in their *Colección de Documentos Inéditos* (Madrid), XIV. 165–191. This text is from an unsigned manuscript in the Archivo General de Indias, Patronato, *est.* 1, *caj.* 1. In the title given it by the editors the authorship is ascribed to Paez. This text and that of Buckingham Smith seem to be from the same original, though there are numerous unimportant differences of spelling, accentuation, and capitalization, the text in Pacheco and Cárdenas being modernized in these respects. Another manuscript copy is in the Muñoz Collection. It bears an annotation ascribing the narrative to Paez. The differences between it and the Buckingham Smith copy are noted by Navarrete on the copy which Smith used.[1]

An English translation by Richard Stuart Evans, made from the Buckingham Smith text, was published in Wheeler, *Report upon United States Geographical Surveys West of the One Hundredth Meridian* (Washington, 1879), VII. 293–314. The title there given is "Translation from the Spanish of the Account by the Pilot Ferrel of the Voyage of Cabrillo along the West Coast of North America in 1542. With Introductory Notes by H. W. Henshaw." Another translation, based on Evans's, but with some differences "in critical passages where important issues were involved," was published in 1886 by Professor George Davidson in his study entitled "An Examination of some of the Early Voyages of Discovery and Exploration on the Northwest Coast of America, from 1539 to 1603," printed in the *Report of the Superintendent of the U. S.*

---

[1] *Col. Doc. Florida*, p. 189.

Coast and Geodetic Survey for 1886 (Washington), pp. 160–241. Numerous inaccuracies and defects in form in the foregoing versions made it seem best to prepare a new translation for this work, which has been done, but with due acknowledgment of indebtedness to my predecessors.

The most important contribution toward the identification of places named or noted by the diary is that by Professor Davidson cited above. Davidson had rare opportunities for this work, and he made excellent use of them. In my identifications and assignments of latitudes I have followed him throughout unless otherwise stated, and I hereby acknowledge my obligation to this great scholar. Davidson made a map identifying the places named by Cabrillo and Vizcaino with modern names.

To the student of exploration the diary is of the first importance. On the whole the record is very good. This is evidenced by the fact that Davidson was able to identify with practical certainty some seventy of the points mentioned by the diary along the coast. Paez's distances are only approximate, and in general his latitudes are too high, those on the coast of Upper California requiring correction from half a degree to a degree and a half. To the student of ethnology the diary is of great interest as the record of the first contact of white men with the Indians of California above latitude 30°.

The translation is based on the Buckingham Smith text, in *Col. Doc. Florida*, pp. 173–189. An awkward feature of the diary, which could not be avoided in the translation without taking too great liberties, is the indiscriminate and sometimes confusing use of the first and the third person. Likewise, tenses are often confused.

RELATION OF THE VOYAGE OF JUAN RODRIGUEZ CABRILLO, 1542–1543

Relation or Diary of the Voyage made by Juan Rodriguez Cabrillo with two Ships, for the Discovery of the Passage from the South Sea at the North, from the twenty-seventh of June, 1542, when he left the Port of Navidad, to the fourteenth of April of the following Year, when he returned to it, having gone as far as the Latitude of Forty-four Degrees; with the Description of the Coast, Ports, Bays, and Islands which he Examined, and their Distances, on the Whole Extent of that Coast.

JUAN RODRIGUEZ set sail from the port of Navidad[1] to explore the coast of New Spain on the 27th of June, 1542. Between the port of Navidad and Cape Corriente,[2] forty leagues, it took him a day and a night, with a southeast wind. From Wednesday until the following Thursday they held their course along the coast thirty-five leagues. Sunday, July 2, they sighted California. On account of the weather, which was not very favorable, it took them almost four days to cross over. On the following Monday, the 3d of the same month, they anchored at the Point of California.[3] Here they remained two days, and from here they went to the port of San Lucas[4] on the following Thursday and took on water. During these days they did not see a single Indian.

---

[1] Navidad is a port on the coast of Mexico in lat. 19° 13′, and twenty miles west-northwest from the harbor of Manzanillo. "This is the port in which were built the ships which discovered the Philippine Islands and with which, as I have said, Cape Mendocino had been discovered. It was to this port that the ships from China used to come before that of Acapulco was discovered" (Torquemada, *Monarchia Indiana*, I. 696).

[2] Cape Corrientes, lat. 20° 25′. Reached on June 28 (Herrera, *Historia General*, dec. VII., lib. V., cap. III.).

[3] Probably Cape Pulmo, lat. 23° 23′.

[4] San Lucas Bay, lat. 22° 52′. Herrera states that on July 2 they were in lat. 24° and examined the Puerto del Marqués del Valle, which they call "de la Cruz" (*Historia General*, dec. VII., lib. V., cap. III.).

They say that this port is in twenty-three degrees. From the point to the port the coast is clear and soundable; the land is bare and rough.

They left the port of San Lucas on Thursday, at night, and on the following Saturday, the 8th of the same month, they anchored under Trinidad Point,[1] which is in twenty-five degrees. It must be about five leagues from San Lucas. The coast is clear, without any irregularity. Inland are seen high, bald, and rugged mountains. They remained at anchor here until the following Wednesday, on account of contrary winds from the west-northwest.

On Wednesday, the 12th of the said month, they left there. At the port of Trinidad[2] a harbor is formed by an island[3] which is there; and it is a good port, sheltered from the west-northwest winds. The port of the island is at its head, on the southeast side. It is a clear and soundable port, but it contains neither water nor wood. The island must be ten leagues long and two leagues wide. They cast anchor that night.

They set sail on the following Thursday, and passed the port of San Pedro,[4] which is in twenty-five and one-half degrees. In this port there is neither water nor wood. Its passage is southeastward. It affords good shelter from west winds. They went sailing along the coast, which forms a large bay,[5] the head of which is in twenty-six degrees. The land is low, with sand dunes, the coast white and clear. They went sailing along it with favorable winds up to twenty-seven degrees, and on Wednesday, the 19th, they landed at a port which they found. Having gone ashore, they found a road used by the Indians and followed it the distance of an arquebus shot, when they found a spring. The interior of the country is level, bare, and very dry. They named it the port of Madalena.[6]

---

[1] Cape Tosco, lat. 24° 17', and 130 miles from Cape San Lucas. "There must be some omission in Ferrelo's narrative wherein he gives the distance of five leagues from Cape San Lucas to Cape Tosco. The actual distance is 43 leagues along the coast" (Davidson, *Early Voyages*, p. 162).

[2] Santa Marina Bay, lat. 24° 20'.

[3] Santa Margarita Island, lat. 24° 17'.   [4] Magdalena Bay, lat. 24° 32'.

[5] *Ensenada*. Evans generally renders this word as "creek." Davidson changes the translation here to "gulf."

[6] Pequeña Bay and Point, lat. 26° 14', thirty leagues from Santa María Bay

From the Bay of San Martin[1] to this port it must be about forty leagues.

On the following Thursday, the 20th of the same month, they left this port and sailed along the coast with contrary winds, and about six leagues from it they found anchorage behind a point which they call Santa Catalina Point.[2] And thus they continued sailing along the coast; and on the following Tuesday, the 25th of the said month of July, they discovered a large bay in twenty-seven and one-half degrees. They made very little headway these days on account of the contrary winds. They anchored in this port and named it the port of Santiago.[3] It must be about twenty-three leagues from the port of Madalena. Five leagues from the port of Santiago there are some very dangerous, rocky shoals, which are invisible except when the sea breaks over them. They are a league from the shore, and are in a little over twenty-seven and one-half degrees. They are called Habre Ojo.[4] They continued sailing along the coast by the same course up to twenty-eight degrees, where they cast anchor in the shelter of a headland. Here there are groves of trees, the first which they had seen since leaving the Point of California. From this headland to the port of Santiago, at its northwestern point, it must be about twenty-three leagues. There are high, rugged mountains with some timber. We named the point Santa Ana.[5] About a league from shore there is a small island.[6]

[1] Santa Maria Bay, lat. 24° 44', four leagues northwestward from the entrance to Magdalena Bay. The diary mentions Puerto de la Madalena and Bahía de San Martín in the reverse order of that in which Cabrillo reached them.

[2] San Domingo Point and anchorage, lat. 26° 19', thirteen miles west-northwest from Pequeña Bay.

[3] Ballenas Bay, lat. 26° 45', under Abreojos Point, seventy-six miles from Pequeña Bay and fifty-four from San Domingo Point.

[4] Abreojos Rocks, lat. 26° 46', three miles west-southwest from Abreojos Point. Navarrete identifies Santiago with Abreojos, but it is seen that the diary distinguishes between them (Navarrete, *Sutil y Mexicana*, Introducción, p. xxix.). "Abre ojos" means "open the eyes," or "look out!"

[5] Asunción Point and anchorage, lat. 27° 7', forty-seven miles in a straight line from Abreojos Point. Navarrete places Puerto de Santa Ana far out of its order in the journey (*Sutil y Mexicana*, Introducción, p. xxix.).

[6] Island of San Roque, lat. 27° 9'. Discovered by Ulloa but not then named. It is only a mile long and half a mile wide.

On Thursday, the 27th of the same month, they left the said port of Santa Ana and went to anchor about six leagues from there in a port which they named Puerto Fondo[1] (Deep Port), because of its great depth, for near the shore it was thirty fathoms; it is clear. Next day they left this port, but three times returned to take shelter in it from contrary winds, and remained in it until the following Monday.

On Monday, the 31st of the said month, they left the said Puerto Fondo and anchored that night about eight leagues[2] from there; next day they continued their voyage.

Tuesday, the 1st day of August, they departed from there and went about ten leagues, when they cast anchor in a port which they named San Pedro Vincula.[3] This port is in sight of Zedros Island. It is in a little over twenty-eight and one-half degrees. The land is high, rough, and bare. From California to this point we have not seen a single Indian.

On Wednesday, the 2d of the month, they left this port; the wind was contrary and they proceeded, beating; they went to cast anchor at an island which is southeast of Zedros Island and four leagues from it. This island, which they called San Esteban,[4] is west of the extremity of the point of the mainland, and its coast runs from northwest to southeast. It is a league from the mainland. From this point the coast of the mainland turns east-northeast and forms a bay so large that the land is not visible. Between the island and the mainland there is a good channel, but they have to pass close to the island because there is a reef underneath which extends a fourth of a league from the point. There is much vegetation on the water which grows on the bottom and is fastened below. This island is northwest of San Pedro Vincula. It must be about three leagues in circumference. We remained at this island, with contrary winds, until the following Saturday, the 5th of the said month of August. It has a good port on the

[1] Table-Head Cove, or San Pablo Bay, lat. 27° 11′, about ten miles from Asunción Point.

[2] Bay of San Christóval, eight miles east of Morro Hermoso.

[3] Port San Bartolomé, lat. 27° 39′, eleven and one-half leagues from Table-Head Cove.

[4] Natividad Island, lat. 27° 53′, discovered by Ulloa but not named. Its southern part is three leagues from Cerros Island (Davidson, *Early Voyages*, pp. 173-174).

southeast side.   There is good fishing with a hook, and there
are many birds.

They left the island of San Estevan on Saturday, the 5th
of August, and went to anchor at the island of Zedros,[1] where
they remained until Thursday, the 10th of the said month,
taking on water and wood.   They found no Indians, although
they found signs of them.   The leeward point of this island,
on the south side, is in twenty-nine degrees, and it has on this
south side good ports, water, and wood.   On this side it is
bare, for it has only some small shrubs.   The island is large,
high, and bare, and trends almost from east to west; on the
south side it must be about twelve leagues long.

They left the island of Zedros on Thursday, the 10th of the
said month of August, to continue their voyage, and followed
the curve of the mainland, sailing north.   They went this
day about ten leagues, and on the Friday following they went
to anchor at a harbor which they called the port of Santa
Clara.[2]   It is a good port.   They went ashore and found four
Indians, who fled.   This port is in thirty degrees, scant.   It
is northeast of the island of Zedros, and from the port toward
the bay this coast runs from north-northwest to south-southeast.   The coast is clear and soundable; the land is bare, and
is not rough; it has plains and valleys.   They remained in
this port till Sunday, the 13th of the said month, on account
of the foul winds.

On Sunday, the 13th of said month, they left this port and
sailed along the coast with light winds, casting anchor every
night; and on the following Tuesday they anchored under a
point which forms a bay which is in thirty and one-half degrees.
It affords little shelter.   They called it Punta del Mal Abrigo[3]
(Point of Poor Shelter).

[1] Cerros Island, lat. 28° 2′ at its southernmost point.   It was discovered by
Ulloa and named by him La Isla de los Cedros, but the name became changed
to Cerros, because it has numerous high peaks (Davidson, *Early Voyages*, p. 174).

[2] La Playa María Bay, lat. 28° 55′, about seventeen leagues northeast of
the north end of Cerros Island.

[3] Probably Point Canoas, lat. 29° 25′, or, possibly, Bluff Point, lat. 29° 34′.
"Working back from San Geronimo Island, one of these points must be that
which Cabrillo intended to designate as Mal Abrijo" (Davidson, *Early Voyages*,
p. 178).   Navarrete identifies Punta del Mal Abrigo with Point Canoas (*Sutil
y Mexicana*, Introducción, p. xxix.).

On the following Wednesday they sailed along the coast, against a strong northwest headwind, and remained in shelter that night without making any headway. The following Thursday they continued amid heavy rains, headwinds, and calms, so that they did not make land. The following night they encountered a heavy west-northwest wind and sought shelter. The following Friday they sailed with favorable winds and found themselves six leagues to the windward of the Point of Mal Abrigo. Thus they continued until the following Saturday, the 19th of the said month, when they cast anchor at a small island which is half a league from the mainland. It must be about ten leagues from the Point of Mal Abrigo. It is in thirty and one-half degrees. It has a good anchorage and good shelter. They called it San Bernardo.[1] It must be about a league long from north to south. The coast of the mainland runs from north-northwest to south-southeast. It is a clear coast. The interior of the country looks very good and level; there are good valleys and some timber, the rest being bare. During these days they saw no sign of Indians.

On Sunday, the 20th of said month of August, they left the island of San Bernardo and approached Point Engaño,[2] which must be about seven leagues from this island, and is in thirty-one degrees. From the point toward the island the coast runs from north-northwest to south-southeast. At Point Engaño the land is not high, and it appears to be good and level; the mountains are bare. We saw no sign of Indians. And thus they sailed along until the next Monday, following the coast to the north and northeast; and about ten leagues from Point Engaño they discovered a good port, in which they cast anchor and took on water and wood. It is in thirty-one and one-half degrees. It is a port suitable for making any kind of repairs on ships, placing them in a secure spot.[3]

On the following Tuesday Captain Juan Rodriguez Cabrillo

---

[1] San Gerónimo Island, lat. 29° 48', eight leagues from Bluff Point and thirteen from Point Canoas.

[2] Punta Baja, lat. 29° 56', eight and one-half miles northwest of San Gerónimo Island. Herrera calls it Cabo del Engaño (*Historia General*, dec. VII., lib. V., cap. III.).

[3] *Poniendoles a monte.*

went ashore, took possession there in the name of his Majesty and of the most Illustrious Señor Don Antonio de Mendoza, and named it port of La Posesion[1] (port of the Possession). He found a lake which has three large[2] . . . . . . , and found some Indian fishermen, who forthwith fled. They captured one of them; giving him a few presents they released him and he departed. The interior of the country consists of high and rugged land, but it has good valleys and appears to be good country, although bare. They remained in this place until Sunday, the 27th of said month, repairing the sails and taking on water. On Thursday they saw some smokes and, going to them with the boat, they found some thirty Indian fishermen, who remained where they were. They brought to the ship a boy and two women, gave them clothing and presents, and let them go. From them they could understand nothing by signs.

On the Friday following, on going to get water, they found in the watering place some Indians who remained quiet and showed them a pool of water, and a saline which contained a large quantity of salt. They said by signs that they did not live there, but inland, and that there were many people. This same day, in the afternoon, five Indians came to the beach; they brought them to the ships and they appeared to be intelligent Indians. Entering the ship they pointed at and counted the Spaniards who were there, and said by signs that they had seen other men like them, who wore beards, and who brought dogs, and crossbows, and swords. The Indians came smeared over with a white paste on the thighs, body, and arms, and wore the paste like slashes, so that they appeared like men in hose and slashed doublets. They made signs that Spaniards were five days from there. They made signs that there were many Indians, and that they had much maize and many parrots. They came covered with deerskins; some wore the deerskins dressed in the way the Mexicans dress the skins which they use for their *cutaras*.[3] They are a large and well-

---

[1] Port of San Quentín, lat. 30° 24', twenty-seven miles northwest of Punta Baja, and five or six miles southwest of the village of San Quentín.

[2] Blank in the original.

[3] *Cotaras*, an Americanism meaning a kind of Indian footwear; also applied to Indians' clothing in general. Rendered "cutters" by Evans.

featured people.   They carry their bows and arrows like those of New Spain, the arrows being tipped with flints.   The captain gave them a letter to carry to the Spaniards who they said were in the interior.

They left the port of La Posesion on Sunday, the 27th of the said month of August, and, continuing their course, they discovered an island two leagues from the mainland.   It is uninhabited; there is a good port in it; they named it San Agustin; it must be about two leagues in circumference. They continued thus along the coast with light winds, holding to windward, until the following Wednesday, the 30th of the said month, when they encountered a heavy northwest wind which forced them to seek shelter at the island of San Agustin.[1] On this island they found signs of people, and two cows' horns, and very large trees which the sea had cast there; they were more than sixty feet long and so thick that two men could not reach around one of them.   They looked like cypresses; and there were cedars.   There was a great quantity of this timber, but this island contains nothing else except a good port.   They remained at this island until the following Sunday.

On Sunday, the 3d of the month of September, they left said Island of San Agustin and continued sailing on their course; and on the following Monday they cast anchor at the shore,[2] about seven leagues to the windward, on a coast running north and south.   At once they continued their course, sailing with favorable though light winds on a coast running north and south, until Thursday, the 7th of said month of September, when they went to cast anchor in a bay which the land forms.   Here the coast ceases to run north and south and turns to the northwest.   At this bay there is a large valley; the land is level at the coast, and inland there are high mountains, and rough land which appears to be good.   All the coast is bold, with a smooth and shallow bottom, for at half a league they were at anchor in ten fathoms.   About here there is much vegetation on the water.

On the following Friday, the 8th of said month, they sailed with light winds, working to windward, and encountering ad-

[1] San Martín Island, lat. 30° 29'.
[2] San Ramón or Virgin's Bay, lat. 30° 49'.   Eight or ten miles inland is the old mission of San Vicente (Davidson, *Early Voyages*, p. 188).

verse currents. They went to anchor under a headland which
forms a cape and affords good shelter from the west-northwest.
They named it Cape San Martin.[1] It forms a spur of land
on both sides; here end some high mountains which come
from behind, and here begin other small mountains. There is
one large valley, and many others; apparently the land is
good. The port is in thirty-two and one-half degrees. It is
a clear port and soundable. Its direction from the island
of San Agustin is north.

While at this Cape of San Martin they went ashore for
water and found a small lake of fresh water, where they got
a supply. To this watering place came forty Indians with
bows and arrows. They could not make each other understood. The Indians were naked; they brought roasted
maguey[2] and fish to eat. They are large people. Here they
took possession. They were at this cape until the following
Monday.

On Monday, the 8th of said month,[3] they left Cape San
Martin and sailed some four leagues on a coast running north-
northeast–south-southwest, and from there the coast turns
northwest. The land is high and bare. Next day they sailed
along a coast running from northwest to southeast a matter
of six leagues. All this coast is bold and clear. The next
day they sailed, with foul winds, a matter of four leagues, still
on a coast running from northwest to southeast. On the land
there are high broken mountains. On the following Thursday
they cast anchor about three leagues farther on, under a headland which extends into the sea and forms a cape on both sides.
It is called Cabo de Cruz[4] (Cape of the Cross); it is in thirty-
three degrees. There is neither water nor wood, nor did
they find a sign of Indians.

Having departed from Cabo de la Cruz, because of head-
winds they found themselves on the following Saturday two
leagues from the same cape on a coast running from north-
northwest to south-southeast. At the shore they saw Indians

---

[1] Point Santo Tomás, or Cape San Tomás, lat. 31° 33'. Navarrete identifies this with Cape San Quentín (*Sutil y Mexicana*, Introducción, p. xxx.).

[2] See Espejo documents, p. 170, above, note 5. [3] The eleventh, of course.

[4] Grajero Point, or Banda Point, lat. 31° 45'. The date of anchoring, according to Herrera, was the 14th (*Historia General*, dec. VII., lib. V., cap. III.).

in some very small canoes. The land is very high, bare, and dry. All the land from California to here is sandy near the shore, but here begins land of another sort, the soil being reddish[1] and of better appearance.

On Sunday, the 17th day of the said month, they sailed on in continuation of their voyage, and about six leagues from Cabo de Cruz they found a good and closed port. To reach it they passed a small island[2] which is near the mainland. In this port they took on water from a small lake of rain-water. There are groves of trees like silk-cotton trees, excepting that they are of hard wood. They found thick and tall trees which the sea brings. This port is called San Mateo.[3] The land appears to be good; there are large savannahs,[4] and the grass is like that of Spain. The land is high and broken. They saw some herds of animals like cattle, which went in droves of a hundred or more, and which, from their appearance, from their gait, and the long wool, looked like Peruvian sheep. They have small horns a span in length and as thick as the thumb. The tail is broad and round and a palm long.[5] This place is in thirty-three and one-third degrees. They took possession here. They remained in this port until the following Saturday.

On Saturday, the 23d of said month, they left said port of San Mateo and sailed along the coast until the Monday following, when they must have gone about eighteen leagues. They saw very beautiful valleys and groves, and country both level and rough, but no Indians were seen.

On the following Tuesday and Wednesday they sailed along the coast about eight leagues, passing by some three islands

---

[1] *Cf.* Evans's translation.   [2] The Todos Santos Islands, lat. 31° 48'.

[3] Perhaps the *ensenada* in Todos Santos Bay, lat. 31° 51' (Davidson, *Early Voyages*, p. 190). Navarrete also maintains this opinion (*Sutil y Mexicana*, Introducción, p. xxx.).

[4] *Cf.* Evans's translation.

[5] Henshaw remarks: "The animal here described seems to have been the product of about equal parts of fact and imagination. Without the wool the account would apply tolerably well to the antelope (*Antilocapra americana*), which it probably was. The only animal with a woolly fleece indigenous to this region is the mountain goat (*Haplocerus montanus*), but this animal inhabits only the highest mountains, and hence could not have fallen under the observation of the Spaniards" (*Voyage of Cabrillo*, in Wheeler's *Report*, vol. II., Archæology, p. 304).

completely denuded of soil.[1] One of them is larger than the others. It is about two leagues in circumference and affords shelter from the west winds. They are three leagues from the mainland, and are in thirty-four degrees. They called them Islas Desiertas[2] (Desert Islands). This day great smokes were seen on the land. The country appears to be good and has large valleys, and in the interior there are high mountains.

On the following Thursday they went about six leagues along a coast running north-northwest, and discovered a port, closed and very good, which they named San Miguel.[3] It is in thirty-four and one-third degrees. Having cast anchor in it, they went ashore where there were people. Three of them waited, but all the rest fled. To these three they gave some presents and they said by signs that in the interior men like the Spaniards had passed. They gave signs of great fear. On the night of this day they went ashore from the ships to fish with a net, and it appears that here there were some Indians, and that they began to shoot at them with arrows and wounded three men.

Next day in the morning they went with the boat farther into the port, which is large, and brought two boys, who understood nothing by signs. They gave them both shirts and sent them away immediately.

Next day in the morning three adult Indians came to the ships and said by signs that in the interior men like us were travelling about, bearded, clothed, and armed like those of the ships. They made signs that they carried crossbows and swords; and they made gestures with the right arm as if they were throwing lances, and ran around as if they were on horseback. They made signs that they were killing many native Indians, and that for this reason they were afraid. These people are comely and large. They go about covered with skins of animals. While they were in this port a heavy storm occurred, but since the port is good they did not feel it at all.

---

[1] *Cf.* Evans's translation.

[2] Los Coronados Islands, lat. 32° 25′. Henshaw thought that they were San Clemente and Catalina, but manifestly without good grounds (*Voyage of Cabrillo*, p. 305).

[3] San Diego Bay. The extremity of Point Loma is near lat. 32° 40′.

It was a violent storm from the west-southwest and the south-southwest. This is the first storm which they have experienced. They remained in this port until the following Tuesday. The people here called the Christians Guacamal.

On the following Tuesday, the 3d of the month of October, they departed from this port of San Miguel, and on Wednesday, Thursday, and Friday, they held their course a matter of eighteen leagues along the coast, where they saw many valleys and plains, and many smokes, and mountains in the interior. At nightfall they were near some islands which are some seven leagues from the mainland, but because the wind went down they could not reach them that night.

At daybreak on Saturday, the 7th of the month of October, they were at the islands which they named San Salvador[1] and La Vitoria.[2] They anchored at one of them and went ashore with the boat to see if there were people ; and when the boat came near, a great number of Indians emerged from the bushes and grass, shouting, dancing, and making signs that they should land. As they saw that the women were fleeing, from the boats they made signs that they should not be afraid. Immediately they were reassured, and laid their bows and arrows on the ground and launched in the water a good canoe which held eight or ten Indians, and came to the ships. They gave them beads and other articles, with which they were pleased, and then they returned. Afterward the Spaniards went ashore, and they, the Indian women, and all felt very secure. Here an old Indian made signs to them that men like the Spaniards, clothed and bearded, were going about on the mainland. They remained on this island only till midday.

On the following Sunday, the 8th of said month, they drew near to the mainland in a large bay which they called Bay of Los Fumos,[3] (Bay of the Smokes), because of the many smokes

[1] Santa Catalina Island, lat. 33° 26½' at Isthmus Cove. It is eighteen miles long and twenty-three and one-half miles from Point Lasuén (Davidson, Early Voyages, p. 194). Navarrete identifies San Salvador with the San Clemente, and La Victoria with the Santa Catalina.

[2] San Clemente Island. The latitude of the southeast head is 32° 49'. This and the foregoing island were named after the ships.

[3] Santa Monica Bay, named from Sierra Santa Monica. Latitude of Point Dume, on the north side, 34°. He landed near the point, where there were large villages of Indians to a very late date (Davidson, Early Voyages, p. 196).

which they saw on it.[1] Here they held a colloquy with some
Indians whom they captured in a canoe, and who made signs
that toward the north there were Spaniards like them. This
bay is in thirty-five degrees and is a good port, and the country
is good, with many valleys, plains, and groves.

On the following Monday, the 9th of the said month of
October, they left the Bay of Los Fuegos (the Fires), and
sailed this day some six leagues, anchoring in a large bay.[2]
From here they departed the next day, Tuesday, and sailed
some eight leagues along a coast running from northwest to
southeast. We saw on the land a pueblo of Indians close to
the sea, the houses being large like those of New Spain. They
anchored in front of a very large valley on the coast. Here
there came to the ships many very good canoes, each of which
held twelve or thirteen Indians; they told them of Christians
who were going about in the interior. The coast runs from
northwest to southeast. Here they gave them some presents,
with which they were greatly pleased. They indicated by
signs that in seven days they could go to where the Spaniards
were, and Juan Rodriguez decided to send two Spaniards into
the interior. They also indicated that there was a great river.
With these Indians they sent a letter at a venture to the
Christians. They named this town the Pueblo of Las Canoas.[3]
The Indians dress in skins of animals; they are fishermen and
eat raw fish; they were eating *maguey* also. This pueblo is in
thirty-five and one-third degrees. The interior of the country
is a very fine valley; and they made signs that in that valley
there was much maize and abundant food. Behind the valley
appear some very high mountains and very broken country.
They call the Christians Taquimine. Here they took possession
and here they remained until Friday, the 13th day of said month.

On Friday, the 13th of said month of October, they left
the pueblo of Las Canoas to continue their voyage, and sailed

[1] "Around it" (Davidson, *ibid.*).

[2] The anchorage off Laguna Mugu, lat. 34° 5', fifteen miles west of Point
Dume and nineteen miles by coast line from San Buenaventura.

[3] "Pueblo of the Canoes," at San Buenaventura, in lat. 34° 17'. "The
name Taquimine seems to be the original of the present Hueneme, and is locally
referred to the name of a celebrated chief" (Davidson, p. 198). Navarrete locates this town on San Juan Capistrano Bay (*Sutil y Mexicana*, Introducción,
p. xxxi.).

this day six or seven leagues,[1] passing along the shores of two large islands. Each of them must be four leagues long, and they must be about four leagues from the mainland. They are uninhabited, because they have no water, but they have good ports. The coast of the mainland trends to the west-northwest. It is a country of many savannahs and groves. On the following Saturday they continued on their course, but made no more than two leagues, anchoring[2] in front of a magnificent valley densely populated, with level land, and many groves. Here came canoes with fish to barter; the Indians were very friendly.

On the following Sunday, the 15th day of the said month, they continued on their course along the coast for about ten leagues;[3] all the way there were many canoes, for the whole coast is very densely populated; and many Indians kept boarding the ships. They pointed out the pueblos and told us their names. They are Xuco, Bis, Sopono, Alloc, Xabaagua, Xocotoc, Potoltuc, Nacbuc, Quelqueme, Misinagua, Misesopano, Elquis, Coloc, Mugu, Xagua, Anacbuc, Partocac, Susuquey, Quanmu, Gua,[4] Asimu, Aguin, Casalic, Tucumu, and Incpupu.[5]

All these pueblos are between the first pueblo of Las Canoas, which is called Xucu, and this point. They are in a very good country, with fine plains and many groves and savannahs. The Indians go dressed in skins. They said that in the interior there were many pueblos, and much maize three days' journey from there. They call maize Oep. They also said that there were many cows;[6] these they call Cae. They also told us of people bearded and clothed.

[1] To the "Rincón," lat. 34° 22', four leagues west of San Buenaventura.

[2] Anchorage off the Carpintería, lat. 34° 24', about a mile west of Sand Point.

[3] Anchorage four or five miles west of Point Goleta, eleven miles west of Santa Barbara lighthouse, in lat. 34° 25'.

[4] A note in Buckingham Smith, p. 189, states that the last two names are united in the manuscript, thus: Quanmugua.

[5] The Indians of this coast were of the Chumashan linguistic stock. The name is from that of the natives of Santa Rosa Island. For a discussion of civilization and divisions of the group, see H. W. Henshaw and A. L. Kroeber in Hodge, *Handbook of American Indians*, I. 296–297, and the authorities there cited.

[6] Henshaw thinks the animal here referred to was the bison (*Voyage of Cabrillo*, p. 307, note), but it was more probably the elk, plentiful in California in early days, which is not true of the bison.

This day they passed along the shore of a large island [1] which must be fifteen leagues long.   They said that it was very densely populated and that there were the following pueblos : Niquipos, Maxul, Xugua, Nitel, Macamo, and Nimitapal. They called this island San Lucas.   From here to the pueblo of Las Canoas it must be about eighteen leagues.   The island must be about six leagues from the mainland.

On Monday, the 16th of the said month, sailing along the coast, they made about four leagues, and cast anchor[2] in the afternoon in front of two pueblos.   All this day, likewise, many canoes came with the ships and made signs that farther on there were canoes much larger.

On the following Tuesday, the 17th of the said month, they made three leagues,[3] with favorable winds.   Many canoes went with the ships from daybreak, and the captain kept giving them many presents.   All this coast which they have passed is very thickly settled.   The Indians brought for them many sardines, fresh and very good.   They say that in the interior there are many pueblos and abundant food.   They ate no maize.   They were dressed in skins, and wore their hair very long and tied up with long strings interwoven with the hair, there being attached to the strings many gewgaws[4] of flint, bone, and wood.   The country appears to be very fine.

On Wednesday, the 18th of the said month, they proceeded along the coast until ten o'clock, seeing that all the coast was populated; and because there was a fresh wind and canoes did not come to them, they drew near to a headland which forms a cape like a galley, and named it Cape Galera.[5]   It is in thirty-six degrees, full.   And because a strong northwest wind struck them they stood off shore and discovered two islands, one large, probably about eight leagues long from east to west, the other about four leagues.   They are inhabited, and

---

[1] The three islands, Santa Cruz, Santa Rosa, and San Miguel.   They overlap each other and were thought to be one.   They afterward discovered that they were separate.   See entries for January, 1543.

[2] Anchorage off the Cañada del Refugio, 34° 27', twenty-one miles from the Santa Barbara lighthouse.

[3] To the anchorage off Gaviota Pass, twelve miles east of Point Concepción, lat. 34° 28'.

[4] *Dagas.*   [5] Point Concepción, lat. 34° 27'.

in this small one there is a good port. They are ten leagues
from the mainland. They are called the Islands of San Lucas.[1]
From the mainland to Cape Galera the coast runs west-northwest. The district from the pueblo of Las Canoas to Cape
Galera is a densely populated province and is called Xexu.
Many languages distinct from each other are spoken in it.
They have bitter wars with one another. From the pueblo
of Las Canoas to Cape Galera it is thirty leagues. They remained in these islands until the following Wednesday because
it was very stormy.[2]

On Wednesday, the 25th of said month, they left these
islands, setting out from the one which was most to windward.
It has a very good port, which within gives shelter from all
storms of the sea. They called it La Posesion.[3] This day they
made little headway because there was no wind. The following midnight they were struck by a wind from the south-southwest and west-southwest, with rain, which put them in peril,
because it was an on-shore wind and they were near land, and
they were unable to double the cape on one tack or the other.
At vespers the following Thursday the wind drove them off-
shore, to the south, whereupon they continued on their course
some ten leagues on[4] a coast running from north-northwest to
south-southeast. All this coast is inhabited and the country appears to be good. That night they held out to sea because the wind was on-shore, and on Friday, Saturday, and
Sunday they sailed with contrary winds, beating about from
one side to the other, without being able to make headway.
They were in thirty-six and one-half degrees, and ten leagues
from Cape Galera. They continued also on Monday, and on

[1] San Miguel, and then Santa Cruz and Santa Rosa as one. "They had
already seen the Island of Santa Rosa, as part of the Island of Santa Cruz when
they overlapped and were named San Lucas. Now they discover San Miguel
separated from the Island of Santa Rosa, which was supposed to be the western
part of San Lucas" (Davidson, *Early Voyages*, p. 204).

[2] Herrera says: "During the eight days that they remained in the port
they were well treated by the Indians, who go naked and paint their faces after
the manner of Axedrèz " (*Historia General*, dec. VII., lib. V., cap. III.).

[3] San Miguel Island. The latitude of the anchorage is 34° 3'. After Cabrillo's death Ferrelo named the island La Isla de Juan Rodríguez. See p. 33.
Herrera adds some information at this point (*Historia General*, dec. VII., lib. V.,
cap. III.).

[4] "To a coast" (Davidson, *Early Voyages*, p. 208).

Tuesday, the 31st of the said month, eve of the Feast of All Saints, tacking back and forth, trying to approach the mainland in search of a large river[1] which they had heard was on the other side of Cape Galera, and because on the land there were signs of rivers. But they found none, neither did they anchor here, because the coast was very bold.

This month they found on this coast the same weather as in Spain from thirty-four degrees and upward, with severe cold in the mornings and at night, and with storms, very dark and cloudy weather, and heavy atmosphere.

On Wednesday, the 1st day of November, at midnight, standing off, they encountered a heavy wind from the north-northwest, which prevented them from carrying a palm of sail, and by dawn it had freshened so that they were forced to seek shelter, and they therefore went to take refuge under Cape Galera. There they cast anchor and went ashore; and although there was a large pueblo which they call Xexo,[2] because wood did not appear to be close at hand they decided to go to the pueblo of Las Sardinas,[3] because there the water and wood were close and handy. This shelter under Galera they called the port of Todos Santos.[4] On the following Thursday they went to the pueblo of Las Sardinas,[5] where they remained three days, taking on water and wood. The natives of the country aided them and brought the wood and water to the ships. This pueblo of the port of Sardinas they call Cicacut; the others, between there and Cape Galera, are Ciucut, Anacot, Maquinanoa, Paltatre, Anacoat, Olesino, Caacat, Paltocac, Tocane, Opia, Opistopia, Nocos, Yutum, Quiman, Micoma, Garomisopona. The ruler[6] of these pueblos is an old Indian woman, who came to the ships and slept two nights on the captain's ship, as did many Indians. The pueblo of Ciucut appeared to be the capital of the rest, for they came there from other pueblos at the call of this ruler. The pueblo which is at the

---

[1] Perhaps the Purísima, or Santa Inez, emptying just north of Point Argüello.

[2] The Indian village at El Coxo anchorage.

[3] The Sardines.   [4] El Coxo anchorage, lat. 34° 28′.

[5] Indian village at Gaviota Pass, lat. 34° 27′. This is the place where they secured so many sardines on October 17. (Davidson, *Early Voyages*, p. 208, where a slight error in chronology occurs.)

[6] *La Señora.*

cape they call Xexo. From this port to the pueblo of Las Canoas is another province which they call Xucu.[1] Their houses are round and very well covered clear to the ground. They wear skins of many kinds of animals. They eat oak acorns, and a seed the size of maize. It is white, and from it they make tamales; it is a good food. They say that in the interior there is much maize, and that men like us are going about there. This port is in thirty-five and two-thirds degrees.

On Monday, the 6th of said month of November, they left the said port of Sardinas; that day they made almost no progress, and until the following Friday they sailed with very light wind. That day we arrived at Cape Galera.[2] During all this course they could make no use of the Indians who came aboard with water and fish, and appeared very friendly. They have in their pueblos large plazas, and have an enclosure like a fence; and around the enclosure they have many blocks of stone set in the ground, and projecting three palms above it. Within the enclosures they have many timbers set up like thick masts. On these poles they have many paintings, and we thought that they worshipped them, because when they dance they go dancing around the enclosure.

On the following Saturday, the day of San Martin, the 11th of the said month of November, they held on their course, sailing along the coast,[3] and that morning found themselves twelve leagues from the cape in the same place where they had first arrived. All this day they had good wind, and they journeyed along the coast from southeast to northwest, making twenty leagues. All this coast which they ran this day is bold and entirely without shelter. All along it runs a chain of very high mountains. It is as high at the seacoast as in the interior, and the sea beats upon it. They saw no settlement nor any smokes, and all the coast, which has no shelter from the north, is uninhabited. They named these mountains the Sierras de San Martin.[4] They are in thirty-seven and one-half degrees. Their northwest extremity forms a cape

---

[1] Elsewhere said to extend from San Buenaventura to Point Concepción.

[2] Point Concepción, lat. 34° 27′.

[3] Driven by a southwester (Herrera, *Historia General*, dec. VII., lib. V., cap. IV.).

[4] The Santa Lucía Mountain.

which juts into the sea.   It is in thirty-eight degrees.   They named it Cape Martin.[1]

At four o'clock this Saturday night, when lying-to at sea about six leagues from the coast, waiting for morning, with a southeast wind, there blew up so heavy a gale from the south-west and south-southwest, with rain and dark clouds, that they could not carry a palm of sail, and were forced to scud with a small foresail, with much labor, the whole night.   On the following Sunday the tempest became much more violent and continued all day, all night, and until noon of the following day.   The storm was as severe as any there could be in Spain.   On Saturday night they lost sight of their consort.

On Monday, the 13th of said month of November, at the hour of vespers, the wind calmed down and shifted to the west, and at once they set sail and went in search of the consort, steering towards the land, praying to God that they might find her, for they greatly feared that she might be lost. They ran to the north and north-northwest with a wind from the west and west-northwest, and at daybreak on the following Tuesday they sighted the land.[2]   They had to run until the afternoon, when they went to reconnoitre a very high coast, and then proceeded along the coast to see if there were any port where they might take shelter.   So great was the swell of the ocean that it was terrifying to see, and the coast was bold and the mountains very high.   In the afternoon they lay-to for shelter.   The coast runs from northwest to southeast.   They examined the coast at a point which projects into the sea and forms a cape.[3]   The point is covered with timber, and is in forty degrees.

On Wednesday, the 15th of said month, they sighted the consort, whereupon they heartily thanked God, for they had thought her lost.   They made toward her, and in the afternoon they joined company.   Those on the other ship had experienced greater labor and risk than those of the captain's

[1] Point Pinos, in lat. 36° 38'.

[2] Davidson says the land sighted was to the northward of Russian River (*Early Voyages*, p. 220).

[3] The bold, high spur of the coast mountains nearly overhanging Ft. Ross Cove, lat. 38° 31'.   Herrera calls it Cabo de Pinos (*Historia General*, dec. VII., lib. V., cap. IV.).

ship, since it was a small vessel and had no deck.   This country where they were sailing is apparently very good, but they saw no Indians or smokes.   There are large mountains covered with snow, and there is heavy timber.   At night they lowered sails and lay-to.

On the following Thursday, the 16th of the said month of November, they found themselves at daybreak in a great bay, which came at a turn, and which appeared to have a port and river.   They held on, beating about that day and night and on the following Friday, until they saw that there was neither river nor shelter.   In order to take possession they cast anchor in forty-five fathoms, but they did not dare go ashore because of the high sea.   This bay is in thirty-nine degrees, full, and its entire shore is covered with pines clear to the sea.   They named it Bay of Los Pinos.¹   That night they lay-to until the following day.

The following Saturday they ran along the coast, and at night found themselves off Cape San Martin.²   All the coast run this day is very bold; the sea has a heavy swell, and the coast is very high.   There are mountains which reach the sky, and the sea beats upon them.   When sailing along near the land, it seems as if the mountains would fall upon the ships.   They are covered with snow to the summit, and they named them the Sierras Nevadas.³   At the beginning of them a cape is formed which projects into the sea,⁴ and which they named Cape Nieve.⁵   The coast runs from north-northwest

---

¹ Drake's Bay, lat. 38°.   Navarrete thought this might be Monterey Bay (*Sutil y Mexicana*, Introducción, p. xxxii.).   For Drake's anchorage in this bay see W. S. W. Vaux, ed., *The World Encompassed by Sir Francis Drake*; J. S. Corbett, *Drake and the Tudor Navy* ; Davidson, *Early Voyages*, pp. 214–218; Davidson, *Identification of Sir Francis Drake's Anchorage on the Coast of California in the Year* 1579 (San Francisco, 1890).

² Either the limit of Sierra Santa Lucía, near Point Carmel, or the San Martín of the earlier part of the voyage, the former being more likely (Davidson, *Early Voyages*, p. 224).

³ "It is evident that Ferrelo runs ahead in his narrative to describe in general terms the appearance of the coast range of Mountains from the Gulf of Farallones to Cape San Martin, and then returns to take up the details" (Davidson, *Early Voyages*, p. 224).

⁴ The San Francisco peninsula.

⁵ "Snow Cape."   Black Mountain, lat. 37° 9'.   Navarrete says "apparently Point Año Nuevo" (*Sutil y Mexicana*, Introducción, p. xxxii.).

to south-southeast. It does not appear that Indians live on this coast. This Cape Nieve is in thirty-eight and two-thirds degrees. Whenever the wind blew from the northwest the weather was clear and fair.

On Thursday, the 23d of the month, they arrived, on the return, in the islands of San Lucas, at one of them called La Posesion.[1] They had run the entire coast, point by point, from Cape Pinos to the islands, and had found no shelter whatever, wherefore they were forced to return to said island because during these past days there was a strong wind from the west-northwest, and the swell of the sea was heavy. From Cape Martin to Cape Pinos we did not see a single Indian, the reason being that the coast is bold, rugged, and without shelter. But southeast of Cape Martin for fifteen leagues they found the land inhabited, and with many smokes, because the country is good. But from Cape Martin up to forty degrees we saw no sign of Indians. Cape Martin[2] is in thirty-seven and one-half degrees.

Passing the winter on the island of La Posesion,[3] on the 3d of the month of January, 1543, Juan Rodriguez Cabrillo, captain of the said ships, departed from this life, as the result of a fall which he suffered on said island when they were there before, from which he broke an arm near the shoulder. He left as captain the chief pilot, who was one Bartolome Ferrelo, a native of the Levant. At the time of his death he emphatically charged them not to leave off exploring as much as possible of all that coast. They named the island the Island of Juan Rodriguez.[4] The Indians call it Ciquimuymu; the next they call Nicalque, and the next, Limu. On this island of La

---

[1] San Miguel Island, lat. 34° 3'. "Ferrelo again runs ahead of events in his narrative in mentioning his approach to the Santa Barbara Islands and then returns and describes the coast from Cabo de Pinos (Northwest Cape at Fort Ross)" (Davidson, *Early Voyages*, p. 224).

[2] Probably Mount Carmel, in lat. 36° 22'.

[3] San Miguel Island. Henshaw remarks: "The three centuries and more that have elapsed have witnessed great changes in the appearance of the island of San Miguel, evidently then well populated. It has become barren and desolate in the extreme by reason of the drifted sand, which lies on it to the depth of many feet and which will doubtless always preserve the secret of Cabrillo's grave" (*Voyage of Cabrillo*, p. 311, note).

[4] San Miguel Island.

Posesion there are two pueblos, one called Zaco and the other Nimollollo. On the next island there are three pueblos, one called Nichochi, another Coycoy, and another Estocoloco. On the third island there are eight pueblos, namely, Niquesesquelua, Poele, Pisqueno, Pualnacatup, Patiquiu, Patiquilid, Ninumu, Muoc, Pilidquay, and Lilibeque.

The Indians of these islands are very poor. They are fishermen, and they eat nothing except fish. They sleep on the ground. Their sole business and employment is fishing. They say that in each house there are fifty persons. They live very swinishly, and go about naked.

They remained on these islands from the 23d of November till the 19th of January. During all this time, which was nearly two months, there were very heavy winter winds and rains. The prevailing winds were west-southwest, south-southwest, and west-northwest. There were very violent winds.

On Friday, the 19th of the said month of January, 1543, they set sail from the island of Juan Rodriguez, which is called Ciquimuymu, to go to the mainland in search of some provisions for their voyage. As they were leaving the port they encountered a heavy wind from the west-northwest, which forced them to seek shelter at the other islands of San Lucas. They anchored at the island of Limun, which they called San Salvador.[1] They were forced to weigh anchor again and depart, because there was no port other than the shelter of the islands. The wind shifted on-shore,[2] and they sailed around these islands eight days with very foul winds, taking shelter from them under the islands themselves; and on the twenty-seventh of said month they entered the same port of the island of Juan Rodriguez where they had been at first. Their greatest difficulty was because the winds were not steady, for they kept changing about from one direction to another. Those most constant are from the west-northwest and west-southwest.

[1] Santa Cruz Island, lat. 34° 2'. This name had already been given to Santa Catalina Island. From Navarrete one would get the impression that this is the same Salvador which he identifies with the San Clemente (*Sutil y Mexicana,* Introducción, p. xxxiii.).

[2] "From all points" (Davidson, *Early Voyages,* p. 226).

Tuesday, the 29th of the said month of January, they set sail from the island of Juan Rodriguez for the island of San Lucas,[1] which is between the others, to get certain anchors which they had left there during a storm, not being able to raise them.[2] They recovered them and took on water.

They left this island of San Lucas on Monday, the 12th of the month of February, not being able to do so sooner because of the bad weather, with winds and heavy snow, which they encountered. It is inhabited and the people are like those of the other island. The Indians call it Nicalque. There are three pueblos on it, called Nicochi, Coycoy, and Coloco. This day they went to the port of Las Sardinas[3] to get wood and other things necessary for their voyage, for there were none on the islands.

On Wednesday, the 14th of the said month, they left the port of Las Sardinas, having secured a boatload of wood. They did not dare remain there longer because of the heavy sea. They did not find so many Indians as at first, nor any fishing at all, because it was winter. The natives were eating acorns from the oaks, and another seed, and raw plants from the field. From here they went to the island of San Salvador,[4] because they were safer there from the storms in setting sail to run out to sea.

On Sunday, the 18th of the said month of February, they left the island of San Salvador with a favorable northeast wind, and ran to the southwest, because they told them that toward the southwest there were other islands. At nightfall of this day, when they were about twelve leagues from the island of San Salvador, they saw six islands, some large and some small. This day a sailor died. On the following Monday, at daybreak, they were at sea about ten leagues to windward of the islands; and with the wind in the west-northwest they stood off to the southwest five days, at the end of which time they had made about a hundred leagues. Finding the winds more violent and a heavy sea, on Thursday, the 22d of said month of February, they turned again toward the land

[1] Santa Rosa Island, lat. 33° 57'.

[2] Davidson thinks that he probably lost his anchors in Becher's Bay (*Early Voyages*, p. 228).

[3] Off Gaviota Pass, lat. 34° 27'.   [4] Santa Cruz Island.

to go in search of Cape Pinos, with a wind from the south-southeast which lasted for three days and became each day more violent. On the following Sunday, at daybreak, they sighted Cape Pinos,[1] and at nightfall of the same day were twenty leagues to windward on a coast running from north-west to southeast. It is bold and without shelter. Not a single smoke was seen on the land. They saw a point[2] which was like a spur of land where the coast turned north-northwest. At midnight the wind shifted to the south-southwest, and they ran west-northwest till next day. In the morning the wind shifted to the west-southwest and became very strong, lasting till the following Tuesday. They ran toward the northwest.[3]

Tuesday, the 27th of said month, the wind shifted to the south-southwest, and continued in that direction all day. They ran west-northwest with foresails lowered, because the wind was high. At night the wind shifted to the west. They ran south all night with but little sail. There was a high sea which broke over them.

On the following Wednesday, the 28th of said month, at daybreak, the wind shifted directly to the southwest, and did not blow hard. This day they took the latitude in forty-three degrees.[4] Toward night the wind freshened and shifted to the south-southwest. They ran this night to the west-north-west, with great difficulty, and on Thursday, in the morning, the wind shifted to the southwest with great fury, the seas coming from many directions, causing them great fatigue and breaking over the ships; and as they had no decks, if God had not succored them they could not have escaped. Not being able to lay-to, they were forced to scud northeast toward the

---

[1] Northwest Cape, lat. 38° 31' just east of Fort Ross anchorage.

[2] Point Arena, the Punta de Arena of later Spanish navigators, lat. 38° 57' (Davidson, *Early Voyages*, p. 247). Called Cabo de Fortunas by Herrera (*Historia General*, dec. VII., lib. V., cap. IV.).

[3] "They saw the great mountain mass which reaches a height of nearly 4300 feet a little to the northward of Point Delgada at Shelter Cove; and continues as a bold range to the north of Cape Mendocino. They could not have seen Point Delgada because it is low and projected on the base of the coast mountains" (Davidson, *Early Voyages*, p. 230).

[4] "On the 28th of February, 1543, they were out of sight of land, and probably in latitude 41½°, allowing a correction of one and a half degrees to his reported latitude" (Davidson, *Early Voyages*, p. 234).

land; and now, thinking themselves lost, they commended themselves to Our Lady of Guadalupe and made their vows. Thus they ran until three o'clock in the afternoon, with great fear and travail, because they concluded that they were about to be lost, for they saw many signs that land was near by, both birds and very green trees, which came from some rivers, although because the weather was very dark and cloudy the land was invisible.[1] At this hour the Mother of God succored them, by the grace of her Son, for a very heavy rainstorm came up from the north which drove them south with foresails lowered all night and until sunset the next day; and as there was a high sea from the south it broke every time over the prow and swept over them as over a rock. The wind shifted to the northwest and to the north-northwest with great fury, forcing them to scud to the southeast and east-southeast until Saturday the 3d of March, with a sea so high that they became crazed, and if God and his blessed Mother had not miraculously saved them they could not have escaped. On Saturday at midday the wind calmed down and remained in the northwest, for which they gave heartfelt thanks to our Lord. With respect to food they also suffered hardship, because they had nothing but damaged biscuit.

It appears to them that there is a very large river, of which they had much notice, between forty-one and forty-three degrees, because they saw many signs of it.[2] This day in the afternoon they recognized Cape Pinos,[3] but because of the high sea they were forced to run the coast in return in search of a port. They experienced great cold.

On Monday, the 5th of the month of March, 1543, in the morning, they found themselves at the island of Juan Ro-

[1] "They were probably in latitude 42° 30', abreast of Rogue River and working their way back to El Cabo de Pinos; but they must have been seventy miles broad off the coast, which was therefore not visible. The logs were brought down the flooded rivers of this part of the coast; and they always have been a feature off the coast north of Mendocino" (Davidson, *Early Voyages*, p. 234). According to Herrera on March 1 they took latitude and found it to be 44° (*Historia General*, dec. VII., lib. V., cap. IV.).

[2] "On Saturday, March 3, 1543, they were approaching the coast south of Point Arena, but Ferrelo goes back in his narrative" (Davidson, *Early Voyages*, p. 236).

[3] Northwest Cape, lat. 38° 31'.

driguez,[1] but they did not dare enter the port because of the high tempest which caused breakers at its entrance in fifteen fathoms. The wind was from the north-northwest. The entrance is narrow. They ran to shelter under the island of San Salvador[2] on the southeast side. The night before, coming with a high tempest, with only two small foresails, they lost sight of the other ship, and feared that she had been swallowed up by the sea; and they were unable to find her again, even in the morning. They think that they must have been in forty-four degrees when struck by the last storm which drove them to shelter.[3]

On Thursday, the 8th of the said month, they left the island of San Salvador to go to the mainland in search of the other ship. They went to the pueblo of Las Canoas,[4] but did not get any news of her. Here they secured four Indians.

On the following Friday, the 9th of the said month, they left the pueblo of Las Canoas and went to the island of San Salvador, but still did not find the consort.

On Sunday, the 11th of said month, they reached the port of San Miguel[5] but did not find the consort there, or any news of her. Here they waited six days; here they secured two boys to take to New Spain as interpreters, and left certain signals in case the other ship should come here.

On Saturday, the 17th of the said month, they left said port of San Miguel. On the following Sunday they reached the Bay of San Mateo,[6] but still did not find trace of the other ship.

On Sunday, the 18th of said month, in the afternoon, they left this Bay of San Mateo, and on the following Wednesday, the 21st of said month, they arrived at the port of La Posesion,[7] but still found no news of the consort. They waited two days

---

[1] San Miguel Island, and Cuyler's Harbor, lat. 34° 3′.

[2] Smuggler's Cove, Santa Cruz Island, lat. 34° 2′. "To reach this anchorage he must have sailed along the north shore of San Miguel Island, Santa Rosa Island, and Santa Cruz Island, and rounded the easternmost point of the latter to find shelter from the northwest wind at Smuggler's Cove" (Davidson, *Early Voyages*, p. 238).

[3] The highest point reached was probably 42½°. See note 1, p. 9.

[4] San Buenaventura, nineteen miles north-northeast of Smuggler's Cove.

[5] San Diego Bay.   [6] Todos Santos Bay.

[7] Port San Quentin, Lower California.

without entering the port, because they did not dare to enter it on account of the high northwest wind; and because they parted their cable they were forced to weigh anchor.

On Friday, the 23d day of said month, they left the port of La Posesion, and on the following Saturday, at midnight, they reached the island of Cedros;[1] and being there on the following Monday, the 26th of the said month, the other ship arrived at the island of Cedros, whereupon they were greatly rejoiced and gave hearty thanks to God. This ship passed by[2] the island of Juan Rodriguez, striking some shoals at night and they thought they would be lost, but the sailors promised Our Lady to make a pilgrimage to her church stripped to the waist,[3] and she saved them.

On Monday, the 2d day of the month of April, they left the island of Cedros to return to New Spain, because they had no supplies with which to again attempt to explore the coast. They arrived in the port of Navidad on Saturday, the 14th day of the said month of April.

As captain of the ships came Bartolome Ferrel, chief pilot of the ships, in lieu of Juan Rodriguez Cabrillo, who died on the island of La Posesion. In said ships came[4] . . . . . . men.

[1] Cerros Island.

[2] *Paso en.* Evans renders this "put into," while Davidson renders it "passed by." Relying on this expression and the narrative in Herrera, Davidson states that the *fragata* did not make port on San Miguel Island (Isla de Juan Rodríguez) but sought shelter on Santa Rosa Island or San Sebastián (*Early Voyages*, p. 238).

[3] *En carnes*, literally, "naked." I here follow a suggestion made by Father Zephyrin Engelhardt in a discussion with me in regard to pilgrimages.

[4] Left blank in the manuscript.

CALIFORNIA

2. THE VIZCAINO EXPEDITION, 1602–1603

INTRODUCTION

ALMOST simultaneously with the voyage of Cabrillo, Villalobos crossed the Pacific Ocean from Mexico and took formal
possession of the San Lázaro Islands, their name now being
changed to the Philippines. It was still twenty years before
the islands were occupied, but in 1565 Legazpi led an expedition from Mexico, and during the next six years subdued the
islands, precisely at the time when the province of Florida was
being founded by Menéndez de Avilés. At once a regular
trade, conducted by means of the annual Manila galleon, was
established between Mexico and the Philippines.

This event gave rise to a new interest in the California
coast. It was soon learned that the most practicable return
route from Manila was northward to the Japan current and
across the Pacific to the California coast in the latitude of
Cape Mendocino. But the security of this route and of the
Strait of Anian, whose existence was generally believed in,
was threatened by the operations of the French and the English in the northern Atlantic, and by the exploits of Drake and
Cavendish in the Pacific. By now, a Spanish writer has said,
"the English had begun to lord it over the South Sea, terroriz-
ing our coasts by outrages, incendiarism, robbery, and notorious piracy." Moreover, a port of call on the California coast
was needed for the Manila galleon, as a place for shelter and
repairs, and for relief for the sailors from the terrible scourge
of scurvy.

With these needs in view, plans were made by Viceroy
Pedro Moya de Contreras (1584–1585) for exploring the entire
northwestern coast of America. But little came of them until

43

1595, when Cermeño was sent from Manila to explore down the California seaboard. At Drake's Bay his vessel, the *San Agustín*, was driven on the coast and wrecked, the crew escaping to Mexico in two barks built from the planks of the ship.

Simultaneously with the despatch of Cermeño, Sebastián Vizcaino was commissioned by Viceroy Velasco to explore the Gulf of California and establish settlements on the Peninsula. Vizcaino had been for several years a trader between Mexico and the Orient. He had been in the Manila galleon, *Santa Ana*, which Cavendish had plundered in 1588. See Hakluyt's *Voyages*.[1] It is significant that at the same time, also, Velasco was arranging with Juan de Oñate for colonizing New Mexico, one of the primary purposes being the protection of the northern strait. The three enterprises were directed to a common end. After some opposition by the new viceroy, the Conde de Monterrey, in 1596 Vizcaino set forth with his expedition, planted a colony at La Paz, on the site formerly occupied by Cortés, and explored many leagues up the inner coast. But an Indian attack, lack of provisions, severe weather, and other difficulties, soon caused the abandonment of the project.

Vizcaino had failed, and while he was on his expedition a royal order had come requiring that his contract be rescinded. Nevertheless, he recommended another attempt, and volunteered to undertake it. His plan was to explore the gulf completely and to colonize its shores, but it did not look to the exploration of the outer coasts. Notwithstanding his former opposition, the viceroy now supported Vizcaino's petition, admitting that he had found in him more ability than he had expected in a mere merchant. He recommended, however, that, before attempting to colonize, an exploration be made of the gulf and its pearl-fisheries. Referring to the wreck of Cermeño, and to the need of a port for the Manila galleons,

[1] VII. 133–135, Everyman ed.

he suggested that the exploration of the outer coast be combined with that of the gulf.

The matter being considered in the Council of the Indies, it was decided that Vizcaino should be ordered to continue with his contract, which had not been fulfilled, and that the coast exploration be undertaken, but that it be done independently of that of the gulf. The royal order for the continuation of the coastwise exploration was dated September 27, 1599. To command the expedition the viceroy selected Vizcaino, whose enterprise of pearl-fishing and colonizing was now turned into one primarily concerned with the outer coast. The royal order specifically provided that the expedition should not stop in the gulf to explore, and so the open instructions of Vizcaino stipulated, but by secret orders Vizcaino was authorized to explore the gulf on his return.

The king had contemplated an expedition in one vessel, but, because of the difficulty of the voyage, the viceroy decided to send two ships and a frigate. The *San Diego*, the captain's ship, was brought for the occasion from Guatemala by Captain Toribio Gómez de Corbán; the *Santo Tomás*, admiral's ship, was a Peruvian trading vessel purchased at the last moment at Acapulco; the *Tres Reyes*, a *fragata* or frigate, was built for the voyage at the last-named port. The enlistments were made primarily in Mexico City. It being difficult to secure men as sailors only, Vizcaino was allowed to raise his standard and enlist men as both soldiers and sailors.

As admiral, in command of the *Santo Tomás*, went Captain Gómez; as commander of the *Tres Reyes*, Sebastián Meléndez; the chief pilot, with the *San Diego*, was Francisco de Bolaños, who had been wrecked with Cermeño at Drake's Bay in 1595. As chief cosmographer the viceroy appointed Captain Gerónimo Martín Palacios, a man of twenty years' experience, who had just come from Spain. To insure dignity and authority, the viceroy sent six old soldiers, with the title of counsellors (*entretenidos*) for his Majesty. Three men in particular were empowered to advise with Vizcaino : Captain Gómez, Captain Peguero, and Ensign Alarcón, "exceptional men," who had seen service in Flanders and Brittany. Spiritual interests were intrusted to three Carmelites, Fray Andrés de la Asumpción, Fray Antonio de la Ascensión, and Fray Tomás de Aquino.[1] Father Ascensión was a cosmographer, and had been pilot in voyages to the Indies before taking the habit in Mexico.

Vizcaino sailed from Acapulco on May 5. In trying to pass San Lucas Bay in June his fleet was three times driven back to that port by headwinds, and before reaching Magdalena Bay the vessels became separated by storms. At Magdalena Bay extensive explorations were made by the *San Diego* and the *Tres Reyes*. At Cerros Island the vessels were all reunited, but, after leaving there on September 9, the *Santo Tomás* again parted company. In November the other vessels spent five days in San Diego Bay, to which they gave its present name. Early in December explorations were made at Santa Catalina Island, where the vessels were again reunited.

The crews were now falling ill, and winter was coming on, and haste was necessary. Proceeding therefore into the Santa Bárbara Canal, so named by Vizcaino, the vessels were driven through it by a storm. Rounding Point Concepción and sailing close under Santa Lucía Mountain, on December 15 they discovered the Bay of Monterey, "the best that could be desired." This was the capital event of the expedition.

But it now became necessary to depart from the original plan of the voyage. Several men had died, forty-five or more were ill of scurvy, and provisions were running short. Accord-

---

[1] For the preparation of the Vizcaino expedition see especially the correspondence printed in Carrasco y Guisasola, *Documentos referentes al Reconocimiento de las Costas de las Californias desde el Cabo de San Lucas al de Mendocino, recopilados en el Archivo de Indias* (Madrid, 1882), pp. 36–46; "Instruccion y horden," *ibid.*, pp. 47–56; Torquemada, *Monarchía Indiana*, I. 693–697; Cesáreo Fernández Duro, *Armada Española*, III. 297–300.

ingly, the *Santo Tomás* was sent back to secure supplies with which to explore the gulf on the return, carrying the sick, and leaving the other vessels to continue up the coast.

Setting out on January 3, 1603, the *San Diego* anchored at Drake's Bay on the 9th. Meanwhile the *Tres Reyes* had parted company. The experiences during the remainder of the voyage were strikingly similar to those of the Ferrelo party, although much more terrible. The two vessels proceeded separately amid storms, and were not reunited until they reached Acapulco. Reaching Cape Mendocino on January 12, the *San Diego* attempted to turn back, but was driven to latitude 42°, returning thence to Mazatlan in direst distress.

The little frigate had succeeded in getting farther north than the *San Diego*. After separation from her companion, she was driven in the storm till a point was seen called Cape Blanco, in latitude reckoned at 43°. Meanwhile the pilot had died, and the vessel was left in charge of the boatswain. In his declaration made in Mexico he told of discovering a great river and bay, which they had tried to enter, in latitude 41°, just below Cape Mendocino. From Cape Mendocino past Cape Blanco, he said, the coast ran northeast. On the basis of the boatswain's declaration the chief pilot of the expedition, Gerónimo Martín Palacios, placed on his chart a large bay and river, which do not exist in fact, just below Cape Mendocino. Torquemada, writing immediately after the expedition, told of the attempt of the *Tres Reyes* to enter a great river, but placed it near Cape Blanco, and concluded that it was the Strait of Anian. He either got his information from some source other than the boatswain's declaration, or else misplaced the river, which seems the more probable, as he said nothing of a river near Cape Mendocino. He also stated that the coast ran northwest above Cape Blanco, whereas the boatswain stated that it ran northeast. Trying to identify the river mentioned by Torquemada as near Cape Blanco, later students have thought it to be the Rogue River. This seems to be a departure from the sources. The Vizcaino party, like that of Ferrelo, missed the Golden Gate and San Francisco Bay.

The principal printed sources of information regarding the Vizcaino expedition of 1602 are contained in Carrasco y Guisasola, *Documentos referentes al Reconocimiento de las Costas de las Californias desde el Cabo de San Lucas al de Mendocino recopilados en el Archivo de Indias* (Madrid, 1882). The work contains documents between the dates 1584 and 1609. Concerning the expedition in 1602, they comprise communications of the governments in Mexico and Spain with each other and with Vizcaino, the viceroy's instructions to Vizcaino, two journals, and a *derrotero*, or description of the route explored. The general diary (pp. 68–107) has no title but begins "Reynando El rrey don phelipe nuestro señor," etc. (printed here, pp. 52–103). Its author is not named, but the attestation at the end states that it was taken from "the original book of his Majesty." It is hereinafter referred to as Vizcaino's diary. The other journal published in Carrasco (pp. 109–148) is entitled "Copia de libro diario llevado por Sebastian Vizcaino durante el descubrimiento y demarcacion de las costas del mar del Sur, desde el puerto de Acapulco al cabo Mendocino, en 1602." It consists of the records of the juntas, or councils, held by Vizcaino with his officers during the voyage. It is referred to hereinafter as the Libro Diario.

The Derrotero (pp. 149–172), written by the cosmographer, is entitled "Derrotero de la navegacion desde el puerto de acap^{co}. Al cabo Mendoçino y Boca de las Californias fecho Por El Cap^{n}. geronimo Mm. Palaçios cosmografo mayor del nuebo descubrimiento," etc. This Derrotero describes the route which should be followed, with "latitudes, landmarks, and other requisites demanded by the art of navigation." It was made in conference with the pilots and in the presence of

Father Fray Antonio de la Ascensión. It gives a most detailed description of the coast, based on the experience of the voyage, but does not relate the incidents of the journey. Appended to the Derrotero is the statement by the boatswain of the *Tres Reyes* regarding the voyage of that vessel above Drake's Bay. It is entitled "Relacion que dio el Contramaestre de la Fragata de los Tres Reyes, La Qual me dio por Escrito el Gen¹. Sevastian Bizcayno es la Sig^te" (pp. 171–172). The Derrotero is accompanied by an "Explicacion que acompaña á cada una de las vistas de costa y planos de este derrotero" (172–182). It consists of an explanation of thirty-three *vistas* or *planos* (charts), which were made to accompany the Derrotero. The *planos* are not printed in Carrasco y Guisasola. In 1603 they were redrawn in colors from the original, by Enrico Martínez, royal cosmographer in New Spain.[1] On the backs of the charts are the descriptions, corresponding to the *vistas* in Carrasco y Guisasola but with different numbering. Two of the charts are reproduced in black in Richman, *California under Spain and Mexico*, pp. 22–23. A map combining the charts was published in Madrid in 1802, in the Navarrete *Atlas para el Viage de las Goletas Sutil y Mexicana al Reconocimiento del Estrecho de Juan de Fuca*. It is referred to hereinafter as the *Carta*. A complete set of the *planos* is in the Bancroft Library, and will be published in facsimile by Professor Frederick J. Teggart. Their publication will be a most important contribution to materials for the Vizcaino expedition.

Most of the documents published by Carrasco y Guisasola concerning the antecedents of the expedition and three of those narrating events of the voyage are translated by George Butler Griffin in Historical Society of Southern California *Publications*, II. (1891) 5–73. The three concerning the events of the voyage are letters written by Vizcaino at Aca-

[1] See Fernández Duro, *Armada Española*, III. 302, note.

pulco, May 5, 1602, on the eve of the departure; at the Bay of Monterey, December 28, 1602, on the eve of the return of the *Santo Tomás*; and at Mexico City, May 23, 1603, after the return of the expedition.

Father Ascensión kept a diary of the voyage and made a map, but neither has been published. In 1620 he wrote an account of the voyage with his original diary in hand. This account (printed hereinafter, pp. 105–134) is published in Pacheco and Cárdenas, *Colección de Documentos Inéditos*, VIII. 539–574, under the title "Relacion breve en que se da noticia del descubrimiento que se hizo en la Nueva España, en la mar del Sur, desde el puerto de Acapulco hasta mas adelante del cabo de Mendocino," etc. It is published from a manuscript in the Biblioteca Nacional, at Madrid. With it is printed a letter by Francisco Ramírez de Arellano transmitting the narrative to the king. The Relación Breve devotes only brief space to the events of the voyage, but elaborates the description of the country, and gives extensive space to recommendations regarding the occupation of California. Between 1602 and 1620 the expeditions of Oñate and Iturbi to the Gulf had given rise to the notion that California was an island instead of a peninsula. This theory Father Ascensión accepts in his narrative. The Relación Breve therefore may be regarded as representing two distinct periods. The narrative of the voyage is an authentic though brief account of an eye-witness; the insular theory represents the result of developments subsequent to 1602, while the recommendations illustrate the ideas held in 1620 regarding the colonization of California.

Most important of all the older accounts by other than eye-witnesses is that contained in Torquemada's *Monarchía Indiana* (I. 693–725), which was completed by 1612. Torquemada wrote from very full sources, having data especially regarding the movements of the *Santo Tomás* which we do not possess. His account was reprinted in Venegas's (Burriel's) *Noticia de la California* (Madrid, 1757), III. 22–139. Venegas states that Torquemada's account was an *extracto* or summary of the relation written by Father Ascensión (I. 191). The version of Torquemada's account in the English translation of Venegas is very incomplete and unsatisfactory at many points. A less important early account is that of Zárate-Salmerón, "Jornada de Sebastian Vizcaino al Cabo Mendocino," in *Relaciones de todas las Cosas que en el Nuevo Mexico se han visto y sabido, asi por Mar como por Tierra, desde el Año de 1538 hasta el de 1626 por el Padre Geronimo de Zarate Salmeron* (*Documentos para la Historia de México*, tercera série, Mexico, 1856).

DIARY OF SEBASTIAN VIZCAINO, 1602–1603[1]

In the reign of our lord, King Philip, the third of this name, the Most Illustrious Señor Don Gaspar de Suñiga y Acevedo, Count of Monte Rey, being viceroy, governor, and captain-general of this New Spain, an exploration was made of the ports, bays, and inlets of the coast of the South Sea from Cape Mendoçino, by order of his Majesty, for certain purposes of the royal service, Sebastian Vizcayno, a resident of Mexico, being the general under whose charge and orders went the seamen and soldiers of the said expedition, in the year one thousand six hundred and two.

CHAPTER 1.

The Departure of the General from Mexico.

The said general left the city of Mexico in prosecution of his voyage on the day of Santo Tomas de Aquino, which was the 7th of March of the said year, taking with him three religious of the Discalced Order of Our Lady of Carmen, the commissary, Fray Andres de la Umsumçion,[2] Fray Antonio de la Asençion, and Fray Tomas de Aquino ; and his son Don Juan Vizcaino ; and as chief cosmographer, Captain Geronimo Martín[3] de Palaçios ; and as counsellors, Captain Alonso Estevan Peguero, Ensign Pasqual de Alarcon, Ensign Martin de Aguilar Galeote, and Ensign Juan de Azevedo y Pereda ; as

---

[1] Carrasco y Guisasola, *Documentos referentes al Reconocimiento de las Costas de las Californias*, pp. 68–107.

[2] A misprint for Asumpción. See Torquemada, *Monarchía Indiana*, I. 695.

[3] The name Martín is here abbreviated into Mm. This frequently occurs elsewhere with the name of the cosmographer, and also with that of Ensign Martín de Aguilar. Frequently the Mm. becomes Rm. and once Mn. in the transcript. But there is no doubt as to the meaning, because both names are sometimes spelled out, when the abbreviations do not occur.

ensign of the company came Juan Francisco Soriano, and as
sergeant, Miguel de Legar; seamen and soldiers, one hundred
and twenty-six.[1]

CHAPTER 2.

The Arrival at the Port of Acapulco.[2]

The general arrived with his men at the port of Acapulco
on the day of the glorious San José, the 19th[3] of the said month
and year.   He found in it the captain's ship *San Diego*, which
had arrived from El Rrealejo,[4] the admiral's ship *Santo Tomas*,
the frigate *Tres Reyes*, and the long-boat.   The general stayed
in this port until May 5, careening and overhauling the ships
and doing other carpentry work, and equipping them with
everything necessary, in which he and his men labored hard,
and in which, by means of his endeavors and of his outlay
with calkers and other persons, great service was rendered
his Majesty, not to mention the large expenditures caused by
the men.

CHAPTER 3.

The Departure from Acapulco.

The fleet left the said port on Sunday, the day of San
Angelo, the 5th of the said month and year.   It consisted of
the said ships, frigate, and long-boat.   As admiral went
Torivio Gomez de Corban;[5] as commander of the frigate,
Sebastian Melendez; as chief pilot, Francisco de Bolaños;
as pilot of the admiral's ship, Juan Pascual; as his assistant
and mate, Estevan Rodriguez and Baltasar de Armas; and
as pilot of the frigate, Antonio Flores.   As patroness and pro-

[1] Father Ascensión says that there embarked from Acapulco about two hundred persons.   Those in excess of one hundred and twenty-six must therefore
have joined the expedition at Acapulco (Relación Breve, cap. I.).

[2] A port on the southern coast of Mexico, in the state of Guerrero, below lat.
17°.   During most of the Spanish régime it was the port of entry for all trade
between New Spain and the Philippine Islands.

[3] Torquemada gives the date as the 20th (*Monarchía Indiana*, I. 695).

[4] A port of Central America, in lat. 12° 28', to which Gómez had been sent
for vessels.

[5] From Torquemada we learn that Gómez had served many years in the
cruising service on the coast of France and had held important offices (*Monarchía
Indiana*, I. 694).

tector, Our Lady of Carmen was carried. We took her on board the day of the Exaltation of the Cross,[1] in procession, with all the sailors and soldiers in order, with a salute of artillery and musketry, the bow of the bark in which she was carried being covered with awning. This gave great pleasure to all the men on board the fleet and on the land.

Sailing out to sea with a light wind, it was necessary to await the long-boat in order to tow it behind by a rope, and when it came alongside it caught its mast in the yard of the sprit-sail and capsized. The men who were in it swam to the captain's ship. The general was put to great pains in giving directions from on board, and it was righted with no little trouble and risk from its beating against the ship. But finally it got clear, and we steered up the coast; and by tacking back and forth, with a head-wind, but aided by the tides, we made the port of La Navidad[2] on Sunday, the 19th of the said month, it being necessary to ballast the captain's ship and to stop a leak which it had sprung through an auger-hole. This was done, and wood and water were taken on; and on Wednesday, the 22d of the said month, we set sail, a council[3] having previously been held of the said admiral, cosmographer, captains, and pilots to consider the order that should be observed in the voyage to the islands of Masatlan, and a report of what was agreed upon and of our arrival at the said port having been despatched to the viceroy by way of Guadalajara.

CHAPTER 4.

The Arrival at and Departure from the Port of Navidad.

We left the port of Navidad, as stated, Wednesday, at eleven at night, in continuation of our voyage, with a land breeze and aided by the currents, which were in our favor, al-

---

[1] The *Invention* of the Cross, May 3, is doubtless intended.

[2] Lat. 19° 13′. See Cabrillo's diary, p. 13, above, note 1.

[3] The original record of the council held on the *San Diego* at Navidad is in the Libro Diario, Carrasco y Guisasola, *Documentos*, pp. 109–112. It was agreed that to reach Cape San Lucas the voyage should be made along the coast to Mazatlan; in case the vessels should become separated on the way the first to arrive must wait there a week and then continue to Cape San Lucas, there to wait a week. If still alone at the end of that time, the crew must carve a cross on the most prominent tree and leave a written message buried at its foot.

though with a light wind. We sighted Cape Corrientes on Monday, the 27th[1] of the said month, the second day of the Feast of Espiritu Santo.[2] This day an observation of the sun was made at a small island near the cape, to which was given the name of Espiritu Santo.

Pursuing the voyage, on the next day, Tuesday, we arrived off the point of Tintoque, and off Saltelga and Chacala.[3] These ports were not made, it not being convenient; and without loss of time, with the wind not very favorable, but aided by the currents, we made the islands of Masatlan.[4] We anchored there at eleven o'clock on Trinity Sunday, the 2d day of the month of June. The general permitted no one to go ashore. He alone went on the said islands in order to see if there was any water, but found none. A great many birds are found on these islands, in such numbers that they gathered in flocks which appeared like flocks of sheep; and with the sardines which they had near their nests we could have fed many people.

CHAPTER 5.

The Departure from the Islands of Masatlan.[5]

Going forward on the voyage, and having passed Culiacan[6] a matter of two leagues, the general gave orders to cross the entrance of the Californias to the Cape of San Lucas. This was done, although with much labor, there being westerly

[1] Lat. 20° 25'. Torquemada says they arrived on the 26th (*Monarchia Indiana*, I. 696).

[2] Pentecost.

[3] The Derrotero, pp. 153–154, mentions Punta de Tintoque, fourteen leagues above Cape Corrientes. It does not mention Saltelga or Chacala under those names.

[4] Islas de San Juan de Maçatlan (Vizcaino, Relación of 1597, in Carrasco y Guisasola, *Documentos*, p. 25). In the Planos, fol. 62, is a map of Islas de Maçatlan. The anchorage was on the islands and not on the mainland.

[5] In the text "Islas de Masatlan" is corrupted into "Velas de Masatlan."

[6] Culiacán, in Sinaloa, near lat. 24° 40'. This place was founded in 1531, by Guzmán, as an outpost of Nueva Galicia. Vizcaino's Relación of 1597 states that from Acapulco to Puerto de Çalagua it was one hundred leagues; thence to Cape Corrientes, sixty leagues; thence to Mazatlan, sixty leagues; thence to Culiacán, forty leagues; thence to Baldehermoso [Vallehermoso] in Sinaloa, fifty leagues; "from this point one crosses the gulf and mouth of the Californias, which is about eighty leagues across" (Carrasco y Guisasola, *Documentos*, p. 25).

head-winds; and going forward by tacking back and forth, after five days we found ourselves to be twelve leagues from the said Cape of San Lucas.[1] Coasting along the land, on Saturday, the 8th day of the month of June, we arrived at the said Cape of San Lucas. We anchored in the Bay of San Bernabe, and because we anchored in it the same day, which was the eleventh of the said month, that saint's name was given to it.[2] The ship being anchored, the admiral, the rest of the captains, and the ensign went ashore with their arms and fifty arquebusiers. We found awaiting us on the beach Indians to the number of a hundred, and the general, the religious, and everyone received them very well, embracing them and giving them food and other things, the Indians giving tiger and deerskins. That night the Indians went to their rancherías, and we remained on the beach. Orders were given to make ready the net for catching fish, but it was not necessary, for God granted that there should be cast upon the beach as many sardines as all could eat, with many left over.

The following day, being the octave of the feast of the Most Holy Sacrament,[3] the general ordered a tent pitched near the beach in the shelter of a large rock, where stopped the men of the ships in which the Englishman Don Tomas plundered.[4] In this place and tent mass was said, and a procession of the most Holy Sacrament held, in which Our Lady of Carmen was carried. The general and many men confessed and received communion. Father Fray Tomas de Aquino preached, and all with much joy, health, and peace gave thanks to God for having reached this place. For, in addition to its having been very much desired, we found in it many fish of different kinds and sardines in abundance, from which the

---

[1] Davidson at this point by mistake places a paragraph from Ferrelo's voyage under the head of Vizcaino, making it appear that Vizcaino arrived at Cape San Lucas on July 2 (*Early Voyages*, p. 161).

[2] San Lucas Bay, lat. 22° 52'; Cabrillo's Puerto de San Lucas (Davidson, *Early Voyages*, p. 162). Martín, Planos, fol. 61, shows on the west coast a "high white sand dune," not shown on the Carta. See Explicación, 1, in Carrasco, *Documentos*, p. 172; Torquemada, *Monarchía Indiana*, I. 697.

[3] Octave of Corpus Christi, June 13, 1602.

[4] There is clearly a mistake in the copy here. The text reads: "la nao Samque Rono El Yngles." I suggest the reading: "Los naos en que rouo El Yngles," which I have followed in the translation. The reference is, of course, to Thomas Cavendish. See Torquemada, I. 699.

men received great satisfaction, as the fish were very wholesome. We found very good fresh water near the beach in a
patch of green canes,[1] and we also found a great number of
rabbits and several hares, and signs of deer; but there was no
fruit. We found incense trees, and some incense was gathered,
as well as some wood; and they finished making the extra
sails, to replace those which were worn out.

Sunday, the 16th of the said month, the general called a
council [2] of the admiral, cosmographer, captains, and pilots
for the purpose of determining the order of navigation from
this place to the island of Serros. It was held, and that
which was decided was noted down in the council book, with
great unanimity of all.[3] It being cold, the men asked the
general that the supply of clothing which was brought be
distributed, which was thereupon done; and he also ordered
an edict proclaimed to the effect that no one should gamble
or sell them, under pain of death; likewise that no one should
harm any Indian, or molest him, or take anything from him
by force.

It was agreed to-day that on Wednesday, the 19th of the
month, the moon being in conjunction, we should set sail in
continuation of our voyage. This we did, and at four o'clock
in the afternoon the captain's ship set sail, the others following. After we had rounded the cape, when six leagues from
it a northwest wind came up which forced us to take shelter
in the same bay, where we remained another two days, until
it grew calm. We set sail a second time, but having arrived
at the place before-mentioned the same wind struck us again
and forced us to put into port.[4] We were there three more

---

[1] See the Carta, and Planos, fol. 61.   [2] See Libro Diario, p. 112.

[3] It was agreed in the council that in case of parting company in a storm
the vessels should put into the nearest and best bay discovered or return to San
Bernabé, to await the others. In order to avoid trouble with the natives, no
landing must be made of less than thirty armed men; orders must be obeyed on
pain of death; Indians must not be ill treated, nor presents received except by
the commander of the landing party (Libro Diario, pp. 113–114).

[4] On June 21 a *junta* was held on the *San Diego*; already two attempts had
been made to sail. It was now agreed that a new attempt should not be made
till a change of weather or till full moon. Later in the same day the wind had
shifted to the southeast and a new *junta* advised sailing with it, lest they be held
in the port by the wind (Libro Diario, pp. 114–115).

days, until the eve of the feast of the glorious San Juan Baptista,[1] when, being desirous of going forward, we that night set sail the third time; but after sailing five days, during which we struggled as best we could, we were driven back with much force to the same bay and cape, where we remained until July 5. Then, with a favoring land breeze, we set sail in continuation of our voyage. A council being held, the long-boat was left in a pool of fresh water, with the concurrence of all, since it was the opinion that it would be lost and would give the captain's ship much trouble in towing it astern, and that it was not fit to sail because of the heavy seas on the coast.

CHAPTER 6.

The Departure from the Cape of San Lucas and the Arrival at Santa María Madalena.

We set out from the said cape and bay of San Bernabé on July 5, as has been said, and after going two leagues out to sea, sailing with a strong wind, we met with a moderate head-wind, and, tacking against it, sailed with great difficulty. After six days we sighted some high, broken mountains, to which we drew near in order to see whether there was any port there, and whether we could find the frigate, which had parted company the day after we left the said bay.

On the 18th of the said month, the day of Samcta Marina, we discovered a bay[2] and tried to enter it. Being near land we found soundings of six fathoms. The tide turned, and for this reason and because it was night, we stood off shore. In the morning we saw that it was a wild coast which showed no safe harbor. We coasted along till the 19th day of said month, when we came upon an inlet, outside of which we remained with lowered sails to await the admiral's ship, which was three leagues to the leeward.

The next morning we could not see her, and we continued

---

[1] June 24.

[2] Santa Marina Bay, lat. 24° 20'; "Bahía engañossa de Santa Marina" (Derrotero, p. 157); Cabrillo's Puerto de la Trinidad (Davidson, *Early Voyages*, p. 164); shown on the Planos, fol. 66. Near this bay the charts show and the Derrotero mentions the point of the Sierra de Santa Margarita, evidently Cabrillo's Punta de la Trinidad (Derrotero, p. 157; *Early Voyages*, p. 164).

our voyage and entered a very large bay, which was named the
Bay of Madalena.[1] The general ordered Ensign Juan Francisco to go on shore and explore it, and to send four arquebusiers to a point made by the bay, and two others to[2] a high
hill, with orders to make smoke signals to the admiral's ship,
thereby to let her know that we were there. Although this
was done, and the men of the admiral's ship saw the smoke
signals, they did not understand them out at sea. The chief
pilot, Francisco de Bolaños, set out in the boat, making every
effort to reach the admiral's ship, but he could not do so because the wind freshened. The chief pilot returned, and this
day, which was the feast of the Magdalene, mass was said on
land.

The following day the general agreed that the bay should
be mapped, and the land and its people examined; that the
cosmographer should sound it and map it; and that Ensign
Pascual de Alarcon, with twenty arquebusiers, should explore
the land, find out who the people were, and search for water,
of which the captain's ship had great need.

They set out upon this undertaking and went twelve
leagues about the bay, but did not find water to any considerable amount, although between two hills, half a league from
the beach, a pool was found where in the rainy season the water
collects. It was not very fresh and was green, but the bottles
we carried were filled with it. A great number of Indians
came to the ensign in different places, with their bows, arrows,
and small, fire-hardened darts, although they were friendly,
for they gave up their arms as a sign of peace. They are a

---

[1] Magdalena Bay, lat. 24° 32'; the Puerto de San Pedro of Cabrillo. Shown
on the Planos, fol. 68. Described in Explicación, *vista* 10. The Derrotero says:
"This Sierra is called Santa Margarita, and between the point which it makes
toward the northeast and the coast behind it it forms a bar, within the Ensenada
Emgañossa de Santa Marina. There are inside of said bar a port and anchorage,
the entry being five fathoms at least; and within there is great depth. It com-
municates with La Vaya de la Madalena. From the southeast point of the
Sierra de Santa Margarita, as they call the very point, to the said bar of Santa
Marina, it is four leagues" (Derrotero, p. 157). Torquemada (*Monarchía
Indiana*, I. 700), says that the flagship entered Magdalena Bay, but that her con-
sort did not enter on account of the fogs; and that mass was said ashore on Santa
Magdalena's day, hence the name given the bay. See *Early Voyages*, p. 165.

[2] In the text *á* is corrupted into *ó*.

well featured and robust race, though naked and living in
rancherías. Their food is commonly of fish and maize, for
there are great quantities of fish of many kinds. They fish
with enclosures of sticks, catching in this way many mussels
and shell fish. There are many whales, which are sometimes
stranded on the beach of this bay, for we found many of their
bones.

Thursday, the 25th of the said month, the frigate arrived,
which gave much pleasure to all the men. Ensign Sebastian
Melendes reported that on account of the strong wind he had
returned to take shelter at Cape San Lucas five days after he
had put out to sea. They had improved the time while there
in caulking the hatchways. Moreover, they said that they
had entered the Bay of Santa Marina, which has been mentioned above, and that at the end of it they had found a very
good port, where many Indians came out to them, like the
others, and in sign of peace gave them their arms, which are
arrows and small wooden darts, which they also use for fishing.
The next day after the frigate had arrived, there being a lack
of water, Ensign Pasqual de Alarcon went in it, with the boat of
the captain's ship, to the pool whence the green water had been
brought before, but he secured only seventy bottles; and although they made great efforts, no other fresh water was found.
This land is very dry and on the side of the mainland is very
flat, the greater part consisting of sand dunes and the rest
being sparsely wooded. During the dry season the Indians
drink brackish water from waterholes which they make near
the salt water. Seeing that there was no water here and that
time was passing, it was agreed to set sail on Saturday, the 27th
of the month. As we sailed out this day from the entrance of
the bay the wind went down, and the tide, setting in, forced
us to anchor. At midnight we stood out with a land breeze,
the boat in tow, and on Sunday at nine o'clock, when four
leagues out at sea, we came up with the frigate. The general
ordered a rope given it so that it might be towed astern and
not become separated again from the captain's ship.

CHAPTER 7.

The Arrival at and Departure from the Bay of Madalena and the Voyage to the Port of San Bartolomé.

We set out, as has been said, on Sunday, with favorable wind, on our way to the island of Serros. Some five leagues from land we discovered the entrance of another large bay,[1] which we attempted to go into in order to protect ourselves from the northwest wind. At its entrance, on the point toward the northwest, there were some shoals which extended out as far as the middle of the mouth of the bay. Having arrived off these, we were obliged to stand away to sea and continue our voyage. This bay was named Santa Marta. Tacking back and forth, on Tuesday, the 30th of the said month, we discovered a bay,[2] and in the middle of it what appeared to be a river or port. The general ordered the cosmographer to go in the frigate to examine it and take soundings and bring back a report of what was there. He did so, and as he drew near with the frigate the breakers were rolling in on all sides. As it was of no importance he returned to the captain's ship, and the general bade him come aboard.

We continued our voyage, skirting along this coast because of our great need of water, and at the end of it we saw another large bay[3] and two leagues of land near it. The general or-

---

[1] Santa María Bay, lat. 24° 44'; the Bahía de San Martín of Cabrillo (*Early Voyages*, p. 165). The Derrotero, p. 159, notes Punta de San Laçaro two leagues above Ensenada de Santa Marta. This is now Cape San Lázaro, lat. 24° 48' (*Early Voyages*, p. 166). See Planos, fol. 69; Explicación, *vista* 11.

[2] Torquemada (*Monarchía Indiana*, I. 701) says: "This place or inlet called San Christoval had been surveyed by the admiral's ship. . . . The inlet was named San Christoval because it was surveyed on the anniversary of that saint." In this inlet is the entrance of Boca de San Domingo, lat. 25° 21'. The southern end of the lagoon heads in Magdalena Bay (*Early Voyages*, p. 167). The Planos, fol. 71, show two "ensenadas" above the "ensenada larga" where the Carta shows only one. The Bay of San Christóval may have been one of these.

[3] Torquemada (I. 701) states that on the night of July 30 they reached Bahía de las Ballenas, seeing, just before reaching it, "another large bay," which they could not enter for the shoals. See *Early Voyages*, p. 169. Bahía de las Ballenas is Ballenas Bay, in lat. 26° 45', and the Puerto de Santiago of Cabrillo. Bahía de las Ballenas had already been explored by the *Santo Tomás* before the *San Pedro* reached it; it was given the name from the multitude of whales seen

dered the launch sent ahead to take soundings and find out whether it had a harbor, so that the captain's ship could anchor and search for water.[1] When he came near land he found a reef more than three leagues long, with breakers throughout its length. Seeing, therefore, that there was no entrance to it, he made the accustomed signal, and we steered out to sea, continuing our voyage with great thirst, and with difficulty on account of head-winds.

On the 8th of the month of August of the said year we arrived at a headland which seemed to us a suitable place for casting anchor; and there, with the boats of the captain's ship and the frigate, we anchored. On inspection the coast was seen to be very wild, without a sign of a river or port. As we had anchored where the southeast wind was onshore, at midnight of this day the general ordered us to set sail in continuation of our voyage.

The next day the headland[2] was rounded, though with difficulty, for out at sea, two leagues from it, we discovered some shoals, to which we gave the name of Los Abreojos.[3] Having rounded these, we tacked back and forth along the coast in search of the island of Serros. On the 11th and 12th of the said month a strong northwest wind struck us, which made us lower the mainsails, there being a heavy sea. That night the wind went down and we veered toward land; but anchorage was not found, and we therefore stood out to sea again with a favorable wind.

there (*Monarchía Indiana*, I. 702; *Early Voyages*, pp. 168–169). The name does not appear on the Planos or the Carta or in the *vistas*, but on the Planos, fol. 73, an unnamed "ensenada" is shown. The bay reached just before Ballenas Bay must be the one shown on the Carta as hemmed in by the "Arecifes." Mapped in the Planos, fol. 73, and described in Explicación, *vista* 14.

[1] This appears to have been August 2. On that day the *San Diego* being in lat. 26¼°, and about two leagues from the shore, near what seemed to be a bay or inlet, Vizcaino took the opinion of his counsellors as to whether it should be examined to search for water and wait for the *Santo Tomás*, which had not been seen for over fourteen days. They agreed that the launch should go in, and, if water were found, that the *San Diego* should follow (Libro Diario, pp. 115–116).

[2] Abreojos Point; Cabrillo's Punta de Santiago (*Early Voyages*, p. 168). The Derrotero, p. 169, gives Punta de Abreojos in 27¼°. Shown in the Planos, fol. 74; described in Explicación, *vista* 15.

[3] Abreojos Rocks, off Abreojos Point, lat. 26° 46'. Vizcaino did not pass between the point and the Abreojos Rocks (Derrotero, p. 160).

The following day, the feast of San Epolito, we arrived at a bay[1] which had good protection from the northwest and which gave indications of having water. At nightfall a north wind blew from the land and obliged us to go outside. As it was strong and favorable, we sailed with it all that night, and at five o'clock in the afternoon of the next day, the fourteenth, eve of the feast of Our Lady of the Assumption, we found ourselves near a little island which had to the north of it an inlet, in which we found anchorage the same day at sunset. As soon as it was morning on the day of Our Lady, the general ordered Ensign Pasqual de Alarcon to embark in the boat with sailors and soldiers and go ashore. He found on the beach some Indians who were peaceful, for they pointed out to them several small wells of scanty, brackish water. Thereupon the ensign returned with this report, which was received with great disappointment.

Because of our great need of water, and because to go forward without finding it would be very rash and to risk our dying of thirst, the general directed Ensign Martin to arrange to go with four soldiers and follow the coast to the windward, to another inlet, three leagues beyond this place, charging him to put forth his utmost endeavors. The said ensign returned at sunset the same day with the report that he had found good water and a saline a little more than two leagues from where we were anchored, which gave us all great joy. The soldiers brought some green tomatoes.

The same night we set sail with a land breeze, passing round and measuring the little island, to which was given the name La Asuncion.[2] About two o'clock of the same day we were off another island, some three leagues distant from the last one, to which was given the name San Roque.[3] We cast

---

[1] San Hipolito Bay, lat. 26° 58′, half-way between Abreojos and Asunción Island (*Early Voyages*, p. 170). Ensenada de San Hipolito on the Carta. See Planos, fol. 75; Explicación, *vista* 16. The feast of St. Hippolytus was August 13.

[2] Asunción Island, off Asunción Point; Planos, fol. 75; Explicación, *vista* 17. By the *Santo Tomás* this and San Roque Island were called Las Islas de San Roque. They were not named by either Ulloa or Cabrillo (*Early Voyages*, p. 170). The Derrotero, p. 161, mentions Punta de San Epolito (Asunción Point, lat. 27° 7′), Isla de la Asuncion, and Isla de San Roque.

[3] San Roque Island, lat. 27° 8½′ (*Early Voyages*, p. 170). Shown in the Planos, fol. 75; described in Explicación, *vista* 17.

anchor between it and the mainland. The general ordered Ensign Alarcon to embark and go ashore where Martin de Aguilar had directed. They carried pickaxes and dug wells, putting in a quarter pipe. The water that ran into it was salty, and that which overflowed it fresh, which was considered a miracle wrought by God. We got thirty quarters and two hundred bottles, although with much trouble, for there was a heavy surf on the beach, which capsized the boat several times. Some bottles were broken and our men escaped drenched, with their arquebuses in their hands; but as we were in great need of the water they did not mind working at such a risk.

As the admiral's ship was missing, the general, desirous of learning about it, ordered Ensign Juan Francisco Serriano[1] to go with four arquebusiers to a very high hill which was about four leagues farther on, and from there to look for the admiral's ship and see whether there was any bay ahead. The ensign went and returned the same day, saying that the ship was not in sight and that there was no bay ahead of any consequence; that he had found some rancherías of Indians, who had in their huts skins of sea-wolves, of which they were making sandals,[2] and that there were many roads leading from there and indications of many people, although they did not wait for them to take some salt from the saline.

Tuesday, the 20th of the said month, we set sail in continuation of our voyage, although with the slack wind we ordinarily had had up to here, and by tacking back and forth we skirted the coast till the 23rd, the eve of the feast of San Bartolomé, when we discovered a very good port, which at first seemed to be the island of Serros. We went into it and cast anchor, and Ensign Pasqual de Alarcon went ashore. Although efforts were made, there were found neither water nor people nor anything of consequence. Captain Gerónimo Martin, cosmographer, observed the said port and said it was very good. We gave it the name of Puerto de San Bartolomé.[3]

---

[1] Suriano.   [2] *Ca, des* in the text, a misprint for *cacles*.

[3] Port San Bartolomé, lat. 27° 39′; Cabrillo's Puerto de San Pedro Vincula. Five leagues above San Roque Island, and before reaching Port San Bartolomé, the Derrotero notes Morro Hermoso, still so called, lat. 27° 30′ (*Early Voyages*, p.

CHAPTER 8.

The Departure from the Port of San Bartolomé and the Arrival at the Island of Serros.

We left this port, as has been stated, on August 23,[1] at eight o'clock at night, in continuation of our voyage. Proceeding along the coast, with the wind generally slack, by tacking back and forth we arrived at some high mountains and a headland on the eve of the feast of San Agustín, the twenty-seventh of the said month. Although great efforts were made to round the headland, the weather would not permit it. It appeared that this land was an island, and that there was another to the leeward, with a large inlet between them.[2] The general directed Captain Gerónimo Martin to go with the frigate to explore it and take soundings, while the captain's ship remained out at sea. The said Captain Gerónimo Martin went with great labor and difficulty because of the strong head-wind. He made land the following day, going ashore and exploring inland, and placing sentinels on the hills to see if the captain's ship was following.

Saturday, the last of the said month, the wind having veered

172). See also the Carta; Planos, fol. 76; Explicación, *vista* 18. Torquemada (*Monarchía Indiana*, I. 704) states that the *capitana* and *fragata* found on the shore at San Bartolomé "a resin which, because it did not have a good odor, no one wished to take. Some have supposed it to be amber, and it would not be surprising if this were so, because there were great numbers of whales there, and, as they say, this is amber. This may be true, and if so there is enough there to load a ship." See *Early Voyages*, p. 173. *Cf.* Father Ascensión's diary (below, p. 116) for a statement concerning the amber (ambergris).

[1] Torquemada (*Monarchía Indiana*, I. 704) states that the *San Pedro* and the tender left Port San Bartolomé in the night of August 24, the day they arrived. See *Early Voyages*, p. 175.

[2] Six leagues above Puerto de San Bartolomé the Derrotero (p. 162) indicates Punta de San Eugenio in lat. 28⅓°, and west of this point Isla de la Natividad de Nuestra Señora, which on approach appeared to be one with the point. The island was eight and one-half leagues around. Between the island and the point there is noted a passage of nearly three leagues (Derrotero, p. 162). Also in Planos, fol. 77, and Explicación, *vista* 19. The island was Natividad Island, lat. 27° 53'. Punta de San Eugenio is now called Point Eugenio, lat. 27° 50'. Davidson, who did not have access to the Derrotero, remarks that Point Eugenio is not described by either Cabrillo or Vizcaino (*Early Voyages*, p. 176). The passage between the point and the island is nearly four miles wide (*ibid.*, p. 174).

with great force to the northwest against the captain's ship, it put in at a harbor on the southeast shore;[1] and having cast anchor with great anxiety because the admiral's ship and launch were missing, God deigned that the admiral's ship should sail round a headland formed by the eastern shore of the same land. This gave great pleasure to the men of both ships because for forty-one days they had not seen each other. Immediately we sent them the shallop, and the admiral told how he had arrived here twelve days before, at a place where there was a good anchorage and water, although the latter was a league inland and was brackish. However, as there was great need for it, it seemed to all of them very good and to be near. There was a great abundance of fish.

Immediately the general gave orders to sail from where they were, and to cast anchor where the admiral had said. This was done, and the two ships setting sail with the same wind, God granted that the captain's ship should make port and cast anchor, the admiral's ship remaining outside, since it was not able to come in, and in order that they might see the frigate which was to windward awaiting the captain's ship, for she had left it out at sea; and thus it was that Captain Gerónimo Martin saw her, and she understanding what the captain's ship wished, he went alongside of her, and at ten o'clock at night recognized her to be the admiral's ship. At this they were greatly pleased, and still more so when told that the captain's ship was anchored further on.

The next day, September 2, they reached the place where the captain's ship was, and the general ordered a council held.[2] It was held, and he proposed to the members, if it were best, that Captain Gerónimo Martin should go in the frigate to circumnavigate and measure this land, for there was doubt as to whether or not it was an island, as it appeared very large. It was agreed that he should go, being given eight days' time for it, and that meanwhile the captain's and admiral's ships should be provided with wood and water, Captain Peguero and Ensign Pasqual de Alarcon being put in charge of this work.

[1] South Bay, on the southeast side of Cape San Agustín, Cerros Island (*Early Voyages*, pp. 174–175). See Planos, fol. 78; Explicación, *vista* 20.

[2] It was held on the *San Diego*, in lat. 29° (Libro Diario, pp. 116–117).

Captain Gerónimo Martin departed on Tuesday at two
o'clock in the afternoon to carry out this undertaking. On the
following day the general, with the religious, went ashore.
After mass was said, he went to the place where they were
getting wood and water and saw that the water was scanty
and poor, and that they were securing it only with much
trouble and that the men were becoming worn out and ill.
Reflecting that so large a land could not lack wood and water,
that the place he was in was convenient for the ships coming
from China, and that it was proper for him to investigate[1] the
resources of the land in order to take back a more complete
report, he held a council of war regarding the matter, consisting of the admiral, captains, counsellors, and ensign. It was
agreed that an entrance into the interior should be made;
that twenty arquebusiers should go, well equipped, since in
the said land there had been seen warlike men who had been
impudent and who had broken twenty bottles which the men
of the admiral's ship had left on land because they could not
get them aboard; and that Ensign Juan Francisco and Sergeant Miguel de Legar should go for three days, with strict
injunction to treat the Indians kindly and to search for wood
and water, which was our greatest necessity.[2]

The ensign set out with twenty men on the 3rd of the said
month to make the attempt, and at the end of two days he
returned, reporting that the country was very rough; that on
the slope of a great mountain range there was a large forest
of pines; and that two leagues beyond the place where they
were anchored, on the very shore of the sea, there was a stream
of fresh spring water which issued from some clumps of rushes
and which was plentiful and good. Upon hearing the good
news the general ordered them to weigh anchor immediately,
and within two hours the watering place was reached,[3] where
anchor was cast. Thursday afternoon, the 5th of the said
month, a landing was made. A pipe of the forge-bellows was

---

[1] The text reads "sta uiesse," evidently a misprint for "sse uiesse."

[2] Libro Diario, p. 118. The reason given for sending Juan Francisco and
Miguel de Lagar (sic) was that Peguero and Alarcón were occupied in preparing
the ships for the voyage.

[3] The Derrotero gives a full description of Cerros Island, pp. 162–163. See
Early Voyages, p. 174; the Planos, fol. 78; Explicación, vista 20.

carried and put into the spring, and a stream filled the pipe. Without more time or labor than putting the bottle or barrel at the pipe it was filled, and it was not two steps[1] from the sea where the boats arrived.   It was regarded as a miracle which God, our Lord, performed for us.   Very good oak, mastic, and sabine wood were found, and a cabin was built on land wherein mass was said.   Wood was taken on and the next day, Saturday, the 7th of said month, the image of Our Lady was brought forth, and was received on shore with a salute of arquebuses and musketry.

The next day, Sunday, mass was sung and there was a procession.   Father Fray Tomas de Aquino preached,[2] and after divine services were over Captain Gerónimo Martin, Father Fray Antonio de la Asemçion, and Ensign Sebastian Melendes, commander of the said frigate, reported that they had been along the land, that it was the island of Serros, and that they had measured around it for twelve leagues when a northwest wind came up and obliged them to turn back southeast to the mainland, where they went ashore, finding neither Indians nor water.   They went to an island two leagues from the mainland,[3] and Captain Gerónimo Martin surveyed it, took soundings, and returned.

Having arrived there, as has been said, the general ordered the frigate supplied with water and wood, and that it should be given canvas for a maintopsail which it needed.   This was done, and immediately the general ordered a conference and sea council,[4] composed of the admiral, cosmographer, pilot, and assistants, concerning the order of navigation from here to Cape Mendoçino.   It was agreed, besides other things which are in the book of decisions, that we should continue our voyage.   Thereupon we set sail in continuation of our voyage Monday, the 9th of the said month of September.

---

[1] The text reads *possos*, a misprint for *passos*.

[2] The text reads *pedrico*, instead of *predico*.

[3] From the description this seems to have been Natividad Island.

[4] Libro Diario, pp. 118–119.   The next stage of the voyage marked off was to Isla de las Cenizas.   It was agreed that the vessels should try to keep together, but in case of a storm from the north they were to return to Cerros Island or some port above it to wait eight days, or, in case of southeast winds, to go to Cenizas Island, to wait twelve days.

CHAPTER 9.

The Departure from the Island of Serros, and the Arrival at the Island of San Gerónimo.

Monday, the 9th of the said month of September, we set sail from the island of Serros in continuation of our voyage, and Wednesday, the 11th of the said month, we sighted the mainland toward the north-northeast. Skirting along the coast in search of some bay and port for shelter from the northwest wind, it being that which troubled us, on Friday, the 13th, we discovered an inlet sheltered from the said northwest wind. It was entered, the captain's and admiral's ships and the frigate cast anchor, and Ensign Pascual de Alarcon, with twenty men, went on shore. They took the net and caught a quantity of white fish, like that of Mechoacan, and of sole, both very good. On land a very broad and long road was found leading to the beach.[1] Not to lose time, we set sail the same night, following along the coast. On the beach the Indians signalled to us by great columns of smoke both day and night, from which we inferred that there were many Indians.

Sunday, the 15th, we sighted the very conspicuous,[2] cliff-like, white sandstone cape of Samta Maria.[3] It seemed best

---

[1] The Derrotero, the Carta, the Planos, fol. 79, and the Explicación, *vista* 21, all mention two bays here three leagues apart. The westernmost was called Ensenada del Pescado Blanco, which seems to have been Blanco Bay, lat. 29° 4′, the other being La Playa María Bay, lat. 28° 55′. Torquemada (*Monarchía Indiana*, I. 706) calls the easternmost bay San Hipolito and the westernmost San Cosme y San Damián, which Davidson identifies as La Playa María Bay and Blanco Bay. From the circumstances mentioned by Torquemada, his San Hipolito Bay seems to be Ensenada del Pescado Blanco. Neither the Carta, the Planos, the Vistas, nor the Derrotero mentions a Bay of San Hipolito here. See *Early Voyages*, p. 178.

[2] The text reads: "Descubrimos un cauo tajado muy conocido de barrial blanco *de Samta Maria*." This is ambiguous, for *muy conocido* may mean either "conspicuous" or "very well known."

[3] Apparently Point Canoas, lat. 29° 25′, the Punta del Mal Abrigo of Cabrillo. The Derrotero, p. 164, calls it El Cavo Blamco de Samta María, gives the latitude as 30½° scant, and locates it five leagues southeast of the Ensenada of San Francisco, which in turn is given as nine leagues from Cavo Bajo y Ysla de San Gerónimo. The distance from San Gerónimo Island corresponds with that of Point Canoas, which is thirteen leagues from San Gerónimo Island.

to go to it in the frigate in order to survey it and take its bearings and altitude, since it is very important for the ships that
may go to the Philippines, for, having sighted it, they may hold
their course to the island of Serros.   Therefore the general
ordered the frigate to come up alongside, whereupon the cosmographer, Captain Gerónimo Martin, went aboard.   On
Monday, the 17th[1] of the month, he set out to make this attempt.   The next day, Tuesday, there came up a very strong
northwest wind, with much fog, so that the ships could not
see one another.   At six o'clock in the afternoon of this day
the captain's and admiral's ships agreed to lie by until dawn
the next day, Wednesday.   This day they resolved to put in
at the Bay of Pescado Blanco previously mentioned,[2] because
the admiral's ship, being old, could not withstand it.   While
coasting along shore it grew dark before they reached the bay,
and for this reason they did not enter, but stood out to sea.

The same night the wind went down, whereupon we turned
back in continuation of our voyage, and Friday and Saturday
we reached the place where we had put in before.   Sunday
evening, the 20th,[3] the eve of the feast of the Apostle San
Mateo, the wind again became heavy, though not so strong,
with the same threatening weather.   That night the admiral's
ship parted company, and although attempts to find her were
made for two days, searching back and forth, she was not to
be seen.   It was thought she had put into the Bay of Pescado
Blanco.   The captain's ship went hugging the land in search
of the frigate, which had been missing for eight days, and on
Sunday, the 29th of the month, we discovered her, which caused
no little satisfaction, great pleasure to the general, and joy to
all, for we had been feeling great anxiety and fear lest she had
met with some accident during the past storm.   Captain
Gerónimo Martin came aboard the captain's ship, the frigate
putting out its canoe to bring him.   He said that during the
past storm he had put into a large bay four leagues from this

---

[1] Evidently this should be the 16th.

[2] Blanco Bay, lat. 29° 4', the Ensenada del Pescado Blanco, mentioned on
p. 69, above, note 1.

[3] This is evidently an error.   The 20th was the eve of St. Matthew, but the
22d was Sunday.   Moreover the *junta* held on September 30 states that the
almiranta strayed on the 22d.

place;[1] that in this bay there was a great number of Indians, who came out to them in reed canoes;[2] that during the second storm they had been under shelter of a small island, which was to leeward; that he had turned back in search of us, and on the 28th of the month had returned to the said bay, because it appeared that we were keeping to leeward, and from there he saw us at four o'clock in the afternoon; that the captain's ship was about to cast anchor, and that it had shelter from the northwest wind. As the weather was favorable the general gave orders to continue our voyage, and by tacking back and forth we found ourselves off the island where the captain had been, to which was given the name San Gerónimo.[3] Having rounded it the northwest wind struck us with greater fury, and the general, seeing that the admiral's ship, which remained behind, and the frigate could not weather so great a storm at sea, decided to put into the bay which has been previously mentioned. In it we, the captain's ship and the frigate, cast anchor October 2.[4]

On the beach were a number of Indians, both men and women. The general agreed with the members of the council to land, to reconnoitre, and to make a complete report of everything.[5] Ensign Pascual de Alarcon, with twenty arquebusiers, at once embarked in the boat, the Indians awaiting them on the beach peacefully. Presents were given them, and they

---

[1] This seems to be the bay entered October 2, as stated below. The latter was Bahía de San Francisco. According to the Derrotero, p. 164, it was nine leagues from San Gerónimo Island. The Carta and the Planos show it, without a name, above Ensenada de Canoas.

[2] De nea, i. e., de enea. Cf. Torquemada, I. 707.

[3] San Gerónimo Island, lat. 29° 48', the Isla de San Bernardo of Cabrillo (Early Voyages, p. 182). Planos, fol. 80; Explicación, vistas 22, 23. Juntas of the officers of the San Diego and the Tres Reyes were held on September 30, October 1 and 2. Finally it was agreed to land (Libro Diario, pp. 120–121). The Derrotero gives San Gerónimo Island as nine leagues from Ensenada de Canoas and five from Cavo Blanco de Santa María, and as in lat. 30⅔°. The Planos, fol. 80, show the little bay, unnamed, six leagues from San Gerónimo Island and three from the Ensenada de Canoas.

[4] Torquemada (Monarchía Indiana, I. 707) states that on the eve of the feast of San Francisco, October 3, they put into La Bahía de San Francisco. See Early Voyages, p. 181.

[5] The junta was held October 1, unless an error has been made in dating it. See above, note 3.

were assured by signs that we were their friends and would treat them well; thereupon Ensign Alarcon re-embarked and conveyed the news to the general. The next day, that of the blessed San Francisco,[1] the general went ashore, taking with him the Father Commissary and Father Fray Tomas de Aquino. Mass was said, and the same day the general ordered Ensign Juan Francisco Suriano, with four arquebusiers, to go to a very high hill more than two leagues from the beach in order from it to look for the admiral's ship, which, as has been said, remained behind. The ensign returned at eight o'clock at night, having carried out his instructions, and reported that the admiral's ship was not in sight and that on top of the hill there was a great number of Indians, both men and women, who were afraid of us. They went inland by a wide trail, followed by people. The next day, which was the day after the feast of San Francisco, the fathers said mass on land. The general and many of the men confessed and received communion.

To this bay was given the name of San Francisco. It has many fish—mackerel, white sea-bass, and many other kinds, of which the soldiers caught a great number with sail-rope and small lines and bent needles and pins. We found in the rancherías of the Indians some horns larger than those of bulls and small ones like those of goats; they say that the large ones are buffalo horns, and the Indians said by signs that there were cattle inland. This country has a good climate and is pleasant to travel in. Monday, the 7th of the said month, we set sail in continuation of our voyage.

CHAPTER 10.

Departure from the Bay of San Francisco and Arrival at that of the Eleven Thousand Virgins.[2]

We set sail, as has been said, from the bay of San Francisco on the 9th[3] of October. The next day we arrived at the island of San Gerónimo, which is nine leagues from this bay. We sailed around it and took its bearings but did not cast anchor, as the weather did not permit it, for it was rough and fitful. We skirted the coast on the lookout for the island

_____

[1] St. Francis.   [2] Port San Quentín.   [3] A mistake for the 7th.

of Senissas,[1] and Saturday, the 12th of the month, we discovered a very large bay[2] and an island toward the northwest. The general directed Ensign Sebastian Melendes and Anton Flores to go ahead in the frigate to take soundings of the bay, instructing them to give a certain sign if it were suitable for the captain's ship to enter and for us to follow.

Having entered it he discovered it to be so large and good that we went in and cast anchor. Immediately there came alongside peacefully more than twenty canoes of Indian fishermen. We gave them some things, which they received with pleasure. They were catching fish with hooks which appeared to be thorns from some tree, and with lines of *maguey*, plaited and better twisted than ours. They caught fish so easily that within two hours they filled their canoes. On the 13th of the month the general, with the members of the council,[3] decided to go ashore to reconnoitre and see the people there and their manner of living, and to search for water, of which we had great need. The cause of this was the quarter pipes which we carried, for as they had been made in Acapulco of old and gaping and worm-eaten staves, when we thought we had water we were without it. This caused the men much labor, and detained us somewhat on land.

When Ensign Juan de Alarcon went with twelve arquebusiers to do this work he found on the beach three rancherías of Indians, with their women and children, as quiet and free from excitement as if we had had dealings with them for many days. He found water in a lagoon a league from the beach

---

[1] There is a confusion of the names Cenizas and San Gerónimo. In Torquemada's account they are identified, but here the name Cenizas is applied to an island north of Port San Quentín. See next note.

[2] Port San Quentín, lat. 30° 24', Cabrillo's Puerto de la Posesión (*Early Voyages*, p. 184). It will be seen that the name San Quentín was applied by Vizcaino to a cape and bay a few leagues above the place now bearing that name.

[3] According to the Libro Diario, pp. 122–123, on the 13th (*tres* for *trese*— the correction is confirmed by the diary), the *San Diego* being at anchor in the bay, in lat. 32° scant, it was decided in a *junta* to send Captain Meléndez to explore an estuary communicating with a lake, and Alarcón, with twenty armed men, to explore by land. Davidson says: "To the eastward of this peninsula [Cape San Quentín] there is low country, with great lagoons penetrating the land for several miles. The entrance to these lagoons is on the east side of the cape and two miles from its extremity" (*Early Voyages*, p. 184). The estuary is shown in the Planos, fol. 81.

and he returned to report it.   The general thought this watering place was too far away and that they would have to work
very hard; and that since toward the northwest shore an entrance like a river or estuary had been discovered, in order to
find out what it was Ensign Melendes should go to reconnoitre
it.   He did so, and brought back the report that it was an
estuary which came from a large lagoon in the interior of the
country, and that it had anchorage in it for the captain's ship.
We set sail immediately and within two hours cast anchor in
it.   The general, his son, and Captain Gerónimo Martin went
ashore to explore it, together with Ensign Juan Francisco Suriano, Sebastian Melendez, Martin de Aguiar Galeote, and some
soldiers, leaving Ensign Alarcon in his place on board the
flagship.

We went more than four leagues along the beach in search
of water but did not find any.   We found in the woods a large
number of hares.   The chief pilot, Francisco de Bolaños, entered the estuary above-mentioned with the boat.   On taking
soundings he found a good depth, but the current was so
strong by reason of the high tide that it whirled the ships
around like a millrace.   The chief pilot and the pilots seeing
this, and that our vessels were not very secure, we set sail
from there, and the general directed that we should return to
the place where we were before.   There he went ashore with
Ensign Alarcon, and with the men and the picks, leaving in
his place Captain Gerónimo Martin.   They made wells near
the beach, in a patch of rushes, and found so much good water
that there was enough for a squadron.   The men were happy
at hearing this news, and the next day the general and the
religious went ashore.   Mass was said, and some Indians
came and listened to it with great attention, as if exalted.
They were told by signs, in answer to their questions, that it
had to do with heaven; and the said Indians bowed their
heads, kissed the cross, and said the prayers and all the words
we told them in our language.   The general gave food to the
Indians at his table, and they said by signs that there were
many Indians inland who shot them with arrows, and that we
should go with them.   They wore in the Mexican fashion
lilmas made of skins of animals, with a knot on the right shoulder, leather sandals, and strings of cotton fibre.   Their food

was generally *mascale*, for there are quantities of *maguey*. This place is very pleasant, for it has a large valley surrounded by lagoons in which are many fish, ducks, and heron, and a grove with hares and deer. The climate of the land is the best in the world, for the night dews last until ten o'clock in the forenoon.

We gave orders to take on water, although it was difficult, owing to the heavy surf on the beach, which flooded the boats. Thursday, the 17th of the month, the general embarked at sunset, though with much trouble and with drenchings, the canoe being flooded when leaving. That night a south wind came up, with a heavy sea oblique to the place where we were —which was in a depth of six fathoms—while near us were the breakers. Seeing our great danger, and that if the wind increased it would drive us on the coast, the general consulted with the cosmographer, chief pilot, his assistant, and experienced seamen as to what should be done to escape the peril which we were in and it was agreed that in the morning we should sail, because at present the fog was so thick that we could not see each other. Accordingly at daybreak we set sail, leaving the anchor and cable to be raised by hand, and with no little effort on the part of the chief pilot, his assistant, and the rest of the crew we went outside, leaving on shore Pasqual de Alarcon, the Father Commissary, Father Fray Tomas de Aquino, Ensigns Melendes and Aguilar, the commander of the squadron, Antonio Luis, and more than forty soldiers, leaving them without food or powder and with only a few ropes. This was what gave the general the most anxiety; however, he remedied the situation by directing the pilot, Anton Flores, to go with the frigate into the estuary, and with the canoe into the lagoon, to aid the men. He did so with great care and no little work, and we at sunset found ourselves off the entrance of the bay. The wind went down, and although there was a heavy sea we cast anchor.[1]

The next day at dawn the general ordered the boatswain,

[1] On October 19, when at anchor at a large *ensenada*, in 32° scant, a *junta* was held. It recited that a storm had arisen from the south-southeast, and that it had been necessary to leave the bay to save the ship. But a number of men and a valuable anchor and the best cable had been left inside. It was decided therefore to send the *capitana* into a near-by inlet, while the *fragata* went inside for the men and the anchor (Libro Diario, pp. 123–124).

Estevan Lopez, to go with ten sailors in the boat, charging him to make every effort to bring back the men, the cable, and the anchor. The anchor was what caused anxiety for it was the best the ship had. He did this so well that at the end of three hours he had removed the anchor and cable and part of the men who were on shore, returning immediately, together with the frigate. All the troops and men embarked; and the same day, at eight o'clock at night, when all were on board, there were many embraces because those who had come from land were with those of us on shipboard, and especially because the ships were safe.

The next day, Sunday, with a sea breeze we set sail in the continuation of our voyage. The name of the Eleven Thousand Virgins[1] was given to this bay.

CHAPTER 11.

Departure from the Bay of the Eleven Thousand Virgins and Arrival at the Port of San Diego.

We sailed, as we have said, on Sunday, the 20th[2] of the said month, from the Bay of the Eleven Thousand Virgins, and at dawn of the following day the general ordered a sailor to the topmast-head, from there to look for the admiral's ship, which was causing much anxiety, lest some misfortune should have happened to her since she had separated from us. The sailor saw a ship about six leagues out at sea, and immediately Ensign Sebastian Melendez was ordered to go in the frigate to inspect her, carrying orders that if she were the admiral's ship she should be told that we were there, and that if she were some other ship she should wait, in order to carry a package of letters to the viceroy. We also approached her, and at two o'clock in the afternoon we were all together. We recognized her to be the admiral's ship,[3] which gave the greatest pleasure.

After we had saluted the general asked the admiral, Father Fray Antonio, and Captain Peguero where they had taken shelter during the past storm, and whether they were in need

---

[1] The celebrated virgins of Cologne.

[2] Torquemada gives the date of sailing as the 24th.

[3] They had not seen the *almiranta* for twenty-eight days, and had given her up for lost (*Early Voyages*, p. 185).

of anything. They said that they carried eight quarters of water, and that the late tempest obliged them to put into the Bay of Pescado Blanco,[1] but, not being very safe there, they went to Serros Island, where they remained during the storm; and that on the 25th of the past month Ensign Juan de Azevedo Tejeda had died. This news gave great pain to the general, for he was a good soldier. After sailing forty leagues from the mainland they had discovered a large island, but the weather did not permit them to go to it.[2]

Seeing that the weather was so favorable the general ordered us to continue our voyage, and, following along the coast, the next day we discovered an island some two leagues from the mainland; we did not cast anchor at it, in order not to lose time. It was given the name of San Marcos.[3] We proceeded, tacking back and forth, and on the eve of the feast of San Simon and San Judas, the 27th of the month, we being in latitude 32° scant, a strong northwest wind came up, with a heavy sea, so that the admiral's ship and the frigate could not weather it unaided. Thereupon the general, with the admiral and the members of the council,[4] determined to put in at a bay[5] which was nine leagues to leeward, to take shelter from the storm, and to provide the admiral's ship with water. This was done, and at sunset of the same day we cast anchor in the said bay.

The next day Captain Peguero and Ensign Juan Francisco, with some soldiers, went on shore with orders to search dili-

---

[1] Blanco Bay, lat. 29° 4'. See p. 70, above, note 2.

[2] Davidson, *Early Voyages*, p. 182, following Venegas, describes the *almiranta's* course.

[3] San Martín Island, lat. 30° 29', Cabrillo's San Agustín. Shown on the Planos, fol. 81, and described in Explicación, *vista* 23. Also called Isla de las Cenizas and Isla de San Hilario by the *almiranta* (*Early Voyages*, p. 186). "San Marcos" is clearly a misprint for "San Martín."

[4] The record of the council is in Libro Diario. It states that on the 28th, the three vessels being together in lat. 32°, and about four leagues from land, a severe northwester came up. A conference was held, speaking from ship to ship, and it was agreed that since there was a prospect that the storm would last several days, and since the *almiranta* was greatly in need of water, they should put in at a bay seven leagues to the leeward. The account in Torquemada varies slightly from this.

[5] Bahía de San Simón y Judas, or de San Quentín. See note 2, p. 73. Davidson describes the Bay of San Ramón, not shown on the Planos, between San Martín Island and Cabo de San Simón y Judas (*Early Voyages*, p. 186).

gently for water and to treat well the Indians who were on the beach. When they arrived on the land they made wells near the sea and found plenty of good water. More than a hundred Indian warriors came to the place with their bows and arrows and with clubs for throwing. These Indians were very insolent, to the extent of drawing their bows and picking up stones to throw at us. Without taking notice of them except to make signs of peace, the captain and ensign embarked, and having come on board reported to the general what had happened.

The next day Captain Peguero, Ensign Pasqual de Alarcon, and the chief pilot, Francisco Bolaños, went ashore to take water. To them the general gave orders to treat the Indians well and to deal with them with great care and prudence, especially in embarking and disembarking. Arriving on land we found a multitude of Indians arrayed for battle, and although, on our part, we gave them to understand that we intended to do them no harm, but to get water, and although we gave them biscuits and other things, the Indians took no notice of what was given them; on the contrary, they tried to prevent the taking of water and to take from us the bottles and barrels. This made it necessary to fire three arquebus shots at them; whereupon, with the noise of the powder and someone's crying at the death of some of the others, they fled with great outcries; but at the end of two hours a multitude of Indians returned, assembling from different rancherías, holding councils among themselves, apparently, as to what they should do, and then, with arms in hand, they came toward us, who to them seemed few, with their women and children, bows and arrows. Ensign Pasqual de Alarcon went out to meet them, telling them by signs that they must be quiet, and that they should be friends. Thereupon the Indians said they would do so upon condition that we would not fire any more arquebuses at them, which appeared to them many. They gave a female dog as a hostage, and with this they went away to their rancherías very well satisfied, and we took on water. At midnight, the 30th of the month, the general ordered us to set sail. This bay was named San Simon y San Judas.[1]

---

[1] Colnett Bay, east of Cape Colnett, whose lat. is 30° 59′ (Davidson, *Early Voyages*, p. 188). Called Ensenada de San Quentín by the Derrotero, p. 166. The

Skirting along the coast with much difficulty because the wind was at the prow, on November 5 we discovered two small islands at the mouth of a large bay.[1] As we were entering it night came on and the wind went down, and the chief pilot told the general that he did not think it best to enter the bay that night, and so he stood out to sea, leaving it for the next day. At dawn we found ourselves at the mouth of the bay. As we were entering it a light breeze came up from the east and prevented our going in. The general consulted the admiral, captains, ensign, counsellors, and pilots as to what should be done and all were of the opinion that he should go on and not lose this wind, which was in our favor; we therefore continued our voyage. This bay was given the name of Islas de Todos los Santos.[2]

On the 9th of the said month we discovered two other islands and three farallones, in latitude 33° full, a little more than two leagues from the mainland, and a very large bay. The general ordered Ensign Melendes to go ahead in the frigate, the captain's and admiral's ships following him. Then, while the frigate sailed along the coast of the mainland, the captain's ship went up to the islands. There was so much kelp around them in the bottom of the sea, that, although the water was fourteen fathoms deep, the kelp extended more than six fathoms above the water. The captain's ship passed over it as if it were a green meadow. Some of the kelp looked as large as gourds and was very highly colored, with fruit resembling very large capers and with tubes like sackbuts. These islands were given the name San Martin.[3] The In-

name San Quentín is now applied to Vizcaino's Bay of the Eleven Thousand Virgins (p. 72, note 2). On the Planos, fol. 81, the cape is called San Quentín or San Simón y Judas. See Explicación, *vista* 23.

[1] Todos Santos Islands, off Grajero Point, whose latitude is 31° 45′. Grajero Point is Cabrillo's Cabo de la Cruz (Davidson, *Early Voyages*, p. 190) and the Cavo de Todos Santos of the Derrotero, p. 166. Shown on the Planos, fol. 82; described in Explicación, *vista* 24.

[2] From Torquemada it is seen that the *fragata* and the *almiranta* went in, but soon went back to follow the *capitana* (see Davidson, *ibid.*, p. 191).

[3] Los Coronados Islands, lat. 32° 25′; the Islas Desiertas of Cabrillo; opposite La Mesa de la Cena on the Carta. Shown in Planos, fol. 83; described in Explicación, *vista* 25. The Derrotero (p. 167) describes the Islas de San Martín as consisting of four, the largest being nearest the land. The distance from the "Puerto Bueno de San Diego" is given as six leagues to the south.

dians made so many columns of smoke on the mainland that at night it looked like a procession and in the daytime the sky was overcast.   We did not land here because the coast was wild.

The next day, Sunday, the 10th of the month, we arrived at a port, which must be the best to be found in all the South Sea, for, besides being protected on all sides and having good anchorage,[1] it is in latitude 33½°.   It has very good wood and water, many fish of all kinds, many of which we caught with seine and hooks.   On land there is much game, such as rabbits, hares, deer, very large quail, royal ducks, thrushes, and many other birds.

On the 12th of the said month,[2] which was the day of the glorious San Diego, the general, admiral, religious, captains, ensigns, and almost all the men went on shore.   A hut was built and mass was said in celebration of the feast of Señor San Diego.   When it was over the general called a council to consider what was to be done in this port, in order to get through quickly.   It was decided that the admiral, with the chief pilot, the pilots, the masters, calkers, and seamen should scour the ships, giving them a good cleaning, which they greatly needed, and that Captain Peguero, Ensign Alarcon, and Ensign Martin de Aguilar should each attend to getting water for his ship, while Ensign Juan Francisco, and Sergeant Miguel de Lagar, with the carpenters, should provide wood.

[1] San Diego Bay.   The end of Point Loma is near lat. 32° 40' (Davidson, *Early Voyages*, p. 192).   This is Cabrillo's Puerto de San Miguel.   Shown in Planos, fol. 83; described in Explicación, *vista* 25.   The Derrotero calls it the "Good port of San Diego," and says: "The tides are like those at Sanlucar, Spain, because the port within is large and good, sheltered on all sides.   No sea enters it.   There is wood, and water, though salty, and to get it wells were dug to the east of the entry near the beach.   Likewise, at a stone's throw there are plentiful fish, both of net and line.   There are numerous Indians, with bows and arrows, good people desirous of dealing with the Spaniards.   This port is in lat. 33½°" (p. 167).

[2] On the 11th, the *San Diego* being at anchor in the bay in 34° scant, Vizcaino called a *junta de mar y guerra*, and stated that the harbor seemed good and in a latitude suitable for a port for the Philippine vessels, and for other purposes of his Majesty.   It was decided to send Bolaños in the *Tres Reyes* to sound the bay and its inlets and rivers, and to find a place for cleaning the snail-covered vessels, and for getting wood, water, and fish (Libro Diario, pp. 125–126).   It would appear that the 12th of the diary should be the 11th.   The feast of San Diego was November 13.

When this had all been agreed upon, a hundred Indians appeared on a hill with bows and arrows and with many feathers on their heads, yelling noisily at us. The general ordered Ensign Juan Francisco to go to them with four arquebusiers, Father Fray Antonio following him in order to win their friendship. The ensign was instructed that if the Indians fled he should let them go, but that if they waited he should regale them. The Indians waited, albeit with some fear. The ensign and soldiers returned, and the general, his son, and the admiral went toward the Indians. The Indians seeing this, two men and two women came down from a hill. They having reached the general, and the Indian women weeping, he cajoled and embraced them, giving them some things. Reassuring the others by signs, they descended peacefully, whereupon they were given presents. The net was cast and fish were given them. Whereupon the Indians became more confident and went to their rancherías and we to our ships to attend to our affairs.

Friday, the 15th of the month, the general went aboard the frigate, taking with him his son, Father Fray Antonio, the chief pilot, and fifteen arquebusiers, to go and take the soundings of a large bay which entered the land. He did not take the cosmographer with him, as he was ill and occupied with the papers of the voyage. That night, rowing with the flood tide, he got under way and at dawn he was six leagues within the bay, which he found to be the best, large enough for all kinds of vessels, more secure than at the anchorage, and better for careening the ships, for they could be placed high and dry during the flood tide and taken down at the ebb tide, even if they were of a thousand tons.

I do not place in this report the sailing directions, descriptions of the land, or soundings, because the cosmographer and pilots are keeping an itinerary in conformity with the art of navigation.

In this bay the general, with his men, went ashore. After they had gone more than three leagues along it a number of Indians appeared with their bows and arrows, and although signs of peace were made to them, they did not dare to approach, excepting a very old Indian woman who appeared to be more than one hundred and fifty years old and who approached weeping. The general cajoled her and gave her some beads and something to eat. This Indian woman, from extreme age, had wrinkles on her belly which looked like a blacksmith's bellows, and the navel protruded bigger than a gourd. Seeing this kind treatment the Indians came peaceably and took us to their rancherías, where they were gathering their crops and where they had made their *paresos* of seeds like flax. They had pots in which they cooked their food, and the women were dressed in skins of animals. The general would not allow any soldier to enter their rancherías; and, it being already late, he returned to the frigate, many Indians accompanying him to the beach. Saturday night he reached the captain's ship, which was ready; wood, water, and fish were brought on board, and on Wednesday, the 20th of the said month, we set sail. I do not state, lest I should be tiresome, how many times the Indians came to our camps with skins of martens and other things. Until the next day, when we set sail, they remained on the beach shouting. This port was given the name of San Diego.

CHAPTER 12.

Departure from the Port of San Diego and Arrival at the Island of Santa Catalina.

We left the port of San Diego, as has been said, on a Wednesday, the 20th of the said month,[1] and the same day the general ordered Ensign Sebastian Melendes to go ahead with the frigate to examine a bay which was to windward some four leagues,[2] and directed that the pilot should sound it, map it,

[1] On November 19 a *junta* was held to draw up sailing orders. It was agreed that in case of any vessel's being driven by head-winds before finding another port, it was to return to the Bay of San Diego; if driven by a southwest wind it was to run with it to 38° or a little above, where there was said to be an island, there to wait eight days, making signals; at the end of that time, if still alone, it should continue to Cape Mendocino (Libro Diario, pp. 126–127).

[2] Apparently False Bay, just north of San Diego Bay, shown as "Ensenada de baxa entrada." It is described by the Derrotero, pp. 167–168, as being a large bay two leagues above the entry of San Diego Bay. It is added that it is shallow at the entry but deep inside, and that it has a great grove of trees on the east shore. From the bay to the Punta de la Arboleda the distance is given as ten leagues; from here to the Ysla y Ensenada de Buena Gente, fifteen leagues; thence to the Ysla de Samta Catalina, eight leagues, southwest. According to

and find out what was there. He did so, and the next day
ordered the return to the captain's ship. He reported to the
general that he had entered the said bay, that it was a good
port, although it had at its entrance a bar of little more than
two fathoms depth, and that there was a very large grove at
an estuary which extended into the land, and many Indians:
and that he had not gone ashore. Thereupon we continued
our voyage, skirting along the coast until the 24th of the
month, which was the eve of the feast of the glorious Samta
Catalina,[1] when we discovered three large islands.[2] We approached them with difficulty because of a head-wind, and
arrived at the middle one, which is more than twenty-five
leagues around.

On the 27th of the month, and before casting anchor in a
very good cove[3] which was found, a multitude of Indians
came out in canoes of cedar and pine, made of planks very well
joined and calked, each one with eight oars and with fourteen
or fifteen Indians, who looked like galley-slaves. They came
alongside without the least fear and came on board our ships,
mooring their own. They showed great pleasure at seeing us,
telling us by signs that we must land, and guiding us like
pilots to the anchorage. The general received them kindly
and gave them some presents, especially to the boys. We
anchored, and the admiral, Ensign Alarcon, Father Fray Antonio, and Captain Peguero, with some soldiers, went ashore.
Many Indians were on the beach, and the women treated us
to roasted sardines and a small fruit like sweet potatoes.[4]

this, Punta de Arboleda would be about at modern Encinitas, although in the
Planos, fol. 84, Punta de Arboleda is shown about half-way from San Diego Bay
to San Pedro Bay. Torquemada mentions a bay a few leagues before reaching
Santa Catalina Island, which Davidson identifies with San Pedro Bay (Davidson,
Early Voyages, pp. 194–195), but it is clear that the one entered by Meléndez on
the 21st was not so far north. I judge, therefore, that Davidson is in error in
his identification.

[1] St. Catherine.

[2] The three shown on the Planos are the Santa Catalina, the Santa Bárbara,
and the San Nicolás, but we know that the San Clemente was also described.

[3] On Santa Catalina Island : the San Salvador of Cabrillo.

[4] Santa Catalina Island is shown on the Planos, fol. 84. From this map,
together with the diary and the Derrotero, it is clear that the first anchorage
was near the middle of the eastern coast. The port near the pueblo is called
Puerto de Santa Catalina. The Derrotero (p. 168) describes the island.

Fresh water was found, although a long distance from the beach.

The next day the general and the Father Commissary went ashore, a hut was built, and mass was said. More than one hundred and fifty Indian men and women were present, and they marvelled not a little at seeing the altar and the image of our Lord Jesus crucified, and listened attentively to the saying of mass, asking by signs what it was about. They were told that it was about heaven, whereat they marvelled more. When the divine service was ended the general went to their houses, where the women took him by the hand and led him inside, giving him some of the food which they had given before. He brought to the ship six Indian girls from eight to ten years old, whom their mothers willingly gave him, and he clothed them with chemises, petticoats, and necklaces, and sent them ashore. The rest of the women, seeing this, came with their daughters in canoes, asking for gifts. The result was that no one returned empty-handed. The people go dressed in seal skins, the women especially covering their loins, and their faces show them to be modest; but the men are thieves, for anything they saw unguarded they took. They are a people given to trade and traffic and are fond of barter, for in return for old clothes they would give the soldiers skins, shells, nets, thread, and very well twisted ropes, these in great quantities and resembling linen. They have dogs like those in Castile.

Thursday, the 28th of the said month, there was an eclipse of the moon, which commenced at a quarter past ten at night and lasted until twelve o'clock, being entirely over at one o'clock; the eclipse commenced on the eastern edge.

On the night of the eve of San Andres, the 29th of the said month, we set sail,[1] for the Indians had told us by signs that farther along on this same island they had their houses and there was food. On the day of San Andres, at four o'clock

[1] On November 29, the *San Diego* being at anchor at Santa Catalina Island in 34½°, a *junta* was held to consider circumnavigating the island and exploring the San Andrés (San Clemente). It was decided not to spend the time, but to go ahead, leaving these explorations for the return, since the weather was good, the men were becoming ill, and supplies becoming short (Libro Diario, pp. 127–128). The general therefore ordered the pilots to set sail as soon as possible.

in the afternoon, we arrived at the place which the Indians
had designated, they piloting us in their canoes into the port,[1]
which is all that could be desired as to convenience and security. On the beach there was a pueblo and more than three
hundred Indians, men, women and children. The general
and Ensign Alarcon went ashore and inspected it. The next
day the general and many of the rest of us went ashore.
The Indian men and women embraced him and took him to
their houses. These women have good features. The general gave them beads and regaled them, and they gave him
prickly pears and a grain like the *gofio* of the Canary Islands,
in some willow baskets very well made, and water in vessels
resembling flasks, which were like rattan inside and very thickly
varnished outside. They had acorns and some very large
skins, apparently of bears, with heavy fur, which they used for
blankets.

The general went inland to see the opposite coast. He
found on the way a level prairie, very well cleared, where the
Indians were assembled to worship an idol which was there.[2]
It resembled a demon, having two horns, no head, a dog at its
feet, and many children painted all around it. The Indians
told the general not to go near it, but he approached it and
saw the whole thing, and made a cross, and placed the name
of Jesus on the head of the demon, telling the Indians that
that was good, and from heaven, but that the idol was the
devil. At this the Indians marvelled, and they will readily
renounce it and receive our Holy Faith, for apparently they
have good intellects and are friendly and desirous of our
friendship. The general returned to the pueblo, and an Indian woman brought him two pieces of figured China silk, in
fragments, telling him that they had got them from people
like ourselves, who had negroes; that they had come on the
ship which was driven by a strong wind to the coast and
wrecked, and that it was farther on. The general endeavored
to take two or three Indians with him, that they might tell
him where the ship had been lost, promising to give them

[1] Puerto de Santa Catalina, mentioned above.

[2] On Vizcaino's chart in Burney a small dot is placed on Santa Catalina
Island, to represent, Davidson thinks, the "so-called Temple of the Sun" (Burney,
Voyages, II., map opp. p. 256; Davidson, *Early Voyages*, p. 196).

clothes. The Indians consented and went with him to the captain's ship, but as we were weighing anchor preparatory to leaving the Indians said they wished to go ahead in their canoe, and that they did not wish to go aboard the ship, fearing that we would abduct them, and the general, in order not to excite them, said: "Very well."

We set sail, and on leaving the port a head-wind struck us, which prevented our going where the Indians indicated; therefore we stood out to sea and the Indians returned to their pueblo. This attempt was given up because we did not have the launch, which had gone to reconnoitre another island,[1] apparently belonging to the mainland, and because the admiral's ship was absent, as it could not make the said port, and because the fog was so very dense that we could not see each other, and also because there seemed to be many islands, keys, and shoals, among which, in such weather, the pilots did not dare take the flagship; and so we continued our voyage.

The next day the admiral's ship and frigate came up with us, for perhaps God willed it that we should be united. On being asked what he had found on the island, Ensign Melendez said that there were many Indians, who had told him by signs that upon it there were men who were bearded and clothed like ourselves. Thinking them to be Spaniards, he sent them a note, and eight Indians came to him in a canoe, bearded and clothed in skins of animals, but they could learn nothing more. Accordingly the general ordered that we should continue our voyage without further delay, because our men were all becoming ill, leaving for the return any efforts to verify what the Indians of the island of Samta Catalina had told us by signs, for, as we could not understand their language, all was confusion and there was little certainty as to what they said.

---

[1] Apparently the island in San Pedro Bay called "Isla vaja de buena gente." This may have been El Moro, or Dead Man's Island.

CHAPTER 13.

The Departure from the Island of Santa Catalina and the Arrival at the Port of Monterrey.

We left this said island of Sancta Catalina and port of San Andres on Sunday,[1] December 1st. On this day, as has been stated, we met the admiral's ship and the frigate, and, after the general had conferred with the admiral and the members of the council as to what should be done, it was agreed that we should continue our voyage, since our men were becoming ill, the cold increasing, and winter coming on, and since there were neither comforts nor medicines with which to cure the sick, and, if we should delay, the voyage could not be completed.[2]

So we went on skirting the coast, and on Monday, the 2d of the said month, we sighted two other large islands. Passing between the first and the mainland,[3] a canoe came out to us with two Indian fishermen, who had a great quantity of fish, rowing so swiftly that they seemed to fly. They came alongside without saying a word to us and went twice around us with so great speed that it seemed impossible; this finished, they came aft, bowing their heads in the way of courtesy. The general ordered that they be given a cloth, with bread. They received it, and gave in return the fish they had, without any pay, and this done they said by signs that they wished to go. After they had gone five Indians came in another canoe, so well constructed and built that since Noah's Ark a finer and

[1] Evidently San Pedro Bay, called on the charts Ensenada de San Andrés. Santa Monica Bay is shown just above it as "Gran Ensenada." Torquemada says, "After taking a survey of several parts of this island, the squadron left it on the third of December, 1602." Quoted in Davidson, *Early Voyages*, p. 197. This does not agree with the official diary.

[2] The reference seems to be to the council recorded in the Libro Diario as of November 29. See above, p. 84, note 1.

[3] They were now in the Santa Bárbara channel. Vizcaino's chart shows Isla de Santa Bárbara (Santa Barbara Island) and Isla de San Nicolás, but he does not mention them in any of the narratives. Davidson states that Vizcaino is the first to call attention to the parallelism of these islands with the continental shore (*Early Voyages*, p. 200). See the Planos, fols. 84, 85, 86, and Explicación, *vistas* 26. 27. 28.

lighter vessel with timbers better made has not been seen. Four men rowed, with an old man in the centre, [singing]¹ as in a *mitote* of the Indians of New Spain, and the others responding to him. Before coming alongside they stopped and he saluted us three times, making many ceremonious gestures with his head and body, and ordering the Indians to row around. This was done so swiftly that in a moment they went around us twice and immediately came aft. Only the old man spoke, he saying by signs that we must go to his land, where they would give us much food and water, for there was a river. He gave us a flask of it which he had brought, and a willow basket of food, a sort of porridge made of acorn meal. This Indian made himself so well understood by signs that he lacked nothing but ability to speak our language. He came to say that as a pledge of the truth of what he said one of us should get into his canoe and go to his land, and that he would remain on board ship with us as a hostage. The general, in order to test the Indian's good faith, ordered a soldier to get into the canoe, and at once the Indian came aboard our ship with great satisfaction, telling the others who were in the canoe to go ashore and prepare food for all of us.

Meanwhile, as the sun was already setting, the admiral's ship arrived near us, whereupon the general called a council ² of the admiral, ensign, and pilots, to consider what should be done, since for our voyage the wind was now behind us, which had not been the case since we had left Acapulco. It was agreed that the Indians should depart, being given to understand by signs that next day we would go to their land; but such were the efforts of this Indian to get us to go to it that as a greater inducement he said he would give to each one of us ten women to sleep with. This Indian was so intelligent that he appeared to be not a barbarian but a person of great understanding. We showed him lead, tin, and plates of silver. He sounded them with his finger and said that the silver was good but the others not.

This Indian left, and the same evening the northwest wind

---

¹ There is evidently some omission in the print. At this point Torquemada has "all singing in their language as the Indians of New Spain sing in the *mitote*" (*Monarchía Indiana*, I. 713).

² This council is not recorded in the Libro Diario.

freshened so well for us that we sailed more than fifteen leagues, but between islands and with no little anxiety and danger, since we knew not where we were going; and next morning we found ourselves hemmed in between islands and mainland. Tacking back and forward on the 4th of the said month, we were struck by a heavy northwester, with a high sea, and were obliged to take off the bonnets and run with lower sails, so that we became separated from each other.

At dawn the captain's ship was near an island, in the shelter of which it was calm. A canoe came out with two Indians and a small boy, their eyes being painted with antimony. They asked us to go to their land; however, there was such a heavy sea and the island presented so many shoals that we did not dare go to it, but veered out to sea, where we found the frigate. We made the usual signals to it and it came to us. When it came alongside it was agreed that we should go ahead of the frigate toward the island to see if there was any protection in which to take shelter from the wind. We did so, and on our going there the admiral's ship appeared and followed us. The launch went in between this island and another, we following it; but it appeared to the chief pilot and pilots that it was not best to follow it, for many shoals and reefs were seen and the night was coming on, with a high sea and wind, and that we should run the risk of being lost. Therefore the general gave orders to go outside, the frigate, which had already gone between the two islands mentioned, remaining.

The next day the wind went down and we skirted the coast, although with great anxiety lest some accident had befallen the frigate, which remained behind and did not appear. We continued our voyage, with a favorable wind, until the 12th of the said month, eve of the feast of Santa Luçia,[1] when the frigate overtook us. This gave great pleasure,

---

[1] As Davidson remarks, it is strange that Vizcaino does not mention Point Concepción in his narrative, though he shows it on his chart (*Early Voyages*, p. 204). The Derrotero, however, does mention it, stating that "La Punta de la Limpia Concessçion is in $35\frac{1}{2}°$ long, and this point is low, with timber. It forms two coasts; on that toward the east, ten leagues from said point, on the seashore, is a very large pueblo of more than two hundred houses" (Derrotero, p. 169).

especially because the ensign and the pilot said that they had gone into the interior of the said island and that there was a pueblo[1] there with more than two hundred large houses, in each one of which lived more than forty Indians; and that in the midst of it two poles were nailed together, with one above, like a gallows. More than twenty canoes came alongside the frigate, and because they were all alone they dared not stay there. In this place there are great numbers of Indians, and the mainland has signs of being thickly populated. It is fertile, for it has pine groves and oaks, and a fine climate, for although it gets cold it is not so cold as to cause discomfort.[2]

The day of Santa Luçia,[3] at four o'clock in the morning, a southeast wind struck us, the first we had had during the voyage. It lasted until sunset the next day, when we reached a place in 37° full.[4] The general ordered Ensign Melendez to go ahead to explore a large bay and see if there were any port, for this country was the most important of the exploration for the purposes of his Majesty.

This was done, and as the bay was found to be large and as night was coming on, we went outside. The said ensign entered the bay, and the next day, the 16th of the month, the frigate came alongside and the pilot told the general that he had found a good port, a sketch of which he had brought back. The general held a council[5] to consider what should be done

[1] This pueblo is shown on the Planos, fol. 86. San Miguel Island (Cabrillo's Isla de la Posesión) is given on Vizcaino's chart as Isla de Baxos.

[2] The reference seems to be to the coast on the Canal de Santa Bárbara.

[3] St. Lucy's Day, December 13. The coast between Point Concepción and the Bay of Monterey is described in the Derrotero, p. 169.

[4] Monterey harbor, lat. 36° 31', now discovered for the first time. It was so named in honor of the ruling viceroy, Gaspár de Zúñiga y Acevedo, Conde de Monterey. Shown on Planos, fol. 88; described in Explicación, *vista* 29; Derrotero, p. 169. Davidson says that Vizcaino applied the name only to the southeast angle of the bay, where the city of Monterey now is (*Early Voyages*, p. 214). The Planos, fol. 88, show Puerto de Monterrey swinging round to a headland about opposite Punta de Pinos, and then another large bight curving clear around to Punta de Año Nuevo, and not showing the convex curve of the coast from Santa Cruz nearly to Point Año Nuevo.

[5] The Libro Diario records the council of December 16. The day before, Meléndez and Flores had been sent in the *fragata* to examine the Bay of Monterey; returning, Flores had boarded the *San Diego* bearing a map of the bay.

and it was agreed that they should put in at the said port, provide themselves with water, and restore the men and the sick, of whom there were many. We arrived this day at seven o'clock in the evening and cast anchor.

CHAPTER 14.

The Arrival at the Port of Monterey, and the Decision made there to despatch the Admiral's Ship with Reports to New Spain; and to continue with the Captain's Ship and the Frigate to Cape Mendoçino.

We arrived, as has been said, at this port of Monterey, on the 16th of the said month of December, at seven o'clock in the evening. The next day the general ordered Ensign Alarcon to go ashore, with orders to make a hut where mass could be said and to see if there was water, and what the country was like. He found that there was fresh water, and a great oak[1] near the shore, where he made the hut and arbor[2] to say mass. The general, commissary, admiral, captains, ensign, and the rest of the men landed at once; and mass having been said and the day having cleared, there having been much fog, we found ourselves to be in the best port that could be desired, for besides being sheltered from all the winds, it has many pines for masts and yards, and live oaks and white oaks, and water in great quantity, all near the shore.[3] The land is fertile, with a climate and soil like those of Castile; there is much wild game, such as harts, like young bulls, deer, buffalo, very large bears, rabbits, hares, and many other animals

Since it seemed promising as a port for the Philippine ships, and as it appeared to have fresh water, for lack of which the men were ill, it was decided to go in, explore, and seek water. There was one dissenting voice, that of Alarcón. He advised going on to the bay where Cermeño had been wrecked (Drake's Bay) and where Bolaños said there was water, he having been with Cermeño. Vizcaino yielded to the majority, and gave orders to enter Monterey Bay (Libro Diario, pp. 128–129).

[1] Until recently an oak stood in Monterey which, according to tradition, was the tree under which mass was said in 1602. The spot is now marked by a cross.

[2] *Recado* for *ramada*.

[3] The bay is well protected from southeast storms, but little from those from the northwest. Davidson states that Vizcaino greatly overpraised the harbor, and thereby misled Costansó. later (*Early Voyages.* p. 212).

and many game birds, such as geese, partridges, quail, crane, ducks, vultures, and many other kinds of birds which I will not mention lest it be wearisome. The land is thickly populated with numberless Indians, of whom a great many came several times to our camp. They appeared to be a gentle and peaceable people. They said by signs that inland there are many settlements. The food which these Indians most commonly eat, besides fish and crustaceans, consists of acorns and another nut larger than a chestnut. This is what we were able to understand from them.

In view of the fact that we had so many sick, that the pilot of the admiral's ship and his assistant were very ill, that there was a shortage of sailors for going forward, and that the supplies were becoming exhausted because of the length of time we had spent in coming, it seemed to the general impossible to complete the exploration this time without a new supply of men and provisions; and he therefore at once called a conference of the admiral and the members of the council [1] to consider what should be done for the best service of his Majesty. It was decided that the admiral's ship should return as a messenger to the viceroy of New Spain with a copy of the records of the discoveries as far as this place, carry back those who were the most ill, ask for further supplies of men and provisions in order to complete at this time the exploration of the remainder of the coast and of the entrance to the Californias, designating the time and place to which they were to be sent; and other things which were treated of in the council and were written to the said señor viceroy; and

---

[1] The council was held on December 18. In it Vizcaino revealed his secret orders to explore on his way back, if there was time, the Gulf of California to 37°, two degrees more or less, and to report on the pearl-fisheries and inhabitants. This conference was the most solemn of all held, and each member gave his opinion separately. It was shown that already eight months had passed, and provisions had been brought for only eleven. Several men had died. Pilot Juan Pascual and his assistant were sick in bed, and in all forty men were ill. This number included some of the helmsmen, who were unable to steer because they were paralyzed. The sick were without suitable medicine and food. The *Santo Tomás* was unseaworthy. Corbán was continued in command of the *almirante*, but since Pilot Juan Pascual was ill, Manuel Sessar Cordero was sent to serve as pilot. The *capitana* and *fragata* were to await the new orders on the return at Puerto de la Paz (Libro Diario, p. 144).

that we, with the captain's ship and frigate, should go on to
Cape Mendoçino, and farther if the weather should permit.

The foregoing having been agreed upon it was at once
put into execution.   The admiral's ship was immediately supplied with wood and water; those who were the most ill went
aboard her; and the journals, maps, relations, and itineraries
were copied, which was no little work, because of the ill health
of the cosmographer and the scrivener, but it was accomplished
with all possible diligence, as was also the taking on of wood
and water, because the men were very ill.   The admiral's
ship left on Sunday night at 8 o'clock, the 29th of the said
month, with orders to make haste.

CHAPTER 15.

*The Departure from the Port of Monterey; What occurred after
the Admiral's Ship had been despatched with Messages;
and the Arrival at Cape Mendoçino.*

Sunday, the 29th of the said month, the admiral's ship set
out with messages, carrying those most ill, and provided with
water, wood, and what was necessary to reach the port of
Acapulco, the admiral carrying instructions not to put in at
any port until he reached that of Acapulco; he was especially
charged with the care of the sick, and with other things which
were provided in the said instructions.   We ourselves remained, making the preparations necessary for our voyage to
Cape Mendoçino.   The men worked under great difficulties in
taking on wood and water because of the extreme cold, which
was so intense that Wednesday, New Year's Day of 1603,
dawned with all the mountains covered with snow and resembling the volcano of Mexico,[1] and that the hole from
which we were taking water was frozen over more than a
palm in thickness, and the bottles, which had been left full
over night, were all frozen so that even when turned upside-
down not a drop ran out.   So urgent was our situation that
necessity compelled us all to act with energy, especially the
general, who aided in carrying the bottles and in the other
tasks, with the good support of Ensign Alarcon and Captain

---

[1] Popocatepetl, popularly called in the neighborhood "El Vulcán"—The
Volcano.

Peguero, who, although ill, aided, while the pilots spared no efforts to forward our preparation, so that by Friday night, the 3d of the said month,[1] we were all ready.

This day the general, with the commissary and ten arquebusiers, went inland, toward the southeast, having heard of a copious stream that ran into the sea and of another good headland, and in order better to see the lay of the land and its people and animals. He proceeded some three leagues when he discovered another good port, into which entered a copious river[2] descending from some high, snow-covered mountains with large pines, white and black poplars, and willows. It had an extended river bottom, and in it were many cattle as large as cows although apparently they were harts, and yet their pelts were different, for their wool dragged on the ground, and each horn was more than three yards long.[3] An effort was made to kill some of them but they did not wait long enough. No people were found because, on account of the great cold, they were living in the interior. He sent Ensign Juan Francisco with four soldiers to a ranchería to see what was there; he found it to be depopulated, and returned.

The general and all the men having reached the flagship, at nightfall we raised all but one anchor, and at midnight, aided by the land breeze, we set sail.[4] On leaving the harbor a northeast wind came up favorably for our voyage, so that at dawn we were more than ten leagues farther on and, although the wind went down, aided by the off-shore breeze we reached the bay[5] where was lost the ship *San Agustin*, of which Sebastian Melendez Rodriguez was pilot; however, although the chief pilot recognized it, we did not stop lest we

---

[1] January, 1603.

[2] Carmel River, which empties into Carmel Bay a few miles to the south of Monterey Bay, in lat. 36° 34' (Davidson, *Early Voyages*, p. 212). It was given this name by the Vizcaino expedition.

[3] Evidently the elk.

[4] January 3, 1603. *Cf.* Father Ascensión's statement (p. 120, below).

[5] Drake's Bay, lat. 38°, where Sebastián Meléndez Rodríguez Cermeño was wrecked in 1595. Davidson states that Vizcaino makes no reference to Point Año Nuevo (*Early Voyages*, p. 214). It is indeed not on the chart as reproduced by Burney, but it is on the Carta and on Planos, fol. 88, which is reproduced in Richman, *California under Spain and Mexico*, opp. p. 23. On this Plano the island southeast of Los Frayles is called Isleo Hendido. El Morro de los Reyes is of course Point Reyes, and Puerto de Don Gaspár is Reyes Bay, or Drake's Bay.

should not have another favorable wind;[1] but the next day an exceedingly strong northwest wind struck us, which obliged us to seek shelter in it. We cast anchor, although outside, with the intention of going ashore next day,[2] but at daybreak the offshore wind struck us and obliged us to set sail. As we were sailing, two canoes, with an Indian in each, came out from the bay calling to us to come to the port, and saying they were awaiting us.[3] They dared not come to the ship, and consequently we left them, in order not to lose time. For it was not well to lose any, since the men were very ill, the cold was increasing, and the frigate did not appear, because in the recent northwest wind it had parted company.

Aided by favoring land breezes, we skirted the coast until the 12th of the said month, when the moon was in conjunction, and we found ourselves to be off Cape Mendoçino,[4] so greatly desired by all, for it was reached with so much toil and difficulty. And in order that our labors should be more highly esteemed, God willed that the new moon of January should begin with so furious a south wind, together with so much rain and fog, as to throw us into great doubt whether to go forward or to turn back, for it was as dark in the daytime as at night. The seas were very high, so that we could neither run nor lie by at sea. All the men had fallen sick, so that there were only two sailors who could climb to the maintopsail.

In view of the great straits and the doubt which we were in,

[1] It will be seen from the note next below that according to the diary the wind shifted on the 8th and not on the 7th.

[2] From the Libro Diario we learn that on January 9, the *San Diego* being in 39°, a council was held. According to the record, at sunset of the day before a strong southwester arose; all night they had sailed with the lower sails, trying without avail to make headway, because the men were too ill to manage the vessel. It was decided, therefore, to take refuge in a port two leagues to the leeward, sheltered from the north, where Bolaños said he had been with Cermeño in the *San Agustín* (Libro Diario, pp. 139–140).

[3] The text is corrupted here.

[4] Lat. 40° 27'. The Derrotero, p. 170, describes Cape Mendoçino, and locates it in latitude 41⅓°, or 53' too far north. See Planos, fol. 91; Explicación, *vistas* 32, 33. The bay and river just below Cape Mendoçino were evidently inserted in the Carta, on Planos, fol. 91, and in the diary, on the basis of the reports of the voyage of the *Tres Reyes* and not of the *San Diego*, as will appear later on. The Derrotero says nothing about them in the original description of the Cape Mendocino region. See Derrotero, p. 170.

the general called a council [1] of the captains, the pilots, and their assistants to consider what should be done for the best interest of his Majesty. It was decided that it would not be best to go forward as there were no men for it, it was very cold, the rains were increasing and winter coming on all at once, and if we were to go on we should all perish. With this decision, the general ordered that when the weather should permit we should return to Cape San Lucas.

The next day the wind calmed and the sun shone, so that the pilots were able to take the latitude,[2] and they found themselves to be in forty-one degrees. Although it had been decided that we should turn back, a wind storm came up from the southeast which made us very cold. Worse than this, on the day of San Anton, the 17th of the said month, at eight o'clock at night, when lying by at sea, the ship was struck by two seas which made it pitch so much that it was thought the keel was standing on end, and that it was even sinking. The pitching was so violent that it threw both sick and well from their beds and the general from his. He struck upon some boxes and broke his ribs with the heavy blow.

This trouble continued until the 20th of the said month, the day of San Sebastian, when the storm abated and we found ourselves in 42 degrees,[3] for the currents and seas were carrying us

[1] This was on the 13th, the *San Diego* being in 41¼°. Vizcaino stated that he had orders to reach Cape Mendocino, in 41°, and, in case the weather would permit without too great risk, to go as far as Cape Blanco, in 44°; arrived there, if the coast did not turn east, to follow it one hundred leagues, but no further. It was decided, however, that it was perilous to continue, since there were not two men who could ascend to the maintopsail, winter was coming on, and navigation of the coast dangerous. Orders were given, therefore, to return to Puerto de la Paz, there to await new orders from the viceroy. Nothing was said of the *Tres Reyes* in the council (Libro Diario, pp. 140–142). No other council is recorded till January 28, at Isla de Santa Catalina.

[2] Davidson concludes that the lat. 41° was based on mere "report," but we learn here that an observation was actually made (Davidson, *Early Voyages*, p. 230).

[3] Of the voyage of the *San Diego* after leaving Puerto de los Reyes, Torquemada says that it sailed slowly northwest in search of the *Tres Reyes*, and on Sunday, the 12th, sighted some high mountains (Davidson says King's Peak), and fourteen leagues farther, Cape Mendocino, in lat. 41°. Next day, the 13th, a heavy southeast wind arose, and they lay to till the 19th, by which time they had drifted to 42°, near Cavo Blanco de San Sebastián (*Monarchía Indiana*, I. 718; Davidson, *Early Voyages*, pp. 231–233).

rapidly to the Strait of Anian. This day we sighted land both on the cape and beyond, covered with great pine forests. There was much snow covering the mountains, making them look like volcanoes, and reaching down to the sea.

On the 21st of the month God sent us a light northwest wind, which had been so unseasonable for us in going but was so desirable for the return, and which brought us out of this trouble. We skirted along the coast, inspecting again what we had seen, as far as this place.

CHAPTER 16.

The Return from Cape Mendoçino, the Arrival at the Islands of Masatlan, and what occurred on the Return.

We returned, as has been said, from Cape Mendoçino, and from another beyond to which was given the name San Sebastian, on the 21st of the month of January. The northwest wind aiding us, we came along skirting the coast, carefully reviewing it all, and on the 25th of the said month we had come as far as the port of Monterrey, where the Indians signalled us with smoke. We did not enter it because the state of our health was so bad and the sick were clamoring, although there was neither assistance nor medicines nor food to give them except rotten jerked beef, gruel, biscuits, and beans and chick-peas spoiled by weevils. The mouths of all were sore, and their gums were swollen larger than their teeth, so that they could hardly drink water, and the ship seemed more like a hospital than a ship of an armada. Affairs were in such a condition that anyone who had ever in his life been at the helm steered, climbed to the maintopsail, and did the other tasks, and all who could walk assisted at the hearth, making gruel and porridge for the sick. Above all, we were greatly distressed because the frigate, the *Tres Reyes*, did not appear, for we feared that she had been lost in the past storm; but our need was so great, as has been said, that we could not wait for her, although it was our intention to do so at the island of Santa Catalina,[1] where we arrived

---

[1] From a *junta* held January 28, the *San Diego* being off Santa Catalina Island in lat. 34°, it is learned that on the return several days were spent re-exploring inlets not completely examined on the way up, and that Captain Gerónimo, Bolaños, and his assistant pilot, had recommended putting in at Santa Catalina Island to await the *Tres Reyes*. But since the men were too ill to get wood and

the 29th of the said month.   Although many canoes of Indians came with fish and other things, inviting us to go to them, the general did not dare cast anchor among them, as he did not have men strong enough to raise the anchors, and as the sick were dying of hunger.

We therefore continued our voyage for the island of Serros, and so great was our need of wood and water that we anchored there February 6th of the said year ; only one small anchor was cast, with the idea that if it could not be raised it could remain there with the cable.   The general went on shore with six men, but the strongest of them could not lift a bottle of water from the ground, and only with the greatest efforts of all could they take on twelve quarters of water.   The Indians of the island came down to the beach where the water hole was made, with their bows and arrows, painted with vermillion, and playing flutes, and although the general called and coaxed them and gave them hardtack, they would not accept it or approach peaceably, but, as before, tried to hinder and prevent the taking of water.   This obliged the general to order some arquebus shots fired, though in the air, in order to terrify them ; thereupon they ran away up the mountain.

The next day the general ordered Ensign Pasqual de Alarcon to go with the men to get wood on land.   He did so, and at midnight on the 8th of the month we set sail, weighing anchor with the greatest efforts of all, and continued our voyage with a fresh wind behind us, skirting the coast, until the 11th of the month, when we drew near Cape San Lucas to bring away the long-boat which we had left there on the outward voyage, as well as to put in at the port of La Paz to await the succor we had sent to the viceroy to ask.   All were of the opinion[1] that

water, or even to weigh anchor once it was cast, it was concluded that no time should be lost, lest all might perish (Libro Diario, pp. 142–143).

[1] A council was held on the *San Diego* on February 13, off Cape San Lucas. The questions considered were whether to enter the Bay of San Bernabé to get the long-boat and await the *fragata* and then go to Puerto de la Paz to await new orders, or to proceed to New Spain as rapidly as possible.   All were agreed that no stop should be made, because of the deplorable condition of the crew.   The two caulkers were dead ; over forty-five men were ill, and not six were able-bodied ; the scanty provisions were foul.   It was decided to go to Mazatlán where help could be had from the villa de San Sebastián (Libro Diario, pp. 143–148).   This is the last council recorded.

we should not put in at the said bay nor go to the port of La Paz, because the men were so sick and exhausted that if anchor were cast the ship would not be able to leave port. Some were of the opinion that we should cross over to the nearest port in New Spain to relieve our necessities, and others that we should go directly to Acapulco. In view of these opinions and considering our great need, and as the sick were dying of hunger because they could not eat what was on board the ship on account of their sore mouths, the general ordered that we go to the islands of Masatlan.

Crossing the entrance of the Californias, we arrived there on the 18th of the said month, in the greatest affliction and travail ever experienced by Spaniards; for the sick were crying aloud, while those who were able to walk or to go on all fours were unable to manage the sails.

We cast anchor between the islands and the mainland and the next day the general determined to go to the mainland with five soldiers, since on all the ship there were no others able to walk. Without knowing the way, he travelled thirteen leagues inland through mountains and rugged places, for the pueblo of Masatlan, but, because there was no travelled road, and because of the wide, grassy plains, the trail was obscured and he followed the one leading to Culiacan. On the way his supply of food gave out and he straightway would have perished of hunger and thirst had not God miraculously provided a remedy in the form of a pack-train which was going to Culiacan from Mexico. The muleteer noticed him and saw how he had lost his way, and gave him wine and *tortillas* and bananas and riding animals, by means of which he went on to the pueblo of Sacarita, subject to the villa of San Sebastian.

Being informed of the necessity which had forced the general to go there to succor his perishing men, the *alcalde mayor*, Martin Ruis de Aguirre, aided him generously with such gifts as were within his jurisdiction, such as hens, chickens, kids, beef, veal, bread, fruits, and vegetables. These the general sent, and from them his men received great refreshment and nourishment. God, like a father of mercy, caused to be provided in these islands a small fruit like agaves, called *jucoystlis*. These, because of their strength, when eaten by the men who had sore mouths caused the ulcers to slough off and bleed profusely; but such was the efficacy of the fruit that within six days there was not a single person whose mouth was not healed.[1] Likewise, his Divine Majesty provided that the paralyzed and lame, without any manner of curing, without medicines, with only the fine climate and food, should all be healed, so that within the eighteen days we were on these islands, up to the 9th of March, when we set sail, all became well and were able to assist in handling the ship and at the helm. Not to be tedious, I do not tell of the hardships which the general endured on land, or of his ruined health, or of his outlay of money; or of those who went with him, namely, Andres Leal, Juan Guerra, Christoval de los Reyes, Gonzalo Fernandes, and Diego Lopez, who can speak as eye-witnesses.

As has been said, we set out from the islands for Acapulco, skirting the coast, and on the morning of the 10th of the said month were off Cape Corrientes, all very happy because the men were improving and becoming well. Continuing the voyage, following the coast, we came to the port of Acapulco and anchored in it on Friday, the 21st of the said month, with great joy. It was marred however by the news that met us of the many deaths among those who had come on the admiral's ship with messages. For lack of necessities the greater part of the men who came on that ship died. The general found orders from the viceroy that the men should be paid what was due them, that they should be thanked for the good work they had done on this voyage, and that such as desired to enter the army or navy should go up to Mexico, in order that his Lordship might reward them in the name of his Majesty. The men received their pay with great satisfaction and the general took them all with him to Mexico at his own expense.

We arrived at Mexico on Saturday, the 18th of March[2] of the said year, and went to Chapultepeque,[3] where his Lordship was, to kiss his hands. The viceroy welcomed the general very warmly and embraced the others, thanking them by word of mouth, and showing himself very grateful for the good work

[1] Since Captain Cook's time, lime-juice has been used for such exigencies.

[2] This must be a misprint for May.

[3] Chapultepec, the famous crag on which the viceroy's palace was located. It is now the site of the principal residence of the presidents of Mexico, and of a military college.

they had done in the exploration. Some of them he appointed as captains and military officers for the aid and escort of the fleet which this year goes from San Juan de Ulúa to Castile because of the news received of the English corsair. Thus ended this exploration, his Lordship sending to his Majesty a copy of the record of all that was done in it, in order that in view of everything he may provide what is best for his royal service.

CHAPTER 17.

What the Frigate discovered after it separated from the Captain's Ship.

We arrived, as has been said, at Mexico, where we found the boatswain, Estevan Lopez, accompanied by the pilot of the frigate, the *Tres Reyes*. He said that during the hurricane that struck us from the south-southwest in latitude 42° they separated from us and kept running on, without being able to stop, as far as latitude 43°, at Cape Blanco.[1] He said that from that point the coast ran northeast, and the cold was so great that they thought they should be frozen, and they were in great danger of being lost. Ensign Martin de Aguilar, their commander, died, and also the pilot, Antonio Flores, and the said boatswain turned back in search of the captain's ship.[2]

[1] This is shown on Burney's chart as Cavo Blanco de Aguilar, distinct from and a degree above Cavo de San Sebastián.

[2] The Relación of the boatswain of the *Tres Reyes* states that six leagues beyond "Puerto de los Reyes, which above they call Puerto de Don Gaspar," they found a "very, very large river" flowing from the southeast. This was evidently Tomales Bay (see Davidson, *Early Voyages*, p. 220). It is shown on the chart as Río Grande de San Sebastián. Farther on, in lat. 41°, near Cape Mendocino, which is placed at 41½°, they found a very large bay into which entered a large river coming from the north. It had such a current that during a whole day they were able to enter it only two leagues. It was on a rise and carried logs. The country was heavily timbered with pine and oak forests. From this river to Cape Mendocino the direction was south. From the river to Cape Blanco in lat. 43° the coast ran northeast and continued in the same direction beyond, though it was scarcely seen, because they turned back there ("Relación que dio el Contramaestre," in Derrotero, p. 171). Torquemada states that the *Tres Reyes*, finding herself alone, continued north looking for the *San Diego*. In lat. 41° she was struck by a southeast wind, and took shelter near Cape Mendocino under a large rocky islet (Davidson thinks this was Redding Rock in 41° 22', *Early Voyages*, p. 232). Continuing close to the shore, on January

In latitude 39¼ ° he discovered a copious river, and an island at the entrance of a very good and secure port, and another large bay in latitude 40½ °, into which another large river emptied.[1] A great number of Indians came out to them in canoes made of pine and cedar planks, but because there were so many people they did not dare to go up the river with the launch, although the Indians invited them to do so, giving them many fish, game, hazel nuts, chestnuts, acorns, and other things to induce them to go with them up the river.

As he said that there were many Indians there, it was decided not to comply, but to go outside instead. And they returned along the coast, entering the port of Monte Rey, that of Los Reyes, the islands of Samta Catalina, and the port of San Diego. The Indians remembered them well, for though but six of our men remained in the said frigate, the rest having died of cold and sickness, the Indians were so friendly and so desirous of our friendship and so grateful for the kind treatment which they had received that they not only did them no harm, but showed them all the kindness possible.

He said that they came hugging the coast all the way and arrived at the port of La Navidad on the 26th of the said month of February. Having no men with whom to take the frigate to Acapulco, he came to the viceroy in this city, who gave him an order to the effect that the *alcalde mayor* there should give him what was necessary for his voyage. Thus, thanks to God, all the ships which the general had taken had returned in safety, with no loss to the Real Hacienda. Thus ended this exploration, the viceroy sending a copy of the reports to his Majesty in order that he may provide what is most fitting for his royal service.

Corrected by the original book of his Majesty, beginning

19 they were at Cape Blanco, in 43°, whence the coast begins to run northwest. Near this place they found a large river, which they could not enter. Here they turned back. It looks as though the boatswain's river, just below Cape Mendocino, had been elevated by Torquemada to 43°.

On the basis of Torquemada's narrative, which gives the direction of the coast incorrectly, Davidson (*Early Voyages*, p. 234) concludes that the Cabo Blanco de Aguilar was the white sand dune in lat. 42° 14', and that the river was the Rogue River, lat. 42° 25'.

[1] This is probably intended for the river and bay in 41° told of by the boatswain and shown on the Carta just under Cape Mendocino.

at the sixty-fifth folio and ending at the eighty-fifth, comprising twenty written folios, which are sent true and correct. There were present, as witnesses, at the copying and correcting, Juan Martin Marques, Antonio Luis, Andres Leal. In testimony whereof I signed and affixed my accustomed rubrics. Done in Mexico, the 8th day of the month of December, 1603.

In testimony of the truth,

DIEGO DE SANTIAGO, chief scrivener.

A BRIEF REPORT OF THE DISCOVERY IN THE SOUTH SEA, BY FRAY ANTONIO DE LA ASCENSIÓN, 1602–1603 [1]

Memorial of Francisco de Arellano

THE name which your Lordship has so established by your eminent Christian works gives me courage to request your Lordship to glance over this letter, and to hold and acknowledge me as a servant of your Lordship's house, and as such to deign to honor and reward me. From the memorial and the papers which will appear in the Council, and from the letter which has been written from this city to his Majesty, in which information is given of my person, according to what, they say, they have been ordered by royal decree, your Lordship will recognize the obligation which constrains me to serve his Majesty, as I have always had very great desire to do and, whenever occasion has arisen, have tried to do. Father Fray Antonio de la Ascension, of the Discalced Order of Carmelites, a person of very great virtue and holiness, concerning whom that Royal Council has information, and who took part in the discovery of the Californias, and as cosmographer surveyed them and made that map of them and their seas and wrote a narrative, which he sent, has given me a full account of this discovery and of how great a service to our Lord and to his Majesty it would be if this land should be reduced to the royal crown, on account of its great riches, and for the conversion of so great a multitude of Indians.

Since your Lordship is so eminent a Christian and so zealous

[1] Pacheco and Cárdenas, *Colección de Documentos Inéditos*, VIII. 537–538; endorsed: "This report has been taken from the folio volume of manuscript in the Biblioteca Nacional which bears the signature 'J. 89,' and contains various papers relating to the Indies. First comes the holographic memorial of Don Francisco de Arellano, which we are publishing, and next the report in the form of a copy which seems to be contemporary."

for the honor of God and the service of his Majesty, it would be fitting that your Lordship should have examined the papers which Sebastian Vizcaino sent to the Council regarding this exploration, which are the same as I am sending, although [these are] more brief. As it is eighteen years since it was made, by order of his Majesty, while the Count of Monterey was viceroy of this New Spain, it may be that your Lordship has not heard of those papers, and that, for this reason, there has been a neglect of a matter so important, and one which might afford a beginning of a settlement and conquest at so little cost, since his Majesty has already[1] . . . [talked] of ordering this realm explored and of sending discalced Carmelites to it for that conversion.

I assure your Lordship that if I myself were in somewhat easier circumstances I would promise to make the beginning at my own expense and cost. But I promise what I can, which is my person, if it should be acceptable, and my very great desire to serve his Majesty, to whose royal feet I should wish to convey the conquered realm and the riches which are said to be therein. May God order everything to his greater honor and glory, and preserve your Lordship most happy years with the greatly merited lustre which your Lordship possesses and which I desire.

Don Francisco Ramirez de Arellano.

Mexico, December 21, 1620.

A Brief Report[2] *in which is given Information of the Discovery which was made in New Spain, in the South Sea, from the Port of Acapulco to a Point beyond Cape Mendocino; containing an Account of the Riches, the Temperate Climate, and the Advantages of the Realm of the Californias, and setting forth how his Majesty will be able at little cost to pacify it and incorporate it into his Royal Crown and cause the Holy Gospel to be preached in it. By Father Fray Antonio*

---

[1] This is illegible.

[2] Pacheco and Cárdenas, *Colección de Documentos Inéditos*, VIII. 539–574, endorsed: "B. N. [*i. e.*, Biblioteca Nacional], J. 89. Found among other manuscript papers that treat of divers matters, in a small folio volume, board binding, at folio 21."

de la Ascension, a Religious of the Discalced Order of Car-
melites, who took part in it and as Cosmographer made a
map of it.

I.

IN the past year of 1602, by order of our very Catholic and most Christian King, Philip III., king of Spain, Don Gaspar de Zúñiga y Acevedo, Count of Monterey, may he be in heaven, being viceroy of New Spain, two small ships and a frigate were equipped by his order and command in the port of Acapulco,[1] which is in New Spain, on the coast of the South Sea. They were supplied with all necessary arms and provisions for a voyage of one year,[2] the time it was thought this expedition would last. Sebastian Vizcaino went as captain and commander of the soldiers and vessels and Captain Toribio Gomez de Corban went as admiral. There embarked in these ships and the frigate two hundred persons,[3] more or less, one hundred and fifty of them select and experienced soldiers, who were also very skilful sailors, to assist in whatever might present itself concerning affairs at sea as well as those of war on land, and to escort the general. Several famous captains and the ensign who had done heroic deeds in his Majesty's service in Flanders and Britain and in the cruise of the galleons embarked as counsellors, all well accustomed and experienced in affairs of war and of the sea. They were Captain Pascual de Alarcon, Captain Alonzo Esteban Pequero,[4] Ensign Juan Francisco Sureano,[5] Ensign Juan de Acevedo Tejeda, and Ensign Melendez. And for steering the ships there went select pilots, very vigilant and experienced, two for each vessel. And for spiritual matters and the guidance of souls, three religious, priests of the Discalced Order of Carmelites, were appointed; they were Father Andrés de la Asumpcion, who went as commissary, Father Tomas de Aquino, and I, Father Antonio de Ascension, who writes this report. They were sent in order that in the name of his Majesty the king our Lord, and of his religion, and of the Province of San Alberto of New Spain, immediate possession might be taken of

---

[1] See Vizcaino's diary, p. 53, above, note 2.

[2] According to the *junta* held in the Bay of Monterey on December 18, the equipment was for eleven months. See Vizcaino's diary, p. 92, note 1.

[3] See Vizcaino's diary, p. 53, note 1.

[4] Peguero elsewhere.   [5] Suriano elsewhere.

the realm of the Californias which was to be discovered and
explored; in order that thenceforward they might take charge
of the conversion and instruction of all the heathen Indians
of that realm; and in order that on the voyage they might ad-
minister the sacraments to those who were in the ships. Besides these, the viceroy appointed two cosmographers, to survey
and map all the coasts, with their ports, inlets, rivers, and bays,
with their latitudes and longitudes. These were Captain
Gerónimo Martin Palacios and I,[1] I having studied this art and
science in the University of Salamanca, where I was born and
reared, and where I studied until I took the holy habit which I
unworthily wear. I have said this and signed here my name
so that persons who may read this brief and concise report
may be convinced that in all its contents I am telling the truth;
and in order not to be prolix I am brief in everything, with a
style plain and simple, as will be seen in what follows.

II.

This armada sailed from the port of Acapulco the 5th day of
the month of May, of the said year, 1602, every one, before
embarking, having confessed and received communion, the captains as well as the soldiers and cabin-boys of the two vessels.

The order which the viceroy gave them was to explore all the
coast from the above-mentioned port of Acapulco to the Point
of California, and everything from there to Cape Mendocino;
and on returning, if there should be time and opportunity, to
explore the Mediterranean Sea of California.[2] Pursuant to
this order, the armada sailed northwest, coasting all along the
shore and land of New Spain as far as the islands of Maçatlan
and thence crossing over so as to reach the Point of California.
It is fifty leagues across the sea from one side to the other.

From the time this armada sailed from the port of Acapulco
until it reached Cape Mendocino there were always strong head-
winds, because almost continually the northwest wind prevails
on all this coast; it was necessary, therefore, to sail with bow-

---

[1] In his correspondence and instructions the viceroy says nothing about
Father Ascensión's being appointed cosmographer. See Carrasco y Guisasola,
Documentos, pp. 41–68.

[2] The order to explore the gulf was in the secret instructions. See p. 92, above.

lines hauled, which was an incredible hindrance, as there were days when it was not able to gain a league's headway. Tacking to the sea or to the land, one way or the other, the voyage was made, and for this reason the outward trip was very prolonged, and all the ports, bays, rivers, and inlets of the entire coast were examined very minutely. It took us nine months from the time we left Acapulco to reach Cape Mendocino, where we arrived on the 20th[1] day of the month of January, 1603. Cape Mendocino is in latitude 42° north, and we went even farther, to the latitude of 43°, to what was named Cape San Sebastian, where the coast turns to the northeast, and where the entrance to the Strait of Anian seems to begin.

III.

This exploration was made with very great care and vigilance and cost a great deal of labor and exertion and tedious illness, and the lives of many who took part in it, because of undergoing so much labor, in continual pain and always struggling against the wild waves which the sea heaved up and against the winds which caused them. Moreover, the provisions became so stale that they finally had no virtue or nutrition. From these two causes there ensued a sickness like a pest, which affected every one and was extremely painful, so that more than forty-four[2] persons died on the voyage. I made a report of all that happened on this voyage, in which is related at length everything that took place during it and what was seen and discovered on it, and upon which I rely. This armada returned to Acapulco, and the captain's ship, in which I came,[3] entered it March 21 of the said year, 1603.

[1] The author is careless here, and confuses Cape Mendocino with Cape San Sebastián. They arrived at the former place on the 12th, and at the latter, in lat. 42°, on the 20th. Cape Blanco was given in the official records as in 43° (see Vizcaino's diary, p. 101). The latitude of Cape Mendocino was variously given as 41°, 41⅓°, and 42½°.

[2] According to Torquemada forty-eight died, including Alférez Juan de Acevedo Texada, Alférez Sebastián Meléndez, Alférez Martín de Aguilar Galeote, pilot Antonio Flores, pilot Baltasár de Armas, Sergeant Miguel de Legar, and Sergeant Juan del Castillo Bueno (*Monarchía Indiana*, I. 724–725). In his letter to the King, dated May 23, 1603, Vizcaino stated that forty-two had died.

[3] On the outward voyage he was on the *almiranta* as far as the Bay of Monterey.

Thus eleven months were spent on the voyage from the time of sailing until port was made. In this short account I will speak briefly of some of the most important things I saw, learned, and observed throughout the land and seacoast which we saw and explored.

IV.

This realm of California is very large and embraces much territory, nearly all inhabited by numberless people. It has a good climate, is very fertile, and abounds in many and various kinds of trees, the most of them like those in Spain, abundant pastures of good grazing land, and a great number of different kinds of animals and birds. The sea of all this coast is full of a variety of savory and wholesome fish, which I will mention later. All the land of this realm is in the temperate zone, which is situated in the northern division, and the climates 2, 3, 4, 5, 6, and 8[1] pass over it. It has the exact form and shape of a casket, being broad at the top and narrow at the point. It is this latter which we commonly call Punta de la California. From there it widens out to Cape Mendocino, which we will describe as being the top and breadth of it. The breadth of this land from here to the other sea, where the Mediterranean Sea of California comes and connects with the sea that surrounds and encircles Cape Mendocino, must be about one hundred leagues.[2] In this part this realm has north of it the Kingdom of Anian, and to the east the land which is continuous with the realm of Quivira. Between these two realms extends the strait of Anian, which runs to the North Sea, having joined the Oceanic Sea which surrounds Cape Mendocino and the Mediterranean Sea of California, both of which are united at the entrance of this strait which I call Anian. Toward the west is the realm of China, and toward the south all the realm of Japan. The most modern maps show that from the meridian corresponding to the Point of California to the meridian corresponding to Cape Mendocino there are sixty degrees of longitude; so that if we give sixteen and a half leagues to each degree, according to the reckoning of

---

[1] Climate in the old astronomical sense—so many degrees of latitude.

[2] This passage is a fair statement of the geographical notions concerning the Northwest after Iturbi's expedition.

cosmographers, it is about one thousand leagues long; but if according to the reckoning of mariners, who give twenty-five leagues to each degree, we should say that its coast and shore is more than fifteen hundred leagues long from north-west to southeast, which is the direction all this realm runs and trends. In latitude, or breadth, it extends from the Tropic of Cancer, that is, from the Point of California, called Cape San Lucas, which is under that tropic, to the latitude of 50°, the highest latitude of this realm—which, I said, is where unite the two seas that surround this realm.

Thus it is plain that this realm of California is a land separate and distinct from the lands of New Mexico and the realm of Quivira, which is continuous with the latter, although there is a long distance and much territory between the one realm and the other. The sea between these two realms, which is the one called the Mediterranean Sea of California, since it is between lands so large and extended, must be about fifty leagues wide. In the middle of it there are many islands, some small and others larger; but I cannot say whether they are inhabited or not. The inhabitants of Cape Mendocino are so opposite and remote from the kingdom of Old Castile in our Spain that it is midnight in the noted city and university of Salamanca when it is noon at Cape Mendocino, and *vice versa:* so that they are the antipodes of each other, being opposite each other, and in the same climate, but with different and diametrically opposite meridians. Hence it follows that they must possess the same atmospheric conditions and climate, having the same winter, summer, and autumn. It is possible that they differ in some conditions and temperatures, because of the different influences of the vertical stars which affect their qualities.

Those who are acquainted with and understand the sphere and cosmography will have no doubt of this; but in order to make myself better understood I made for those who do not understand it a geographic map of it all, which I have with me; and I am sending a copy of it to his Majesty and to his Royal Council of the Indies, that they may understand the great size and the situation of this great realm. And I believe it will be indispensable and important, in order that the present maps of the world may be compared with it and corrected, because many of the things which are depicted in them relating to matters of this realm are very different from what they actually are. This is not to be wondered at, since the land and seacoast of this realm have never been viewed or explored so exactly and designedly as on this expedition, which went solely for this purpose.

V.

The Cape of San Lucas,[1] which is at the extremity of California, whence all this realm begins and takes its name, forms in its shelter a bay called San Bernabé, so spacious that it is a good bay and will accommodate many ships, although it is not protected on all sides. This bay, or cape, of San Lucas is under the Tropic of Cancer, and off the islands of Maçatlan, which, on the coast of New Spain, are the frontier and limit on this side of the bishopric of Guadalajara and of the kingdom which they call Nueva Galicia. It is fifty leagues, more or less, across the sea, which is the width of the Mediterranean Sea of California between the realm of California and that of Galicia. This latter joins the kingdom of New Spain and extends to New Mexico, continuing to the kingdom of Quivira, and terminating at the Strait of Anian, as has already been said. Some call it the Mediterranean because it flows between these two large realms; others call it the Vermillion Sea, since in this passage the water looks a bright reddish color, perhaps because the land at the bottom is red, or it may be from the spawn brought here by the river-fish that come to swim in that sea, this color being caused by the blood; for once I saw that the water at the port of Acapulco was of this bright reddish color, and they told me that it was because of the fish spawn. On the old maps it is called the bay, or gulf, of Ballenas,[2] because there, as on all the coast as far as Cape Mendocino, there are so many whales that they cannot be numbered, nor would it be believed by anybody who had not seen them. And because until now[3] it has been understood to be a bay or large gulf, formed there by the sea, and not a regular and continuous sea, which it is, they gave it this name.

[1] See Vizcaino's diary, p. 56, above, note 1.   [2] Whales.
[3] The allusion is perhaps to the results of the Iturbi and Oñate expeditions.

In this passage are the islands called the Marías, and another small one called San Andrés; and through all this sea there are many other islands. Among them, facing the port formed by the Tizon River,[1] which flows into this sea from New Mexico in latitude 35°, is the island of Giganta,[2] where lives the queen of the neighboring peoples. In this sea, on both shores, other islands also, as well as the land of California, have many oyster-beds, which produce pearls, many, rich, and large. They are found as far as latitude 36°, as I say in the last chapter of the report which I made of this discovery.

VI.

I will say that the wealth and abundance of pearls in this sea is very great, a thing which is well known and remarked upon by persons who have coasted along the sea; and they are, indeed, large and beautiful, choice, and very perfect. The oysters are not very deep, for the Indians search for and bring them up. This is not to make use of the pearls, because they do not understand or value them, but only to eat the fish within. In order to open the oysters and more easily extract their contents they put them in the fire, whereupon they open and the pearls are burned or smoked. When found they are thrown away, as if they were stones of no value.

There are many different kinds of fish in this sea, large and small, which are seen to go in shoals or schools. As they are fish known in other seas, I will here name some of those I have caught, had in my hands, and eaten,[3] so that the abundance, excellence, and wealth of that sea may be understood. There are, as I have said, multitudes of very large whales, and a great quantity of sardines, large and small, slender and thick, which are, according to what they say, the common sustenance of the whales, and may be it is for this reason there are so many. There are ruffles, porgy, sea-bass, corrundas, small sharks, or dog-fish, sturgeon, *esmirigalas*, skate, salmon, tunny, ray, *chucos*, sea-horse, little bass, striped tunny, gilt-

---

[1] The Colorado, named Rio del Tizón (Firebrand) by the Alarcón expedition in 1540.

[2] See the account of Oñate's journey to California, p. 276.

[3] When in California with Vizcaino, presumably.

head, sole, mutton-fish, porpoise, newts, *tirgueros*, common oysters, those that bear pearls, and many other never seen and unknown. And there are octopus. One was caught so large that it wrapped itself around the buoy-rope or line by which the buoy was fastened to the anchor; although it was very heavy, as it had a firm hold, the ship raised it and dragged it behind.[1] It had a mouth like a half-moon. I measured it from one point to the other, crosswise, and it was a *vara* and three quarters, and from the head to the end of the tail it was five and one quarter *varas*. It was broad and flat like a mantle. These fish are of fine flavor, palatable, and wholesome. All these varieties were caught every year by casting the net, or seine. Sometimes the seine was so full that it broke.

VII.

The country of this Cape San Lucas is very fertile and healthful, with a fine climate and clear sky. It has good level land and is not very mountainous. All of it is perfectly adapted to cultivation and to keeping and raising stock, both cattle and sheep, goats and swine. There is plenty of wild game for hunting and fowling, such as rabbits, hare, deer, lions, tigers, armadillos, ringdoves, quail, and many ducks. Of trees, there are figs, broccoli, agaves, mangroves, mastick, and, near the beach, a grove of plum trees.

In place of gum or resin, they exude in great quantities very good and fragrant incense. The fruit which they produce is very delicious, as I have been told by those who have tried it on other occasions. There is also on the shore of this land which encircles the Bay of San Bernabé, where I saw all the things mentioned, a lagoon of good fresh water,[2] all surrounded and hedged in with brambles. On the other side, near the rocks and the beach, there is a little lagoon of salt water, left by the sea in high winds, which was covered, all around, with very good salt, plentiful, white, and of a good taste. Here also are many robust Indians, of good disposition, who use bows, arrows, and darts for arms. They gave indications of being bellicose and spirited; for, when some

[1] Evidently an incident of the Vizcaino voyage.
[2] For this lagoon see the Carta.

natives came to see us at this port, they said that if the soldiers would put away the arquebuses they carried they would also come without arms. Laying them aside, they seated themselves, saying in a loud voice "Vtesi," that is to say, "Seat yourselves" or "be seated," which is the surest and most certain sign of peace in use among them. With this ceremony they came peaceably, and treated us with friendliness and civility, although always with extreme caution and suspicion, and on hearing an arquebus discharged they immediately ran away. When they came, they always brought with them such little things as they had, showing themselves to be a people grateful and thankful for what the soldiers and religious gave them.

VIII.

It is at this port that his Majesty should order the first settlement of Spaniards to be made when he sends people to pacify the country, in order that the pacification of all this realm and the preaching of the Holy Gospel may begin here. It is situated near and convenient for trade and communication with New Spain and Peru, as the ships to New Spain touch at this place when they come from Peru by the new mode of navigation now in use, and they come in one month. Besides these, it has other advantages for sustaining human life, and for enabling the Spaniards to keep their trade and commerce in good and secure communication, because, besides the pearl-fisheries near by, there is, on the south coast, a neighboring land which we call Sierra Pintada or del Enfado.[1] It has many minerals of various kinds; and one can go by land to extract them, and to get the gold and silver which they may contain. Apparently they are very abundant, according to experience and trustworthy information upon which I rely.

It is the best place that could be found in the world for the maintenance and mode of life of the Discalced Carmelite religious (who, by order of the king, our lord, have charge of the conversion of this realm), and for their abstemious and penitent life, because of the good mild climate as well as the great abundance of many kinds of good fish, as is stated above. The heat of the climate is not so excessive as to need linen,

[1] See Vizcaino's diary, p. 57, above.

nor does it require much protection against the cold, so that one kind of clothing can be worn all the time. Moreover, the proximity of the country to New Spain and the facility of navigation from one realm to the other is very important for providing it with the religious, for governing them by one provincial, and for conveying some and bringing back others, according as the necessity of the religious may require; for, having settlements as far as the port of Navidad where they can embark if they do not wish to go to Acapulco, in a month one can go from Mexico to the Californias with great ease and comfort.

IX.

After remaining in this port and bay of San Bernabé some days, we set sail[1] for the purpose of making the exploration of Cape Mendocino. As the coast runs from southeast to northwest, and as the wind is continually from that quarter, that is, northwest, we found it so severe and strong that four times against our will it forced us to put back into the port from which we sailed. Finally, at the end of some days, with bowlines hauled, we made our way and arrived at the port of Magdalena,[2] which was formerly called the port of Santiago.[3] Here the Indians received us peacefully and, as an acknowledgment of submission, offered the Spaniards their bows and arrows, very nicely wrought, and brought some incense like that we had procured in the Bay of San Bernabé, a sign that there are here a great number of these trees which produce it. An arm of the sea enters this port, unless it is some large river which disembogues here and empties into the sea. But it was ascended only about a league, being left for exploration when we should return from Cape Mendocino. Here many Indians came out to us in their canoes and showed themselves friendly and gentle.

This port is very good and spacious, and has two mouths or entrances. By one, small vessels only can enter; by the other large ones can enter, as it has good soundings. Here

---

[1] They set sail the first time on June 19, finally on July 5. See Vizcaino's diary, pp. 57, 58, above.

[2] See Vizcaino's diary, p. 59, above, note 1.

[3] By Cabrillo it was called Port of San Pedro. See p. 14, note 4.

and all along this coast there are many whales, and, if it is true that amber comes from their filth, as I understand, from what I saw on this voyage, there must be much amber on this coast; for not far from this place, though farther up on the same coast, we found another port, which was named San Bartolomeo, on whose shore was a large quantity of ambergris,[1] in cakes, like soft, whitish pitch. We did not recognize it as such, and for this reason we took no notice of it. Afterward, when giving a description of it to those who are well acquainted with amber, they said that it was very fine ambergris. There was a large quantity of it in this port. Perhaps God our Lord allowed none of those who went there to know this, since it may be that in the interest of going to obtain it his Majesty will send ministers with the design of converting those Indians, for according to the signs which they gave it will be easy to bring them into our Catholic faith.

X.

We went forward, making the exploration carefully and slowly, because head winds impeded it. Other ports and islands were discovered along the coast, and all along it there were many Indians, who signalled us with smoke columns and other signs; but, in order to reach Cape Mendocino, everything was left to be examined on our return. Finally, after much labor we reached the port of San Diego,[2] which is very good and capacious and offers many very good advantages for Spanish settlement. Here the ships were cleaned and oiled again, the place being quiet, and there being many friendly and affable Indians there. They use bows and arrows and appear warlike and valiant, since, notwithstanding they came to see us every day, they always treated us with so great a distrust that they never had complete confidence in us. They pronounced so very well in our language what they heard us speak that anyone hearing them and not seeing them would say they were Spaniards. Every day they would come in order that we might give them some of the fish we caught in the net, and they would go away quietly after they had helped to haul it in.

[1] Port of San Bartolomé. See Vizcaino's diary, p. 64, above, note 3.
[2] November 10, 1602. See Vizcaino's diary, p. 80, above, note 1.

The harbor is large and secure, and has a large beach within, like an island of sand,[1] which the sea covers at high tide.   In the sand on this beach there is a great quantity of yellow pyrites, all full of holes, a sure sign that in the neighboring mountains and adjacent to this port there are gold mines; for the water, when it rains, brings it from the mountains, and the whole watershed converges here.   On the sandy beach which I said was in this harbor we found some large pieces, like adobe, brown or dark red in color, and very light in weight, like dried cowdung.   They had neither a good nor a bad odor, and they are said to be amber.   If this is so, there are great riches and an abundance of amber here.

There are many different kinds of fish, of very good taste and flavor, such as ray, sea-horse, lobster, crab, *guitarras*, sardine, turtle, and many other kinds.   There is much wild game for hunting and fowling; and there are many large, grassy pastures.   The Indians paint themselves white, and black, and dark London blue.   This color comes from certain very heavy blue stones, which they grind very fine, and, dissolving the powder in water, make a stain, with which they daub the face and make on it lines which glisten like silver ribbons.   These stones seem to be of rich silver ore, and the Indians told us by signs that from similar stones a people living inland, of form and figure like our Spaniards,[2] bearded, and wearing collars and breeches, and other fine garments like ours, secured silver in abundance, and that they had a name for it in their own language.   To ascertain whether these Indians knew silver, the general showed them some silver bowls and a plate.   They took it in their hands and spun it around, and, pleased by the sound, said it was good, and was the same as that possessed and valued highly by the people of whom they had told us.   Then he put in their hands a pewter bowl, but when they struck it the sound did not please them and, spitting, they wanted to throw it into the sea.[3]

The people of whom the Indians told us might have been

[1] The Peninsula.   See Davidson, *Early Voyages*, p. 194.

[2] The Spaniards of the Oñate Expedition had recently entered New Mexico, and the Indians perhaps referred to their activities.

[3] In the official diary this incident or one very similar is related as occurring on the San Buenaventura coast.   See Vizcaino's diary, p. 88, above.

foreigners, Hollanders or English, who had made their voyage by the Strait of Anian and might be settled on the other coast of this land, facing the Mediterranean Sea of California. Since the realm is narrow, as has been said, it may be that the other sea is near that place; for the Indians offered to guide and take us to the place where they say the people are settled. If this is so, it is probable they have large interests and profits there, since their voyage is so long and difficult. Still, it is true that by passing through the Strait of Anian and reaching their land by that latitude, their voyage is only half as long as that from the port of San Juan de Ulúa to Spain. This will be clearly seen from evidence furnished by the globe. In this case, it will be to his Majesty's interest to endeavor to assure himself of the fact: first, in order to know the route, and secondly, in order to expel from there such dangerous enemies, lest they contaminate the Indians with their sects and liberty of conscience, by which great harm to their souls will follow, whereby instructing them and leading them in the paths of the true law of God will be made very difficult. Besides this, his Majesty will be able to secure many other advantages, as I shall show later.

XI.

After we left the Port of San Diego we discovered many islands placed in a line, one behind another.[1] Most of them were inhabited by many friendly Indians, who have trade and commerce with those of the mainland. It may be that they are vassals of a petty king who came with his son from the mainland in a canoe with eight oarsmen, to see us and to invite us to go to his land, saying that he would entertain us and provide us with anything which we needed and he possessed.[2] He said that he came to see us on account of what the inhabitants of these islands had reported to him. There are many people in this land, so many that the petty king, seeing that there were no women on the ships, offered by signs to give to everyone ten women apiece if they would all go to his land, which shows how thickly populated it all is. And besides,

[1] Particularly the Santa Bárbara Islands. See Vizcaino's diary, p. 83, above.
[2] See Vizcaino's diary, ibid.

all along, day and night, they made many bonfires, the sign
in use among them to call people to their land. Since there
was no convenient port where the ships could be secure in
the country whence this petty king came, the acceptance of
his invitation was deferred until the return voyage.

Thereupon we went forward with our voyage, and at the
end of some days arrived at a fine port, which was named
Monterrey.[1] It is in latitude 37°, in the same climate and
latitude as Seville. This is where the ships coming from the
Philippines to New Spain come to reconnoitre. It is a good
harbor, well sheltered, and supplied with water, wood, and
good timber, both for masts and ship building, such as pines,
live oaks, and great white oaks, large and frondose, and many
black poplars on the banks of a river that near by enters the
sea and was named the Carmelo.[2] In climate, in birds and
game, in variety of animals and trees, in everything it is essentially like our Old Spain. When the ships from China arrive
at this place they have already sailed four months and they
come in need of repairs, which in this harbor they can make
very well, and with perfect convenience; therefore it would
be a very good thing for the Spaniards to settle this port for
the assistance of navigators, and to undertake the conversion
to our Holy Faith of those Indians, who are numerous, docile,
and friendly. And from here they might trade and traffic
with the people of China and Japan, opportunity for that
being favorable because of propinquity.

The land of this country is very fertile and has good pastures and forests, and fine hunting and fowling. Among the
animals there are large, fierce bears, and other animals called
elks, from which they make elk-leather jackets,[3] and others
of the size of young bulls,[4] shaped and formed like deer, with
thick, large horns. There were many Castilian roses here.
There are pretty ponds of fresh water. The mountains near
this port were covered with snow, and that was on Christmas
day. On the beach was a dead whale, and at night some
bears came to feed on it.

There are many fish here, and a great variety of mollusks
among the rocks; among them there were certain barnacles,

[1] December 16.   [2] See Vizcaino's diary, p. 91, above.   [3] *Cuiras.*
[4] See Vizcaino's diary, p. 91. Possibly the antelope.

or large shells, fastened to the lowest part of the rocks. The Indians hunt for them to extract from them their contents to eat. These shells are very bright, of fine mother-of-pearl.[1] All along this coast, there is a great abundance of sea-wolves or dogs,[2] of the size of a yearling calf. They sleep on the water, and sometimes go ashore to take the sun; and there they place their sentinel in order to be secure from enemies. The Indians clothe themselves in the skins of these animals,which are healthful, fine, beautiful, and convenient. Finally, I will say that this is a good and commodious port, and might be settled, but this should be done in the way which I shall set forth hereafter.

XII.

We set sail from here after dispatching the admiral's ship to New Spain with the news of what had been discovered and with the sick who were unfit for service. Among them returned Father Tomás de Aquino, one of the three religious who were going in this fleet, because he had been ill many days, and in order that the sick might have someone to confess them should God desire to relieve them of this life. Our departure in quest of Cape Mendocino was made on the first Sunday after Epiphany,[3] of the year 1603. On the coast we noted the port of San Francisco,[4] where in times past there was lost a ship from China which was coming with orders to explore this coast. I believe that much of the wax and porcelain which the vessel carried is there to-day. And we arrived at Cape Mendocino[5] in latitude 42°, which is the highest latitude at which the China ships sight land. Here, because of the severity of winter in this climate, and of the cold, and the stiffness of the rigging, and because almost all the crew were ill, the sails were lowered. The captain's ship got into the trough of the sea, and, as it could not be steered, the currents that

---

[1] Clearly the abalone.

[2] Probably the sea lion instead of the seal proper.

[3] January 5. See Vizcaino's diary, p. 94. The day of sailing is given there as Friday, January 3.

[4] Drake's Bay, called San Francisco by the Cermeño expedition. See Vizcaino's diary, p. 94.

[5] January 12, according to Vizcaino's diary, p. 95.

run to the Strait of Anian whose entrance begins here, carried
it little by little toward land.   In eight days we had ascended
more than one degree of latitude, which was up to 43°, in sight
of a cape that was named San Sebastian.[1]   Near it empties
a river that was called Santa Inez.[2]   No one landed here, as
all the crew were very ill, only six persons being able to walk.
Here the coast and land turns to the northeast, and here is
the head and end of the realm and mainland of California
and the entrance to the Strait of Anian.   If on this occasion
there had been on the captain's ship even fourteen sound men,
without any doubt we should have ventured to explore and
pass through this Strait of Anian, since all were of good courage to do this.   But the general lack of health and of men
who could manage the sails and steer the ship obliged us to
turn about toward New Spain, to report what had been discovered and seen, and lest the whole crew should die if we remained longer in that latitude.[3]

With this decision and agreement the return voyage was
begun.   It was made by coasting along shore with favorable
winds, exploring all the ports, bays, and inlets that we had
sighted on our outward voyage.[4]   As the northwest wind is
so usual and continual on this coast, one can easily come from
Cape Mendocino to the port of Acapulco in one month, if the
pilot knows how to choose the correct routes at the proper
times, as I set them down in an itinerary which I made for
this voyage.   The course which we took on our return was
along the coast, and so near it that everything on it was
seen with great clearness and distinctness.[5]   The Indians, as
they saw us pass at a distance, sent up columns of smoke and
other signals to attract us; and wherever we landed they gave
indications of their good natures and intelligence, hence it ap-

[1] Father Ascensión is again careless with his latitudes.   Cape San Sebastián
was estimated as at or near 42° and Cape Blanco, reached by the *Tres Reyes*,
in 43°.   See Vizcaino's diary, pp, 95, 96, 101.

[2] By the Vizcaino diary and the Planos this river, not named, was placed
below Cape Mendocino.   See Vizcaino's diary, p. 102, note.

[3] See Vizcaino's diary, p. 96, note 1, for an account of the *junta* which decided to return.

[4] See Vizcaino's diary, p. 97, note 1, for a statement regarding the exploration made on the return.

[5] Yet they missed San Francisco Bay.

peared to us all that they might easily and with very little labor be taught our Holy Catholic faith, and that they would receive it well and lovingly.   But this should be done with great prudence and in the manner that our Master and Redeemer, Jesus Christ, taught us in his Holy Gospel.

As to how persons should be sent to new lands for the conversion of the heathen Indians, I wrote a brief treatise, which I sent to the king, our lord, Philip III.   In it I discuss what ought to be done that the people may be converted and that his Majesty may with just title become the lawful emperor and lord of their lands;   and to this I refer the reader. Nevertheless, as there I have treated of the general instruction for all, here, for the sake of greater clearness, I will set forth briefly what his Majesty can and ought to do for the conversion of the Indians of this great realm of the Californias in particular, and to pacify their lands and become lord over them with good conscience, as will be seen by beginning with number 23[1] below of this little treatise.

Finally, returning to our voyage, I will say that we returned to the port of Acapulco on March 22,[2] of the year 1603, having passed through great labor and severe illness, of which died the number of people that I mentioned at the beginning; and I made a full report of all that happened on the voyage, and a map of the situation of this realm.

XIII.

The Method to be observed in Subduing and Settling the Realm of Californias.[3]

All this realm of the Californias can be pacified and settled, and by this means and by the preaching of the Holy Gospel its natives can be led to the fold of our Holy Mother, the Roman Catholic Church, and converted to our Holy Catholic Faith.   Now, in order that this may become an accomplished fact, and that his Majesty may effect it at a moderate ex-

---

[1] A mistake for 13.

[2] On page 108 he gives the date as March 21, as does the Vizcaino diary, p. 100.

[3] The following is an excellent outline of an ideal missionary "pacification" of a new Spanish frontier.

pense, that which must be commanded, ordered, and provided is as follows :

There should be prepared and equipped in the port of Acapulco two small vessels of two hundred tons burden, and a frigate, with boats and skiffs for their service ; and they should be abundantly supplied with stores and munitions of war, as well as with food, rigging, canvas, and everything that may seem necessary for settling in infidel and heathen lands.

While these things are being provided and prepared, there should be raised in Mexico as many as two hundred soldiers, care being taken that they should be good seamen, and also that they be old soldiers, expert and experienced as well in arms as in seamanship, in order that all, uniformly and without distinction, may aid in everything as occasion may offer. And let care be taken that they be good and honorable men in order that on the journey both on sea and land there may be peace, union, and brotherhood among all. Plenty of men of these parts and talents will very easily be found in Mexico if his Majesty will increase their pay in proportion as the double service they have to render demands, and if their pay and allowance be given them punctually when due.

The duty of raising this troop should be assigned to one or two captains, good Christians and God-fearing men, and persons of merit, who have served his Majesty faithfully on other occasions, in war on land as well as in the fleets at sea. To them should be entrusted the appointment of officers to accompany them, who should be persons they are satisfied will perform their service in a Christian and careful manner, and men of experience, who know how to fulfill the offices committed to them, for on these officers depend the good order and discipline of the soldiers. This expedition must be entrusted to a person of courage and talents, of long experience, and accustomed to such charges, in order that he may know how to treat all with love and dignity, and each one individually as his character deserves. Let care be taken that such a person be God-fearing, scrupulous in his conscience, and zealous in the service of his Majesty and in the things relating to the conversion of these souls. To a person of these qualities can be given the office of general of the armada, to whom all, both captains and soldiers, will be subject, and whom they will obey in everything, and whose orders they will follow.

To the general, captains, soldiers, and all who go on this expedition, must be given express order and command that they shall hold themselves in strict obedience and subjection to the religious who are in their company, and that without their order, counsel, and advice, war may not be made, or the heathen Indians be otherwise molested, even if they should give occasion, in order that by this means matters may be conducted with peace and Christianity, and with love and quiet, which is the method to be used in the pacification of that realm, and in the preaching of the Holy Gospel, to which end and aim these expenses and preparations are directed. Not to do this, but the contrary, will be to waste everything, to lose time, and to render the expenditure ineffectual, as has been found by experience many times in this New Spain, in other conquests and pacifications of new lands, whereby God our Lord has been more injured than served.

XIV.

The religious who should go on this expedition are the Discalced of Our Lady of Carmel, the ones to whom are intrusted by his Majesty the conversion, instruction, and teaching of the Indians of this realm of the Californias. On this first entrance there should be six religious, four priests and two lay brothers; and it will be requested of the superiors of this order, in the name of his Majesty, that those whom they assign and appoint for this voyage be persons such as the occasion and enterprise demand, holy, affable, full of love and wisdom, that they may know how to counsel, guide and direct these souls, and to deal with such cases as may present themselves conformably with sound Catholic doctrine.

By observing the indulgences and benefits which the Supreme Pontiffs have granted in favor of new conversions, for their greater increase, these holy friars, with their piety, modesty, simplicity, and religious graciousness, will succeed in winning the wills and hearts of both general and captains, as well as of all the soldiers, in order thereby to lead them in the holy path of virtue; and may they with loving arguments persuade and admonish all, before embarking, to confess their sins and receive the most holy sacrament of the Eucharist, with all the devotion and inclination possible, offering their souls and lives to the service of his divine Majesty, asking of him success for their voyage and expedition. By doing this, with the proper spirit and devotion, the religious will make themselves lords over the hearts and wills of all, and will have authority over all to keep them in peace, love, and unity; and if perchance there should be any dissension among them, they will calm it at once with discretion, and thus animosities, vexations, and enmities, and the mutinies, insurrections, and disobedience to superiors which ordinarily occur on such enterprises, will be avoided.

These religious will be provided with everything necessary for their voyage, such as vessels for saying mass and administering the sacraments, books and vestments and, in particular, something in the way of delicacies that they may have wherewith to give to the sick if there should be any. Likewise, there should be taken on board at the cost of his Majesty a quantity of trifles, Flemish trinkets, such as beads of colored glass, artificial garnets, hawks' bells, mirrors, knives, cheap scissors, Parisian tops, and some articles of clothing.

These things should be divided among the religious and soldiers, so that in places where they may go on shore or where they may choose sites for settlements in the lands of the heathen, they may distribute them, with signs of love and good will, in the name of his Majesty, in order that with these pleasing gifts the heathen Indians may come to feel love and affection for the Christians, and may realize that they are coming to their lands to give them of that which they bring, and not to take away their possessions, and may understand that they are seeking the good of their souls. This is a measure of great importance, to the end that the Indians may become quiet, humane, and peaceable, and obey the Spaniards without opposition or repugnance, and receive with pleasure those who go to preach to them the Holy Gospel and the mysteries of our Holy Catholic faith; to the end, moreover, that the Indians may be grateful and thankful, and, in recompense and pay for what is given them, may assist with what-

ever of value they may have in their land, things to eat as well
as other articles, as they did with us.

With this preparation, the soldiers and religious should
embark in the ships provided, no woman going or embarking
with them, to avoid offenses to God and dissensions between
one another. With the ocean currents that run toward the
entrance of California, even if winds favorable to navigation
should fail, one can within a month at the most succeed in
landing in the Bay of San Bernabé, which is at Cape San Lucas
and the extremity of California, the point best fitted for the
first settlement.

XV.

After a landing is made in the Bay of San Bernabé, effort
should be made at once to establish the camp in the place that
seems most convenient; and it should be of such a style and
plan as that some of the houses may serve as a guard and protection to the others. First of all a church should be built,
in order that there the priests may celebrate mass every day;
and it would be very holy and well if immediately on entrance into this realm the general with his captains and all
the soldiers should confess and receive the sacrament, for this
would be a very good beginning for making the entrance in
proper form, and for following out, with the aid and favor of
our Redeemer and Lord Jesus Christ, that which is attempted,
namely, the pacification of the realm and the conversion of
its inhabitants to our holy Catholic faith.

As to the location of a stronghold to serve as a castle
and watch-tower and as a defense in adverse chances, it
should be a strong location, high and commanding; and if a
secure passage could be made from it to the sea it would
be very advantageous as a means of receiving aid or of sending for aid by sea in case any necessity should arise. The
Portuguese have generally done this way in the places where
they have established themselves in India, and the observance
of this stratagem and precaution has succeeded very well with
them. This castle and stronghold should be stocked with
artillery carried there for that purpose, together with other
defenses customary in such fortresses; and in it should be

kept the arms and supplies. Above it there should be a watch-tower in which there should be continually a guard or sentinel, in order that all coming and going to the camp may be carefully watched; for when in lands of heathen Indians, although they may have declared themselves friendly and peaceable, they must not be trusted much; rather, one must live with them and among them with great circumspection, vigilance, and watchfulness, and be gracious and kindly, with wisdom and prudence, showing them love and all good treatment, regaling and giving them gratis of the trifles which, at his Majesty's expense, may have been taken for the purpose of coaxing and winning them.

Besides these buildings, a trading house should be erected, whither the Indians may repair to barter with the Spaniards for whatever they may desire, and in order that they may trade and bargain among themselves; for thereby their communication with us will be greatly facilitated and love and friendship thus engendered.

From this place, with the ships, frigate, and other vessels, they can send to the land of Culiacan,[1] which is a settlement of Christians, or to the islands of Macatlan,[2] or to the pueblo of La Navidad,[3] to bring from there whatever may seem necessary both for the settlement of the land and for sustenance, such as cows, sheep, goats, mares, and hogs, which in two or four days at the most can be sent alive from one side to the other, as the sea lying between is about fifty leagues in width, and is safe and smooth. These animals will grow and multiply as well in this land, since it is suitable for that purpose and is fertile. Likewise it will be possible to cultivate fields of wheat and maize, and to plant vines and gardens, in order that sustenance may be had from within and it may not be necessary to carry it from without. The Indians can be taught and instructed to do the same, and will take everything well, seeing it redound to their advantage.

[1] See Vizcaino's diary, p. 55, above, note 6.
[2] Mazatlan. See Vizcaino's diary, p. 55, note 4.
[3] See Cabrillo diary, p. 13, note 1.

XVI.

Besides what is said above, the Spaniards in this place will be able to establish fisheries for pearls and other fish, of which there is abundance, to send to New Spain, to sell in Mexico. Very good salt-works can be established; likewise they can work mines, of which there are some near by, as I have said in number VIII.[1] These things being settled with the peace, love and good will of the natives, the religious will give their attention to their ministry, and make a beginning and commencement of converting the Indians, in the way which may seem best to them, founding with great prudence and gentleness the new Christian church to be planted there.

And it would be well to bring from New Spain Indian minstrels, with their instruments and trumpets, that the divine services may be celebrated with solemnity and pomp, and to teach the Indians of the land to sing and play. Likewise it would be well and proper to choose from among the Indians some of the brightest, selecting among the young men and boys such as appear the most docile, talented and capable; and they should be taught and instructed in the Christian doctrine and to read the Spanish primers, in order that along with the reading they may learn the Spanish language, and that they may learn to write and sing, and to play all the musical instruments;[2] because a good foundation makes the edifice firm, and according as care is given in this matter to the beginnings, so will the middle parts and the ends be good.

It is a very easy matter, by this method, to teach the children our language, and they, as they grow up, will teach it to their companions and to their children and families, and in a few years all will know the Spanish language, which will be a very great boon; for they will not lack ministers to teach, guide, and direct them in the path leading to heaven and to their salvation. From here they can continue the planting of settlements of Christians and of the Indians who may be scattered through the mountains, draw-

---

[1] The reference is to Sierra Pintada or del Enfado. See p. 114.

[2] For instruction given Indians in Spanish missions, see Father Zephyrin Engelhardt, *Missions and Missionaries of California*, I. 99–102, 123–125.

ing them to the settlements with love, suavity, and gentleness; taking care that the Christian soldiers do not disperse themselves so much that the guard will be diminished and impaired, so that, if the Indians, instigated by the evil one, should try to effect some uprising or to rebel against the Spaniards, there may be someone who can make resistance, and hold them in line, and even punish their insolence if the case demands it.

XVII.

In number VIII. I told how with very little trouble it would be possible to explore a certain land that is near here, on the coast of the South Sea, called the land of Enfado, or Pintada. I say that I believe that it has very rich silver ores. This can be explored by land, for it is near, and it might be developed if the ores proved to be of high grade and easily worked; and should they be rich and profitable, the expense which may have been entailed by building this fleet and bringing it to this country might be reimbursed from the fifths of the silver and pearls secured belonging to his Majesty. And this, once established, will necessarily bring great profits to his Majesty and to his royal patrimony, and great increase to his estate, with which there can be sent to this realm whatever number of people may seem to be necessary to pacify and settle it, and the ministers necessary for the conversion and instruction of the natives.

Before making the second settlement, it is well that with the two ships all the Mediterranean Sea of California be explored, examining everything on the coast running from Culiacan to Quivira, as far as the Strait of Anian, to see what rivers, ports and inlets there are on it; as well as along the coast encircling the realm of California,[1] until Cape Mendocino is turned, with all the rivers, ports, bays, and straits which there may be in its whole extent; and to learn on the way where and how are settled the strangers which the Indians said were in the realm near there and in their lands, as I have mentioned above in number X.,[2] and, also, to try

---

[1] That is, the eastern coast of the island of California.

[2] See p. 117.

to acquire knowledge and information of what the country contains.

By making this exploration with proper care and diligence it will be learned at once what there is along the sea and its coasts, and what people and wealth the region contains; and in what places settlements of Spaniards can be made, from which the religious may go to preach the Holy Gospel and convert souls to our holy Catholic faith. It will be learned, likewise, in what place and region is situated the Tizon River, which comes from New Mexico, how it is situated, what advantages it possesses, and what the distance is from there to the Spanish pueblos;[1] for if it is as they say, and as I mentioned in the last chapter of the report which I made of this exploration, his Majesty could order it settled, so that by this route supplies might be taken to the people of that realm. And from the settlements could be brought to them the necessary live stock and supplies, both for settling the coast and for sustenance. For it is said that it is no more than fifty leagues from one place to the other.

Personally, I think it will be very well that the pacification of the realm of New Mexico should begin at the port of Tizon River, since it is said that the best and richest settlements are on that border; for near there are the Lake of Gold,[2] and the pueblos of the Crowned King (Rey Coronado), and many people. For the preservation of the settlement on the Tizon River it will be very important that opposite it, in the realm and on the coast of California, another Spanish settlement be made, that they may communicate and trade one with another, and lend aid in case of need. Thereby each will stimulate the other to discover new lands and riches, and all may enjoy very good pearl fisheries and mineral wealth, those of New Mexico enjoying the wealth from the Lake of Gold, and those of the Californias that from some rich mountains which are on that border or near it and have an abundance of rich silver ore. Both of these God created for the service of man, as lures, I think, so that in the interest of these temporal things the king, our lord,

[1] Of New Mexico.

[2] For reference to the Laguna de Oro, see the documents of the Espejo and Oñate expeditions, pp. 156, 184, 186.

might send his vassals to discover and enjoy them, and, in their company, friars and ministers of the Gospel to undertake the conversion of those natives.

XVIII.

Of the reports brought back by those who may go on the ships for this exploration, both of what they may have seen and what they may have heard and learned, one may be given to his Majesty and his Royal Council of the Indies, that he may provide and order what is most fitting to his royal service and to the aggrandizement of his royal crown. I think it would be a matter of great importance to all these western nations of his Majesty if the navigation of the Strait of Anian should be discovered for Spain, as well as the rich city of Quivira, and the position of the realm of Anian, which is understood to be continuous with the realms of China. This will be discovering here another new world, to the end that in all of it may be preached the Holy Gospel, and the conversion undertaken of the many souls throughout its whole extent who live without religion or knowledge of the true God or of his most sacred law. Since all have been ransomed by the most precious blood of Our Redeemer and Lord Jesus Christ, it is a very great pity that they should be condemned for want of this light and the knowledge of the truth. May His most Holy Majesty, for He created them and died for them, grant that to so many and various nations of lands so remote and as yet undiscovered, knowledge be given of His most holy law, that they may receive and believe it, and that by means of holy baptism their souls may be saved, and that they may enjoy it.

As this realm of the Californias becomes pacified and its natives become converted to our holy Catholic faith, the Spaniards can go on settling other districts and places suitable for effecting the conversion of souls, and affording them profits and advantages; for if the Spaniard does not see any advantage he will not be moved to do good, and these souls will perish without remedy if it is understood that no profit will be drawn from going there. But if they are lured by self-interest they will go on discovering new lands every day, so much, indeed, that it will be necessary to keep them in check lest the forces be weakened, as I have already observed above. If it should seem best to his Majesty, he can command that his Spaniards go by land to settle, some at the port of San Diego, of which I have treated in number X., and others at the port of Monterey, of which I have treated in number XI.; for to endeavor to go by sea to settle there will be a very great and difficult task, on account of the head-winds that prevail along that coast, and because of the great difficulty of sailing there, as I have seen and experienced.[1]

XIX.

As time and occasion offer themselves for dealing with the Indians, the Spaniards will have opportunity to learn how to treat them and how to conduct themselves toward them, and on what occasions and for what causes they may make war upon them, or aid the friendly Indians against their enemies and opponents. Of this I treated at length in a tract which I composed in regard to these things, entitled, "Concerning the method to be observed in preaching the Holy Gospel to the heathen Indians," which is in a preceding part of this note-book. There I state that it is not meet that any war should be made upon the Indians without the counsel and consent of the religious whom the general, captains, and soldiers accompany, in order that everything may be done with devotion and a Christian and pious heart, and the gospel preached with peace, suavity, quietude, love, and sweetness, as our Master and Redeemer Jesus Christ commands us, of which I treated in paragraph VII.

It is well founded in reason and justice that, since the king makes this expedition at his own expense, no other than his own Spanish subjects should undertake it, for they are earning their wages, and they run like faithful vassals to fulfill the orders and mandates given them, not departing in the least from them, as is the practice of Spanish soldiery everywhere; and for this and other reasons, which I have set forth in the treatise mentioned, paragraph V., it is well that his Majesty should

---

[1] This suggestion forecasts the method of settling California pursued by the Portolá and Anza expeditions, of 1769 and 1775.

make these pacifications at his own expense, and that he should commit them to no one else. And in order that the soldiers may go with subjection and obedience to their superiors, the Spaniards who may be sent by his Majesty on this expedition for the pacification and settlement of this region should be warned that they go not to win land or vassals for themselves, but for the monarchs of Castile, who send them; for it is not right that his Majesty should make rewards of pueblos, or of Indians who are being pacified and converted to our holy faith, to any Spaniard, however great services he may have rendered his Majesty in these realms.[1] For his Majesty will not be able to do so with a good conscience, and it will cause the total ruin and destruction of all the Indians, as happened in the beginning, when all these realms of New Spain were conquered, and as was experienced in the Windward Islands and on the Tierra Firme, as the Bishop of Chiapa, Don Fray Bartolomé de las Casas, relates and discusses at very great length in a treatise[2] written in regard to this point, namely, that it is not fitting to give the Indians in *encomienda* to the Spaniards. He proves it with great erudition, and I refer to it in the treatise cited in paragraph XII.

XX.

Our very Catholic and most Christian King Philip, king of Spain and supreme emperor of the Western Indies, by reason of the sovereign rule he exercises over them, is obliged in conscience and in justice, and by human and divine law, to procure the conversion of all the Indians of the Western Indies, the obligation being the greater toward those realms already known and discovered, as is now this realm of the Californias, which has been treated of here; since it is already known and discovered, and the people in it are known, and since it is known how apt and inclined they are to receive our holy

---

[1] Father Ascensión makes it plain here as elsewhere that he favors the supremacy of the religious in the pacification. He clearly does not favor proprietary *entradas* like that of Oñate, nor *encomiendas*, which were granted in New Mexico.

[2] The reference is to Bishop Bartolomé de las Casas's *Brevissima Relacion de la Distruycion de las Indias* (Seville, 1552).

Catholic faith. And here I have discussed the manner by which his Majesty will be able at very little cost to send people to pacify this realm and to preach the Gospel to the natives, to convert them to our holy faith.

This obligation of his Majesty to hasten to the conversion of these souls, devoting to it all care, solicitude, and diligence, even if it be at a great expense to his royal estate, is treated of by the Bishop of Chiapa, Don Fray Bartolomé de las Casas, in a book[1] entitled "A Treatise proving the sovereign empire and universal principate which the monarchs of Castile and Leon hold over the Indies," to which I refer in the treatise cited, paragraph I. This being granted, I do not know what security his Majesty can have in his conscience for delaying so long to send ministers of the Gospel to this realm of the Californias. By coming to their aid, conscience will be satisfied and obligation fulfilled. It can be done with ease and little cost, and the result will be the winning of so many souls for God, while to his Majesty will follow increased rewards in heaven, and on earth the lordship over a new world and infinite riches. May God our Lord dispose his mind so to lend aid as will please Him best. Amen.

Written in the convent of San Sebastian, of the Order of Discalced Carmelites, in the City of Mexico, on the 12th of October of the year 1620. And to give it greater credence I signed it with my name.

Fray ANTONIO DE LA ASCENSION.

---

[1] The reference is evidently to Las Casas's *Treynte Proposiciones muy juridicas*, etc. (Seville, 1552).

II. EXPLORATION AND SETTLEMENT IN NEW MEXICO AND IN ADJACENT REGIONS, 1581–1605

1. THE RODRÍGUEZ EXPEDITION, 1581

INTRODUCTION

THE renewed activities on the Pacific coast at the turn of the century, as exemplified by the two expeditions of Vizcaino, were preceded and stimulated by a new advance into the northern interior. Coronado's expedition into New Mexico had proved disappointing and for nearly four decades no further explorations were made in the region, according to the present state of our knowledge. Nevertheless, during that time the frontier of settlement was pushed rapidly northward, and a new line of approach to New Mexico was opened by way of the great central plateau. In the forward moving column were explorers, missionaries, miners, and cattlemen. Zacatecas was founded in 1548, Durango in 1563, and with the opening of the mines of Santa Bárbara, Parral, San Bartolomé, and other places in their vicinity, before 1580, the frontier of settlement reached the head of the Conchos River. It was this stream which furnished the new avenue of approach to New Mexico.

The military frontier had proceeded even further, for, in pursuit of marauding Indians, as well as in search of mines and slaves, the frontier garrisons had made many forays to the interior beyond Santa Bárbara. In this way they had heard new reports of the Pueblo region, which had never been forgotten. About 1579 an Indian captured during one of these raids told at Santa Bárbara of a country to the north where there were large settlements of people who raised cotton for clothing, and had a plentiful food supply. Upon hear-

ing this report, Fray Agustín Rodríguez, a Franciscan lay
brother, stationed at San Bartolomé, began to plan with some
of the soldiers to make an expedition to the region thus described.   Fray Agustín went to Mexico to get permission from
the viceroy, and the outcome was the expedition narrated in
the documents which follow.

The party comprised three friars, nine soldiers, and some
sixteen Indian servants.   Fray Agustín Rodríguez, the or-
ganizer of the enterprise, was a native of Niebla, Spain.   Fray
Francisco López, who went as superior to the missionaries,
was an Andalusian.   The third friar, Juan de Santa María,
was a Catalan, versed in astrology.   The commander of the
soldiers was Francisco Sánchez, commonly called Chamuscado.
The career and calling of Hernando Gallegos, one of the followers of Sánchez, were typical of that far northern frontier
and significant of the interests in whose behalf the frontier
was being extended.   He was a native of Spain, had spent
eight years in Mexico as a prospector and soldier, and was
among those who had made expeditions beyond the mines
against the Indians.

Leaving Santa Bárbara on June 5, 1581, the party of about
twenty-eight persons passed down the Conchos River to the
Rio Grande.   Following that stream for many leagues through
a settled country and then for nineteen or twenty days through
a desert, they reached the first pueblos in the region of Socorro.
From there they continued up the river, fifty leagues according to one witness, passing numerous pueblos on the way, to
the Tigua towns about Bernalillo.   Against the advice of the
rest, Father Santa María now set out alone to report the discoveries in Mexico but was killed within a few days by the
Maguas Indians.   The rest of the party visited the salinas
east of the Manzano Mountains, and the buffalo plains beyond

the Pecos. West of the river they visited Ácoma and Zuñi. Leaving the other missionaries at Puaray, near the present Bernalillo, the soldiers returned to Nueva Vizcaya.

The expedition had important consequences. The reports made by Bustamante and Gallegos in Mexico in May, 1582, greatly interested the viceroy, and he thought at once of sending out another expedition, to aid the missionaries if they were still alive, and to explore in any case. News received later that Father López had been killed at Puaray somewhat changed his plans but did not lessen his interest. Rodrígo del Río de Losa, lieutenant-captain-general of Nueva Galicia, of whom the viceroy sought advice, now recommended an expedition of three hundred men, equipped to overawe the natives, settle New Mexico, explore and occupy the country beyond Quivira, and build two vessels on the northern strait if it should be reached. The men were to serve without pay, but were to be rewarded with titles of nobility, encomiendas, haciendas, and exemption from taxation. Truly the journey of Father Rodríguez had stirred up large ideas. When the matter was reported to the king he immediately ordered a contract made for the proposed undertaking.

The principal published sources of information regarding the Rodríguez expedition are those printed hereinafter. In addition, there is a declaration by Hernando Gallegos, made before the viceroy on May 16, 1582, at the time when Bustamante gave his testimony. It is so nearly identical with that of Bustamante that it is not included here, but all essential variations are indicated in the foot-notes to Bustamante's statement. All of these documents are published in Spanish in Pacheco and Cárdenas, *Colección de Documentos Inéditos*, XV. 80–150, under the title "Testimonio dado en Méjico sobre el descubrimiento de doscientas leguas adelante, de las minas de Santa Bárbola, Gobernación de Diego de Ibarra; cuyo descubrimiento se hizo en virtud de cierta licencia que pidió Fr. Agustín Rodríguez y otros religiosos franciscos: Acompañan Relaciones de este descubrimiento y otros documentos (Años de 1582 y 1583)." This collection covers both the Rodríguez and the Espejo expeditions. The originals are in the Archivo de Indias at Seville, Patronato, *est.* 1, *caj.* 1. Two documents in the collection (pp. 137–146) not reproduced here are the opinions of Rodrigo del Río referred to above. The "Relacion Breve" of Escalante and Barrando (the same as Barrado) is also printed in Spanish in the *Cartas de Indias* (pp. 230–233), published at Madrid in 1877 by the Ministerio de Fomento of Spain. So far as the editor is informed, none of these documents have hitherto been published in English. Some additional information regarding the Rodríguez expedition is contained in the documents of the Espejo journey (see *post*). Bancroft, in his *Arizona and New Mexico* (pp. 79–80), gives extensive notes concerning accounts of the expedition in the older Spanish works.

Two manuscript accounts of the greatest importance have recently come to light and will add much to our present knowledge of the Rodríguez expedition. They are: (1) Hernan Gallegos, "Relacion y concudío de el viage y subseso que Francisco Sanchez Chamuscado con ocho soldados sus compañeros hizo en el descubrimiento del Nuevo Mexico en Junio de 1581" (Archivo General de Indias, Patronato, 1–1–3/22). Gallegos was a member of the Rodríguez party. In his declaration (*Col. Doc. Inéd.*, XV. 88–95) he states that he has "made a book, written by his hand, wherein he gives an account of all this journey which he has made, and which he has delivered to His Excellency." The "Relacion" noted above is doubtless the same. (2) Baltasár de Obregón, "Cro-

nica comentario ó relaciones de los descubrimientos antiguos
y modernos de N.E. y del Nuevo Mexico," 1584 (Archivo
General de Indias, Patronato, 1–1–3/22).   Obregón had been
a member of the Ibarra exploring expedition, and had secured
first-hand information regarding the Rodríguez and Espejo expeditions.   The purpose of his Relation was to offer his services for further exploration and conquest in New Mexico.[1]

[1] Copies of these two manuscripts are in the Edward E. Ayer Collection in
the Newberry Library, Chicago, and have been used by the editor.

DECLARATION OF PEDRO DE BUSTAMANTE, 1582[1]

In the City of Mexico, New Spain, on the 16th day of the month of May, 1582, his Excellency Señor Don Lorenso Suarez de Mendoza, Count of Coruña, viceroy, governor and captain-general for his Majesty in this New Spain, and president of the Royal Audiencia which is located there, etc., said that, having been informed by Fray Agustín Rodríguez, of the order of San Francisco, and other religious of that order, that they desired to go to preach the gospel beyond the mines of Santa Bárbola[2] and the government of Diego de Ibarra[3], in a certain new land which they heard must be a place where they could obtain very fruitful results, he gave them permission in the name of his Majesty to go to discover said land and the people who might be in it; and that for the safety of their persons, and in order that thereby they might be able to preach the gospel, he granted that as many as twenty men might go with them. And it appears that, conforming to said permit, these religious and eight[4] of the said men

[1] Pacheco and Cárdenas, *Col. Doc. Inéd.*, XV. 80–88.

[2] Santa Bárbara is a mining town in Chihuahua, near the southern boundary of the state. It was founded about 1563 by Rodrigo del Río de Losa, under the direction of Francisco de Ibarra, founder of Nueva Vizcaya (Bancroft, *North Mexican States*, I. 106).

[3] Diego de Ibarra was evidently the successor of Francisco de Ibarra. In 1576 the Licenciate Ibarra was sent from Spain to take the place of his brother, Francisco, as governor of Nueva Vizcaya. On October, 1576, the viceroy wrote to the king: "Dize V.M. quen lugar de Francisco de Ybarra, governador que fué de la Nueva Vizcaya, a hecho V.M. merced de proveer al licenciado Ibarra, su hermano, y que vendria en esta flota." (*Cartas de Indias*, p. 325; see also Bancroft, *North Mexican States*, I. 112).

[4] Evidently there were eight men besides the leader, Francisco Sánchez Chamuscado. The "Relación Breve y Verdadera," by Escalante and Barrado (Barrando), translated hereinafter, gives the number as nine, and Bancroft was able to find the names of nine. See pp. 138, 168.

set forth; and yesterday, the 15th of the present month, there came to this city two of the men who accompanied the said religious, who report that they discovered and explored, two hundred leagues beyond the said mines of Santa Bárbola, which are within the government of Diego de Ibarra, a land thickly settled with pueblos of Indians who wear clothes and who live in a civilized way like the people of this New Spain, and that they had learned that beyond was much more land, settled by many pueblos of civilized people. In order to learn the facts in the case, he ordered taken the sworn testimony of these two men, who, as has been said, have come out and come to this city; all of which was done in the following manner:

At once oath was administered to and sworn in due form, in the name of God and Holy Mary, and with a sign of the cross, by Pedro de Bustamante, who is one of the said two men who came to this city. Under this oath he promised to tell the truth, and after he had taken it the following questions were asked him:

He was asked his name and his birthplace, and he replied that his name was Pedro de Bustamante, and that he was a native of a pueblo called Carancejas, of La Montaña del Valle de Cavezon, near the Villa de Santillana.

He was asked how long since he had come to this New Spain, and he replied that it was some ten years, more or less.

He was asked what had been his occupation since coming to this New Spain, and he said that the first three years he spent in prospecting for mines, and that the remaining seven he had been a soldier serving his Majesty in the government of Diego de Ibarra.

He was asked if he was one of the eight soldiers who had accompanied Fray Agustín Rodríguez, of the Order of San Francisco, and the other religious[1] who went with him; and who had solicited his services for the said journey; and with what object and purpose he had gone. He answered that it was true that he was one of those who accompanied the said religious, and that what particularly influenced him to make the journey with them was his desire to serve our

---

[1] The names of the other friars are given on p. 138.

Lord and his Majesty; that no one persuaded him to do so, but, on the contrary, with the desire already stated, he and the said religious had planned for more than two years to go on the journey, and that he had tried to enlist the others who went.

He was asked, since he said that for more than two years he was talking of and planning to make the journey, what information he had of the country leading him to believe that it was worth while; and he replied that the reason why they planned the journey was because an Indian[1] had told him that beyond the government of Diego de Ibarra there was a certain settlement of Indians who had cotton, and made cloth with which they clothed themselves; and that besides he was influenced by hearing of the account given by Alvar Nuñez Cabeza de Baca,[2] in a book which he wrote regarding a journey that he made coming from Florida to this New Spain.

Being asked what authority he and the rest who went with him had for making the journey; and how they provided themselves with arms, horses, and the other necessary equipment which they carried to make it, and what servants they had, he said that the journey having been decided and agreed upon between the witness, his companions, and the religious, they equipped and provided themselves with arms for their persons, that is, coats of mail, arquebuses, armored horses, and an Indian servant apiece, while the friars took seven Indians from the mines of Santa Bárbola, amongst whom was a half-breed.

Being asked what route they took, having set out from the mines of Santa Bárbola and the journey having been

---

[1] Gallegos says that he "had made, together with leaders and captains named for this purpose, many journeys into the interior beyond Santa Bárbola in pursuit of thieving Indians," and that through an Indian captured in an expedition he had learned of the country beyond. He states also that for two years he had discussed the matter with Fray Agustín and Francisco Sánchez (Chamuscado), and that together they had persuaded the others to go. Thus it is not quite clear who played the leading part in organizing the party (Declaration of Hernando Gallegos, in *Col. Doc. Inéd.*, XV. 88–89).

[2] Gallegos puts it somewhat differently, saying that they were guided (*guiandose*) by the relation of Cabeza de Vaca. He perhaps means that they were guided by it in forming their opinion (*ibid.*, p. 89).

begun, and through what pueblos and provinces they passed, he replied that on the 6th of June[1] of last year, 1581, he, his companions, and the religious set out from the valley of San Gregorio,[2] of the jurisdiction of Santa Bárbola, Nueva Vizcaya, and went down the same valley until they came to the river called Concha,[3] where they found a little settlement of the wild[4] Indians, who were naked and lived on roots and other things found in the fields; and following down the river, they came to another to which they gave the name of the Guadalquivir,[5] because it was large and carried an abundance of water. On this river they found other Indians of different nation and tongue from those of the Concha, although they too are naked like the latter. These and the others received them peacefully, and willingly offered them of what they had, and when inquiry was made of them as to whether there were more settlements beyond, they said yes, and that they were a people naked like themselves, and hostile to and at war with them.

And so they continued up the same river for twenty days,[6] through eighty leagues of uninhabited country, until they came to a settlement to which they gave the name of the province of Sant Felipe.[7] There they found a permanent

[1] It will be seen by comparing these documents that the expedition left Santa Bárbara on the 5th, and San Gregorio on the 6th. See *post*, p. 154. Bancroft and those who follow him give the 6th as the date of leaving San Bartolomé (Bancroft, *Arizona and New Mexico*, p. 76; Twitchell, *Leading Facts of New Mexican History*, I. 256).

[2] San Gregorio is in the valley of a small stream running northeastward from Santa Bárbara to the Río Florido, the main southern branch of the Conchos River. The route evidently was directly northeastward to the neighborhood of the present Jiménez.

[3] The Conchos River. It heads in southern Chihuahua and flows northeastward into the Río Grande at Ojinaga, Chihuahua.

[4] *Chichimeco*, at first applied to a single wild tribe of Indians of central Mexico, came to be a generic term for the wild tribes, as opposed to the settled and more civilized tribes.

[5] In honor, of course, of the Guadalquivir River of Spain.

[6] The account of Escalante and Barrado (Barrando) given later, says nineteen days. Gallegos says twenty days.

[7] Bancroft located San Felipe in the Socorro region, which Coronado had visited (*Arizona and New Mexico*, pp. 76, 77); Twitchell identifies it, a little more exactly, with San Marcial, the Piro village named Tre-na-quél, visited by Coronado's men, in 1542 (*Leading Facts of New Mexican History*, I. 256).

pueblo with houses two stories high and of good appearance, built of mud walls and white inside, the people being dressed in cotton *mantas* with shirts of the same.   They learned that away from the river on both sides there were many other pueblos of Indians of the same nation, who also received them peacefully and gave them of what they had, namely, maize, gourds, beans, chickens, and other things, which is what they live upon.   Inquiry being made as to whether there were more settlements of people, by signs the natives replied in the affirmative.

With this information they passed on up the same river, and found many pueblos along the road they travelled, as well as others off to the sides, which were to be seen from the road; and they came to another nation of Indians of different tongue and dress, where they were also received peacefully and gladly by the Indians, who kissed the hands of the religious.   These Indians are also clothed[1] and have three-story houses, whitewashed and painted inside; and they plant many fields of maize, beans, and gourds, and raise many chickens.

From there they passed on to another nation,[2] dwelling further up the same river.   These were the finest people of all they had met, possessing better pueblos and houses, and were the ones who treated them best, giving them the most generously of whatever they had.   They have well-built houses of four and five stories,[3] with corridors and rooms twenty-four feet long and thirteen feet wide, whitewashed and painted.   They have very good plazas, and leading from one to the other there are streets along which they pass in good order.   Like the others, they have a good supply of provisions.   Two or three leagues distant are other pueblos of the same nation, and consisting of three or four hundred

---

[1] Gallegos says "dressed in cotton cloth and shirts."

[2] Probably the Puaray mentioned farther along in the narrative.   Puaray was the principal pueblo of the province of Tiguex in Coronado's time.   Its ruins have been located by Bandelier opposite Bernalillo (A. F. Bandelier, *Final Report*, II. 226; Hodge, *Handbook of American Indians*, II. 313).   For new light on the location of Puaray, see Charles W. Hackett, "The Location of the Tigua Pueblos of Alameda, Puaray, and Sandía in 1680–1681," in *Old Santa Fé*, II. 381–391.

[3] Gallegos says "four, five, and six stories."

houses, built in the same fashion. They dress in cotton like the foregoing nations.

He said that up to this point they had always been travelling north. Leaving the river one day's journey and continuing north, they saw a large pueblo of four or five hundred dwellings, more or less. On reaching it they saw that the houses of the Indians were of four or five stories, and they named it Tlascala,[1] because it was so large. They were received peacefully there, as they had been in the other pueblos. There they were informed by the natives themselves that there was a very large settlement of Indians ten days' journey in the same northerly direction which they were following; but because of a lack of shoes for the horses and of clothing for himself and the rest of the men, they did not dare to go farther, but returned over the same road by which they had gone. From one of the pueblos which they had passed through and had named Castildavid, they crossed the river to the south,[2] following along a small river[3] which joined the other, and went to see three pueblos of which they had heard. The first two of them had as many as two hundred dwellings and the other as many as seventy.[4] In this last pueblo they learned of eleven others, further up the river, of a different nation and tongue from these. To the valley where the three pueblos were they gave the name of Valleviciosa.[5] They did not go to see them [the eleven] because they wished to go to find the cows which they had been informed existed in large numbers some thirty leagues distant, more or less.

Accordingly, they went in search of them, travelling the said thirty leagues in a roundabout course, because the guide

---

[1] This may have been northwest of Bernalillo, in the Xemes River valley. Gallegos says: "They named it Tlaxcala because of its size and because it resembled the city of Tlaxcala" (*Col. Doc. Inéd.*, XV. 92). The allusion is to Tlascala, an important city in Mexico east of the capital. During the conquest it gave stubborn resistance to Cortés, but later became a firm ally of the Spaniards.

[2] "South" here probably means "west."

[3] This was probably the Jémez River.

[4] Gallegos says "about seventy or eighty."

[5] Gallegos is directly in conflict with Bustamante here, stating that "Valle Viciosa" was the name given to the valley of the eleven pueblos of which they had heard, instead of that of the three where they were (*Col. Doc. Inéd.*, XV. 92).

who conducted them took them that way, which appeared different from the route described to them by the natives, for if they had gone by a direct road they would have arrived more quickly. Reaching some plains and water-holes, which they gave the name Los Llanos de San Francisco and Aguas Zarcas, they saw many herds of cows that come there to drink. They go in herds of two and three hundred; they are hump-backed, shaggy, small-horned, thick set, and low of body. There they found a ranchería of naked Indians of a different nation from those they had left behind, going to kill cattle for their food. They carried their provisions of maize and dates[1] loaded on dogs which they raise for this purpose. This witness and his companions killed with their arquebuses as many as forty cattle, made jerked beef, and returned to the settlement whence they had set out.

From there they returned down the river through the same country they had traversed, until they came to a pueblo called Puaray.[2] Here they heard of a certain valley and settlement of a different tongue, called Valle de Camí, south of the river.[3] On hearing this news they went forth and reached the said valley, where they found six pueblos of thirty, forty, and even one hundred houses, with many Indians clothed in the same

---

[1] The word is *dátil*, which means the fruit of the common date palm.

[2] See note 2, p. 146, above. According to Gallegos's "Relacion" and Obregón's "Cronica," Father Santa María set out from the Province of San Felipe alone and against advice to tell in Mexico the news of the discoveries. He was killed shortly afterward by wandering people of the Sierra Morena, but the others did not hear of his death till they returned from the buffalo plains. On September 28 they left Pueblo de Malpartida to go to the buffalo; on October 10 they reached Valle de San Francisco, and on the 19th set out to return. Reaching the Rio Grande they set up camp at Pueblo de Piedra y Taques, where they demanded provisions with threats of force. They now heard of Father Santa María's death, but tried to conceal it, lest they be considered vulnerable. An Indian attack was threatened, and they moved to Pueblo de Mal Puesto, where the Indians killed three of their horses. Three Indians were captured and sentenced by Chamuscado to be hanged, but the missionaries interfered. During the remainder of their explorations the party was constantly in danger. When the soldiers set out to return they left horses, goats, merchandise, and ornaments with the missionaries at Puaray. It was for these things, says Obregón, that the Indians killed them.

[3] "South" here means "west." Gallegos (*Relacion*) mentions both Ácoma and Zuñi as pueblos visited.

manner as the others,[1] the houses being of two and three
stories and built of stone. While there they told them of the
Valle de Asay,[2] where there were five large pueblos with many
people. According to the signs which the Indians made,
they understood that two of the pueblos were very large,
and that in all of them large quantities of cotton were raised,
more than in any other place which they had seen.

But, owing to a snowfall,[3] they could not go forward and
were forced to return to the said pueblo of Puaray, whence
they had set out. Learning there of some salines lying fourteen leagues from the said pueblo, they went to see them and
found that they were behind a mountain range which they
named Sierra Morena.[4] They are the best that have been
discovered up to the present, and extend, in the opinion of
this witness and the rest, five leagues. They provided themselves with what they needed, and of it brought to his Excellency the quantity which he has seen.[5] Near these salines
were seen many other pueblos, which they visited. They
had the same appearance as the others. The natives informed
them of three other pueblos, which they represented as being[6]
near these salines and very large.

From here they returned to the pueblo of Puaray, where
they had left the religious, the horses, and the rest of the
things which they possessed, and from this pueblo they returned along the same route by which they had gone. In
the said pueblo the religious remained with the Indian servants whom they had taken, among them being a half-breed.[7]
This witness and the rest of the soldiers returned with their
leader to Santa Bárbola, whence they had set out with the com-

---

[1] Gallegos says "dressed in shirts, cotton blankets, and hide shoes with
soles" (*Col. Doc. Inéd.*, XV. 93).

[2] Gallegos says "Osay." Bandelier was of the opinion, and I concur in it,
that Camí was Zuñi (*Final Report*, II. 228). In that case Osay, or Asay, might
have been Oraibi, one of the Moqui pueblos.

[3] Gallegos adds that it was now December.

[4] The Sierra Morena was evidently the Manzano Mountains, east of which
lie extensive salines (Bandelier, *Final Report*, II. 253-254).

[5] Gallegos says the viceroy was pleased with the samples (*Col. Doc. Inéd.*,
XV. 94).

[6] *Bigurificaban.*

[7] Gallegos tells us that his name was Juan Bautista (*Col. Doc. Inéd.*, XV. 94).

mission of his Excellency, and came to report to him what they had seen and discovered.

He said that in the course of the journey, in some pueblos, they found and explored five[1] mine prospects which appeared to them good, but because they did not go prepared they did not assay them; nor did they dare to bring any Indians from those parts, although they attempted to do so through kindness and the promise of gifts, but the Indians would not agree to it,[2] and they did not dare to use force lest they should anger them. He said that besides the aforesaid mine prospects, they told them of many others, and that this is the truth by the oath he has taken; and he approved, ratified, and signed it in his name.[3] He said that he was thirty-four years of age, and that their leader, named Francisco Sanches Chamuscado, died[4] thirty leagues from Santa Bárbola while coming hither with this witness and Hernan Gallegos, his companion, to report what they had seen.—PEDRO DE BUSTAMANTE. Before me, JUAN DE CUEVA.[5]

---

[1] Escalante says that eleven mines were discovered (see p. 157, *post*). Gallegos says that besides those discovered, many more, rich in silver, were heard of (*Col. Doc. Inéd.*, XV. 95).

[2] Gallegos says that the Indians refused to mount the horses (*ibid.*).

[3] Gallegos adds (*ibid.*) that the distance from Mexico City to the country discovered was four hundred leagues, mainly over level road, passable for men on horseback, with pack trains, or with carts.

[4] On the way back from New Mexico Chamuscado, who was more than sixty years old, fell ill. He was bled, and long halts were made to give him rest. As he got no better, he was carried between two horses on a litter made of poles cut with sabres, and of thongs from the hide of a horse killed for the purpose. Thirty leagues before reaching Santa Bárbara he died (Gallegos's *Relacion*, cap. XV).

[5] The declaration of Hernando Gallegos which follows here in the *Colección*, pp. 88–95, is omitted, since it is nearly identical with the foregoing deposition.

DECLARATION OF HERNANDO BARRADO, 1582.[1]

AFTER the foregoing, in the said city of Mexico, on the 20th day of the month of October, 1582, the said Señor Viceroy stated that whereas he was informed that the Indians who were discovered in this new land had killed the religious who had remained with them to teach and instruct them in matters pertaining to the holy Catholic faith, in order that his Majesty might be informed of everything he ordered that new testimony relative thereto be obtained; and to this end oath was administered in legal form to Hernando Barrado, a Spaniard who, it is said, went to the new land with the other soldiers who went to it. He took the oath in the name of God our Lord and of Holy Mary His Mother, making the sign of the cross with his right hand, under charge of which he promised to tell the truth.

And being asked in regard to the foregoing, this witness said that what he knows of the matter is that he is one of the eight soldiers who went into the interior with the leader, Francisco Sanchez Chamuscado, in company with Fray Agustín Rodríguez, of the order of San Francisco, and two other religious; that they succeeded in seeing all the settlements of the Indians which are referred to in the declaration of the two soldiers,[2] his companions, which has been shown to him; and that he knows that what they said and declared about the matter is the truth, and so happened, because he was a witness to it all.

At the time when this witness went into the interior, he took in his service an Indian named Geronimo, of the Concho nation, from near Santa Bárbola, of the kingdom of Nueva

[1] Pacheco and Cárdenas, *Col. Doc. Inéd.*, XV. 95–97.
[2] The reference is to the declarations by Bustamante and Gallegos. See pp. 139, 142–149.

Vizcaya, and when they agreed with the said leader and the other companions to return to this New Spain to report what they had seen and discovered, the said Indian, with two others, called Francisco and Andrés, and a mestizo and some Indian boys, remained voluntarily with the religious in the settlement which they call Puaray. And after having returned to Santa Bárbola, of the said kingdom of Nueva Galicia [sic], this witness being in the convent of the said pueblo, some three months ago, he saw there the said Francisco, one of the Indians who had remained with the religious. Being surprised at this, he spoke to him, and asked him how he happened to be there, and to have returned from the new land where he had left him. He replied that the Indians of that land of Puaray had killed Fray Francisco Lopez, the guardian, and that he had seen him buried. On telling Fray Agustín, his companion, of it, they became excited, and without waiting to see more he and the other two Indians, Andrés and Gerónimo, came away, through the Concho country, coming roundabout by almost the same route as they had gone. When they came away they heard many outcries and a tumult in the pueblo, wherefore he believed that they had killed[1] the rest of the religious and the Indian boys who remained there and had been unable to come with them. The one of his companions called Andrés had been killed by certain Indians in a settlement which they came upon between those of the Concho nation and the Tatarabueyes,[2] and only the Indian Geronimo, who had been a servant of this witness, had escaped with him.

And this witness, coming afterwards through the mines of Zacatecas, came across the said Indian Geronimo, who was being brought to this city by the other soldiers, companions of this witness; and he talked with him, and learned the same as what the other Indian, Francisco, had told him. From the said mines they all came together to this city of Mexico, and the said Indian saw his Excellency and spoke with him. A

---

[1] For the different versions of the death of the missionaries, see Bancroft, *Arizona and New Mexico*, p. 79, note 7; Bandelier, *Final Report*, II. 227-228. See also p. 148, note 2, and p. 168, note 3.

[2] The Patarabueyes, or Jumanos, who lived on the Rio Grande near the junction with the Conchos River. See p. 172, below.

few days ago he disappeared, and the witness has not seen him since, but he understands that he has returned to his own country. He says that this is the truth by the oath he has taken; and he affirmed, ratified, and signed it. He said he was more than fifty years old.—HERNANDO BARRADO. Before me, JUAN DE CUEVA. Copied and compared with the original which is in my possession. JOAN DE CUEVA. There is a rubric.

BRIEF AND TRUE ACCOUNT OF THE EXPLORATION
OF NEW MEXICO, 1583[1]

*Brief and true Account of the Exploration of New Mexico, which
we Nine[2] Companions explored, when we went from Santa
Bálbola in company with three Religious of the Order of
Saint Francis.*

WE, the said nine companions, set out from Santa Bálbola to undertake our journey, our sole object being to serve
God our Lord and his Majesty, by establishing the Holy
Gospel wherever we might find a suitable place and wherever
the Divine Majesty might guide us. We left on the 5th of
June,[3] 1581, and travelled thirty-one days[4] from the time
when we departed from Santa Bálbola through a country of
naked barbarian people. They are very poor and have nothing to eat except roots and prickly pears. Continuing our
journey from here, we left this people and travelled nineteen[5] days with great hardship and disappointments, and
without being able to see any people or any living thing.
At the end of that time, on the eve of the feast of the Assumption of Our Lady,[6] our Lord was pleased to show us a
naked Indian. We asked him by signs where maize could
be found, and he replied that one day's journey from there
we should find it in plenty. This information was obtained
by showing him two or three kernels of maize. He said there
was a great quantity, and told us that the natives were dressed

---

[1] Pacheco and Cárdenas, *Col. Doc. Inéd.*, XV. 146–150.

[2] This is one of the evidences that there were eight men besides the leader,
Francisco Sánchez Chamuscado. See p. 142, note 4.

[3] The other documents give June 6 as the date of leaving Valle de San
Gregorio. Some secondary authorities have failed to note the full evidence of
the documents on this point.

[4] This passage is our source for the time spent in reaching the Rio Grande.

[5] Bustamante and Gallegos say twenty. See p. 145.

[6] Nuestra Señora de Agosto, day of the Assumption of the Blessed Virgin
Mary, August 15.

in clothing the color of our shirts, and that they had houses. All this was by gestures and by signs which he made upon the ground.

This pleased us greatly, for already we were in need of provisions, and we kept the Indian for three days, so that he might take us where he said. He did so and we found all to be true as he had stated, for on August 21[1] we discovered a pueblo of forty-five houses of two and three stories.[2] We also found great fields of maize, beans, and gourds, whereat we gave thanks to our Lord for having provided us with supplies. We all entered into the said pueblo, well equipped, ready for war in case it should be necessary. That, however, was not our intention, for we were guided only by peace and love, and by a desire to bring the natives to the fold of our holy Catholic faith. In our midst we took three religious, bearing crosses in their hands and around their necks. Thus we entered into the pueblo, but we found no one there,[3] for they had not dared to wait for us, not knowing what we were, as our entrance was made upon armored horses. Seeing this, we immediately left the pueblo, travelling through fields of maize for about half a league, when we discovered five more pueblos. In the open we pitched our camp and agreed not to go on until we had won over those natives and made friends of them. At the end of two days a cacique came with three Indians to see who we were, and by signs we saluted one another. They came near to us and we gave them iron hawk's bells, playing cards, and other trinkets, and thus made them friends. They went and summoned the rest of the people, who came in great numbers to see us, saying to each other that we were children of the Sun. They gave us maize, beans, gourds, cotton *mantas* (blankets), and tanned cowhides. We remained four days in their midst, and in that space of time we learned from them, through signs, that beyond as well as to the sides there were great numbers of pueblos.

[1] Bancroft calls attention to the discrepancy here in dates (*Arizona and New Mexico*, p. 77, note 4).

[2] See 7, p. 145, above.

[3] Note a discrepancy between this and Bustamante's account of the reception. See p. 146.

From there we travelled up stream for fifty leagues,[1] and along the river and to the sides, within the distance of about a day's journey, we discovered, saw, and passed sixty-one pueblos, all peopled with clothed natives. These pueblos are in good sites and on good and level land. The houses are close together and the plazas and streets all well arranged. They have turkeys, which they raise. It seemed to us all that the sixty-one pueblos which we saw and visited must contain more than one hundred and thirty thousand natives, all of whom wore clothes.

In the said province there were more than as many more pueblos, equal to the largest, which we did not see, as we dared not go to them. Much cotton is raised there. Father Fray Bernaldino Beltran, of the Order of St. Francis, who went in after us, recently, ten months ago, with Antonio Despejo[2] and fifteen soldiers, brought the news that he had discovered five pueblos in the said province containing[3] more than fifty thousand souls. They gave them two thousand cotton *mantas*. Soon afterwards they discovered eleven more pueblos, of many people, as they report. They informed them of a very large lake,[4] with many settlements and people, where the people travel in canoes, carrying in the prows large balls of brass color. They report that Antonio Despejo with eight companions is going in search of this lake. Of all this Father Fray Barnaldino Beltran will give complete and detailed information.

We, the said nine companions and the three fathers, discovered also, about thirty leagues to one side of said pueblos, an immense number of humpbacked cows, which have on their shoulders humps a cubit high. These cows are found over a continuous space of more than two hundred leagues in length;[5] the width we do not know. They are not very wild

[1] This seems to be an estimate of the whole distance travelled up the river within the settled district.

[2] Antonio de Espejo. Beltrán went with Espejo but returned before him. Espejo had not yet returned when this relation was written. See *post*, p. 192.

[3] Moqui. See p. 186.

[4] The Laguna de Oro. See pp. 130, 184, 186.

[5] This information must have come from the Coronado expedition, or from reports given by the natives of New Mexico, for Chamuscado's men did not see two hundred leagues of buffalo plains.

cattle, and they run but little. Their meat is better than that of this country, and the cattle are larger than those of this country.

We also discovered in the said country eleven[1] mine prospects, all having great veins of silver. From three of them ore was brought to this city and given to his Excellency. He sent it to the assayer of the mint to be assayed; he assayed them and found one of the samples to be half silver; another contained twenty marks per quintal, and the third five marks. For all this I refer you to the assayer for verification, for I repeat only what he stated.

We also discovered in the said settlement a very rich saline containing a great quantity of granulated salt of good quality. Of it a sample was brought to his Excellency. The saline measures five leagues around.[2]

After stating the above I will add that we are ready and equipped, if his Majesty will give us permission, to go and settle and save so many souls which the devil holds captive, by teaching and instructing them *berbo ad berbo*,[3] as we say here.

There are reports of much more wherein God our Lord may be served and the royal crown increased, as regards both vassals and royal fifths, for after the Spaniards have once entered into the said land, besides the mines which we have already discovered they will seek and discover many more, for the land abounds in them, as also in forests, pastures, and water. It is a land whose climate is a little cold, although not excessively so. Its temperature is like that of Castile. And if it is not settled soon those souls who are there will be in danger, and the royal crown of his Majesty will suffer great injury, as is patent.—PHELIPE DE ESCALANTE. HERNANDO BARRANDO. By order of the Illustrious Archbishop of Mexico, I ordered this account copied from the original, with which it agrees, Mexico, October 26, 1583.[4] JOAN DE ARANDA. There is a rubric.

---

[1] Bustamante and Gallegos say five. See p. 150.

[2] Bustamante and Gallegos say five leagues in extent. See p. 149.

[3] Word for word.

[4] The date of the declaration fell between the return of Beltrán and this date given here.

REPORT OF THE VICEROY TO THE KING, 1583[1]

His Very Catholic and Royal Majesty:

In November of last year, 1580, a friar named Fray Agustín Rodríguez, of the Order of San Francisco, came to me and told me that he desired to go to the interior to preach the Holy Gospel beyond the mines of Santa Bárbola, which are in Nueva Vizcaya; and seeing his great zeal, and that it was reported that along the Conchas River were people where this good purpose might be effected, I granted him permission to do so, and to take with him other religious, and as many as twenty men who might voluntarily wish to go with him, to protect them and as company; and that they might take some things for barter; and that the one whom the friar should name should go as leader,[2] whom the others should obey, that they might not cause disorder. I did not give permission for more men to go, because your Majesty had issued instructions that no entries or new discoveries should be made without express permission from your Majesty.

They entered with as many as eight men,[3] who desired to go with them; and it appears that they went along discovering some pueblos in a good country, fertile, and having a food supply, the people having better dress and appearance than those of the Conchas River. Fray Agustín Rodríguez decided to remain in one of them with a companion, and that the eight men should come to report what until then had been seen and discovered. I have had their depositions taken and am sending[4] them herewith, attested, so that your Majesty may see them. And Rodrigo del Rio de Losa, lieutenant-captain-general in the province of Nueva Galicia, a man well informed and of much experience in expeditions,

---

[1] Pacheco and Cárdenas, *Col. Doc. Inéd.*, XV. 97–100.
[2] This is evidence that the purpose of the expedition was primarily religious.
[3] See p. 142, note 4.
[4] The text says *envió*, which is clearly a misprint for *envio*.

158

because he was in Florida with Don Tristan de Arellano[1] and in Nueva Vizcaya with Francisco de Ibarra, being here at the time, I consulted with him as to what he thought was necessary in order to send men to learn about the friars and to endeavor to obtain information about all the country, and, particularly, that they might report of it here; and he gave me the statement which I send[2] herewith, signed by himself.[3]

While this was taking place there arrived a soldier with one of the Indians who had remained with the friars, who said that they had killed one of them in his presence, and that as he was fleeing hither that they might not kill him he heard cries and shouts in the pueblo, by which he understood that they must be killing the other friar. And I having consulted with the said Rodrigo del Rio, concerning this event also, and concerning what would be necessary to make a military expedition, both as to the number of men and the supplies, if your Majesty should deign so to order it, he made a full report, which is the one accompanying this, signed by himself, so that your Majesty may order it examined.

From what can be gathered from the account given by these men, that country is densely populated and fertile; although they say they saw signs of mines, among the Indians no signs of gold or silver are found, or evidence that any metal has been taken out. Your Majesty will command the whole matter to be investigated, and will order what best suits your royal service, for in the meantime nothing more will be done in the affair. May God preserve the Very Catholic Royal person of your Majesty and increase your kingdoms and domains, as we the servants of your Majesty desire.

Mexico, November 1, 1582. His very Catholic Royal Majesty. Your Majesty's servant kisses your Majesty's royal hands. The Count of CORUÑA. Rubric.

[Endorsement.] On the cover is the following: "New Spain. To his Majesty, 1582. The viceroy, the Count of Coruña, November 1. Examined. Give this, with the papers

---

[1] See Lowery, *Spanish Settlements within the Present Limits of the United States*, 1513–1561, pp. 357–374.

[2] *Envió*, clearly a misprint for *envio*.

[3] Del Río's statements are printed in Pacheco and Cárdenas, *Col. Doc. Inéd.*, XV. 137–146.

referred to, to a relator.　There are two rubrics.　Issue a cédula addressed to the viceroy of New Spain, or to the person who in his place may be governing, so that, with respect to the exploration concerned in this letter and in the declaration and reports which he sends with it, he may make there a contract[1] with the person whom he may think best fitted for it, in conformity with the ordinances relative to the matter, so that the expedition may be made without any expenditure whatsoever from the treasury of his Majesty; and when the contract is made, before any of the conditions therein agreed upon are put into effect, let it be forwarded to the Council, so that, it having been examined, what is best may be provided for.　Madrid, March 29, 1583.　Licentiate BAÑOS. Two rubrics.　Before me, FRANCISCO DE LEDESMA.　Rubric."

[1] The contract was finally made with Juan de Oñate.　See *post*, p. 201.

NEW MEXICO

2. THE ESPEJO EXPEDITION, 1582–1583

INTRODUCTION

WHILE the viceroy was discussing an expedition to New Mexico, more effective measures were being taken by the Franciscan order and a private citizen. On learning through the returning soldiers that the friars who went with Chamuscado had been left alone in New Mexico, the Franciscans feared for the safety of their brethren and at once considered the organization of a rescue party. To lead it, Fray Bernaldino Beltrán, of the monastery of Durango, volunteered. Hearing of the project, Antonio de Espejo, a wealthy citizen of Mexico, who was in Nueva Vizcaya at the time, offered to equip and lead some soldiers as an escort, and to pay the expenses of Father Beltrán. Through the efforts of the friar a license was secured from Captain Juan Ontiveras, *alcalde mayor* of Cuatro Ciénegas, a settlement seventy leagues east of Santa Bárbara, then in Nueva Vizcaya, but now in Coahuila.

Enlisting fourteen or fifteen soldiers, on November 10, 1582, the expedition was begun at San Bartolomé, a place nine leagues east of Santa Bárbara. Besides Father Beltrán, Espejo, the soldiers, and servants, there were several other persons in the party, as is shown by the documents.[1] They

[1] The above account is based on the statement by Espejo, who does not give all the facts. The exact process by which the license was secured is not clear. The departure was attended by trouble and a conflict of interests. When the party set out on November 10 it consisted of Espejo, twelve other soldiers, Fray Pedro de Heredia, and Fray Bernaldino Beltrán, servants, and interpreters. At that time Father Heredia was evidently the superior of the missionaries of the party and no captain had been appointed. The *justicia* of Santa Bárbara forbade their departure, but Father Heredia exhibited a license from Juan de Ibarra, *teniente de gobernador* of Nueva Vizcaya, permitting all who wished to go with him. The first night they were overtaken in camp by one Fray Luis with an

were equipped with one hundred and fifteen horses and mules. The start was made three or four months after news of the death of Father López reached Santa Bárbara and it can hardly be supposed that the report was unknown to Father Beltrán and Espejo. Perhaps they hoped to find one at least of the friars still alive. No doubt Espejo at least was curious to see the country and regarded the journey as an opportunity for exploration.

The route followed was that of the Rodríguez party, but the records tell us more of what they saw than do those of the earlier journey. Passing down the Rio Conchos, they went through the tribes of the Conchos, Pazaguantes, and Tobosos. On the Rio Grande, at the junction and for twelve days above, they passed through Jumano villages. Above the Jumano country, and apparently before reaching the river bend near El Paso, they encountered two tribes who lived in rancherías. They were probably the tribes later known as the Sumas and the Mansos. Next they travelled fifteen days, or eighty leagues, through an unsettled region. It was evidently the same unsettled stretch of eighty leagues reported by the Rodríguez party. Going twelve leagues further, passing a ranchería on the way, they entered the pueblo region. After passing for two days through a province in which they visited ten pueblos, seeing others at the right and left, they reached

order from his *custodio* requiring Father Heredia to return, because Fray Luis, Fray Juan Bautista, and Fray Francisco de San Miguel were equipped for the journey. The soldiers insisted that Heredia should continue, since some of them would be ruined by the expense of the outfit if the enterprise were abandoned. He replied in writing that he would proceed. Fray Luis went back to San Gregorio to get his companions, and while there engaged in a quarrel with Father Heredia, who also returned. In the midst of it Heredia got a message from Ibarra asking him to await for ten or twelve days his coming with a license from Heredia's *custodio*. Thereupon Heredia sent word to the party to go ahead slowly and that he would overtake them. Meanwhile Miguel Sánchez Valenciano had returned to Valle de San Bartolomé and got his wife, Casilda de Amaya, and three sons, Lázaro, Pedro, and Juan, of whom the last two were aged three and one-half years. and twenty months, respectively (Luxán, *Entrada*).

the borders of the province of the Tiguas, and learned that Fathers López and Rodríguez had been killed at Puaray. The avowed purpose of the expedition had now been accomplished, but Espejo, seconded by Father Beltrán, decided to explore the country before returning. Going two days east with two companions, to the province of the Maguas, adjacent to the buffalo country, Espejo learned that there Father Santa María had been killed before Chamuscado left New Mexico.

Returning to the Tiguas, the whole party went six leagues to the Quires, and then visited Sia, fourteen leagues to the northwest, and the Emeges (Jemez), six leagues further northwest. Turning southwest, they now went to Ácoma, and thence to Zuñi. At this point Father Beltrán and about half of the party decided to return to Nueva Vizcaya. But Espejo and nine companions set out northward in search of a lake of gold said to be in that direction. He did not find the lake, but he visited the province of Mohoce (Moqui), and was given there a present of four thousand cotton blankets (mantas). Sending these back to Zuñi by five men, with the remaining four Espejo went west in search of mines of which he had heard. After travelling forty-five leagues he found them in western Arizona, and secured rich ores. Returning to Zuñi by a shorter and better route, he found Father Beltrán and his companions still there.

His party being increased by another of Espejo's men, Fray Beltrán now returned to San Bartolomé; but Espejo, bent on further explorations, turned east again and ascended the Rio Grande to the Quires. Going east from there six leagues, he visited the Ubates, and found mineral prospects near by. One day from the Ubates he visited the Tanos pueblos, who would neither admit him nor give him food. In view of this hostility and of the smallness of his party, Espejo now set out for home, but by a different route from that of the entrance. Going to Cicquique (Cicuye), he descended the Rio de las Vacas (Pecos) one hundred and twenty leagues, over a trail followed by Alvarado forty years before. From here, conducted by Jumano Indians, he crossed over to the mouth of the Conchos. Thence he returned to San Bartolomé, reaching it on September 20, 1583, nearly a year after setting out. Fray Beltrán had preceded him by several days. The report brought back by Espejo of the Lake of Gold (Laguna de Oro) and of the mines in western Arizona played a large part in directing the western exploration of Oñate and his subordinates two decades later.

The principal published source of information regarding the expedition is Espejo's own account (printed hereinafter), written at Santa Bárbara shortly after his return from New Mexico. This was published by Pacheco and Cárdenas in their *Colección de Documentos Inéditos*, XV. 101–126, under the title "Relacion del viage, que yo Antonio Espejo, ciudadano de la ciudad de México, natural de Cordoba, hize con catorce soldados y un relijioso de la orden de San Francisco, á las provincias y poblaciones de la Nueva México, a quien puse por nombre, la Nueva Andalucía, á contemplacion de mi patria, en fin del año de mill e quinientos e ochenta e dos."[1] This version of the relation will be designated here as A. It is preceded in the *Colección* by a letter of transmittal to the king, dated at San Salvador, April 23, 1584. Another version of the relation, bearing the same title as A, is in the same volume of the *Colección*, pp. 163–189.[2] This version will be referred to as B. With it is printed (pp. 162–163) the letter of transmittal by Espejo to the viceroy, at the end of October,

---

[1] It is comprehended in the *expediente* entitled "Testimonio dado en Méjico," etc., noted on page 139, above.

[2] It is comprehended in a group of documents entitled "Expediente sobre el Ofrecimiento que hace Francisco Diaz de Vargas, de ir al Nuevo México, y refiere la Historia de este Descubrimiento, con documentos que acompañan. Año de 1584." The originals are in the Archivo de Indias, Patronato, *est.* 1, *caj.* 1.

1683. The two versions differ very little, but A, though of slightly later date, is marred by fewer misprints than the other, and on it the translation is therefore based. All essential differences in B are indicated in the foot-notes.

Other documents in the same volume of the *Colección* containing incidental information regarding the expedition are the Relación Breve by Escalante and Barrado (pp. 146–150), printed hereinbefore, pp. 154–157; the petition of Francisco Días de Vargas for license to make a new expedition (pp. 126–137); the memorial of Espejo to the king, asking authority to settle the country he had discovered, pp. 151–162; the power of attorney by Espejo to Pedro González de Mendoza, his son-in-law, Joan García Bonilla, and Diego de Salas Barbadillo, April 23, 1583 (pp. 189–191). So far as the editor knows, none of the documents have been published in English heretofore.

Another relation of this expedition, still unpublished, was written by Diego Pérez de Luxán, a member of the expedition, under the title, "Entrada que hizo en el Nuevo Mexico Anton de Espejo en el año de 82" (A. G. de I., 1–1–3/22). A copy of this manuscript, which has recently come to light, is contained in the Ayer Collection. The "Cronica" of Obregón cited above also contains a detailed account of the expedition. So far as the editor knows, these important sources have not been used hitherto.

In Mendoza's *History of the Kingdom of China* (trans. in Hakluyt Society Publications, London, 1854), II. 228–252, is a contemporary account of the Espejo expedition; also in Hakluyt, *Voyages* (London, 1599–1600), III. 383–396.

ACCOUNT OF THE JOURNEY TO THE PROVINCES AND SETTLEMENTS OF NEW MEXICO, 1583

Account of the Journey which I, Antonio Espejo, Citizen of the City of Mexico, native of the City of Cordoba, made at the close of the year 1582, with Fourteen Soldiers and a Religious of the Order of San Francisco, to the Provinces and Settlements of New Mexico, which I named Nueva Andalucía, in Honor of my Native Land.[1]

In order that this account may be better and more easily understood it should be observed that in the year 1581 a friar of the Order of San Francisco, named Fray Agustin y Ruiz,[2] who resided in the valley of San Bartolomé, having heard through certain Conchos Indians who were communicating with the Pazaguates, that to the north there were certain undiscovered settlements, endeavored to obtain permission to go to them for the purpose of preaching the Gospel to the natives. Having obtained permission from his prelate and from the viceroy, the Count of Coruña, this friar and two others, named Fray Francisco Lopez and Fray Jhoan de Santa Maria, with seven or eight soldiers of whom Francisco Sanchez Chamuscado was leader, went inland in the month of June of 1581, through the said settlements, until they arrived at a province called Tiguas, situated two hundred and fifty leagues north of the mines of Santa Bárbola, of the government of Nueva Vizcaya, where they began their journey. There Fray Jhoan de Santa Maria was killed,[3] and as they saw that

---

[1] Pacheco and Cárdenas, *Col. Doc. Inéd.* (A), XV. 101–126; (B), *ibid.*, 163–189.

[2] This name should be Rodríguez.

[3] Father Santa María was killed among the Maguas, as Espejo himself tells further on.

there were many people, and that for any purpose either of
peace or of war they themselves were too few, the soldiers and
their leader returned to the mines of Santa Bárbola, and from
there went to Mexico, which is one hundred and sixty leagues
distant, to report to the viceroy, in the month of May, 1582.

The two religious who remained, with the desire to save
souls, believing that they were safe among the natives, did
not wish to come away, but preferred to stay in the said province of the Tiguas, through which Francisco Vasquez Coronado
long ago passed on his way to the conquest and discovery of
the cities and plains of Cibola.[1]   And thus they remained
with three Indian boys and a half-breed, whereat the Order of
San Francisco was greatly grieved, regarding it as certain that
the Indians would kill the two religious[2] and those who remained
with them.   Entertaining this fear, they wished and endeavored to find someone who would enter the said land and bring
them out and succor them.   For this purpose another religious of the same order, named Fray Bernaldino Beltran, a resident of the monastery of the Villa of Durango, capital of
Nueva Vizcaya, offered to make the journey, with the authority and permission of his superior.

And as at that time it happened that I was in that jurisdiction, and that I heard of the wise and pious desire of the
said religious and of the entire order, and knowing that by so
doing I would serve our Lord and his Majesty, I offered to
accompany this religious and to spend part of my wealth in
paying his expenses and in taking some soldiers, both for his
protection and defense and for that of the religious whom he
was going to succor and bring back, if the royal justice, in his
Majesty's name, would permit or order me to do so.   Accordingly, having learned of the holy zeal of the said religious and
of my intention, and at the instance of the said Fray Bernardino, Captain Joan de Ontiveros,[3] *alcalde mayor* for his Maj-

---

[1] For references to the province of the Tiguas (Tiguex) in the report of the
Coronado expedition, see Winship, "The Coronado Expedition," in the *Fourteenth Annual Report of the Bureau of Ethnology* (Washington, 1896), pp. 491,
497, 500, 503, 519, 520, 524, 569, 575, 587, 594.

[2] This would imply that the Franciscans knew that Father Santa María
had been killed before Chamuscado returned.

[3] B gives this name as "Onteveros" (p. 165).

esty in the pueblos called the Cuatro Cienegas,[1] which lie within the said jurisdiction of Nueva Vizcaya, seventy leagues east of the mines of Santa Bárbola, gave his order and commission that I, with some soldiers, should enter the new land to succor and bring out the religious and men who had remained in it.

And so, by virtue of said order and commission, I enlisted fourteen soldiers, whose names are Joan Lopez de Ibarra, Bernardo de Luna, Diego Perez de Lujan, Gaspar de Lujan, Francisco Barreto,[2] Gregorio Hernandez, Miguel Sanchez Valenciano, Lazaro Sanchez and Miguel Sanchez Nevado, sons of the said Miguel Sanchez, Alonso de Miranda, Pedro Hernandez de Almansa, Joan Hernandez, Cristóbal Sanchez, and Joan de Frias, all of whom, or the major part of whom,[3] I supplied with arms, horses, munitions, provisions, and other things necessary for so long and unaccustomed a journey. Beginning our journey at Valle de San Bartolomé, which is nine leagues from the mines of Santa Bárbola, on November 10, 1582, with one hundred and fifteen horses and mules, some servants, and a quantity of arms, munitions, and provisions, we set out directly north.

After two days' march of five leagues each we found in some rancherías a large number of Indians of the Conchos nation, many of whom, to the number of more than a thousand, came out to meet us along the road we were travelling. We found that they live on rabbits, hares, and deer, which they hunt and which are abundant, and on some crops of maize, gourds, Castilian melons, and watermelons, like winter melons, which they plant and cultivate, and on fish, *mascales*, which are the leaves of *lechuguilla*, a plant half a *vara*[4] in height, the stalks of which have green leaves. They cook the stocks of this plant and make a preserve like quince jam. It is very sweet, and they call it *mascale*.[5] They go about naked, have

---

[1] Regarding this place see p. 163, above.

[2] B gives this name as "Barrero" (p. 166).

[3] Elsewhere Espejo says that he supplied all of them.

[4] The *vara* was equivalent to about thirty-three inches.

[5] The maguey plant. "The fleshy leaf bases and trunk of various species of agave. It was roasted in pit ovens and became a sweet and nutritious food among the Indians of the states on both sides of the Mexican boundary" (Walter

grass huts for houses, use bows and arrows for arms, and have caciques whom they obey. We did not find that they have idols, nor that they offer any sacrifices. We assembled as many of them as we could, erected crosses for them in the rancherías, and by interpreters of their own tongue whom we had with us the meaning of the crosses and something about our holy Catholic faith was explained to them. They went with us six days beyond their rancherías, which must have been a journey of twenty-four leagues to the north. All this distance is settled by Indians of the same nation, who came out to receive us in peace, one cacique reporting our coming to another. All of them fondled us and our horses, touching us and the horses with their hands, and with great friendliness giving us some of their food.

At the end of these six days we found another nation of Indians called Pazaguantes,[1] who have rancherías, huts, and food like the Conchos. They were dealt with as had been those of the Conchos nation, and they continued with us four days' march, which must have been fourteen leagues, one cacique informing another, so that they might come out to receive us, which they did. In places during these four days' travel we found many mines[2] of silver which, in the opinion of those who know, were rich.

We left this nation, and on the first day's march we found another people called Jobosos.[3] They were shy, and therefore they fled from all the settlements through which we passed, where they lived in huts, for as it was said some soldiers had been there and carried away some of them as slaves. But we called some of them, making them presents, and some of them came to the camp. We gave some things to the caciques, and through interpreters gave them to understand that we had not come to capture them or to injure them in any manner. Thereupon they were reassured, and we erected crosses for

Hough, in Hodge, *Handbook of American Indians*, I. 845, *q. v.* for further data.)
See p. 321, below, note 5.

[1] B says Pazaguate (p. 167).

[2] "Minas de plata." B says "barras de plata" (bars of silver), which is probably a misprint (p. 167).

[3] Probably a misprint for Tobosos, as it appears in B, and as the name is commonly known.

them in their rancherías and explained to them something about[1] God our Lord. They appeared pleased, and being so, some of them went on with us till they had taken us beyond their territory. They live on the same things as the Pazaguates, use bows and arrows, and go about without clothing. We passed through this nation, which seemed to have few Indians, in three days, which must have been a distance of eleven leagues.

Having left this nation we came to another who call themselves the Jumanos,[2] and whom the Spaniards call, for another name, Patarabueyes. This nation appeared to be very numerous, and had large permanent pueblos. In it we saw five pueblos with more than ten thousand Indians, and flat-roofed houses, low and well arranged into pueblos. The people of this nation have their faces streaked, and are large; they have maize, gourds, beans, game of foot and wing, and fish of many kinds from two rivers that carry much water. One of them, which must be about half the size of the Guadalquivir,[3] flows directly from the north and empties into the Conchos River. The Conchos, which must be about the size of the Guadalquivir, flows into the North Sea. They have salines consisting of lagoons of salt water, which at certain times of the year solidifies and forms salt like that of the sea. The first night, when we pitched camp near a small pueblo of this nation, they killed five of our horses with arrows and wounded as many more, notwithstanding the fact that watch was kept. They retired to a mountain range, where six of us went next morning with Pedro, the interpreter,[4] a native of their nation, and found them, quieted them, made peace with them, and took them to their own pueblo. We told them what we had told the others, and that they should inform the people of their nation not to flee nor hide, but to come out to see us. To some of the caciques I gave beads, hats, and other

---

[1] "Algunas cosas de Dios Nuestro Señor." B says "Algunas cosas de la ley de Dios Nuestro Señor" (p. 168).

[2] B reads "Xumarias" (p. 168), evidently a misprint. For the Jumano Indians, see Hodge, *Handbook*, I. 636; Hodge, "The Jumano Indians," in *Proc. Am. Antiq. Soc.*, April, 1909; Bolton, "The Jumano Indians in Texas," in *Texas State Hist. Assoc. Quarterly*, XV. 66–84.

[3] B reads "Guadalquibí" (p. 168).   [4] *Naguatato.*

things, so that they would bring them in peace, which they did; and from these pueblos they accompanied us, informing one another that we came as friends and not to injure them; and thus great numbers of them went with us and showed us a river from the north, which has been mentioned above.

On the banks of this river Indians of this nation are settled for a distance of twelve days' journey. Some of them have flat-roofed houses, and others live in grass huts. The caciques came out to receive us, each with his people, without bows or arrows, giving us portions of their food, while some gave us *gamuzas* (buckskins) and buffalo hides, very well tanned. The *gamuzas* they make of the hides of deer; they also are tanned, as it is done in Flanders. The hides are from the humpbacked cows which they call *civola*, and whose hair is like that of cows of Ireland. The natives dress the hides[1] of these cows as hides are dressed in Flanders, and make shoes of them. Others they dress in different ways, some of the natives using them for clothes. These Indians appear to have some knowledge of our holy Catholic faith, because they point to God our Lord, looking up to the heavens. They call him Apalito in their tongue, and say that it is He whom they recognize as their Lord and who gives them what they have. Many of them, men, women, and children, came to have the religious and us Spaniards bless them, which made them appear very happy. They told us and gave us to understand through interpreters that three Christians and a negro had passed through there, and by the indications they gave they appeared to have been Alonso[2] Nuñez Cabeza de Vaca, Dorantes Castillo Maldonado, and a negro, who had all escaped from the fleet with which Pánfilo Narvaez entered Florida. They were left friendly and very peaceful and satisfied, and some of them went with us up the Río del Norte, serving and accompanying us.[3]

---

[1] "Antas" (p. 107). B (p. 169) reads "cintas," evidently a misprint.
[2] A mistake for "Alvar." It is the same in B.
[3] Luxán, in his *Entrada*, gives a day-by-day diary of the expedition, which clears up many of Espejo's very general statements. The Rio del Norte was reached on December 9 after twenty-one days, or seventy-two leagues, of actual travel. On November 15 they passed the junction of the Florido with the

Continuing up that river, always to the north, there came out to receive us a great number of Indians, men, women, and children, dressed or covered with buckskins; but we did not learn of what nation they were,[1] through lack of interpreters. They brought us many things made of feathers of different colors, and some small cotton *mantas*, striped with blue and white, like some of those they bring from China; and they gave us to understand by signs that another nation that adjoined theirs, towards the west, brought those things to barter with them for other goods which these had and which appeared from what they told us by signs to be dressed hides of cows and deer; and showing them shining ores, which in other places usually bear silver, and others of the same kind which we carried, they pointed towards the west five days' journey, saying they were taking us to where there was an immense quantity of those metals and many people of that nation. They went forth with us four days' journey, which must have been a distance of twenty-two leagues.

Conchos; on the 23d they reached Rio de San Pedro, and next day crossed the Conchos at El Xacal, forty leagues from San Gregorio, where Lope de Ariste had built a hut during a slave-hunting expedition. Here Chamuscado had been buried the year before. December 4, twenty-three leagues further on, they left the Conchos tribe and entered that of the Pasaguates, friends of the Conchos and Patarabueyes, and speaking all three languages. Four leagues beyond, on December 6, they reached the first ranchería of the Patarabueyes. This name, Luxán tells us, was made up by the soldiers of Mateo González during a previous slaving expedition to this ranchería. The Indians called themselves Otomoacos. It was at this ranchería that the Indians killed Espejo's horses. On the ninth the expedition reached the Rio del Norte, five leagues above the junction. The Indians here and at the junction were called Abriaches, and spoke a language different from the Otomoacos, though related to them. By the Spaniards both tribes were called Patarabueyes. Here and at the junction eight days were spent awaiting Father Heredia and resting the horses. At the junction they visited the village of chief Baysibiye, on the south side, and across the river those of chief Casicamoyo and head-chief Qbisise. The previous year Luxán's brother, Gaspár, had been at this point on a slaving expedition for Juan de la Parra, of Indeche (Indé). Hearing while here through the Indians that Father López and his companion were still alive, Father Beltrán insisted on hurrying on, without awaiting Father Heredia. As yet no captain had been formally elected, as Heredia was to name one. Accordingly, Espejo was chosen captain and *justicia mayor*, and the march was continued.

[1] Later the Spaniards found the Suma and Manso tribes settled between El Paso and the Jumanos. It may have been these whom Espejo saw. See p. 176, note 4, below.

These Indians having stopped, and we having travelled four days more up the said river, we found a great number of people living near some lagoons[1] through the midst of which the Río del Norte flows. These people, who must have numbered more than a thousand men and women, and who were settled in their rancherías and grass huts, came out to receive us, men, women, and children. Each one brought us his present of *mesquital*,[2] which is made of a fruit like the carob bean,[3] fish of many kinds, which are very plentiful in those lagoons, and other kinds of their food in such quantity that the greater part spoiled because the amount they gave us was so great. During the three days and nights we were there they continually performed *mitotes*, balls, and dances, in their fashion, as well as after the manner of the Mexicans. They gave us to understand that there were many people of this nation at a distance from there, but we did not learn of what nation they were, for lack of interpreters. Among them we found an Indian of the Concho nation who gave us to understand, pointing to the west, that fifteen days' journey from there there was a very large lake, where there were many settlements, with houses of many stories, and that there were Indians of the Concho nation settled there, people wearing clothes and having plentiful supplies of maize and turkeys and other provisions in great quantity, and he offered to take us there. But because our course led us north to give succor to the religious and those who remained with them, we did not go to the lake. In this ranchería and district the land and the climate are very good ; and nearby there are cows and native cattle, plentiful game of foot and wing, mines, many forests, pasture lands, water, salines of very rich salt, and other advantages.

Travelling up the same river, we followed it fifteen days from the place of the lagoons mentioned above without finding any people, going through country with mesquite groves, prickly pears, mountains with pine groves having pines and pine-nuts like those of Castile, sabines, and cedars. At the

---

[1] From note 4, p. 176, below, this place would seem to have been some distance below El Paso.

[2] B, p. 171, reads "Mezquitama," obviously a misprint.

[3] The mesquite bean.

end of this time[1] we found a ranchería, of few people but containing many grass huts, many deer skins, also dressed like those they bring from Flanders, a quantity of very good and white salt, jerked venison, and other kinds of food. These Indians received us[2] and went with us, taking us two days' journey[3] from that place, to the settlements, always following the Río del Norte. From the time when we first came to it we always followed this river up stream, with a mountain chain on each side of it, both of which were without timber throughout the entire distance until we came near the settlements which they call New Mexico, although along the banks of the river there are many groves of white poplars, the groves being in places four leagues wide. We did not leave the river from the time when we came to it up to the time of reaching the said provinces which they call New Mexico. Along the banks of the river, in many parts of the road, we found thickets of grape vines and Castilian walnut trees.[4]

After we reached the said settlements, continuing up the river, in the course of two days we found ten inhabited pueblos[5] on the banks of this river, close to it and on all sides, be-

[1] B adds, p. 171, "in which we had travelled about eighty leagues." This is important, for it helps to interpret the accounts of the Rodríguez expedition. It would seem that the eighty leagues mentioned by Bustamante and the rest after leaving the first Indians encountered on the Guadalquivir, refer to the distance travelled after leaving the settlements, rather than to that travelled after reaching the Guadalquivir. This being the case, the accounts of the two expeditions tally at these points.

[2] B adds "bien" (p. 172).

[3] B adds "about twelve leagues from there" (p. 172).

[4] Luxán gives the following account of the journey from the camp five leagues above the junction to the first pueblos. The pueblos were reached on February 1, after twenty-nine days, or one hundred and twenty-three leagues, of actual travel. Otomoacos Indians were met all the way up for forty-five leagues, till January 2, when the Caguates were met. They were related to the Otomoacos and spoke nearly the same language. Eleven leagues farther up they encountered large marshes and pools (charcos). Three leagues up, in this lake country, they met the Tampachoas, people similar to the Otomoacos. Thirty-seven leagues up, on January 26, they crossed the river and from that point went straight north. Twenty-one leagues from here they reached the first inhabited pueblos, thirteen days of actual travel after reaching the great marshes.

[5] These towns were in the general region of Socorro and above. Twitchell thinks the group began about at San Marcial (Leading Facts, I. 274–275).

sides other pueblos which appeared off the highway, and which in passing seemed to contain more than twelve thousand persons, men, women, and children. As we were going through this province, from each pueblo the people came out to receive us, taking us to their pueblos and giving us a great quantity of turkeys, maize, beans, tortillas, and other kinds of bread, which they make with more nicety than the Mexicans. They grind on very large stones. Five or six women together grind raw corn in a single mill, and from this flour they make many different kinds of bread. They have houses of two, three, and four stories, with many rooms in each house. In many of their houses they have their *estufas*[1] for winter, and in each plaza of the towns they have two *estufas*, which are houses built underground, very well sheltered and closed, with seats of stone against the walls to sit on. Likewise, they have at the door of each *estufa* a ladder on which to descend, and a great quantity of community wood, so that the strangers may gather there.

In this province some of the natives wear cotton, cow hides, and dressed deerskin.[2] The *mantas* they wear after the fashion of the Mexicans, except that over their private parts they wear cloths of colored cotton. Some of them wear shirts. The women wear cotton skirts, many of them being embroidered with colored thread, and on top a *manta* like those worn by the Mexican Indians, tied around the waist with a cloth like an embroidered towel with a tassel. The skirts, lying next to the skin, serve as flaps of the shirts. This costume each one wears as best he can, and all, men as well as women, dress their feet in shoes and boots, the soles being of cowhide and the uppers of dressed deerskin. The women wear their hair carefully combed and nicely kept in place by the moulds that they wear on their heads, one on each side, on which the hair is arranged very neatly, though they wear no headdress. In each pueblo they have their caciques, the number differing according to the number of people. These caciques have under them caciques, I mean *tequitatos*, who

[1] These were *kivas*, or ceremonial chambers. See Hodge, *Handbook*, I. 710–711.

[2] For a description of the ancient dress of the Pueblo Indians see Hodge. *Handbook*, II. 322–323.

are like *alguaciles,* and who execute in the pueblo the cacique's orders, just exactly like the Mexican people. And when the Spaniards ask the caciques of the pueblos for anything, they call the *tequitatos,* who cry it through the pueblo in a loud voice, whereupon they bring with great haste what is ordered.

The painting of their houses, and the things which they have for balls and dancing, both as regards the music and the rest, are all very much like those of the Mexicans. They drink toasted *pinole,* which is corn toasted and ground and mixed with water. It is not known that they have any other drink or anything with which to become intoxicated. In each one of these pueblos they have a house to which they carry food for the devil, and they have small stone idols which they worship. Just as the Spaniards have crosses along the roads, they have between the pueblos, in the middle of the road, small caves or grottoes, like shrines, built of stones, where they place painted sticks and feathers, saying that the devil goes there to rest[1] and speak with them.

They have fields of maize, beans, gourds, and *piciete*[2] in large quantities, which they cultivate like the Mexicans. Some of the fields are under irrigation,[3] possessing very good diverting ditches, while others are dependent upon the weather. Each one has in his field a canopy with four stakes and covered on top, where they take him food daily at noon and where he takes his siesta, for ordinarily they are in their fields from morning until night, after the Castilian custom. In this province are many pine forests which bear pine-nuts[4] like those of Castile, and many salines on both sides of the river. On each bank there are sandy flats more than a league wide, of soil naturally well adapted to the raising of corn. Their arms consist of bows and arrows, *macanas* and *chimales;* the arrows have fire-hardened shafts, the heads being of pointed flint, with which they easily pass through a

---

[1] A reads "Va alli ha de poxar" (p. 111). This is a corruption. B reads, "Va allí a reposar" (p. 174), which is obviously correct.

[2] B reads "*piciere,* which is a good and healthy herb" (p. 174).

[3] For a discussion of pueblo irrigation before the coming of the Spaniards, see Hodge, *Handbook,* I. 620–621, and works cited therein.

[4] For a discussion of the range of the *piñon,* see Ponton and McFarland, in the Texas State Historical Association *Quarterly,* I. 180–181.

coat of mail. The *chimales* are made of cowhide, like leather
shields; and the *macanas* consist of rods half a vara long,
with very thick heads. With them they defend themselves
within their houses. It was not learned that they were at
war with any other province. They respect their boundaries.[1]
Here they told us of another province of the same kind which
is farther up the same river.

After a stay of four days in this province we set out, and
half a league from its boundary we found another, which is
called the province of the Tiguas. It comprises sixteen pueblos, one of which is called Pualas.[2] Here we found that the
Indians of this province had killed Fray Francisco Lopez and
Fray Augustin Ruiz,[3] three boys, and a half-breed, whom
we were going to succor and take back. Here we secured a
very correct report that Francisco Vasquez Coronado had
been in the province, and that they had killed nine of his
soldiers and forty horses, and that because of this he had completely destroyed the people of one pueblo of the province.[4]
Of all this the natives of these pueblos informed us by signs
which we understood. Believing that we were going there
to punish them because they had killed the friars, before we
reached the province they fled to a mountain two leagues
from the river. We tried to bring them back peacefully,
making great efforts to that end, but they refused to return.
In their houses we found a large quantity of maize, beans,
gourds, many turkeys, and many ores of different colors.
Some of the pueblos in this province, as also the houses, were
larger than those of the province we had passed, but the
fields and character of the land appeared to be just the same.
We were unable to ascertain the number of people in this
province, for they had fled.

Having arrived at this province of the Tiguas and found
that the religious in quest of whom we had come, and the
half-breed and the Indians who had remained with them,
were dead, we were tempted to return to Nueva Vizcaya,
whence we had started. But since while we were there the

---

[1] This sentence is lacking in B.

[2] B gives this name as "Paula" (p. 175).   [3] This should be *Rodríguez*.

[4] For the revolt of the Tiguex and their punishment by the Spaniards under
Coronado, see Winship, *The Coronado Expedition*, p. 497.

Indians informed us of another province to the east which they said was near, and as it seemed to me that all that country was well peopled, and that the farther we penetrated into the region the larger the settlements we found, and as they received us peacefully, I deemed this a good opportunity for me to serve his Majesty by visiting and discovering those lands so new and so remote, in order to give a report of them to his Majesty, with no expense to him in their discovery. I therefore determined to proceed as long as my strength would permit. Having communicated my intention to the religious and soldiers, and they having approved my decision, we continued our journey and discovery in the same way as heretofore.

In this place we heard of another province,[1] called Maguas, which lay two days' journey to the east.[2] Leaving the camp in this province I set out with two companions for the place, where I arrived in two days. I found there eleven pueblos, inhabited by a great number of people. It seemed to me they must comprise more than forty thousand souls, between men, women, and children. They have here no running arroyos or springs to use, but they have an abundance of turkeys, provisions, and other things, just as in the foregoing province. This one adjoined the region of the cows called *cíbola*. They clothe themselves with the hides of these cows, with cotton *mantas*, and with deerskins. They govern themselves as do the preceding provinces, and like the rest have idols which they worship. They have advan-

[1] "Tubimos noticia de otra provincia" (p. 114). B, evidently corrupt, reads, "tubimos noticia como el dicho, otra provincia," etc. (p. 176).

[2] In Espejo's memorial (*Col. Doc. Inéd.*, XV. 156) Maguas (Magrias) is said to join the Tiguas on the northeast. Bancroft notes a difficulty regarding the location (*Arizona and New Mexico*, p. 85, foot-note). Obregón and Luxán state that the Indians in San Felipe, on the border of the Tiguas, told Espejo of the death of the two friars at Puaray, and that the Tiguas, knowing of Espejo's coming, were preparing to destroy his party. Thereupon a division arose in Espejo's camp, some, led by Fray Bernaldino, Miguel Sánchez, and Gregorio de Hernández, desiring to go back; but the rest, led by Espejo and Diego Pérez de Luxán, voted to continue. From this point they went to visit the Magrias (Maguas) pueblos, behind the sierra, returning thence to the river, which they ascended fifteen leagues to Puara. This statement clarifies Espejo's narrative in regard to the location of the Maguas. They were southeast of Puara. The party reached Puara February 17.

tages for mines in the mountains of this province, for as we travelled toward[1] them we found much antimony[2] along the route, and wherever this is found there are usually ores rich in silver. In this province we found ores in the houses of the Indians. We likewise discovered that here they had killed one of the religious, called Fray Jhoan de Santa Maria, who had entered with the other religious, Francisco Chamuscado, and the soldiers. They killed him before the said Francisco Chamuscado went to the pacified country.[3] However, we made friends of them, saying nothing of these murders. They gave us food, and having noted the nature of the country, we departed from it. It is a land of many pine forests, with Castilian pine-nuts and sabines. We returned to the camp and the Río del Norte, whence we had come.

Having reached the camp we heard of another province called Quires[4] up the Río del Norte one day's journey, a distance of about six leagues from where we had our camp. With the entire force we set out for the province of the Quires, and one league before reaching it many Indians came out to greet us peacefully, and begged us to go to their pueblos. We went therefore and they received us very well, and gave us some cotton *mantas*, many turkeys, maize, and portions of all else which they had. This province has five pueblos, containing a great number of people, it appearing to us that there were fifteen thousand souls. Their food and clothing were the same as those of the preceding province. They are idolatrous, and have many fields of maize and other things. Here we found a parrot in a cage, just like those of Castile, and sunflowers like those of China, decorated with the sun, moon, and stars. Here the latitude was taken, and we found ourselves to be in exactly 37½° north. We heard of another province two days' journey to the west.

Leaving this province, after two days' march, which is fourteen leagues, we found another, called Los Pumames,[5]

---

[1] "La Ví á ella" (p. 115); B reads "hacia ella" (p. 177); the former is doubtless a corruption, and the latter correct.

[2] *Artimonia.* B adds, "ques una quemazon de metales de plata" (p. 177).

[3] *Tierra de paz.* Frequently used in this sense in these documents.

[4] For a brief discussion of the Keresan family, see Hodge, *Handbook,* I. 675.

[5] "Punames" in B, p. 178.

consisting of five pueblos, the chief pueblo being called Sia.[1] It is a very large pueblo, and I and my companions went through it; it had eight plazas, and better houses than those previously mentioned, most of them being whitewashed and painted with colors and pictures after the Mexican custom. This pueblo is built near a medium-sized river which comes from the north and flows into the Río del Norte, and near a mountain. In this province there are many people, apparently more than twenty thousand souls. They gave us cotton *mantas*, and much food consisting of maize, hens, and bread made from corn flour, the food being nicely prepared, like everything else. They were a more deft people than those we had seen up to this point, but were dressed and governed like the others. Here we heard of another province to the northwest and arranged to go to it. In this pueblo they told us of mines nearby in the mountains, and they showed us rich ores from them.

Having travelled one day's journey to the northwest, a distance of about six leagues, we found a province, with seven pueblos, called the Province of the Emexes,[2] where there are very many people, apparently about thirty thousand souls. The natives indicated to us that one of the pueblos was very large and in the mountains, but it appeared to Fray Bernardino Beltran and some of the soldiers that our numbers were too small to go to so large a settlement and so we did not visit it, in order not to become divided into two parties.[3] It consists of people like those already passed, with the same provisions, apparel, and government. They have idols, bows and arrows, and other arms, as the provinces heretofore mentioned.

We set out from this province towards the west, and after going three days, or about fifteen leagues, we found a pueblo called Acoma,[4] where it appeared to us there must

[1] "Siay" in A, a misprint for "Sia a," as it is in B, p. 178. Sia is now a Keresan tribe on the north side of the Jemez River, about sixteen miles northwest of Bernalillo (Hodge, *Handbook*, I. 562).

[2] Jemez, now a pueblo on the Jemez River, about twenty miles northwest of Bernalillo (Hodge, *Handbook*, I. 629).

[3] That is, in order not to disagree.

[4] Ácoma is situated about sixty miles west of the Rio Grande, in Valencia County. The rock on which it is built is 357 feet above the plateau (Hodge,

be more than six thousand souls. It is situated on a high rock more than fifty *estados*[1] in height. In the very rock stairs are built by which they ascend to and descend from the town, which is very strong. They have cisterns of water at the top, and many provisions stored within the pueblo. Here they gave us many *mantas*, deerskins, and strips of buffalo-hide, tanned as they tan them in Flanders, and many provisions, consisting of maize and turkeys. These people have their fields[2] two leagues from the pueblo on a river of medium size, whose water they intercept for irrigating purposes, as they water their fields with many partitions of the water near this river, in a marsh. Near the fields we found many bushes of Castilian roses. We also found Castilian onions, which grow in the country by themselves, without planting or cultivation. The mountains thereabout apparently give promise of mines and other riches, but we did not go to see them as the people from there were many and warlike. The mountain people come to aid those of the settlements, who call the mountain people Querechos.[3] They carry on trade with those of the settlements, taking to them salt, game, such as deer, rabbits, and hares, tanned deerskins, and other things, to trade for cotton *mantas* and other things with which the government pays them.

In other respects they are like those of the other provinces. In our honor they performed a very ceremonious *mitote* and dance, the people coming out in fine array. They performed many juggling feats, some of them very clever, with live snakes.[4] Both of these things were well worth see-

Handbook, I. 10). The native name of the town is Áco and of the people, Acóme. For Castañeda's description of Ácoma see Winship, *The Coronado Expedition*, p. 491.

[1] An *estado* is the height of a man, *i. e.*, between five and six feet.

[2] Hodge says that these fields were "probably those still tilled at Acomita (Tichuna) and Pueblito (Titsiap), their two summer, or farming, villages, 15 m. distant" (*Handbook*, I. 10).

[3] Querecho was a Pueblo name for the buffalo-hunting Apache Indians east of New Mexico (Hodge, *Handbook*, II. 338).

[4] The snake dance is now characteristically a Hopi (Moqui) ceremony, where it is primarily a prayer for rain. It was formerly widespread among the Pueblo tribes, and traces of it are still found at Ácoma and other places (Walter Hough, in Hodge, *Handbook*. II. 605–606, *q. v.* for a bibliography of writings on the subject).

ing. They gave us liberally of food and of all else which they had. And thus, after three days, we left this province.

We continued our march toward the west four days, or twenty-four leagues, when we found a province comprising six pueblos, which they call Amí,[1] or by another name Cibola. It contains a great many Indians, who appeared to number more than twenty thousand. We learned that Francisco Vazquez Coronado and some of the captains he had with him had been there. In this province near the pueblos we found crosses erected; and here we found three Christian Indians, who said their names were Andrés of Cuyuacan, Gaspar of Mexico, and Anton of Guadalajara, and stated that they had come with the said governor Francisco Vasquez. We instructed them again in the Mexican tongue, which they had almost forgotten. From them we learned that the said Francisco Vazquez Coronado and his captains had been there, and that Don Pedro de Tobar had gone in from there, having heard of a large lake where these natives said there were many settlements. They told us that there was gold in that country, and that the people were clothed and wore bracelets and earrings of gold; that these people were sixty days' march from there; that the men of the said Coronado had gone twelve days beyond this province and then had returned, not being able to find water and the supply of water they had carried being exhausted. They gave us very clear signs regarding that lake and the riches of the Indians who live there. Although I and some of my companions desired to go to that lake, others did not wish to assist.

In this province we found a great quantity of Castilian flax, which appears to grow in the fields without being planted. They gave us extended accounts of what there was in the provinces where the large lake is, and of how here they had

---

[1] "Zuñi" in B, p. 180. Perhaps "Amí" is a misprint. At any rate, there can be no doubt of its identity with Zuñi. Zuñi is situated in Valencia County, near the western border of New Mexico. It was first visited by Spaniards in 1539. The only remaining pueblo of the province is on the Zuñi River. Obregón writes that by the time they left Acuco (Ácoma) for Ciboro (Zuñi) the party was seriously divided over the matter of returning to Santa Bárbara, and that Gregorio Hernández Gallegos was elected *alférez* to appease the malcontents. Luxán gives the names of the Zuñi pueblos visited as Malaque, Cuaquema, Agrisco, Oloná, Cuaquina, and Cana.

given to Francisco Vazquez Coronado and his companions
many ores, which they had not smelted for lack of the necessary equipment. In this province of Cibola, in a town they
call Aquico, the said Father Fray Bernaldino, Miguel Sanchez Valenciano, his wife Casilda de Amaya, Lázaro Sanchez
and Miguel Sanchez Nevado, his sons, Gregorio Hernandez,
Cristóbal Sanchez, and Juan de Frias, who were in our company, said that they wished to return to Nueva Vizcaya,
whence we had set out, because they had learned that Francisco Vazquez Coronado had found neither gold nor silver and
had returned, and that they desired to do likewise, which they
did.[1] The customs and rites here are similar to those of the
provinces passed. They have much game, and dress in cotton
mantas and others that resemble coarse linen. Here we heard
of other provinces[2] to the west.

We went on to the said provinces toward the west, a four
days' journey of seven leagues per day. At the end of this
time we found another province called Mohoce, of five pueblos, in which, it seemed to us, there are over fifty thousand
souls. Before reaching it they sent us messengers to warn
us not to go there, lest they should kill us. I and nine companions who had remained with me, namely: Joan Lopez
de Ibarra, Bernardo de Cuna,[3] Diego Perez de Luxan, Francisco Barroto, Gaspar de Luxan, Pedro Fernandez de Almansa, Alonso de Miranda, Gregorio Fernandez, and Joan
Hernandez, went to the said province of Mohoce, taking with
us one hundred and fifty Indians of the province whence we
started and the said three Mexican Indians. A league before we reached the province over two thousand Indians,
loaded down with provisions, came forth to meet us. We
gave them some presents of little value, which we carried,
thereby assuring them that we would not harm them, but
told them that the horses which we had with us might kill
them because they were very bad, and that they should make
a stockade where we could keep the animals, which they did.
A great multitude of Indians came out to receive us, accompanied by the chiefs of a pueblo of this province called

[1] They did not do so immediately, however, as appears later.
[2] B says "another province," p. 181.
[3] B gives this name as Bernardo de Luna, p. 182.

Aguato.[1] They gave us a great reception, throwing much maize flour where we were to pass, so that we might walk thereon.   All being very happy, they begged us to go to see the pueblo of Aguato.   There I made presents to the chiefs, giving them some things that I carried for this purpose.

The chiefs of this pueblo immediately sent word to the other pueblos of the province, from which the chiefs came with a great number of people, and begged that we go to see and visit their pueblos,[2] because it would give them much pleasure. We did so, and the chiefs and *tequitatos* of the province, seeing the good treatment and the gifts that I gave, assembled between them more than four thousand cotton *mantas*,[3] some colored and some white, towels with tassels at the ends, blue and green ores, which they use[4] to color the *mantas*, and many other things.   In spite of all these gifts they thought that they were doing little for us, and asked if we were satisfied.   Their food is similar to that of the other provinces mentioned, except that here we found no turkeys.   A chief and some other Indians told us here that they had heard of the lake where the gold treasure is and declared that it was neither greater nor less than what those of the preceding provinces had said.   During the six days that we remained there we visited the pueblos of the province.

Thinking that these Indians were friendly toward us, I left five of my companions with them in their pueblos, in order

[1] This was Awatobi, a now extinct Hopi pueblo, about nine miles southeast of Walpi, in northeastern Arizona.   It was visited by Tobar and Cárdenas in 1540, and by Oñate in 1598.   Later it was the seat of a Christian mission (Hodge, *Handbook*, I. 119).

[2] From Zuñi to the Moqui pueblos Luxán gives the following itinerary: April 11, six leagues to Laguna de los Ojuelos; April 12, five leagues to El Cazadero; April 13, five leagues to a marsh; April 16, six leagues to Ojo Hediondo; April 17, six leagues to a Moqui pueblo destroyed by Coronado, a league from Aguato; April 18, a fort was built near Aguato; April 19, to Aguato; April 21, to pueblo of Gaspe, very high up; April 22, to two pueblos called Comupani and Majanani; April 24, three leagues to Olallay, the largest of the province.   Obregón gives the names of the pueblos: Aguato, Oalpes, Moxanany, Xornupa, and Oloxao.

[3] The raising of cotton was widespread among the ancient Pueblos, but especially among the Hopi (Moqui), who to-day are the only ones among whom the industry survives (Walter Hough, in Hodge, *Handbook*, I. 352).

[4] A reads "que buscan dellos," p. 120.   B reads "que usan dellos," "which they use," p. 183.   The latter reading is more probably the correct one.

that they might return to the province of Amí[1] with the baggage. With the four others whom I took with me I went directly west for forty-five leagues, in search of some rich mines there of which they told me, with guides whom they furnished me in this province to take me to them. I found them, and with my own hands I extracted ore from them, said by those who know to be very rich and to contain much silver. The region where these mines are is for the most part mountainous, as is also the road leading to them.[2] There are some pueblos of mountain Indians, who came forth to receive us in some places, with small crosses on their heads.[3] They gave us some of their food and I presented them with some gifts. Where the mines are located the country is good, having rivers, marshes, and forests; on the banks of the river are many Castilian grapes, walnuts, flax, blackberries,[4] maguey plants, and prickly pears. The Indians of that region plant fields of maize, and have good houses. They told us by signs that behind those mountains, at a distance we were unable to understand clearly, flowed a very large river which, according to the signs they made, was more than eight leagues in width and flowed towards the North Sea;[5] that on the banks of this river on both sides are large settlements; that the

---

[1] "Zuñi" in B, p. 183.

[2] Luxán gives the following itinerary from the Moqui province to the mines: From Olallay they returned to Aguato. Leaving Aguato that day they went five leagues to Ojo Triste; May 1, ten leagues to a fine river; May 2, six leagues through cedars and past pools and marshes, to a large marsh, near a pine and cedar forest; May 6, seven leagues through a rough and difficult forest, and down a steep slope to a fine river running south, called Rio de las Parras; May 7, six leagues, part of the time along Rio de las Parras, to a marsh, called Cienega de San Gregorio; May 8, four leagues to a marsh. On the way a fine river running south was crossed, and named Rio de los Reyes. At the marsh they met Indians with crosses on their heads. Near the marsh were the mines in a rough mountain. Finding no silver and only a little copper, they returned to Zuñi. Espejo probably reached the region of Bill Williams Fork, west of Prescott, Arizona. See Bancroft, *Arizona and New Mexico*, p. 88, for a somewhat different opinion. It seems clear that Farfán, in 1598, went over essentially Espejo's ground.

[3] They were tied to the hair. See p. 242, note 2.

[4] "Xorales" in A, a misprint for "morales," as it is in B, p. 184.

[5] It is to be presumed that it was the Colorado River of which Espejo was told, but if so he evidently misunderstood what they said about the direction of the current, or else the text is defective.

river was crossed in canoes; that in comparison with those provinces and settlements on the river, the province where we were then was nothing; and that in that land were many grapes, nuts, and blackberries. From this place we returned to the one whither I had sent my companions, it being about sixty leagues from the said mines to Amí.[1] We endeavored to return by a different route so as to better observe and understand the nature of the country, and I found a more level road than the one I had followed in going to the mines.

Upon arriving at the province of Amí, I found my five companions whom I had left there,[2] and also Father Fray Bernaldino, who had not yet gone back with his companions. The Indians of that province had supplied them all they needed to eat, and he[3] with all of us greatly rejoiced. The caciques came forth to receive me and my companions and gave us plentiful food, and Indians for guides and to carry the loads. When we bade them adieu they made us many promises, saying that we must return again and bring many "Castillos," as they call the Spaniards, and that with this in view they were planting a great deal of maize that year so that there would be ample food for all. From this province Fray Bernaldino and the others who had remained with him returned, and with them Gregorio Hernandez, who had accompanied me as ensign, although I urged them not to leave, but to remain and search for mines and other treasures, in the service of his Majesty.

Fray Bernaldino and his companions having departed, with eight soldiers I returned, determined to go up the Rio del Norte, by which we had entered. After having travelled ten days, or about sixty leagues, to the province of the Quires, we went east from there two days' journey of six leagues each, and reached a province of Indians called the Ubates,[4] having five pueblos. The Indians received us peacefully and gave us much food, turkeys, maize,[5] and other things. From there

---

[1] "Zuñi" in B, p. 184.   [2] He had left them in the Moqui country.

[3] A reads, "y él con todos nosotros, se holgaron mucho," p. 122. B reads, "y con todos nosotros se holgaron mucho," p. 184.

[4] This was evidently a Tano settlement north of Santa Fé. This being the case, Espejo went northeast instead of east from the Queres (Twitchell, *Leading Facts*, I. 282).

[5] B omits "maiz," p. 185.

we went in quest of some mines[1] of which we had heard and found them in two days, travelling from one place to another. We secured shining ore and returned to the settlement from which we had set out. The number of people in these pueblos is great, seeming to us to be about twenty thousand souls. They dress in white and colored *mantas*, and tanned deer and buffalo hides. They govern themselves as do the neighboring provinces. There are no rivers here, but they utilize springs and marshes. They have many forests of pine, cedar, and sabines.[2] Their houses are three, four, and five stories in height.

Learning that at one day's journey from this province there was another, we went to it. It consists of three very large pueblos, which seemed to us to contain more than forty thousand souls. It is called the province of the Tamos.[3] Here they did not wish to give us food or admit us. Because of this, and of the illness of some of my companions, and of the great number of people,[4] and because we were unable to subsist, we decided to leave the country,[5] and, at the beginning of July, 1583, taking an Indian from the said pueblo as a guide, we left by a different route from that by which we had entered. At a distance of half a league from a town of the said province, named Ciquique,[6] we came to a river which I named Rio de las Vacas,[7] for, travelling along its banks for six days, a distance of about thirty leagues,[8] we found a great number of the cows of that country. After travelling along this river one hundred and twenty leagues toward the east we found three Indians hunting. They were of the Jumana nation. From them we learned through an interpreter whom

---

[1] B reads "ruinas," obviously misprint for "minas," p. 185.

[2] B reads "salinas," evidently a misprint for "sabinas," p. 185.

[3] Tanos. See Hodge, *Handbook*, II. 686–687.

[4] *I. e.*, the Indians.   [5] The last clause is omitted from B, p. 186.

[6] Cicuye, or Pecos, a Tanoan settlement, now extinct, but formerly the largest pueblo of New Mexico. It was situated on the Pecos River, about thirty miles southeast of Santa Fé (Hodge, *Handbook*, II. 220–221).

[7] The Pecos.

[8] Alvarado had gone over the same route in 1540, and Coronado in 1541. In the eighteenth century it was followed in opening a highway to San Antonio, Texas (manuscript diaries of Pedro Vial, 1786–1789, Santiago Fernández, 1788, and Francisco Xavier Fragoso, 1788).

we had that we were twelve days' journey from the Conchas River, a distance which we thought must be a little over forty leagues. We crossed over to this river,[1] passing many watering places in creeks and marshes on the way, and found there many of the Cumano[2] nation, who brought us fish of many kinds, prickly pears and other fruits, and gave us buffalo hides and tanned deerskins. From there we came out to the Valley of San Bartolomé, whence Fray Bernaldino Beltran and I, with the companions named herein, had started. We found that the said Father Fray Bernaldino and his companions had arrived many days before at the province of San Bartolomé, and had gone to the Villa of Guadiana.[3]

Everything narrated herein I saw with my own eyes, and is true, for I was present at everything. Sometimes I set out from the camp with a number of companions, sometimes with but one, to observe the nature of that country, in order to report everything to his Majesty, that he may order what is best for the exploration and pacification of those provinces and for the service of God our Lord and the increase of His holy Catholic faith; and that those barbarians may come to know of it and to enter into it. My companions and I have employed in this narrative, as also in the *autos* and *diligencias*[4] which we drew up on the way, all possible and necessary care, as is shown by testimony as authoritative as we were able to procure there. Not all that occurred could be written, nor can I give an account of it in writing, for it would be too long, for the lands and provinces through which we travelled on this journey were many and large.

By the direct course which we took from the Valley of San Bartolomé until we reached the borders of the provinces we visited, it is over two hundred and fifty leagues, and by the route over which we returned it is more than two hundred

---

[1] The route followed must have been approximately that of Juan Domínguez de Mendoza, almost exactly a century later. Mendoza was thirteen days in going from the mouth of the Conchos to the Pecos, and estimated the distance at seventy leagues. See *post*, pp. 325–328, and Bolton, "The Jumano Indians," in the Texas State Historical Association *Quarterly*, XV. 73–74.

[2] Evidently a misprint for "Jumano." B reads "Jumanas," p. 186.

[3] Guadiana, an early name for Durango.

[4] The *autos* and *diligencias* were the authenticated records of their acts, drawn up on the spot.

leagues.   Besides this, we travelled more than three hundred[1] more leagues in the exploration of the said provinces and in going through them from one part to another, over both rough and level lands, over lagoons, marshes, and rivers, with great dangers and many difficulties.   We found many different tongues among the natives of those provinces, different modes of dress, and different customs.   That which we saw and of which I write gives but an inkling of what actually exists in those provinces, for in travelling through them we heard of large settlements, very fertile lands, silver mines, gold, and better governed peoples.

As we saw, dealt with, and heard of large settlements, and as our numbers were few, and as some of my companions were afraid to continue further, we did not explore more than what I have stated.   But even to accomplish this much has required of us great courage, which we mustered because we realized that thereby we were serving God our Lord and his Majesty, and that thereby the Indians might obtain some light, and in order that we might not lose our opportunity. We therefore endeavored by all means at our disposal to see and understand everything, learning the facts through interpreters where there were any, or by signs where there were none, the Indians of those provinces showing us by lines which they made on the ground and by their hands the number of days' journey from one province to another, and the number of pueblos in each province, or by the best means at our command for understanding.

The people of all those provinces are large and more vigorous than the Mexicans, and are healthy, for no illness was heard of among them.   The women are whiter skinned than the Mexican women.   They are an intelligent and well-governed people, with pueblos well formed and houses well arranged, and from what we could understand from them, anything regarding good government they will learn quickly.   In the greater part of those provinces there is much game of foot and wing, rabbits, hares, deer, native cows, ducks, geese, cranes, pheasants, and other birds, good mountains with all

---

[1] For a general estimate of distances travelled, see Espejo's letter to the viceroy, p. 193. B (p. 187) gives the figure as fifty, "cincuenta," obviously a misprint.

kinds of trees, salines and rivers, and many kinds of fish. In the greater portion of this country carts and wagons can be used; there are very good pastures for cattle, lands suitable for fields and gardens, with or without irrigation, and many rich mines,[1] from which I brought ores to assay and ascertain their quality. I also brought an Indian from the province of Tamos[2] and a woman from the province of Mohoce, so that if in the service of his Majesty return were to be made to undertake the exploration and settlement of those provinces they might furnish us with information regarding them and of the route to be travelled, and in order that for this purpose they might learn the Mexican and other tongues. For all of this I refer to the *autos* and *diligencias* which are made in the matter, from which will be seen more clearly the good intentions and good-will with which I and my companions served his Majesty in this journey, and the good opportunity there was for doing so in order to report to his Majesty, in whose service I desire to spend my life and my fortune.

I wrote this narrative at the mines of Santa Bárbola, of the jurisdiction of Nueva Vizcaya, at the end of October, 1583, having arrived at the Valle of San Bartolomé, in the said jurisdiction, on the 20th of September of the said year, the day we arrived from the said journey.

Antonio Despejo.
(Between two rubrics.)

[1] A reads "muchas ánimas ricas," literally "many rich souls." This obviously is a misprint for "muchas minas ricas," as given by B, p. 188.

[2] Apparently the person referred to in Zaldívar's account of his journey to the buffalo, p. 223, below.

LETTER OF ESPEJO TO THE VICEROY, 1583[1]

Very illustrious Sir:

Some twenty-five days ago I reached these mines of Santa Bálbola,[2] of this jurisdiction, very much wearied and fatigued from having travelled, within the past year and over, more than eight hundred leagues,[3] visiting and exploring the provinces of New Mexico, to which I gave the name of Nueva Andalucia, as I was born in the district of Cordoba. I entered those lands with a pious purpose, as your Lordship, if you so desire, may see from the account of my entire journey which I transmit. I trust in God that therefrom great results will accrue to your service, to that of his Majesty, and to the exaltation of the Catholic faith. For, besides the lands and settlements which I traversed, and the great number of pueblos and people which I saw, I heard of many more, larger and richer, beyond and on the borders of the others; but our numbers being few and provisions being already consumed, we did not go further.

I would have been glad to go and kiss the hands of your Lordship as soon as I learned in Santa Bálbola that his Majesty had entrusted to your Lordship the inspection[4] of that Royal Audiencia. But not until I shall have proved my innocence of the charge against me,[5] which I hope in God will be soon, shall I venture to appear before your Lordship. I am determined however to send a suitable person,[6] who in my name

[1] Pacheco and Cárdenas, *Col. Doc. Inéd.*, XV. 162–163.

[2] Santa Bárbara.   [3] See Espejo's relation, p. 192.

[4] The word is *visita*, which was more than a mere inspection. It involved wide powers of instituting reforms.

[5] When Espejo returned to Santa Bárbara the *alcalde mayor* confiscated his papers, and the Indians and three thousand blankets which he had brought. Later, at the order of the Real Audiencia, they were restored (Obregón, *Relacion*, pt. II., cap. IX.).

[6] On April 23, 1584, Espejo named Pedro González de Mendoza, his son-in-law, his representative before the court, and stated that González was about to start for Spain. Espejo, "Memorial," April 23, 1584, in Pacheco and Cárdenas, *Col. Doc. Inéd.*, XV. 189.

shall give a report to his Majesty of my wanderings, and beg him to favor me by entrusting to me the exploration and settlement of these lands and of the others which I may discover, for I shall not be satisfied until I reach the coasts of the North and South seas.   Although they have attached part of my estate, I shall not lack the necessary means to accomplish the journey with a sufficient number of men, provisions, arms, and ammunition, should his Majesty grant me the favor, as one has a right to expect from his most Christian and generous hand.   I would not dare to write to your Lordship if this undertaking were not of such importance to God and his Majesty, in whose name your Lordship acts.   May our Lord guard and preserve the illustrious person and state of your Lordship many years, as we all, your humble servants, desire. From the Valley of San Bartholomé, of Nueva Vizcaya, at the end of October, 1583.

Most Illustrious Sir: Your servant kisses the hands of your most Illustrious Lordship.

ANTONIO DE ESPEJO.

[Superscription] : To the illustrious Archbishop of Mexico,[1] Visitor-general of New Spain, my lord.

[1] This was Pedro Moya de Contreras.

LETTER OF ESPEJO TO THE KING, 1584[1]

His Very Catholic Royal Majesty:

Since from the relation which accompanies this letter your Majesty will be informed of the lands and provinces which, by God's favor, and with the desire to serve your Majesty and increase the royal crown, like a loyal and faithful vassal, I have discovered and traversed since the month of November, 1582, when I set out from the government of Nueva Vizcaya with a religious and fourteen soldiers whom I took with me, moved and compelled by a very pious and charitable occasion, I will omit telling of them now; but I beg your Majesty to please be assured of my zeal, so dedicated to the service of your Majesty, and consider it well that I should finish my life in the continuation of these discoveries and settlements; for with the estate, prominence, and friends which I possess, I promise to serve your Majesty with greater advantage than any others who are attempting to make a contract with you regarding this enterprise. I beg your Lordship to please order that it be made with me, your Majesty granting me the mercy, honor, and favor corresponding to my very great desire to increase the realms of your Majesty and the Catholic faith, by the conversion of millions of souls who lack the true knowledge, and to elevate my name and my memory the better to serve and to merit the favor of your Majesty, whom God our Lord exalt and preserve many years, as the vassals of your Majesty have need. San Salvador, April 23, 1584.—His Very Catholic Royal Majesty.—Your Majesty's most humble vassal,

ANTONIO ESPEJO (two rubrics).

[1] Pacheco and Cárdenas, *Col. Doc. Inéd.*, XV. 100–101.

NEW MEXICO

3. THE OÑATE EXPEDITIONS AND THE
FOUNDING OF THE PROVINCE OF
NEW MEXICO, 1596–1605

INTRODUCTION

The expeditions of Rodríguez and Espejo stirred up an enthusiasm for northern exploration much like that which had preceded the expedition of Coronado. There were now dreams, not only of conquering and settling New Mexico, but of going beyond the Llanos del Cíbolo and Quivira to plant settlements on the Strait of Anian, and soon there was a crowd of competitors for the position of adelantado of New Mexico.

First among the applicants was Cristóbal Martín. In October, 1583, he proposed to conquer and colonize the region, leading thither an expedition of two or three hundred men, in exchange for titles of honor and extensive privileges, among them being the right to explore and settle one thousand leagues beyond the first pueblos of New Mexico and to establish ports on either ocean.

Espejo, soon after his return, addressed a memorial to the king asking permission to undertake at his own expense the conquest and settlement of New Mexico. He proposed taking four hundred soldiers, one hundred with their families, and a large outfit of live-stock. He recommended making the new province dependent directly on Spain rather than on the viceroy; and as a means to this end he proposed looking for a port on the North Sea as a base of communication and supplies. He would thus be master of another viceroyalty.

About the same time Francisco Díaz de Vargas, *alguacil mayor* and *regidor* of Puebla, asked for the title of adelantado of the north country. He gave the opinion that all the region seen by Coronado, Ibarra, Chamuscado, and Espejo was poor in provisions and minerals; but beyond. it was said, was a great salt river, and lakes where the people used gold and silver. He presumed that the river was the northern strait, or an arm of either the North Sea or the South Sea; and he offered to take at his own expense sixty or seventy men, and pass two hundred leagues beyond New Mexico, to explore, and, if desirable, to settle the country.

Five years later (in 1589) Juan Bautista de Lomas y Colmenares, a wealthy resident of Nueva Galicia, proposed to undertake the task, asking for the right to exclude all other adventurers from territory beyond his own conquests. A contract with Lomas was made by the viceroy on March 11, 1589, but it was not approved by the king, and the new viceroy made an agreement with Francisco de Urdiñola; but before he could fulfil it Urdiñola was arrested on a criminal charge. In 1592 and again in 1595 Lomas attempted to have his contract renewed, but without avail.

While these men were seeking to secure contracts with the king, others entered the coveted field without governmental sanction. In 1590 Gaspar Castaño de Sosa, lieutenant-governor in Nuevo León, hearing of the excitement regarding New Mexico, formed his mining camp of Nuevo Almadén, now Monclova, into a colony and started north with more than one hundred and seventy persons.

Crossing the Nadadores, Sabinas, and Rio Grande, he ascended the Salado or Pecos. Reaching a pueblo, probably Pecos, he captured it after a battle, and from there continued his conquest through the Tehua, Queres, and Tiguas towns, having also ascended to Taos. In the midst of his successes he was arrested by Captain Juan Morlete, sent for the purpose from Saltillo by the viceroy.

Some three years later Francisco Leyva de Bonilla and Antonio Gutiérrez de Humaña led an unauthorized expedition from Nueva Vizcaya to New Mexico. They spent about a year among the pueblos, making Bove, later San Ildefonso, their principal headquarters. Setting out from there they went far to the northeastward, entered a large Indian settlement on the Arkansas, in eastern Kansas, and continued to a still larger stream some twelve days' journey beyond. The stream would seem to have been the Platte. On the way Humaña murdered Leyva and took command, but later he and nearly all his party were destroyed by Indians.[1]

The contract for the conquest and settlement of New Mexico was finally awarded in 1595 to Juan de Oñate, a member of a family which had taken a prominent part in the conquest of New Spain. His wife was granddaughter of Cortés and great-granddaughter of Montezuma. His father, Cristóbal de Oñate, had been prominent among the conquerors of Nueva Galicia and one of the founders of Zacatecas; he himself was one of the wealthy citizens of that place.

By his contract Oñate was made governor, adelantado, and captain-general of the new conquests, and was granted a government subsidy and extensive privileges, while the usual

---

[1] Much new light is thrown on the Humaña expedition by the now accessible declaration of the Indian Jusephe (Joseph) who had been with Humaña and returned to New Mexico. The declaration was made at San Juan, February 16, 1599. Jusephe stated that Humaña went through Pecos and a great pueblo of the Vaqueros. At the end of a month of leisurely wandering from side to side, crossing many streams, they reached great herds of buffalo. Going northward now fifteen days, they reached two large rivers, beyond which were rancherías, and, farther ahead, a very large pueblo in a great plain ten leagues long, which they crossed in two days. Through the pueblo flowed one of the rivers, both of which they had crossed. The houses were grass lodges and the Indians had plentiful crops. Humaña continued three days to a most amazing buffalo herd. Going still farther, they found no Indian rancherías, and only ordinary buffalo herds. Three days after having left the large pueblo Humaña murdered Leyba. Ten days from the pueblo they came to a large river about a quarter of a league wide. Upon reaching the river, Jusephe and five other Indians fled and returned toward New Mexico. On the way four were lost, and a fifth was killed. Jusephe was taken prisoner by the Apaches and kept for a year. At the end of that time he heard that there were Spaniards in New Mexico and made his way to one of the Pecos pueblos, and was later found by Oñate at Picuries ("Relacion que dió un indio de la salida que hicieron Umaña y Leyba del Nuevo Mexico," MS.). It is clear that the large pueblo reached by Humaña was the one north of the Arkansas reached by Oñate in 1601 (see p. 260, below).

privileges and exemptions of first settlers (*primeros pobladores*) were promised to his colonists. Captain Vicente de Zaldívar, Oñate's nephew, was made recruiting officer. The lists were opened with great pomp and ceremony at the viceroy's palace, and the enterprise was popular. Spiritual charge of the conquests was assigned to the Franciscans, and Fray Rodrigo Durán was made commissary.

A change of viceroys and jealousy of Oñate on the part of his rivals caused long delays and a modification of his contract. Early in 1596, however, he began his march north from Mexico City, but underwent inspections and suffered long delays at Zacatecas, Caxco, San Bartolomé, San Gerónimo, and Río de Conchos. After having spent nearly two years on the way, on February 7, 1598, the start was made from the last-named place. The colony now consisted of four hundred men, of whom one hundred and thirty had their families. For carrying baggage there were eighty-three wagons and carts, and a herd of more than seven thousand head of stock was driven on foot. At Río de San Pedro Oñate was joined by a new commissary, Father Martínez, with a band of new missionaries, Father Durán having been recalled.

Previous expeditions had followed the Conchos, but Vicente de Zaldívar opened up a new trail direct to the upper Rio Grande, leaving the Conchos on the right. Early in April the party reached the Médanos, those great sand-dunes lying south of El Paso. Here the party was divided, and on April 19 a little over half of the wagons began the passage of the sand-dunes, leaving the rest to await reinforcements of oxen. On the 26th the caravan was reunited on the Rio Grande, and on the 30th Oñate took formal possession "of all the kingdoms and provinces of New Mexico, on the Rio del Norte, in the name of our Lord King Philip. There was a sermon, a great religious and secular celebration, a great salute, and much rejoicing. In the afternoon a comedy was presented and the royal standard was blessed."

Continuing five and one-half leagues up-stream, on May 4 they reached El Paso, the ford, a place ever since important in the history of the Southwest. A short distance after crossing over, Oñate took sixty men and went ahead with the commissary "to pacify the land" and to prepare for settlement. Passing through the pueblo region, on July 7, at Santo Domingo, Oñate received the submission of the chiefs of seven provinces. Continuing north, on July 11 he reached the pueblo of Caypa, christened San Juan, where he made his headquarters which were established a few years later at Santa Fé.[1] The caravan, which had been met above El Paso by Vicente de Zaldívar, arrived at San Juan on August 18, and thus the colony reached its destination. Oñate had already begun to visit the surrounding pueblos, and on August 11 work had been begun at San Juan on an irrigating ditch for "the city of San Francisco," the Spaniards being assisted by fifteen hundred Indians. On August 23 a church was begun and its completion was celebrated on September 8. Next day a general assembly was held of representatives from all the country thus far explored; rods of office were given to the chiefs, and the various pueblos were assigned to eight Franciscan missionaries, who soon afterward departed for their respective charges. Thus was the province of New Mexico founded.

The colony having been established and the pueblos having been placed under the friars, Oñate turned his attention to the search for more attractive fields beyond, which was an

[1] Until as late as March, 1599, Oñate's headquarters were at Pueblo de San Juan. In June, 1601, and also in December of the same year, they were at Pueblo de San Gabriel. The contemporary map of Oñate's journey to Quivira, which is of unquestioned authenticity, shows San Gabriel to be west of the Rio Grande, below the junction with the Chama. In April, 1605, Oñate's headquarters were still at San Gabriel. See p. 280, below.

essential part of his task. In the middle of September he sent Vicente de Zaldívar, accompanied by sixty men and guided by an Indian who had been with Humaña, to hunt buffalo on the plains to the northeast. Going through Pecos, where they left two missionaries, they continued to a point seventy leagues from San Juan. Though they failed in their attempt to capture buffalo alive, they secured a large supply of hides and meat, and made the acquaintance of the Vaquero Apaches and of a large stretch of country.

While Zaldívar was away Oñate went southeast and visited the great salines and the Jumano pueblos, then turned west with the intention of going to the South Sea, where he hoped to find wealth in pearls. He made his way to Zuñi, where a rich saline was discovered, and to the Moqui towns, whence he sent Captain Marcos Farfán with a party to find the mines discovered by Espejo. Farfán made the journey to Bill Williams Fork, found rich veins, staked out claims, and brought back detailed reports. In the course of the journey he visited Jumanos near San Francisco Mountains, and the Cruzados, further southwest.

In November Juan de Zaldívar followed Oñate, intending to join him in his expedition to the South Sea, but at Ácoma he was killed, with fourteen companions, by the Indians. News of this misfortune reached Oñate while on his way back to San Juan, in December, and in January he sent Vicente de Zaldívar to avenge his brother's death. After a two days' assault, with hand-to-hand fighting, the Indians surrendered. The diary laconically adds: "Most of them were killed and punished by fire and bloodshed, and the pueblo was completely laid waste and burned."

In 1599 Vicente de Zaldívar, with twenty-five companions, made a three months' journey in an attempt to reach the South Sea. On the way he had difficulty with the Jumanos, and Oñate went in person with fifty soldiers to punish the offenders. Zaldívar continued his journey till he reached impassable mountains and a hostile tribe, at a point which he was told was three days from the sea.[1] So interested was Oñate in the project of reaching the South Sea that he now planned to go in person with a hundred men and prepared to build boats. In April, 1601, he was all ready to start, but he changed his plans and went northeast instead.

In June, 1601, Oñate set out to see the country traversed by Humaña. He was accompanied by two friars and more than seventy picked men; he had in his caravan more than seven hundred horses and mules, eight carts, four cannon, and a retinue of servants to carry the baggage. His guide was the Indian Joseph who had led Zaldívar to the Llanos del Cíbolo. Going by way of Galisteo, he crossed the Pecos to the Rio de la Madalena (Canadian River). Descending that stream to a great bend one hundred and eleven leagues from the pueblo of San Gabriel, he continued northeast to a point on the Arkansas more than two hundred and twenty leagues from the starting-point. Before crossing the stream he had dealings with a roving tribe called the Escanjaques. Fording the Arkansas, Oñate visited the extensive settlement called Quivira, through which Humaña had passed. It was evidently at Wichita, Kansas. The Quiviras appearing hostile, the journey was now discontinued. On starting homeward a battle was fought with the Escanjaques.

Before Oñate had set out for the northeast he had engendered hostility, and when he returned he found that most of the colonists and friars had deserted to Santa Bárbara;

---

[1] The principal source at my command regarding the Zaldívar expedition to the west has not been known before. It is a manuscript in the Archivo de Indias consisting of an abstract of reports sent by Oñate, March 22, 1601 (see p. 209, doc. c.). In an investigation regarding the work of Zaldívar, December, 1601, this expedition is recorded briefly. *Doc. Inéd.*, XVI. 219. Bancroft, *Arizona and New Mexico*, evidently overlooked this source, for he rejects a statement by Peñalosa that Zaldívar made such an expedition.

Zaldívar was accordingly sent to recover them. In 1602 Zaldívar went to Spain to secure a confirmation of Oñate's titles and a force of three hundred men with whom to continue explorations beyond Quivira.

Oñate still planned for reaching the South Sea, and in 1604 he carried out his intention. Setting out in October with thirty men, he followed in the footsteps of Espejo and Farfán to Bill Williams Fork. Descending that stream to the Colorado he followed its left bank to the Gulf of California, returning to New Mexico in 1605, where he ruled till 1608. He had now re-explored practically all of the ground covered by the Coronado and Espejo expeditions and opened new trails.

The principal printed original sources for the work of Oñate are those in Pacheco and Cárdenas, *Documentos Inéditos*, XVI. 38–66, 88–141, 228–322. These, given in order, consist of:

1. "Treslado de la posesion que en nombre de Su Magestad tomó Don Juan de Oñate, de los Reynos y Provincias de la Nueva Mexico; y de las obediencias y vassalaje que los Judios [Indios] de algunos pueblos de los dichos Reynos y provincias le dieron en el dicho nombre, Año de 1598" (pp. 88–141). This contains the act of possession proclaimed on the Rio Grande April 30, 1598; acts of "obedience and vassalage" by the pueblos of Santo Domingo, San Juan Baptista, Acolocú, Cuelóce, Ácoma, Aguscobi, and Mohoquí; and the assignment of pueblos to the different friars. The act of possession is also printed in Villagrá, *Historia de la Nueva Mexico*, fols. 114–132.

2. "Discurso de las jornadas que hizo el Campo de Su Magestad desde la Nueva España á la provincia de la Nueva Mexico, Año de 1526 [1596]." The subtitle, by which it will be cited, is "Ytinerario de las minas del Caxco . . . hasta el Nuevo México," etc. (pp. 228–276). It is a brief diary, based on the official documents, of all the operations of Oñate, from

November 1, 1596, to December 20, 1598. It was written by one of the friars.

3. "Copia de Carta escripta Al Virrey Conde de Monterrey, Don Juan de Oñate, de la Nueva México, á 2 de Marzo de 1599 Años: Corresponde al Capítulo Primero de Materia de Guerra, fecha en Mexico á 4 de Octubre de 1599" (pp. 302–315). Printed hereinafter, pp. 212–222. The letter is a summary of events after leaving Río del Nombre de Diós. With this letter were sent, evidently, nos. 1 and 2 above, besides other documents noted below. They were carried to Mexico by Father Alonso Martínez, Gaspar Pérez de Villagran, and companions.

4. "Don Alonso de Oñate pide se confirme la capitulacion que hizo el Virrey con Don Joan de Oñate sobre el Nuevo México: y que se declare aber cumplido las capitulaciones y se le dé titulo de Adelantado y otras cosas, en orden al cumplimiento de lo que al principio se asentó con él: Mayo de 1600" (pp. 316–319).

5. "Don Alonso de Oñate, á 5 de Mayo de 1600.—Al Presidente del Consejo de Yndias" (pp. 320–322). This document and no. 4 are requests by Oñate's brother that the conqueror's titles and privileges be confirmed.

6. "Memorial sobre el descubrimiento del Nuevo México y sus acontecimientos, Años desde 1595 á 1602" (pp. 188–227). This is a memorial presented by Vicente de Zaldívar in 1602 requesting that Oñate be equipped with three hundred men to continue explorations left off at the Arkansas River in 1601, followed by a summary of Oñate's negotiations and of investigations made in Mexico in 1602 regarding Oñate's work.

7. "Discurso y Proposicion que se hace á Vuestra Magestad de lo tocante á los descubrimientos del Nuevo México por sus capítulos de puntos diferentes" (pp. 38–66). This is a discussion by the viceroy of the negotiations with and the

work of Oñate, written at the time when Zaldívar went to
Spain to present his petition. It is in four parts. Part I.
is a statement of reasons why Oñate should not be granted
the concessions which the viceroy had withheld. Part II.
tells of investigations made to determine whether Oñate had
fulfilled his contract. Part III. discusses what he has accomplished in New Mexico and the advantages and difficulties
of maintaining the province. Part IV. is a brief account
("Breve relación") of Oñate's expedition to the Arkansas,
based on the correspondence, and a discussion of the importance of the expedition.

Besides the above printed official sources, there are unprinted documents of the same class in the Archivo de Indias,
of even greater importance. Of these the following are represented by transcripts in the Lowery Collection at the Library
of Congress, while transcripts of several others are in the Ayer
Collection at the Newberry Library in Chicago:

a. "Relacion de como los Padres de San Francisco se encargaron de las Provincias de la Nueva Mexico, con testimonio autorizado. Sep're 8" (Nuevo Mexico, 1598). This is
the act of possession given by Oñate to the friars. It contains important data not contained in no. 1 above.

b. "Relaciones que envió Don Juan de Oñate de algunas
jornadas descubrimientos y ensayes que se hicieron en Nuevo
Mexico" (Nuevo Mexico, 1599). These documents consist of
first-hand accounts, hitherto unused by modern scholars, of
Oñate's explorations and of the Humaña expedition. They include (1) "Relacion del descubrimiento de las Vacas de cibola"
(printed hereinafter, pp. 223–232). This is the original report of Zaldívar's expedition to the buffalo plains in 1598.
(2) "Relacion de la jornada que hicieron á la Mar y la visita
de salinas y Xumanas" (printed hereinafter, pp. 233–238).
This is the original account of Oñate's expedition in 1598 to
the Salines, the Jumanos, and the Moqui. (3) "Relacion

del descubrimiento de las salinas de cuni." This is the declaration of Farfán and others regarding the saline discovered
near Zuñi in 1598. (4) "Relacion é informacion del descubrimiento de minas" (printed hereinafter, pp. 239–249). This
is the declaration of Farfán and his companions regarding
their journey to the mines of Arizona in 1598. (5) "Relacion que dió un indio de la salida que hicieron Umana y Leyba
del Nuevo Mexico." This contains the declaration of the
Indian Jusephe (Joseph) and of Zaldívar regarding the Humaña
expedition. (6) "Relacion de los ensayes que se hicieron de
ciertas minas." This is the testimony given in 1599 regarding
the assays of ores brought from Arizona by the Farfán party.

c. "Relacion sacada de las cartas que envia Don Juan de
Oñate Gobernador de las provincias de la Nueva Megico.
Vino con carta de veinte y dos de Marzo de 1601" (Nuevo
Mexico, 1601). This document tells of events of 1599–1600
not recounted elsewhere, among them being the unknown
journey of Zaldívar to discover the South Sea in 1599.

d. "Relacion Verdadera de los sucesos de la entrada que
hizo el gobernador D. Juan de Oñate en las poblaciones de
Nueva Megico hacia el norte" (printed hereinafter, pp. 250–
267). This is the original account of Oñate's expedition to
the Arkansas in 1601.

e. "Parecer de la Audiencia de Mexico cerca de la propo-
siçion de la conquista y descubrimiento del Nuevo Mexico."
This is a part of the documents of which no. 6 above ("Memorial sobre el descubrimiento") is a summary. It is the document summarized in Pacheco and Cárdenas, XVI. 200, last
paragraph.

Among the contemporary histories three are especially
important: (1) In 1610 there was published at Alcalá, Spain,
the *Historia de la Nueva Mexico, del Capitan Gaspar de Villagrá* (24 + 287 folios). This work, while written in verse, is
in reality an important source based upon the author's per-

sonal experience and documentary data. The account is
especially important for the preparation of the expedition and
the march to New Mexico, and for the revolt and the punishment of Ácoma. Incorporated in it are several official documents, some of which are not elsewhere available (fols. 55–60,
119–132, 208–212). A reprint of this work was published in
Mexico in 1900 by Sr. Don Luis González Obregón. As ap-
pendices it contains important documents regarding Villagrá's
personal history, besides other documents relating to the history of New Mexico. (2) Father Zárate-Salmerón, "Relaciones
de Todas las cosas que en el Nuevo-Mexico se han visto y
Savido, asi por mar como por tierra, desde el año de 1538 hasta
el de 1626" (printed in *Documentos para la Historia de México*,
tercera série, Mexico, 1856) gives a chapter on the "Entrada
de D. Juan de Oñate al Nuevo Mexico" (paragraphs 33–36) ;
one on the "Jornada de D. Juan de Oñate a la Gran Ciudad
de Quivira" (paragraphs 37–43) and another on the "Jornada
de D. Juan de Oñate a la California por tierra" (paragraphs
44–57). The account of the Quivira expedition contains many
details not accessible elsewhere, while that of the expedition
of 1604–1605 is practically our sole reliance. It was evidently
based on full first-hand reports. When Father Zárate wrote,
in 1626, he had spent eight years as missionary in New Mexico.
A translation of the Zárate "Relaciones" was published by
Charles F. Lummis in 1899 and 1900, in *Land of Sunshine*,
vols. XI. and XII. The translation published hereinafter,
though made independently, owes much to that one. (3)
Torquemada, *Monarchía Indiana*, which was finished just
after the Oñate conquest, contains (tomo I., libro V., caps.
XXXVI.–XL.) a brief account of events to 1608, in which is
incorporated a letter by Fray Juan de Escalona to the com-
missary, San Gabriel, October 1, 1601, and a letter by Fray
Francisco de San Miguel to the provincial, Fray Diego Muñoz,
Santa Bárbara, February 29, 1602.

A map of Oñate's route from Mexico to Quivira in the
Archivo de Indias, hitherto unpublished, is reproduced opposite p. 212. A map, or drawing, by an Indian named Miguel
captured by Oñate on the Arkansas, is also in the Archivo de
Indias, and a copy is in the editor's possession.

LETTER WRITTEN BY DON JUAN DE OÑATE FROM NEW MEXICO, 1599

Copy of a letter written by Don Juan de Oñate from New Mexico to the Viceroy, the Count of Monterey, on the second day of March, 1599.[1]

FROM Rio de Nombre de Dios[2] I last wrote to you, Illustrious Sir, giving you an account of my departure, and of the discovery of a wagon road to the Rio del Norte,[3] and of my certain hopes of the successful outcome of my journey, which hopes God has been pleased to grant, may He be forever praised; for greatly to His advantage and that of his royal Majesty, they have acquired a possession so good that none other of his Majesty in these Indies excels it, judging it solely by what I have seen, by things told of in reliable reports, and by things almost a matter of experience, from having been seen by people in my camp and known by me at present. This does not include the vastness of the settlements or the riches of the West which the natives praise, or the certainty of pearls promised by the South Sea from the many shells containing them possessed by these Indians, or the many settlements called the seven caves,[4] which the Indians report at the head of this river, which is the Rio del Norte; but includes only the provinces which I have seen and traversed, the people of this eastern country, the Apaches, the nation of the Cocoyes,[5] and many others which are daily being dis-

---

[1] Pacheco and Cárdenas, *Col. Doc. Inéd.*, XVI. 302–315.

[2] Nombre de Diós was reached March 12, 1598, and was left on the 14th. See Ytinerario, entries for those days, pp. 234–235.

[3] The reference is to the exploration made by Vicente de Zaldívar. See Ytinerario, p. 234; Villagrá, *Historia*, cantos XI.–XII.

[4] This may be a survival of the older tradition regarding the Seven Caves existing somewhere to the northward of Mexico. The text is evidently corrupt at this point. It reads, "ni las muchas poblazones que el nacimiento destos indios, que es el del Rio del Norte, llamada las siete quebas."

[5] Cicuyé, or Pecos.

covered in this district and neighborhood, as I shall specify in this letter. I wish to begin by giving your Lordship an account of it, because it is the first since I left New Spain.

I departed, Illustrious Sir, from Rio de Nombre de Dios on the sixteenth[1] of March, with the great multitude of wagons, women, and children, which your Lordship very well knows, freed from all my opponents, but with a multitude of evil predictions conforming to their desires and not to the goodness of God. His Majesty was pleased to accede to my desires, and to take pity on my great hardships, afflictions, and expenses, bringing me to these provinces of New Mexico with all his Majesty's army enjoying perfect health.

Although I reached these provinces on the twenty-eighth day of May (going ahead with as many as sixty soldiers to pacify the land and free it from traitors, if in it there should be any, seizing Humaña and his followers,[2] to obtain full information, by seeing with my own eyes, regarding the location and nature of the land, and regarding the nature and customs of the people, so as to order what might be best for the army, which I left about twenty-two leagues from the first pueblos,[3] after having crossed the Rio del Norte, at which river I took possession,[4] in the name of his Majesty, of all these kingdoms and pueblos[5] which I discovered before departing from it with scouts), the army did not overtake me at the place where I established it and where I now have it established, in this province of the Teguas, until the nineteenth[6] day of August of the past year. During that time I travelled through settlements sixty-one leagues in extent toward the north, and thirty-five in width from east to west. All this district is filled with pueblos, large and small, very continuous and close together.

---

[1] See note 2, p. 212.

[2] It was not yet known that Humaña had been slaughtered by the Indians of the plains.

[3] He refers here to reaching the first pueblos above El Paso, having left the caravan at El Sepulcro de Robledo. See Ytinerario, pp. 247–250; Villagrá, *Historia,* canto XV.

[4] April 30, 1598. See Ytinerario, p. 242; Villagrá, *Historia,* canto XIII., where the formal act of possession is printed.

[5] The text reads *pueblo,* but *pueblos* seems required to convey the sense.

[6] The Ytinerario in two places says they reached San Juan on the 18th.

At the end of August I began to prepare the people of my camp for the severe winter[1] with which both the Indians and the nature of the land threatened me; and the devil, who has ever tried to make good his great loss occasioned by our coming, plotted, as is his wont, exciting a rebellion among more than forty-five soldiers and captains,[2] who under pretext of not finding immediately whole plates of silver lying on the ground, and offended because I would not permit them to maltreat these natives, either in their persons or in their goods, became disgusted with the country, or to be more exact, with me, and endeavored to form a gang in order to flee to that New Spain, as they proclaimed, although judging from what has since come to light their intention was directed more to stealing slaves and clothing and to other acts of effrontery not permitted. I arrested two captains and a soldier, who they said were guilty, in order to garrote them on this charge, but ascertaining that their guilt was not so great, and on account of my situation and of the importunate pleadings of the religious and of the entire army, I was forced to forego the punishment and let bygones be bygones.

Although by the middle of September I succeeded in completely calming and pacifying my camp, from this great conflagration a spark was bound to remain hidden underneath the ashes of the dissembling countenances of four[3] of the soldiers of the said coterie. These fled from me at that time, stealing from me part of the horses, thereby violating not only one but many proclamations which, regarding this matter and others, I had posted for the good of the land in the name of his Majesty.

Since they had violated his royal orders, it appeared to me that they should not go unpunished; therefore I immediately sent post-haste the captain and procurator-general Gaspar Perez de Villagran and the captain of artillery Geronimo Marques, with an express order to follow and overtake them and give them due punishment. They left in the middle of September, as I have said, thinking that they would

[1] See Ytinerario, pp. 262–264. For the establishment of headquarters at San Juan, see Villagrá, *Historia*, canto XVI.

[2] See Ytinerario, entries for August 20–21; Villagrá, *Historia*, canto XVI.

[3] For the names of those who fled, see Ytinerario, entry for September 12.

overtake them at once, but their journey was prolonged more than they or I had anticipated, with the result to two of the offenders[1] which your Lordship already knows from the letter which they tell me they wrote from Sancta Barbara. The other two who fled from them will have received the same at your Lordship's hands, as is just.

I awaited their return and the outcome for some days, during which time I sent my *sargento mayor* to find and utilize the buffalo to the east, where he found an infinite multitude of them, and had the experience which he set forth in a special report.[2] Both he and the others were so long delayed that, in order to lose no time, at the beginning of October, this first church having been founded, wherein the first mass was celebrated on the 8th of September, and the religious having been distributed[3] in various provinces and *doctrinas*, I went in person to the province of Abo and to that of the Xumanas and to the large and famous salines of this country, which must be about twenty leagues east of here.[4]

From there I crossed over to the west through the province of Puaray to discover the South Sea, so that I might be able to report to your Lordship. When Captain Villagran arrived I took him for this purpose.[5]

What more in good time it was possible to accomplish through human efforts is in substance what I shall set forth in the following chapter. For this purpose it shall be day by day, and event by event,[6] especially regarding the death of my nephew and *maese de campo*, who, as my rear-guard, was following me to the South Sea. His process,[7] along with

---

[1] They were beheaded. See Ytinerario, p. 265; Villagrá, *Historia*, canto XVI.

[2] The reference is to Zaldívar's report printed hereinafter. See pp. 223–232. Villagrá treats this expedition in his *Historia*, canto XVII.

[3] The pueblos were assigned to the friars on the 9th, and the missionaries went to their new posts within the next few days (Ytinerario, pp. 264–266).

[4] A special account of the journey is printed hereinafter, pp. 233–238. See also Ytinerario, pp. 266–267; Villagrá, *Historia*, canto XVII.

[5] See Ytinerario, entry for December 5; Villagrá, *Historia*, canto XIX.

[6] The reference here is apparently to the Ytinerario.

[7] Villagrá, *Historia*, canto XXV., recounts the *proceso*. A transcript of it is in the Ayer Collection.

many other papers, I am sending to your Lordship. To despatch them earlier has been impossible. I have, then, discovered and seen up to the present the following provinces:

The province of the Piguis,[1] which is the one encountered in coming from that New Spain; the province of the Xumanás; the province of the Cheguas, which we Spaniards call Puaray; the province of the Cheres; the province of the Trias; the province of the Emmes; the province of the Teguas; the province of the Picuries; the province of the Taos; the province of the Peccos; the province of Abbo and the salines;[2] the province of Juni; and the province of Mohoce.

These last two are somewhat apart from the rest, towards the west, and are the places where we recently discovered the rich mines, as is attested by the papers which your Lordship will see there. I could not[3] work or improve these mines because of the death of my *maese de campo*, Joan de Zaldivar, and of the rectification of the results of it, which I completed at the end of last month.[4] Nor could I complete my journey to the South Sea, which was the purpose with which I went to the said provinces, leaving my camp in this province of the Teguas, whence I am now writing.

There must be in this province and in the others abovementioned, to make a conservative estimate, seventy thousand[5] Indians, settled after our custom, house adjoining house, with square plazas. They have no streets, and in the pueblos, which contain many plazas or wards, one goes from one plaza to the other through alleys. They are of two and three stories, of an *estado*[6] and a half or an *estado* and a third

---

[1] I do not know what tribe this was. For each of the other tribes listed in this paragraph, see Hodge, *Handbook of American Indians*, under the following names: Jumano, Tigua, Keres, Sia, Jemez, Tewa, Picuris, Taos, Pecos, Abo, Zuñi, Moqui (or Hopi).

[2] See Oñate's relation, pp. 233–238.

[3] The text here reads "puede," which seems to be a misprint for "pude."

[4] He refers to the punishment of the pueblo and the investigation of the uprising. See Villagrá, *Historia*, cantos XXV., XXVII., XXXIII.; Ytinerario, pp. 270–272.

[5] An exaggerated estimate, no doubt. For actual figures at different dates see Hodge, *Handbook*, II. 325.

[6] An *estado* is a unit equivalent to the height of a man.

each, which latter is not so common; and some houses are of four, five, six, and seven stories. Even whole pueblos dress in very highly colored cotton *mantas*, white or black, and some of thread—very good clothes. Others wear buffalo hides, of which there is a great abundance. They have most excellent wool, of whose value I am sending a small example.

It is a land abounding in flesh of buffalo, goats with hideous horns, and turkeys; and in Mohoce there is game of all kinds. There are many wild and ferocious beasts, lions, bears, wolves, tigers, *penicas*, ferrets, porcupines, and other animals, whose hides they tan and use. Towards the west there are bees and very white honey, of which I am sending a sample. Besides, there are vegetables, a great abundance of the best and greatest salines in the world, and a very great many kinds of very rich ores, as I stated above. Some discovered near here do not appear so, although we have hardly begun to see anything of the much there is to be seen. There are very fine grape vines, rivers, forests of many oaks, and some cork trees, fruits, melons, grapes, watermelons, Castilian plums, *capuli*, pine-nuts, acorns, ground-nuts, and *coralejo*, which is a delicious fruit, and other wild fruits. There are many and very good fish in this Rio del Norte, and in others. From the ores here are made all the colors which we use, and they are very fine.

The people are in general very comely; their color is like those of that land, and they are much like them in manner and dress, in their grinding, in their food, dancing, singing, and many other things, except in their languages, which are many, and different from those there. Their religion consists in worshipping idols, of which they have many; and in their temples, after their own manner, they worship them with fire, painted reeds, feathers, and universal offering of almost everything they get, such as small animals, birds, vegetables, etc. In their government they are free, for although they have some petty captains, they obey them badly and in very few things.

We have seen other nations such as the Querechos,[1] or herdsmen, who live in tents of tanned hides, among the buf-

[1] See p. 183, note 3, above.

falo. The Apaches, of whom we have also seen some, are innumerable, and although I heard that they lived in ran- cherías, a few days ago I ascertained that they live like these in pueblos, one of which, eighteen leagues from here, con- tains fifteen plazas.[1] They are a people whom I have com- pelled to render obedience to His Majesty, although not by means of legal instruments like the rest of the provinces. This has caused me much labor, diligence, and care, long journeys, with arms on the shoulders, and not a little watching and circumspection; indeed, because my *maese de campo* was not as cautious as he should have been, they killed him with twelve companions in a great pueblo and fortress called Acóma, which must contain about three thousand Indians. As punishment for its crime and its treason against his Maj- esty, to whom it had already rendered submission by a public instrument, and as a warning to the rest, I razed and burned it completely, in the way in which your Lordship will see by the process of this cause. All these provinces, pueblos, and peoples, I have seen with my own eyes.

There is another nation, that of the Cocóyes,[2] an innu- merable people with huts and agriculture. Of this nation and of the large settlements at the source of the Rio del Norte and of those to the northwest and west and towards the South Sea, I have numberless reports, and pearls of remark- able size from the said sea, and assurance that there is an infinite number of them on the coast of this country.[3] And as to the east, a person in my camp, an Indian who speaks Spanish and is one of those who came with Humaña, has been in the pueblo of the said herdsmen.[4] It is nine contin-

[1] I know of no permanent Apache settlement which would correspond to the one here described.

[2] Cicuyé, or Pecos.

[3] Extended notice of pearls in the South Sea was brought back from Arizona by Farfán. See *post*, pp. 245–246.

[4] The Indian Jusephe, who had been with Humaña and had made his way back to New Mexico, declared among other things that he had been in the pueblo of the Vaqueros. He did not give the distance from Pecos to the pueblo ("Relacion que dió un indio de la salida que hicieron Umaña y leyba del Nuevo Mexico," MS.). The next statement might be taken to mean that Zaldívar had been to the pueblo described by Jusephe. See Zaldívar's account of his journey to the buffalo country, p. 224, below.

uous leagues in length and two in width, with streets and houses consisting of huts.[1] It is situated in the midst of the multitude of buffalo, which are so numerous that my *sargento mayor*, who hunted them and brought back their hides, meat, tallow, and suet, asserts that in one herd alone he saw more than there are of our cattle in the combined three ranches of Rodrigo del Rio,[2] Salvago, and Jeronimo Lopez, which are famed in those regions.

I should never cease were I to recount individually all of the many things which occur to me. I can only say that with God's help I shall see them all, and give new worlds, new, peaceful, and grand,[3] to his Majesty, greater than the good Marquis[4] gave to him, although he did so much, if you, Illustrious Sir, will give to me the aid, the protection, and the help which I expect from such a hand. And although I confess that I am crushed at having been so out of favor when I left that country, and although a soul frightened by disfavor usually loses hope and despairs of success, it is nevertheless true that I never have and never shall lose hope of receiving many and very great favors at the hand of your Lordship, especially in matters of such importance to his Majesty. And in order that you, Illustrious Sir, may be inclined to render them to me, I beg that you take note of the great increase which the royal crown and the rents of his Majesty have and will have in this land, with so many and such a variety of things, each one of which promises very great treasures. I shall only note these four, omitting the rest as being well known and common:

First, the great wealth which the mines have begun to reveal and the great number of them in this land, whence proceed the royal fifths and profits. Second, the certainty of the proximity[5] of the South Sea, whose trade with Pirú, New Spain, and China is not to be depreciated, for it will give birth in time to advantageous and continuous duties, because of its close proximity, particularly to China and to that land. And what I emphasize in this matter as worthy

---

[1] *Xacales.*   [2] Evidently the official by this name mentioned on p. 139.

[3] The word in the text is "ganados," which must be a miscopy for "grandes."

[4] Cortés, the Marquis of the Valley.

[5] The text reads "cercana," which seems to be a miscopy for "cercanía."

of esteem is the traffic in pearls, reports of which are so certain, as I have stated, and of which we have had ocular experience from the shells.   Third, the increase of vassals and tributes, which will increase not only the rents, but his renown and dominion as well, if it be possible that for our king these can increase.   Fourth, the wealth of the abundant salines, and of the mountains of brimstone,[1] of which there is a greater quantity than in any other province.   Salt is the universal article of traffic of all these barbarians and their regular food, for they even eat or suck it alone as we do sugar.   These four things appear as if dedicated solely to his Majesty.   I will not mention the founding of so many republics, the many offices, their quittances, vacancies, provisions, etc., the wealth of the wool and hides of buffalo, and many other things, clearly and well known, or, judging from the general nature of the land, the certainty of wines and oils.

In view, then, Illustrious Sir, of things of such honor, profit, and value, and of the great prudence, magnanimity, and nobility of your Lordship, who in all matters is bound to prosper me and overcome the ill fortune of my disgrace, I humbly beg and supplicate, since it is of such importance to the service of God and of his Majesty, that the greatest aid possible be sent to me, both for settling and pacifying, your Lordship giving[2] your favor, mind, zeal, and life for the conservation, progress, and increase of this land, through the preaching of the holy gospel and the founding of this republic, giving liberty and favor to all, opening wide the door to them, and, if it should be necessary, even ordering them to come to serve their king in so honorable and profitable a matter, in a land so abundant and of such great beginnings of riches.   I call them beginnings, for although we have seen much, we have not yet made a beginning in comparison with what there is to see and enjoy.   And if the number should exceed five hundred men, they all would be needed, especially married men, who are the solid rock on which new republics are permanently founded; and noble people, of whom

---

[1] The Itinerary mentions deposits of *piedra azufre* at Xemez.   It is perhaps to these that Oñate refers.

[2] The participle "dando" is ambiguous, but from what follows the subject seems to be "your Lordship."

there is such a surplus there. Particularly do I beg your Lordship to give a license to my daughter Mariquita, for whom I am sending, and to those of my relatives who may wish so honorably to end their lives.

For my part, I have sunk my ships and have furnished an example to all as to how they ought to spend their wealth and their lives and those of their children and relatives in the service of their king and lord, on whose account and in whose name I beg your Lordship to order sent to me six small cannon[1] and some powder, all of which will always be at the service of his Majesty, as is this and everything else. Although on such occasions the necessities increase, and although under such circumstances as those in which I now find myself others are wont to exaggerate,[2] I prefer to suffer from lack of necessities rather than to be a burden to his Majesty or to your Lordship, feeling assured that I shall provide them for many poor people who may look to me if your Lordship will grant the favor, which I ask, of sending them to me.

To make this request of you, Illustrious Sir, I am sending the best qualified persons whom I have in my camp, for it is but reasonable that such should go on an errand of such importance to the service of God and his Majesty, in which they risk their health and life, looking lightly upon the great hardships which they must suffer and have suffered. Father Fray Alonso Martinez, apostolic commissary of these provinces of New Mexico, is the most meritorious person with whom I have had any dealings, and of the kind needed by such great kingdoms for their spiritual government. Concerning this I am writing to his Majesty, and I shall be greatly favored if your Lordship will do the same. I believe your Lordship is under a loving obligation to do this, both because the said Father Commissary is your client as well as because of the authority of his person and of the merits of his worthy life, of which I am sending to his Majesty a special report, which your Lordship will see if you desire, and to which I refer. In his company[3] goes my cousin, Father

---

[1] "Piecezuelas pequeñas ó esmerilejos."
[2] The text has "muchos los," where "muchas las" seems to be required.
[3] "En su compañero" evidently should be "en su compañía."

Fray Cristobal de Salazar, concerning whom testimony can be given by his prelate, for in order not to appear an interested witness in my own cause I refrain from saying what I could say with much reason and truth. For all spiritual matters I refer you to the said fathers, whom I beg your Lordship to credit in every respect as you would credit me in person. I say but little to your Lordship as to your crediting them as true priests of my father Saint Francis. With such as these may your Lordship swell these your kingdoms, for there is plenty for them to do.

For temporal matters go such honorable persons as Captain and Procurator-general Gaspar Perez de Villagran, captain of the guard, Marcos Farfan de los Godos, and Captain Joan Pinero, to whom I refer you, as also to the many papers which they carry.[1] In them your Lordship will find authentic information regarding all that you may desire to learn of this country of yours.

I remain as faithful to you, Illustrious Sir, as those who most protest. Your interests will always be mine, for the assurance and confidence which my faithfulness gives me is an evidence that in past undertakings I have found in your Lordship true help and love; for although when I left I did not deserve to receive the cédula from my king dated April 2, I shall deserve to receive it now that I know that I have served him so well.

And in order to satisfy his royal conscience and for the safety of the creatures who were preserved at Acóma, I send them to your Lordship with the holy purpose which the Father Commissary will explain, for I know it is so great a service to God that I consider very well employed the work and expense which I have spent in the matter. And I do not expect a lesser reward for your Lordship on account of the prayers of those few days. Honor it, Illustrious Sir, for it redounds to the service of God. May He prosper and exalt you to greater offices. In His divine service, which is the highest and greatest I can name, I again beg for the aid requested, much, good, and speedy—priests as well as settlers and soldiers.

---

[1] The papers clearly were those printed hereinafter, pp. 223–249.

ACCOUNT OF THE DISCOVERY OF THE BUFFALO, 1599[1]

THE *sargento mayor* Vicente de Saldivar Mendoca, the *proveedor general* Diego de Cubia, Captain Aguilar, and other captains and soldiers, to the number of sixty, set out from camp[2] for the cattle herds on the 15th day of September,[3] well provided with many droves of mares and other supplies. They reached the Pecos River on the 18th and set out from there on the 20th, leaving Father Fray Francisco de San Miguel of the Order of San Francisco as prelate of that province, and Juan de Dios, lay brother and interpreter of that tongue. That province is the one Espejo named Tamas,[4] from which came a certain Indian named Don Pedro Oros, who died in Tlanepantla under control and instruction of the friars of San Francisco.

Having travelled four leagues they reached the place called Las Ciruelas, where there are very great quantities of Castilian plums, Almonacid plums of Cordoba.[5] On the following day they travelled five more leagues, finding water after going three leagues, although they camped for the night without it. Next day they travelled two leagues to a small

[1] "Relaciones que envió Don Juan de Oñate de algunas jornadas," ff. 1–7 (manuscript in Lowery Collection, Library of Congress).

[2] At San Juan de los Caballeros. Villagrá gives an account of this expedition in cantos XVI.–XVII. He says that Zaldívar went to discover "the main herd of the cattle" (fol. 145).

[3] The Ytinerario states that Father San Miguel and the Zaldívar party set out on September 16. See entry of that date.

[4] See Espejo's narrative, p. 192, above.

[5] "Ciruela almonaci de la cordoba." Almonacid de Toledo is a village in Spain twelve miles southeast of Toledo. Almonacid de Zorita is a village in Spain nineteen miles southeast of Guadalajara. Both are in Castile. The Indian Joseph declared that five or six leagues beyond the Pecos the Humaña party had encountered a great quantity of plums. This is an indication that Zaldívar went by the same route. ("Relacion que dió un indio.") See Villagrá, *Historia*, canto XVI., fol. 45.

223

stream[1] carrying but little water but containing a prodigious quantity of excellent fish, pilchard, sardines, prawn, shrimp, and *matalote*. That night five hundred catfish were caught with only a fishhook, and many more on the following day.[2] At that place four Indian herdsmen[3] came to see him; they ordered that the Indians be given food and presents. One of them arose and with a loud voice called many Indians who were hidden and they all came to where the Spaniards were. They are powerful people and expert bowmen. The *sargento mayor* gave presents to all and won them over. He asked them for a guide to the cattle and they furnished one very willingly.

Next day they travelled six leagues and reached some rain water. There three Indians came out from a mountain, and, being asked where their ranchería was, they said that it was a league from there, and that they were very much excited because of our being in that land. In order that they might not become more excited by many people going, the *sargento mayor* went to their ranchería with but one companion, telling the three Indians to go ahead and quiet the people, and that he wished only to go and see them and to be their friend. He told them by means of an interpreter whom he had with him, named Jusepillo, one of the Indians who had been brought by Humayna and Leyba, and who had gone with them to a very great river to the east, in the direction of Florida. We all understand this to be the famous Rio de la Magdalena[4] which flows into Florida, and that this was the route followed by Dorantes, Cabeça de Vaca, and the negro who came thence

[1] They were now eleven leagues—twenty-five or thirty miles—from Pecos. The stream was probably the Gallinas, near Las Vegas.

[2] The names here given by the writer to the fish evidently were incorrect in some cases. Villagrá says they caught forty *arrobas*—a thousand pounds— of fish in less than three hours, with hooks only. *Historia*, canto XVI., fol. 145.

[3] *Vaqueros.*

[4] The name Magdalena is given on the Martínez map to what is clearly the Canadian. Saldívar probably referred to the large river beyond the Arkansas reached by Humaña. The name Magdalena as applied to a stream flowing into the Gulf of Mexico dates from the Narváez expedition, in 1528. When at Aute (identified by Lowery as at St. Mark's, Florida), Narváez decided to go to the sea, whose proximity was suspected "from a great river to which we had given the name of the Rio de la Magdalena" (*The Journey of Alvar Nuñez Cabeza de Vaca*, Bandelier edition, p. 33). The only large stream in that vicinity is the

to this land and to the rancherías and mountains of the Patarabueyes.

When he was about three-quarters of a league from his camp a great number of people came out to meet him, by fours and sixes.   They asked for the Spaniards' friendship, their method of making the request being to extend the palm of the right hand to the sun and then to bring it down on the person whose friendship they desire. He made them presents also, and they importuned him to go to their ranchería, and although evening was approaching he had to comply so that they would not think he was afraid to go. He reached the ranchería and remained with them in great friendliness, returning to his camp very late at night.

Next day as he travelled many Indians and Indian women came out to meet him, bringing *pinole*.[1]   Most of the men go naked, but some are clothed with skins of buffalo and some with blankets.   The women wear a sort of trousers made of buckskin, and shoes or leggins, after their own fashion. He gave them some presents and told them by means of the interpreter that Governor Don Juan de Oñate had sent him that they might know that he could protect those who were loyal to his Majesty and punish those who were not. All were friendly and very well pleased. They asked him for aid against the Xumanas,[2] as they call a tribe of Indians who are painted after the manner of the Chichimecos.[3] The *sargento mayor* promised them that he would endeavor to insure peace to them, since he had come to this land for that purpose.

Bidding them goodby, he left that place and travelled ten more leagues in three days, at the end of which time he saw the first buffalo bull,[4] which, being rather old, wandered alone and ran but little. This produced much merriment and was regarded as a great joke, for the least one in the

Apalachicola, which it may have been.   The name was later applied to various streams farther west, probably with reference to the stream mentioned by Cabeza de Vaca.   See Lowery, *Spanish Settlements*, 1513–1561, p. 186; Winsor, *Narrative and Critical History*, II. 288.

[1] See Espejo, narrative, p. 178, above.

[2] Jumano.   See p. 172, note 2.

[3] See Bustamante's declaration, p. 145, note 4.

[4] The party had now travelled twenty-seven leagues, or perhaps seventy-five miles, from Pecos.

company would not be satisfied with less than ten thousand head of cattle in his own corral.

Shortly afterward more than three hundred buffalo were seen in some pools. During the next day they travelled about seven leagues, when they encountered as many as a thousand head of cattle. In that place there were found very good facilities for the construction of a corral with wings. Orders having been given for its construction, the cattle went inland more than eight leagues. Upon seeing this the *sargento mayor* went on ahead with ten of his soldiers to a river six leagues from there, which flows from the province of the Picuries and the snow-covered range where they are,[1] and where the guide had told him that there were great numbers of cattle. But when he reached the river the cattle had left, because just then many Indian herdsmen crossed it, coming from trading with the Picuries and Taos, populous pueblos of this New Mexico, where they sell meat, hides, tallow, suet, and salt in exchange for cotton blankets, pottery, maize, and some small green stones[2] which they use.

He camped for the night at that river, and on the following day, on his way back to the camp, he found a ranchería in which there were fifty tents made of tanned hides, very bright red and white in color and bell-shaped, with flaps and openings, and built as skilfully as those of Italy and so large that in the most ordinary ones four different mattresses and beds were easily accommodated. The tanning is so fine that although it should rain bucketfuls it will not pass through nor stiffen the hide, but rather upon drying it remains as soft and pliable as before. This being so wonderful, he wanted to experiment, and, cutting off a piece of hide from one of the tents, it was soaked and placed to dry in the sun, but it remained as before, and as pliable as if it had never been wet.[3] The *sargento mayor* bartered for a tent and brought it to this camp,

---

[1] They were now forty leagues—a hundred miles or more—from Pecos, and the river must have been the Canadian, near Alamosa. It issues from the Sangre de Cristo Mountains.

[2] *Chalehiquitillos.* For an account of this trade see Espejo documents (*ante*) and Benavides, "Memorial," translation in *Land of Sunshine*, vols. XIII., XIV.

[3] Villagrá makes almost exactly the same statement, indicating that he wrote from this account (*Historia*, canto XVII., fol. 151).

and although it was so very large, as has been stated, it did not weigh over two *arrobas*.[1]

To carry this load, the poles that they use to set it up, and a knapsack of meat and their *pinole*, or maize, the Indians use a medium-sized shaggy dog, which is their substitute for mules. They drive great trains of them. Each, girt round its breast and haunches, and carrying a load of flour of at least one hundred pounds, travels as fast as his master. It is a sight worth seeing and very laughable to see them travelling, the ends of the poles dragging on the ground, nearly all of them snarling in their encounters, travelling one after another on their journey.[2] In order to load them the Indian women seize their heads between their knees and thus load them, or adjust the load, which is seldom required, because they travel along at a steady gait as if they had been trained by means of reins.

Having returned to camp they had a holiday that day and the next, as it was the feast of Señor San Francisco, and on the 5th of October they continued their march so as to reach the main herd of the cattle. In three days they travelled fourteen leagues, at the end of which they found and killed many cattle. Next day they went three more leagues farther in search of a convenient and suitable site for a corral, and upon finding a place they began to construct it out of large pieces of cottonwood.[3] It took them three days to complete it. It was so large and the wings so long that they thought they could corral ten thousand head of cattle, because they had seen so many, during those days, wandering so near to the tents and houses. In view of this and of the further fact that when they run they act as though fettered, they took their capture for granted. It was declared by those who had seen them that in that place alone there were more buffalo

---

[1] An *arroba* is twenty-five pounds.

[2] This is an excellent description of the *travois*. See also Castañeda, in Winship, *The Coronado Expedition*, p. 527.

[3] They were now fifty-one leagues, or perhaps from one hundred and twenty-five to one hundred and forty miles from Pecos. This took them near to, if not beyond, the borders of New Mexico. Since they found cottonwood timber, they must have been near a stream, which, I infer, was the Canadian. Details of the construction of the corral are given by Villagrá, *Historia*, canto XVII., folios 150–151.

than there are cattle in three of the largest ranches in new Spain.[1]

The corral constructed, they went next day to a plain where on the previous afternoon about a hundred thousand cattle had been seen. Giving them the right of way, the cattle started very nicely towards the corral, but soon they turned back in a stampede towards the men, and, rushing through them in a mass, it was impossible to stop them, because they are cattle terribly obstinate, courageous beyond exaggeration, and so cunning that if pursued they run, and that if their pursuers stop or slacken their speed they stop and roll, just like mules, and with this respite renew their run. For several days they tried a thousand ways of shutting them in or of surrounding them, but in no manner was it possible to do so. This was not due to fear, for they are remarkably savage and ferocious, so much so that they killed three of our horses and badly wounded forty, for their horns are very sharp and fairly long, about a span and a half, and bent upward together. They attack from the side, putting the head far down, so that whatever they seize they tear very badly. Nevertheless, some were killed and over eighty *arrobas*[2] of tallow were secured, which without doubt is greatly superior to that from pork; the meat of the bull is superior to that of our cow, and that of the cow equals our most tender veal or mutton.

Seeing therefore that the full grown cattle could not be brought alive, the *sargento mayor* ordered that calves be captured, but they became so enraged that out of the many which were being brought, some dragged by ropes and others upon the horses, not one got a league toward the camp, for they all died within about an hour. Therefore it is believed that unless taken shortly after birth and put under the care of our cows or goats, they cannot be brought until the cattle become tamer than they now are.

Its shape and form are so marvellous and laughable, or frightful, that the more one sees it the more one desires to see it, and no one could be so melancholy that if he were to

---

[1] Three such are specified in Oñate's letter, p. 219. It is evidently from here that Oñate gets his information.

[2] This would be more than a ton.

see it a hundred times a day he could keep from laughing heartily as many times, or could fail to marvel at the sight of so ferocious an animal. Its horns are black, and a third of a *vara* long, as already stated, and resemble those of the *búfalo;*[1] its eyes are small, its face, snout, feet, and hoofs of the same form as of our cows, with the exception that both the male and female are very much bearded, similar to he-goats. They are so thickly covered with wool that it covers their eyes and face, and the forelock nearly envelops their horns. This wool, which is long and very soft, extends almost to the middle of the body, but from there on the hair is shorter. Over the ribs they have so much wool and the chine is so high that they appear humpbacked, although in reality and in truth they are not greatly so, for the hump easily disappears when the hides are stretched.

In general, they are larger than our cattle. Their tail is like that of a hog, being very short, and having few bristles at the tip, and they twist it upward when they run. At the knee they have natural garters of very long hair. In their haunches, which resemble those of mules, they are hipped and crippled, and they therefore run, as already stated, in leaps, especially down hill. They are all of the same dark color, somewhat tawny, in parts their hair being almost black. Such is their appearance, which at sight is far more ferocious than the pen can depict. As many of these cattle as are desired can be killed and brought to these settlements, which are distant from them thirty or forty leagues, but if they are to be brought alive it will be most difficult unless time and crossing them with those from Spain make them tamer.[2]

In this region and on this road were found some camps and sleeping places made by Leyba and Humaña when they left this land, fleeing from the men who were coming from New Spain to arrest them.[3]

---

[1] That is, the Asiatic buffalo, or wild ox.

[2] The copy has *aman,* where *amansen* seems to be intended.

[3] Noting this statement in Zaldívar's declaration, Oñate had him make a more explicit statement under oath, on February 17, 1599, and attached it to the declaration of Jusephe (see p. 201). He states that the first camping place of Humaña was encountered about twenty-four leagues from San Juan Baptista,

These cattle have their haunts on some very level mesas[1] which extend over many leagues, for, after reaching the top of them by a slight grade, as of low hills, thirty leagues were travelled, continuously covered with an infinite number of cattle, and the end of them was not reached. The mesas have neither mountain, nor tree, nor shrub, and when on them they were guided solely by the sun. To the north in their highest part flows a medium-sized river, which appears to be a marvel, for at that point it is higher than at its source, and seems rather to flow up than down. It contains many fish and crustaceans. At the base of these mesas, in some places where there are glens or valleys, there are many cedars, and an infinite number of springs which issue from these very mesas, and a half league from them there are large cotton groves.

The Indians are numerous in all that land. They live in rancherías in the hide tents hereinbefore mentioned. They always follow the cattle, and in their pursuit they are as well sheltered in their tents as they could be in any house. They eat meat almost raw, and much tallow and suet, which serves them as bread, and with a chunk of meat in one hand and a piece of tallow in the other, they bite first on one and then on the other, and grow up magnificently strong and courageous. Their weapons consist of flint and very large bows, after the manner of the Turks. They saw some arrows with long thick points,[2] although few, for the flint is better than spears to kill cattle. They kill them at the first shot with the greatest skill, while ambushed in brush blinds made at the watering places, as all saw who went there, and who in company with the said *sargento mayor* consumed in the journey fifty-four days and returned to this camp on the 8th of November, 1598, thanks be to God.

In the pueblo of San Juan Baptista, on the 23d day of the

and the second about thirty-six leagues further on. He based his opinion on the statement of Jusephe, who went with them as a guide and interpreter ("Relación que dió un indio de la salida que hicieron Umana y leyba del nuevo Mexico").

[1] A *mesa* is a tableland. The term is commonly used in the Southwest, and stands for a definite natural feature.

[2] He evidently means the spear.

month of February, 1599, before Don Juan de Oñate, governor,
captain-general, and *adelantado* of the provinces and kingdoms
of New Mexico, conqueror, settler, and pacifier of these lands
for the king our lord, etc., Vicente de Saldivar Mendoça,
sargento mayor, captain, and commander of the companies of
the said kingdoms and army of his Majesty, presented this
account of the journey which he made by order of his Lordship to the buffalo ; and the said Señor governor, in order that
to his Majesty and his audiencias and viceroys it may be evident and known that it is all true, ordered that it all be read
to some of the captains and soldiers who went with the said
sargento mayor and who were present, and that they all should
respond and sign with their hands.   For this purpose the said
governor had them all take oath in the name of God and by the
sign of the cross, in legal form.   They did so, and promised
to tell the truth.   They were the said *sargento mayor*, Vicente
Saldivar de Mendoça, the Proveedor and Captain Diego de
Çubia, Captain Pablo de Aguilar Inojosa, Captain Marcelo
de Espinosa, Ensign Domingo de Liçama, Marcos Cortes,
Juan de Pedraça, Alonso Sanchez, Hernando Inojosa, Esteban
de Sosa, Juan de Olague, Juan de Salas, Diego Robledo, and
Diego de Ayerde.   To all of them, as has been said, I, the
undersigned secretary, read the foregoing account word for
word, and one and all replied and said that all contained therein
is correct and true and what happened in their presence in the
said journey to the cattle ; and it being read to them, under
charge of the said oath which all had taken, they ratified it,
and those who knew how signed it, they being those whose
signatures appear herein.   And I, the said secretary, testify
that all the foregoing took place before me and was witnessed
by the *contador* of the Real Hacienda, Juan Ortiz, Juan Velas-
ques de Cavanillas, and other persons, Don Juan de Oñate,
Vicente de Saldivar Mendoça, Diego de Çubia, Pablo de
Aguilar Inojosa, Marcello de Espinosa, Domingo de Liçama,
Alonso Sanchez, Esteban de Sosa, Juan de Pedraça, Diego
Robledo, Juan de Salas.   Before me, Juan Gutierrez Bocanegra, secretary.   And I, the said Juan Gutierrez Bocanegra, captain for the king our lord and government secretary
of New Mexico and of its kingdoms and provinces, was
present at the aforesaid with the said governor, who herein

signed his name; and upon his order I made this copy, which is correct and true, and has been corrected by the original, which remains in my possession. In witness whereof I signed it.

JUAN GUTIERREZ BOCANEGRA, secretary.

ACCOUNT OF THE JOURNEY TO THE
SALINES, THE XUMANAS, AND
THE SEA, 1599[1]

Account of the Journey which they made to the Sea and of the Visit to the Salines and the Xumanas.[2]

On the 6th of October in the year of '98 the governor set out from this pueblo of San Juan, province of the Teguas.[3] On the first day we travelled four leagues, to the first pueblo of the Cañada[4] de los Teguas; on the next day six leagues to San Marcos;[5] on the following day six leagues to the Pueblo del Tuerto;[6] on the next, two leagues to the first pueblo over the mountain, last pueblo of Puaray; next day five leagues to the first pueblo of the salines;[7] next day four leagues

---

[1] "Relaciones que envió Don Juan de Oñate de algunas jornadas," ff. 7–10 (manuscript in Lowery Collection).

[2] Villagrá gives an account of this journey in his *Historia*, canto XVIII.

[3] Tewa, Tehua.

[4] Apparently one of the Tewa pueblos in the group to which Santa Cruz de la Cañada belonged. But as Santa Cruz is only some four miles southward of San Juan, the pueblo reached by Oñate would seem to be farther south. See Hodge, *Handbook*, II. 458; Bandelier, *Final Report*, I. 82–83.

[5] Shown on the Martínez map as no. 27. The ruins of San Marcos are eighteen miles south-southwest of Santa Fé. The place here mentioned may have been the same. See Hodge, *Handbook*, II. 448.

[6] The town of the Crooked or Twisted. This name is still borne by the Rio Tuerto, a small stream entering the Rio Grande opposite San Felipe, and by mountains in the same general region. Rio Tuerto affords a pass through the mountains through which runs an old trail from Albuquerque to Galisteo. In this pass along the trail was the place called Tuerto. For a discussion of pueblo ruins about Galisteo see Bandelier, *Final Report*, I. 100–106.

[7] The salines lie near the Manzano Mountains, in eastern Valencia County. To the southeast of them is the Mesa de los Jumanos. The saline country was inhabited in the early seventeenth century by Tigua, Piro, and Jumano villages (see Hodge, *The Jumano Indians*, pp. 8–9; Bandelier, *Final Report*, I. 167). The salines are evidently the same as those visited by the Chamuscado party.

to the last pueblo of the salines, or Gallinas.[1] We remained there three days and visited the salines which lie to the east five or six leagues from there. They consist of white salt; there are many very large and good ones, and they are seven or eight leagues in circumference. Next day we went three leagues to the pueblo of Abbo,[2] and the next day four leagues to the Xumanas.[3] There are three pueblos, one of them large like Cia[4] and two small ones. The said pueblos of the salines and the Xumanas all rendered obedience to his Majesty.

From this point his lordship decided to go to the sea, and therefore on the following day we came from there to the second pueblo of Abbo, a league and a half. The next day we returned to the last pueblo of the said Gallinas and then to the first pueblo of the Gallinas or salines; next day to the pueblo of the Portezuelo; next day seven leagues to the pueblo of Father Claros,[5] where we remained two days.

From there we set out for the pueblo of Acoma[6] towards the west, going four leagues to the Torrente de los Alamos. Midway is the Arroyo de los Mimbres. Next day seven leagues to the Manantial de la Barranca; next day two leagues to Acoma,[7] a pueblo of five hundred houses, where the Indians received him very well with maize, water, and turkeys, and rendered obedience to his Majesty. This place is almost im-

[1] The railroad station of Gallinas and Gallinas National Forest still preserve this name in the same general region.

[2] Abo was a Tompiros pueblo located in Arroyo del Empedradillo, in the southeastern corner of Valencia County. The ruins of the mission of San Gregorio, founded in 1629, are still there. Hodge, *Handbook*, I. 6.

[3] The direction from Abo to the Xumana pueblos is not clear. There were four instead of three Jumano pueblos in this region. See Hodge, *The Jumano Indians*, p. 8; *Doc. Inéd.*, XVI. 123–124.

[4] Sia.

[5] Father Claros was assigned to the pueblo of Chiguas. See Ytinerario, entry for September 16. According to the "Relacion de como los Padres de San Francisco se encargaron de las Provincias de la Nueva Mexico," the province of the Chiguas extended from Puaray to the Queres. That they set out west from Puaray, located near Bernalillo, is shown by the Ytinerario, entry for October 23, 1598.

[6] See Ytinerario, entry for October 23; Villagrá, *Historia*, canto XVIII.

[7] Ácoma is about sixty miles west of the Rio Grande. If the pueblo of Father Claros was on the Rio Grande, the estimate gives about five miles to the league. In the assignment of the pueblos to the missionaries, Tziaas, Tamaya, and Acco were grouped together ("Relacion de como los Padres," etc.).

pregnable, for except by climbing over the very rocks by holes which they have made one cannot ascend.[1]

We rested one day, and on the next we set out for the province of Zuñi, going to the head of the river which is called De la Mala Nueva;[2] next day four leagues, camping for the night in a forest, without water; next day to the Agua de la Peña, four leagues. It snowed furiously, the horses stampeded, and some were lost for good. Next day four leagues to a spring which flows to the province of Cuni.[3] We saw three ruined pueblos. The following day, which was the feast of All Saints,[4] three leagues to the first pueblo of the people belonging to the province of Zuñi, which consists of six pueblos. The Indians received us with a large quantity of maize, tortillas, and rabbits. Remaining here one day, on Tuesday we went three leagues to visit the last pueblo, which they call Cibola, or by another name, Granada,[5] where Francisco Vazquez Coronado nearly sixty years ago had the encounter with the Indians. They received us very well with maize, tortillas, gourds, beans, and quantities of rabbits and hares, of which there are a great many. They are a very amiable people and all rendered obedience to his Majesty.

In all these pueblos we found crosses which the Indians reverence and to which they are accustomed to make the same offering as to their idols, which consist of flour, small sticks painted with different colors, and turkey feathers. The Indians speak a few Mexican words, as two of Coronado's Indians, now dead, had remained there. One of them, called Gaspar, left two sons. We saw the one named Alonso.[6] He spoke a few Mexican words but understood none. Each house there gave us a *manta* of *istle*,[7] very good cloth.

We remained there until the 8th of November of '98 and during that time the governor sent Captain Farfan to see a saline which we heard was nine leagues from there. He returned on the third day, convinced that it must be the best saline in the world, and truly its salt would indicate this, for

---

[1] See Hodge, *Ascent of the Enchanted Mesa* (1898).
[2] Bad news.   [3] Zuñi.   [4] November 1.
[5] This was the pueblo of Hawikuh. See Hodge, *Handbook*, II. 1017.
[6] See the Espejo documents, p. 184, above, for references to these men.
[7] *Yxtle*, a fibre produced from a species of pine in Mexico.

besides being exceedingly white and of marvellous grain he said the saline was a league around, and that in the centre of it there was a spring from which the saline is engendered, and therefore is very salty; that it has a depth of over a spear's length, and that in all this depth the salt forms a hardened[1] crust, so that in order to extract the salt it is necessary to use a bar or pick-axe. Of all this, lengthy testimony was taken.[2]

During these days Captain Villagran arrived,[3] being brought in by three soldiers who had gone to round up the horses which the snow-storm had scattered and had found him almost dead at El Agua de la Peña, without horse or arms, and not having eaten for two or three days, for he had lost everything near Acoma by falling into a pit, and only the mercy of God prevented his perishing as his horse had done. He was coming from the country of New Spain.

From there, on the said Sunday, the 8th, we set out for the province of Mohoqui,[4] or Mohoje, going four leagues without water. It snowed all the time, for it was mid-winter. Next day, after travelling five leagues, we came across water near the road in a marsh. We camped for the night without water. Next day five leagues to some springs to get water, which was small in quantity. After travelling six leagues we camped for the night without water. On the following day we went five leagues to Mohoqui, and on the road only the men drank at a small spring which was underneath a rock. After going two leagues, at the first pueblo of Mohoqui or Mohoce they came out to receive us with tortillas, scattering

---

[1] *Oxaldrada.*

[2] On November 8, at the pueblo of Zuñi, Farfán made a sworn statement regarding the saline. It was eight leagues westward of Granada, or Zuñi, round in shape, twelve or more leagues in circumference, and composed of fine, white, crystallized salt. Near the edge of the saline the crust was a span thick, and at the centre "a good spear's length"; wagons might travel over it without breaking the crust. Farfán was "certain that neither in all Christendom nor outside of it is there anything so grand, nor has the king anything to equal it" ("Relacion del descubrimiento de las salinas de cuni"). This statement would place the saline well into Arizona. The Ytinerario states that it was east of Zuñi.

[3] See Villagrá's *Historia*, canto XIX. The Ytinerario (p. 274) mentions this incident as happening to Captain Marqués instead of to Villagrá.

[4] Moqui.

fine flour upon us and upon our horses as a token of peace and friendship, and all of those provinces, which are four pueblos, rendered obedience to his Majesty and treated us very well.

We rested there one day. Next day we travelled three leagues to another small pueblo. On the following day we spent the night at the last pueblo, four leagues distant, having passed through the third one. In all of them they received us as in the first. We rested for one day and on the following day we retraced the same ground, returning to the second pueblo of the said province. Next day we went to the first, where we rested three days.

From there on Friday, November 17, because of the reports of the rich mines, the governor sent Captain Marcos Farfan de los Godos with eight companions to make the exploration. Then, on Saturday, we set out on the return, by the same marches and places, to the province of Cuni, where we awaited the said explorers of the mines for seventeen days; and at the end of twenty-one days from their departure Captain Farfan and Captain Alonso de Quesada returned, having left the other seven companions in Mohoqui, as the animals were worn out. They brought flattering reports[1] of the good mines discovered thirty leagues from the said province of Mohoqui, and they brought very good ores from which silver was later extracted by many and divers very rich assays,[2] by means of mercury. This infused new life into over a hundred lifeless residents of this camp. They are ores which can be smelted. The description of their route is in a separate report, on which I rely.

The said Captain Farfan having returned, and the governor seeing the great delay of the thirty men who had gone with his *maese de campo*, Don Juan de Saldivar, and who were to overtake him in order to make the said journey to the South Sea, he having sent for them to the camp which he had established in the province of Teguas, he determined to return to the said camp to celebrate Christmas, which was near, so that immediately after Christmas he could make the journey

---

[1] They are printed hereinafter, pp. 239–249.

[2] The details concerning these assays are set forth in "Relacion de los ensayes que se hicieron de ciertas minas," etc.

to the sea with all the soldiers necessary.[1]   Therefore, on the twelfth of December we left Cuni and camped for the night in the first pueblo of that province; the following day at El Agua de la Peña, where we found Ensign Bernabe de las Casas, with six companions, who was going in search of his Lordship with the sad news of the occurrence at Acoma, and of the death of the above-mentioned *maese de campo* and other captains and soldiers.[2]

Next day, from that point his Lordship sent Don Tomas, Indian interpreter, who was the one who had remained in the country from Castano's expedition and who has been of great service, to inform the seven explorers who remained in Mohoqui of what had happened and to warn them not to come by way of Acoma, but to follow our trail, so that they might arrive safely at the camp.   We made our journey directly to the said camp, which we reached in seven days, may God be praised.   Amen.   Don JUAN DE OÑATE.

[1] See Villagrá, *Historia*, canto XIX.

[2] See Ytinerario, entry for January 7, for additional data regarding this incident.

ACCOUNT OF THE DISCOVERY OF THE MINES, 1599[1]

In the pueblo of Cibola, which the natives call Cuni,[2] on the 11th day of the month of December, 1598, Don Juan de Oñate, governor, captain-general, and adelantado of the kingdoms and provinces of this New Mexico, explorer, pacifier, and colonizer of the same for the king our Lord, said that his Lordship sent Marcos Farfan de los Godos, his captain of the guard and of the horses, with eight companions,[3] from the province of Mohoqui, which is twenty leagues distant from this one, to make a certain exploration of settlements and mines, which captain returned to his presence on this day to report his experiences on the said expedition and journey. And in order that this may be on record forever and a memorandum of it be had he ordered evidence taken, and that the said captain of the guard and his companions should testify under oath and give an account of all that had occurred and of what they had discovered. Thus he provided and ordered, and signed with his name. Don JUAN DE OÑATE. Before me, JUAN VELARDE, secretary.

And after the foregoing, in the said pueblo of Cibola, on the 11th day of the month of December, 1598, the said Señor governor caused to appear before him Marcos Farfan de los Godos, captain of the guard, to whom oath was administered in the name of God our Lord and with the sign of the cross, in due form, and in virtue of which he promised to tell the

---

[1] "Relaciones que envió Don Juan de Oñate de algunas jornadas," ff. 11–20 (manuscript in Lowery Collection). For reference to this expedition see Ytinerario, pp. 275–276.

[2] Zuñi.

[3] The eight companions were: Captain Alonso de Quesada, Captain Bartolomé Romero, Francisco Vido, Antonio Conte de Herrera, Sargento Hernan Martín, Marcos García, Juan Rodríguez, and León de Ysasti. See *post*, p. 248.

truth. The foregoing order[1] having been read to him, the witness said that he had set out[2] with the said eight companions from the province of Mohoqui at the order of his Lordship in the month of November of this year. They travelled six leagues[3] towards the west through a land of sand dunes without timber, and where they camped for the night they found a small spring of water, where the horses could not drink, although there was plenty of water for the men. Next morning they set out from this place in the same direction, and having travelled about three leagues they found a river[4] which flowed towards the north, of moderate width and carrying considerable water, with many cottonwoods, level banks, and little pasture.

And travelling on in the same direction they reached the slope of a mountain range[5] in time to camp for the night, having gone about another [three] leagues.[6] They camped without water, and the next morning they set out from this place; and after going two leagues they arrived at a grove of small pines, and at a very deep pool,[7] which was ample to water all the horses and more if there had been more. Travelling on for two leagues along the mountain range, which was covered with snow, they camped for the night on a slope where was found a small amount of grass for the horses. They

[1] *Cabeça de proceso.* This is the technical name applied to the account and order constituting the first paragraph above.

[2] They set out on November 17. See p. 237.

[3] The Ytinerario, p. 276, gives a summary of the route to the mines, taken obviously from this document. Farfán's general route and the general region of the terminus of his route are quite clear from the topographical data given. The direction was west-southwest. The terminus was evidently just east or just west of the Big Sandy River, the indications pointing rather to the former. The distance covered is given by Farfán as thirty-five leagues. The air-line distance is about two hundred miles, and by the trails more than that. Farfán's leagues therefore, average about six miles. Espejo, who clearly went to the same region, gave the distance as forty-five leagues.

[4] The Little Colorado.

[5] The San Francisco Mountain. They passed south of this mountain, and apparently not far from Flagstaff.

[6] The Ytinerario supplies the omission here.

[7] Southwest of Flagstaff on one of the old trails there is a laguna, which may have been the place where Farfán camped. In the same general locality, on the old trails, there were several springs, as Antelope Spring, Volunteer Spring, Snively's Holes, but a study of the map points to Laguna as the place mentioned.

camped without water. After they had unsaddled the horses and placed the sentinels, two of the Indians whom they were taking as guides said that they knew where there was water very near there, and that they wanted to go and bring some in some gourds. But the witness did not give his consent, as he feared they would flee unless accompanied by a trustworthy person, and accordingly Captain Alonso de Quesada went with them.

He took the Indians ahead of him, and after travelling about three arquebus shots from where we were lodged the Indians saw lights and dwellings,[1] and signalled to the captain that there were the Jumana Indians. The captain, finding himself so near, told them to go over there, and having arrived there he found many Indians and Indian women in four or five rancherías, who surrounded them with their bows and arrows. The captain told them that he had a message for them; that he was not coming to do them harm, but, instead, to give them of what he had. Thereupon they were reassured, and two Indian chiefs of the said ranchería came on with the captain and friendly Indians to where the witness and his companions were. The witness treated them very well, showing them marks of friendship, caressing them, giving them beads and other presents. He then sent them back to their own rancherías, telling them by signs that they should reassure the rest of the people, because they were not going to injure them but to be their friends, and to find out where they secured the ore which the witness showed them.

Next morning the witness and his companions went to the said ranchería,[2] which he found deserted, there being in it only the two chiefs and a woman. They received him with signs of gladness, and as a token of peace gave them pulverized ore and a great quantity of ground dates,[3] which is their food, and a few pieces of venison. The witness in return gave them more beads and presents, and begged them to go with him to show him where they got that ore. One of the Indian chiefs complied willingly.

[1] *Ranchos.*
[2] This is the Ranchería de los Gandules given in the Ytinerario, which supplies the distance of two and one-half leagues.
[3] *Datil.*

They left their ranchería, going up a smooth hill. They reached a plain and a very large pine grove with many large and tall pines, which is the beginning of the mountain range, all of which, as stated, was covered with snow which reached to their knees. The Indian chief always going ahead as a guide, they travelled about six leagues along the mountain range,[1] and at the end of this distance they found a rather low valley, without snow and with very good grass, water, and wood, where they spent the night.[2] Leaving this place, on the following day they came in sight of another ranchería because they saw the smoke from it. And when they came near it the witness took with him three companions, leaving the rest of the men and the horses behind, and went to the said ranchería, where he found a petty Indian chief with about thirty Indians, stained with ores of different colors, and as many as eight or ten dwellings in which were women and children. The witness dismounted and embraced the captain and the other Indians, making signs of peace and friendship, giving them beads and presents of what he had with him, as a token of peace, and making a cross with his fingers, which is the sign they make when they desire peace. The Indians gave them powdered ores of different colors and apparently rich. The witness, after reassuring them, and peace having been made, begged the captain to bring the women and children there, as he wanted to see them and give to them of what he had with him. The Indian chief did so, and within about an hour he brought about forty women and as many children, all dressed in the skins of deer, otter, and other animals, with which they clothe themselves.

The Indian who had come as guide, saying that he felt too tired to go on to the exploration upon which they were going, remained in this ranchería, and begged the chief of it to go on with the witness and his two companions. He con-

---

[1] They were evidently now crossing the range south of Bill Williams Mountain.

[2] The Ytinerario calls this the Ranchería de los Cruzados, and gives the distance as two leagues. Espejo told of the Cruzados on the way to the Arizona mines, a people with small crosses on their heads. See Espejo, p. 187, above. They have been identified as the Yavapai (see Bandelier, in Arch. Inst. of America *Papers*, III. 109).

sented willingly, and after they had given them venison and
of what they had in their ranchería, they set out from it,
travelling through a land of pine groves, with the finest of
pastures, many cattle, very good prickly pears, and many
and large maguey patches, where they saw Castilian partridges, a great many deer, hares, and rabbits.[1]

Having travelled about three leagues, they saw the smoke
of another ranchería. Taking ahead of them the other chief
as a guide, he said that he wished to go ahead to notify the
ranchería, so that they would not become excited, and to tell
them that we were men who would do them no harm but were
friends. The witness permitted the Indian to go. He reached
the ranchería, which was about a league[2] beyond, and reassured the people thereof, who came out to meet him. They
arrived at the ranchería and received the chief of it and the
rest with signs of joy and peace. They found many women
and children, to whom they gave of what they had with them,
and the Indians gave them powdered ore of different colors,
mescale, and venison.

As it was late they camped for the night about two arquebus shots from there, on the bank of a river[3] of fair width and
much water, with good pasture and a cottonwood grove. The
following morning, as the chief whom they had as a guide wished
to return, the witness begged the chief of this ranchería to
go with him and show him the mine from which they got
ores. He consented willingly, and having travelled about
four leagues through very fine, fertile land, with extensive
pastures, they came to another river, wider than the first,
where they spent the night. This river flowed almost from
the north. They crossed it, and having travelled about two
leagues they came to another river, much larger, which flowed
from the north. They crossed it, and having travelled about

[1] Compare Espejo's description of the country near the mines.

[2] The Ytinerario does not account for this league.

[3] This would seem to correspond with the northwestern branch of the
Verde River, which was crossed between Bill Williams Mountain and Prescott.
The old trail from Antelope Springs, south of Bill Williams Mountain, crossed
the river at Postal's Ranch. It is just possible that they crossed Black Forest
farther north, and went through old Camp Hualpai, where the trail forked,
but I doubt it.

a league, arrived at the slopes of some hills[1] where the Indian chief said the mines were whence they got the ore.

And arriving at the slope of the said hills, the banks of the said rivers were seen, with deep ravines having the finest of pastures, and extensive plains. As it was late, they camped that night on the slope of these hills, at a spring of water which issued from one of them, very large and carrying much water, almost hot.[2] Here six Indians from different rancherías of those mountains joined him, and next morning they took him up to the said mine, which was at a good height, although one could go up to it on horseback, for these Indians had opened up a road. There they found an old shaft, three *estados* in depth, from which the Indians extracted the ores for their personal adornment and for the coloring of their blankets, because in this mine there are brown, black, water-colored, blue, and green ores. The blue ore is so blue that it is understood that some of it is enamel. The mine had a very large dump, where there were many and apparently very good ores, which are the ones which have been enumerated.

The vein is very wide and rich and of many outcrops, all containing ores. The vein ran along the hill in plain view and crossed over to another hill which was opposite, where they took from twenty-eight to thirty claims for themselves and for the companions who remained at the camp as a guard to the Señor governor. At one side of the said hill they found another vein of more than two arms' length in width, which they named the vein of San Francisco. Here they took fourteen or fifteen claims. On the other side of the other part of the outcrop[3] they found another vein which they named San Gabriel, wide and rich in ores, where they took fourteen or fifteen more claims; and on the other side, on the hill of the outcrop, they found another vein which they named the

---

[1] I am in doubt as to whether the last stream was the Big Sandy or the Spenser River, a branch of the Santa María, but the indications seem to point to the latter. In that case the mines were in the Aquarius Range; in the other case, they were in the Hualpai Range. Both of these ranges have become mining districts.

[2] The identification of this spring may become the key to the locality.

[3] *La descubridora.*

vein of Guerfanos, wide and rich in ores, where they took ten
or twelve more claims.

As it was late they descended and slept at the said camp
and spring of water; and complying with the instructions which
he had from his Lordship he assembled all the Indians he
could in order to learn about everything else which there
was in the country. When everybody from the rancherías
and the mountains had come together he asked them through
what country the three rivers which they had seen came,
and where they went. They said and indicated by signs,
joining them on the ground with a rod, that the said three
rivers and two others which joined them further on,[1] all
united and passed through a gorge which they pointed out
to them, and that beyond the gorge the river was extremely
wide and copious, and that on the banks on both sides there
were immense settlements of people who planted very large
fields of maize, beans, and gourds in a very level country
of good climate; and (referring to the snow which they showed
him on the mountain which they were leaving behind) they
said that neither on the mountain of the mines nor in the
settlements of the rivers does it ever snow, because the climate is mild and almost hot. Conditions described on this
river and settlements were understood to extend to the sea,
which they showed to be salty by dissolving a small quantity of salt in water in order to demonstrate the condition
of the sea water.

When the witness asked them where they got some shells
which they wore suspended from their noses and foreheads,
which are pearl-bearing, they said by signs that they got
them from this said salt water, which is thirty days' journey
from their rancherías, which, according to their rate of travel,
must be eighty or ninety leagues. And making signs with
the hands, placing one hand over the other in the form of
a shell, they opened it on one side. They said that there
these shells were to be found, and that they opened them
and found some white and round objects as large as grains

---

[1] This confirms my opinion that the mines were on the eastern slope of the
Aquarius Mountains. In that case the Big Sandy and the main Colorado
would be referred to as the other two streams uniting with the three to form the
Colorado.

of maize; and that it is from the shells that they get them; and that in that neighborhood there are many and very large settlements.

After this was over the captain and his companions set about returning to examine and consider with care the qualities of the country and the mines wherein they found, as has been stated, the said veins, besides many other reports which the Indians give. The veins are so long and wide that half of the people of New Spain can have mines there. At a quarter of a league, half a league, or a league, there is a very great quantity of water from the said rivers and spring, where many water mills can be constructed, with excellent water wheels, and water can be taken out with the greatest ease.

Near to the very mines themselves are enormous pines, oaks, mesquites, walnuts, and cottonwoods, and, as has been stated, great pastures and plains and fine lands for cultivation. The maize which the Indians gather gives most excellent evidence of the bounty of the land, because this witness got down to cut off with his own hand a stalk of that which the Indians had planted and had, and although it appeared to have been broken in the middle, yet this half which he brought to his Lordship so that he might see it was two fathoms and three spans long, and as thick as the wrist. In all this land the good pasture lands continue, and there is much game, as deer, hares, and partridges, and although no fish were seen in the river, because of the little we saw of it, they found on it many Indians clothed in the skins of beavers, which were very fine and well tanned. They found two lizards hung in a ranchería to dry. In the groves on the rivers mentioned there are a great number of birds of all kinds, which is an excellent indication of the good climate of the country, and from what this witness saw in it, the said mountains are without doubt the richest in all New Spain, for the witness has been in almost all the mines of New Spain and he has seen that this country has the same qualities, especially the rich mines of San Andrés.

Hereupon the witness and his companions returned to report to his Lordship all that they had seen and explored and all that they had heard of, as he did. He returned to his presence for two reasons: first, because they lacked provisions, and secondly, because the time allotted for the said journey was up. And this which he has stated is what occurred, what he saw and learned, and is the truth by the oath which he has taken. And it being read to him he reaffirmed and ratified it. He said he was about forty years of age, and was a legally qualified witness. And he signed in his own name with his Lordship. MARCOS FARFAN DE LOS GODOS. Don JUAN DE OÑATE. Before me, JUAN VELARDE, secretary.[1]

Witness. And after the above, in the said pueblos of Cíbola, on the 11th day of the month of December, 1598, his Lordship the governor caused to appear before him Captain Quesada, to whom he administered oath in the name of God our Lord and with a sign of the cross, in legal form, and in virtue of which he promised to tell the truth. And being shown the above order and the narrative given regarding this matter by Captain Marcos Farfan de los Godos on this day, he declared that the said account is true, and that all is literally as happened, and is what occurred to them in the said journey, and that, in addition to what the said Captain Marcos Farfan de los Godos declared, they found and discovered another rich vein about a half-league from the other mines, towards the north, which they named the vein of La Cuesta; and also another, a quarter-league away, more or less. This witness found two veins where he and the others who were with him took up claims; and he understands and is very certain that there are an infinite number of mines throughout all that land, because the indications are extremely favorable. He said that this is the truth, and he

---

[1] On the return to New Mexico, the samples of ore brought from the west were distributed among various men of mining experience, to be assayed. On February 18, 1599, at the pueblo of San Juan Baptista, Oñate ordered declarations regarding the results. It was stated that as Farfán had set out from Moqui, his party was unprepared with tools, and could only get samples extracted with daggers and knives. Alonso Sánchez, *real contador*, declared that from one sample the assay showed eleven ounces of silver per quintal. In his testimony it is clearly implied that the mines explored by Farfán were the same as those discovered by Espejo. Diego de Çubia, *proveedor general*, also made a declaration, on the basis of an assay, to the effect that he believed the mines to be rich ("Relacion de los ensayes que se hicieron de ciertas minas," MS.).

reaffirmed and ratified it and the account of the said Captain
Marcos de los Godos, under the oath which he has taken.
He said that he was about thirty years of age, and was a
legally qualified witness; and he signed his name with the said
governor. ALONSO DE QUESADA. Don JUAN DE OÑATE. Before me, JUAN VELARDE, secretary.

In the pueblo of San Juan Baptista of this New Mexico,
on the 15th day of the month of January, 1599, the said
Señor governor, for the said inquiry, caused to appear before
him Captain Bartolomé Romero, Antonio Conte de Herrera,
his chief equerry, Francisco Vido, his chief page, Sargento
Hernan Martin, Marcos Garcia, Juan Rodriguez, and León
de Ysasti, to whom he administered oath in the name of
God our Lord and with the sign of the cross, in legal form;
and the foregoing order and the statement and account given
by Captain Marcos Farfan de los Godos, and the statement
and deposition of Captain Alonso de Quesada being read to
them, they all and severally said that the said statement
and relation, as rendered and declared, are true and what
happened, by the oath which they have taken; and they
reaffirmed and ratified the same, and again said and stated
it in the form stated and declared by the said captains. And
they signed it with their own names, with the said governor.
Captain ROMERO, ANTONIO CONTE DE HERRERA, FRANCISCO
VIDO, JUAN RODRIGUEZ, HERMAN MARTIN, LEON DE YSASTI,
MARCOS GARCIA, Don JUAN DE OÑATE. Before me JUAN
VELARDE, secretary.

In the pueblo of San Juan Baptista of New Mexico on
the sixteenth day of the month of January, 1599, his Lordship Governor Don Juan de Oñate, having seen this inquiry,
ordered that one, two, and more copies be made, in order
to send it to the king our Lord and to his royal council.
And this he provided, ordered, and signed with his name.
Don JUAN DE OÑATE. Before me JUAN VELARDE, secretary.

This copy was corrected and compared with the original,
which remains in possession of the Señor governor who here
signed his name; and at his request and order I had this
written in the pueblo of San Juan Baptista of this New Mex-

ico on the twenty-second day of the month of February, 1599, the correction being witnessed by Antonio Conte, Cristobal de Herrera, and Francisco de Villalva. In witness whereof I signed and sealed it with the seal of his Lordship. Don JUAN DE OÑATE. In testimony of the truth. JUAN VELARDE, secretary.

TRUE ACCOUNT OF THE EXPEDITION OF OÑATE TOWARD THE EAST, 1601[1]

Faithful and true account of the events which took place in the expedition made by the Adelantado and Governor Don Juan de Oñate, in the name of his Majesty, from these first settlements of New Mexico, toward the north, in the year of 1601.[2]

WITH particular care, I mean with the consent and counsel both of our Father Commissary, Fray Juan Descalona,[3] and the other fathers who resided in these kingdoms occupied in ministering to souls, and of the officers of the royal troops which his Majesty has herein, and after many supplications, suffrages, sacrifices, and prayers to God our Lord, that his Majesty might reveal His divine will, knowing that that of our most Catholic king and lord Philip, God guard him through infinite years, has been and is that the most holy name of God be proclaimed in these his realms, and His holy gospel preached to these barbarous nations, bound by the power of Satan, the enemy of humankind, the governor and adelantado Don Juan de Oñate determined to make an expedition from these first settlements where at the present time this camp of his Majesty is established, to the interior, by a northern route and direction, both because of the splendid reports which the native Indians were giving of this land, and also

[1] "Relacion Verdadera de los sucesos de la entrada que hizo el governador D. Juan de Oñate en las poblaciones de Nueva Megico hacia el Norte" (manuscript in Lowery Collection).

[2] For other data regarding this expedition see especially "Breve relacion en sustancia del nuevo descubrimiento que intentó y dexó comenzado Don Juan de Oñate en la jornada que hizo entre Norte y Levante," etc., in Pacheco and Cárdenas, *Doc. Inéd.*, XVI. 52-60; Zárate Salmerón, *Relaciones*, paragraphs 37-43.

[3] Fray Juan de Escalona was made commissary after the return of Father Martínez to Mexico in 1599.

because of what an Indian named Joseph, who was born and reared in New Spain and who speaks the Mexican tongue, saw while going with Captain Umaña.[1]

The most necessary things having been arranged for the journey, with the supply of provisions, arms, ammunition, and other requisite military stores, with more than seventy picked men for the expedition, all very well equipped, more than seven hundred horses and mules, six mule carts, and two carts drawn by oxen conveying four pieces of artillery, and with servants to carry the necessary baggage,[2] the journey was begun this year of 1601, the said adelantado, Don Juan de Oñate, governor and captain-general, going as commander, with Vicente de Çaldivar Mendoça as his *maese de campo* and *sargento mayor*, and two religious of the order of our father San Francisco, Fray Francisco de Velasco, priest, and Fray Pedro de Vergara, lay brother. For reasons which prevented all the people from setting out together, it was necessary that some should go out ahead of the others to a convenient place where all should unite. The first left this camp of San Gabriel on the 23d of the month of June, eve of the Most Blessed Precursor, San Juan Bautista,[3] and having travelled for four days they reached the post or pueblo which is called Galisteo,[4] which is one of these first settlements.

There the greater part of the men came together in five or six days, and from there they commenced to march toward the east; and although at two leagues from this post there arose the difficulty of a large mountain which it was feared the carts could not ascend, our Lord was pleased to overcome it by opening a road through which they passed very

[1] It must be remembered that one of the avowed purposes of settling New Mexico was to explore beyond Quivira. Interest was greatly stimulated also by the report given by the Indian Jusephe.

[2] The Breve Relacion (*Doc. Inéd.*, XVI. 54) says that Oñate took eighty men, half of whom were rather a hindrance than a help. . . . The number of men is given in "Memorial sobre el Descubrimiento" (*Doc. Inéd.*, XVI. 198) as one hundred. In an inquiry made in Mexico by Factor Valverde, an eye-witness said that besides the carts Oñate had a hundred sumpter loads of provisions (*ibid.*, p. 221).

[3] St. John the Baptist.

[4] They descended the Rio Grande valley and crossed the mountains through the Galisteo Pass (see the Martínez map).

easily.   Having travelled five days we all came to a river in an opening, with peaceful waters, covered with shady groves of trees, some bearing fruits, and with very good fish.   Having reached the river on the eve of the learned and seraphic San Buenaventura, we named it San Buenaventura River.[1]

Next day we continued through some extensive plains with very abundant pasturage to another river which they call River of the Bagres[2] and justly so, because of the many catfish which it contains.   After the horses had rested we continued our journey, always going east, and in three days arrived at another river, which we named Magdalena,[3] having reached it on her day.   Although at first it did not appear promising, we having seen it at a point where it flowed sluggishly among some rocks, and as its banks were not inviting at this point, yet next day and on the other days during which we travelled along it we found it to be so verdant, pleasant, and so covered with vines and other fruits on all sides that we clearly saw that it was one of the best rivers which we had seen in all the Indies.   Here some Indians of the nation called Apachi came out with signs of peace.   The governor and the other men who were with him made them so many presents that they felt compelled, in view of the small number who had come at the first to see us, to return, and in a little while to come back to our camp with men, women and children, who ratified [the actions of the others] by raising their hands to the sun, which is the ceremony they use as a sign of friendship, and brought to us some small black and yellow fruit of the size of small tomatoes, which is plentiful on all that river.   It was as healthful as it was pleasant to taste, for although eaten freely it injured no one.

We took joyous leave and, enjoying the great improvement in the land which we saw each day, we travelled on, following the course of this river, although upon entering the

---

[1] The map shows the route to have been nearly south from Galisteo for some distance, parallel to the mountains, and then to turn sharply east, around the range.   The San Buenaventura was the Pecos, which was crossed above the junction.

[2] The River of Bagres was the Gallinas.

[3] The Canadian, which was reached just below the sharp turn to the east. The route from the Gallinas to that point evidently had been close to the south line of San Miguel County.

plains which they call Cibola or Cebolo we encountered some openings of rocks half detached, which are those which the mountains of this land give off. They caused the carts trouble, but with the great diligence of the good soldiers who were in charge of them they passed this difficult threshold very well and came out at some very extensive and pleasant plains, where scarcely any mountains like those passed could be seen.

Learning from the guide whom we were taking with us that all the country was now level, we began to travel with greater rapidity and with pleasure occasioned by the coming of the *maese de campo* with the rest of the men who remained behind. And like good soldiers, desirous of serving God our Lord and his Majesty, they were undismayed by the absence of four or five cowardly soldiers, who, frightened by military service as by a nightmare, turned their backs, just when the hopes of seeing grander things were becoming brighter. For these the country promised, since each day, as we descended, it seemed warmer, and it doubtless was warmer than the settlements from whence we had started.

At times it became necessary for us to depart from the main river in order to find a road for the carts; and although we feared the lack of watering places for the cattle, there are so many in this country that throughout the journey at distances of three or four leagues there was always sufficient water for the cattle and for the men; and in many places there were springs of very good water and groves of trees.

In some places we came across camps of people of the Apache nation, who are the ones who possess these plains, and who, having neither fixed place nor site of their own, go from place to place with the cattle always following them. We were not disturbed by them at all, although we were in their land, nor did any Indian become impertinent. We therefore passed on, always close to the river, and although on one day we might be delayed in our journey by a very heavy rain, such as are very common in those plains, on the following day and thereafter we journeyed on, sometimes crossing the river at very good fords.

Each day the land through which we were travelling became better, and the luxury of an abundance of fish from the river greatly alleviated the hardships of the journey. And the fruits gave no less pleasure, particularly the plums, of a hundred thousand different kinds, as mellow and good as those which grow in the choicest orchards of our land. They are so good that although eaten by thousands they never injured anybody. The trees were small, but their fruit was more plentiful than their leaves, and they were so abundant that in more than one hundred and fifty leagues, hardly a day passed without seeing groves of them, and also of grapevines such that although they hid the view in many places they produced sweet and delicious grapes. Because of this the people were very quiet and [not] inclined to injure us in any way, a favor granted by our Lord, for which we did not cease to praise Him and to render a thousand thanks, and in acknowledgment of which the majority of the people endeavored to unburden their consciences and their souls; and God being pleased that on the feast of the Porciuncula, which is the 2d of August, we should reach a place which from times past had been called Rio de San Francisco,[1] with very special devotion to the Most Blessed Confessor the greater part of the army confessed and received communion.

Proceeding on the day of the Glorious Levite and Martyr, San Lorenzo, God was pleased that we should begin to see those most monstrous cattle called *cibola*. Although they were very fleet of foot, on this day four or five of the bulls were killed, which caused great rejoicing. On the following day, continuing our journey, we now saw great droves of bulls and cows, and from there on the multitude which we saw was so great that it might be considered a falsehood by one who had not seen them, for, according to the judgment of all of us who were in any army, nearly every day and wherever we went as many cattle came out as are to be found in the largest ranches of New Spain;[2] and they were so tame that nearly always, unless they were chased or frightened,

---

[1] This is an indication that the country was known to this point. Forty leagues from the Pecos, Zaldívar had celebrated the feast of San Francisco, near a stream flowing from the Taos and Picuries. It was clearly the Canadian or a branch of it. He could hardly have been as far east as Oñate now was.

[2] Some of these are named on p. 219.

they remained quiet and did not flee. The flesh of these cattle is very good, and very much better than that of our cows. In general they are very fat, especially the cows, and almost all have a great deal of tallow. By experience we noted that they do not become angry like our cattle, and are never dangerous.

All these cattle are of one color, namely brown, and it was a great marvel to see a white bull in such a multitude. Their form is so frightful that one can only infer that they are a mixture of different animals. The bulls and the cows alike are humped, the curvature extending the whole length of the back and even over the shoulders. And although the entire body is covered with wool, on the hump, from the middle of the body to the head, the breast, and the forelegs, to just above the knee, the wool is much thicker, and so fine and soft that it could be spun and woven like that of the Castilian sheep. It is a very savage animal, and is incomparably larger than our cattle, although it looks small because of its short legs. Its hide is of the thickness of that of our cattle, and the native Indians are so expert in dressing the hides that they convert them into clothing. This river is thickly covered on all sides with these cattle and with another not less wonderful, consisting of deer which are as large as large horses. They travel in droves of two and three hundred and their deformity causes one to wonder whether they are deer or some other animal.[1]

Having travelled to reach this place one hundred and eleven leagues, it became necessary to leave the river, as there appeared ahead some sand dunes;[2] and turning from the east to the north, we travelled up a small stream until we discovered the great plains covered with innumerable cattle. We found constantly better roads and better land,

[1] Perhaps elk. The viceroy rather contemptuously remarks that besides buffalo Oñate saw "naught else but some birds and animals, particularly some deer out of all proportion in size" ("Breve relacion en sustancia del nuevo descubrimiento," in *Doc. Inéd.*, XVI. 53).

[2] Sand dunes are found at various places along the Canadian. The place where the turn was made seems to have been the Antelope Hills, just east of the Texas Panhandle. In this case the arroyo ascended was Commission Creek. From this point the route was apparently close to the line of the present Santa Fé Road from the Canadian to Wichita, Kansas.

such that the carts could travel without hindrance or difficulty, and although we encountered some large ravines and
broken hills, nowhere were there any over which the carts
had to pass, as the land was in general level and very easy
to traverse. We continued in this direction for some days,
along two small streams[1] which flowed toward the east, like
the one previously mentioned. We wandered from the direction we had been following, though it did not frighten
us much, as the land was so level that daily the men became
lost in it by separating themselves for but a short distance
from us, as a result of which it was necessary to reconnoitre
the country from some of the stopping places. Therefore the
camp continued its march by the most direct route possible.

In order to further insure our safety, the governor and
adelantado decided to send ahead the *maese de campo* with
some companions, and, with the lucky star which ever guides
him, in a short time he returned, having found many signs
of people, and a country full of pasture lands, which was
the matter of deepest concern, since they had been lacking
for several days, as there had been none for many leagues,
for the fields there were covered with flowers of a thousand
different kinds, so thick that they choked the pasture. The
cattle of this territory must eat these flowers far better than
ours are wont to do, because wherever they were there were
multitudes of cattle. Great was the joy felt by all at this
good news, because it was what they were hoping for. With
the forethought and diligence of the *maese de campo*, which, like
a good soldier, he always displayed in matters of war, he had
his people prepared and ordered for whatever might happen;
and all together we continued our journey and route and
reached a small river, carrying little water but so grown with
timber that its banks resembled thickly wooded mountains.
Here we found many walnut trees loaded with nuts which were
nearly as good as those of our country, the trees being taller
and having more abundant foliage, and the land being so
grown with pasture that it could scarcely be seen. Having
slept one night in this pleasant spot, we went on next day
three leagues from this point to where flowed a river carrying more water than the last one, and with many fish and

---

[1] These were Beaver Creek (North Fork) and Cimarron River.

larger groves, both of walnuts and of oak, and other valuable timbers. The land was better than that which we had hitherto seen, so good indeed that all said that they never had seen any better in their lives. The cattle were innumerable, and of all kinds of game there was a great abundance—Castilian partridges, turkeys, deer, and hares.

From this point the *maese de campo* began again to explore the country, and having travelled three leagues he discovered a large ranchería, with more than five thousand souls; and although the people were warlike, as it later developed, and although at first they began to place themselves in readiness to fight, by signs of peace they were given to understand that we were not warriors, and they became so friendly with us that some of them came that night to our camp and entertained us with wonderful reports of the people further on. Having heard these reports, at daybreak next day the whole camp marched on through this good country, bounded on both sides by the coolest of rivers and by pleasant groves.

At three in the afternoon we arrived within an arquebus shot of this ranchería, and at some pools that were there we stopped with due care and precaution. From there the governor and the religious went with more than thirty armed horsemen to reconnoitre the people and the ranchería,[1] and they, all drawn up in regular order in front of their ranchos, began to raise the palms of their hands towards the sun, which is the sign of peace among them. Assuring them that peace was what we wanted, all the people, women, youths, and small children, came to where we were; and they consented to our visiting their houses, which all consisted of branches an *estado* and a half long, placed in a circle, some of them being so wide that they were ninety feet in diameter. Most of them were covered with tanned hides, which made them resemble tents. They were not a people who sowed or reaped, but they lived solely on the cattle. They were ruled

[1] Called on the map and in other sources the Escanjaques. Sometimes corrupted to Escansaques. The map gives it six hundred houses, and other sources give it five thousand or six thousand inhabitants. It was not a permanent village, but a temporary camp (see "Breve relacion en sustancia del descubrimiento," p. 53; "Memorial sobre el Descubrimiento," p. 199).

and governed by chiefs, and like communities which are freed from subjection to any lord, they obeyed their chiefs but little. They had large quantities of hides which, wrapped about their bodies, served them as clothing, but the weather being hot, all of the men went about nearly naked, the women being clothed from the waist down. Men and women alike used bows and arrows, with which they were very dexterous.

We learned while here that this nation was at war with the people settled eight leagues distant towards the interior, and they, thinking that we were going to avenge the murder of the Spaniards who had entered with Umaña, of course took the opportunity to throw the blame upon their enemies and to tell us that it was they who had killed them. Thinking that we were going for this purpose only, they were much pleased, and offered to accompany us, and as we were unable to prevent it, lest we should cause them to make trouble, they went.

They guided us to a river[1] seven leagues from this place, with wonderful banks, and, although level, so densely wooded that the trees formed thick and wide groves. Here we found a small fruit the size of the wild pear or yellow sapodilla, of very good flavor. The river contained an abundance of very good fish, and although at some points it had good fords, in other parts it was extremely deep and vessels could sail on it with ease. It flowed due east,[2] and its waters were fresh and pleasant to taste. Here the land was fertile and much better than that which we had passed. The pastures were so good that in many places the grass was high enough to conceal a horse. The Indians who came with us to this place, in a few hours quickly built a ranchería as well established as the one left behind, which caused no little wonder to all, with the intention of there awaiting the result of our journey, or of awaiting us on our return with evil intent, as later developed, when they threw off their disguise and shamefully made war on us.

We set out from this place the next day, and, leaving the river and passing through some pleasant plains, after having

---

[1] This stream was clearly the Arkansas.

[2] See p. 252, note 3. These two emphatic statements regarding the course of the great river where it was encountered cannot be overlooked.

travelled four leagues we began to see people who appeared upon some elevations of a hill. Although hostile to this nation they came on, inviting us to battle and war, shouting and throwing dirt into the air, which is the sign used in all this region to proclaim cruel war. Three or four hundred people awaited us in peace, and by the signs which one side was able to make to the other we were assured of friendship. Peace being made, some of these people came to us, and throwing among us some beads which they wore about their necks, proclaimed themselves our friends. They invited us to their houses, but as it was already late it was not possible to go that day, and it became necessary to go to the banks of a large river[1] called the Rio de San Francisco, whose banks in these parts were most beautiful to look upon and were covered with mulberry trees and other trees bearing fruit of very fine flavor. Many people constantly came and went to see us, bringing ears of maize, which were the first we had seen in this good country, and some round loaves of bread, as large as shields and three or four fingers thick, made of the same maize.

All that night we took the necessary care and precaution, but at dawn the following day the people who had represented themselves as friendly to us were stationed at our rear in a great multitude, threatening the other tribe "to beat a Roldan," and awaiting their chance to attack them. We inquiring again regarding the country, they told us that in this region they had murdered the Spaniards,[2] surrounding them with fire and burning them all, and that they had with them one who had escaped, injured by the fire.[3] Counsel and opinion being taken as to what must be done in a matter of such importance, it was decided to seize some Indians, both to take with us as guides and also to verify the statements of their enemies, and it was a fortunate coincidence that their chief, or captain, whom they call Catarax, was there at the time. It was remarkable to note how they obeyed him and served him, like a people more united, peace-

---

[1] This was evidently the same river as that just previously mentioned.

[2] The Humaña party.

[3] Presumably the mulatto woman told of by Father Zárate (*Relacion*, in *Land of Sunshine*, XII. 45).

ful, and settled.   As evidence of this it is enough to say that
while they might with justice have become aroused because
of his arrest, they did not do so, merely because he signalled
to them that they should withdraw.[1]

We took him with us, treating him well, as was proper,
and in order to carry out our plans we crossed the river, at
a very good ford.   Having travelled half a league we came
to a settlement containing more than twelve hundred houses,
all established along the bank of another good-sized river
which flowed into the large one.[2]   They were all round, built
of forked poles and bound with rods, and on the outside
covered to the ground with dry grass.   Within, on the sides,
they had frameworks or platforms[3] which served them as
beds on which they slept.   Most of them were large enough
to hold eight or ten persons.[4]   They were two lance-lengths
high and all had granaries or platforms, an *estado* high, which
they must have used in summer, and which would hold three
or four persons, being most appropriate for enjoying the
fresh air.   They entered them through a small grass door.
They ascended to this platform by means of a movable wooden
ladder.   Not a house lacked these platforms.   We found the
pueblo entirely deserted but not lacking maize, of which
there was much and of good quality.   For this reason the
enemy wished to sack it; but in no manner were they per-

---

[1] Father Zárate says that Catarax was rescued.   He says: "The ambassa-
dor did not dare to cross the river which separated them from the Spaniards;
but the adelantado sent some soldiers to try to catch him from behind, which
they did, and put irons on him.   He was an Indian of importance.   But the
Indians had a sharper trick; for making a feint of attack, while the Spaniards
were getting the arms, they took care to carry off the prisoner bodily, ironed as
he was" (*Relacion*, par. 38, *Land of Sunshine*, XII. 45).

[2] The stream was the Arkansas.   The two streams crossed just below were
branches of the Ne-Ne-Schah, as is clear from the Martínez map, where the second
is called Rio del Robredal.   Such a network of streams is found on the border
of Sedgwick and Kingman counties, and another in Reno County.   After leaving
the ranchería, Oñate turned north and reached the Arkansas opposite the mouth
of a stream coming in from the north.   This could be either the Little Arkansas,
at Wichita, or Cow Creek, at Hutchinson.   The statement that the river flowed
east points to Hutchinson, but ethnological considerations point to Wichita.
The Indians were probably the Jumano (Wichita, Panipiquet).

[3] *Canicos, i. e.,* cañizos.

[4] This description fits the Wichita grass lodges.

mitted to do so,[1] nor to do any damage except to take away a little maize. Thereupon the governor dismissed them and gave them express commands to go to their ranchería, which they did.

We remained here for one day in this pleasant spot surrounded on all sides by fields of maize and crops of the Indians. The stalks of the maize were as high as that of New Spain and in many places even higher. The land was so rich that, having harvested the maize, a new growth of a span in height had sprung up over a large portion of the same ground, without any cultivation or labor other than the removal of the weeds and the making of holes where they planted the maize. There were many beans, some gourds, and, between the fields, some plum trees. The crops were not irrigated but dependent on the rains, which, as we noted, must be very regular in that land, because in the month of October it rained as it does in August in New Spain. It was thought certain that it had a warm climate, for the people we saw went about naked, although they wore skins. Like the other settled Indians they utilize cattle in large numbers. It is incredible how many there are in that land.

Here we took new information from the Indian, who appeared to be one of the *caciques* or lords of the land, regarding what there was further ahead, and he informed us that up the river were settled people like these in large numbers, and that at one side was another large river which divided into six or seven branches,[2] on all of which there were many people, and that the people whom Umaña had brought had been killed eighteen days' journey from here. We compared the statements of these Indians with those of Indians of the ranchería who had remained in our company, and without discrepancy in any point they said the same, adding that down the river also, going due east, it was all settled by

[1] Eyewitnesses declared in Mexico that the Escanjaques had already begun to burn some of the houses when Oñate forbade it (*Doc. Inéd.*, XVI. 225). Zárate adds that Oñate's interference was at the instance of Father Velasco, who, "moved with pity for the damage which those Indians kept doing, prayed the adelantado that they be on hand amid the damage" (*Land of Sunshine*, XII. 45).

[2] The Kansas River answers this description. Between Manhattan and Saline, a distance of some fifty miles or more, it divides into the Big Blue, the Republican, the Solomon, the Saline, and the Smoky Hill Rivers, not to mention several smaller streams.

people. They accordingly persuaded us that under no circumstances should we proceed, saying that the people who
had withdrawn from this settlement had done so in order
on the third day to assemble their friends, who were so numerous that in the course of a whole day they would not be
able to pass by their houses, and that undoubtedly, our number being so small, they would soon put an end to us, not a
single person escaping.

Although this spurred us on to go ahead, on the following
day, having travelled three leagues, all the way through a
populated district,[1] and seeing that the houses continued
beyond, and having positive knowledge of the large assem-
blage of people which was awaiting us, it was necessary to
take counsel as to what should be done. And seeing that
the horses and mules were tired out and exhausted, because
of the many leagues travelled, and that the chief purpose
of our journey had been achieved, and that his Majesty
would be better served by learning the wonders of this land,
that he might issue the orders most necessary to the royal
service and to the acceleration of the salvation of these souls,
and seeing that it would be foolhardy for our small number
to proceed where more than three hundred persons[2] were
necessary, it was unanimously agreed to present a petition
to the governor and adelantado, representing to him the
combination of just reasons for not proceeding, making known
to him how much greater service would be rendered to his
Majesty by informing him of the fertility of the soil, of its
many people, of the wealth of the innumerable cattle, so
beyond number that they alone would suffice to enrich thousands of men with suet, tallow, and hides; of the suitable-
ness of the land for founding many important settlements,
fortunately possessing all materials necessary for the purpose;
and above all, of how important it was that the King our
Lord should speedily learn what all the world had so much
desired to know, so that his Majesty's orders might be carried

---

[1] This assertion is borne out by other documents. For the doings of the
Spaniards at the pueblo see *Doc. Inéd.*, XVI. 54, 199, 225; Zárate, *Relacion*,
pars. 38–39, in *Land of Sunshine*, XII. 45–46.

[2] That number was asked for later by Oñate through Zaldívar for the purpose.

out; and although it was a hard blow to the governor's courage and bravery, and though he was very sorry to curtail
his journey, upon realizing the justness of the petition[1] made
in his Majesty's name, he granted it.

Having travelled up to this point more than two hundred and twenty leagues,[2] matters were rearranged so as to
return as speedily as possible. On reaching the place whence
we had set out the previous day, which was that of the first
settlement, unsuspecting any treason, we found therein the
Indians who at first had pretended to be friends, now converted into cruel enemies, and entrenched within the same
houses,[3] ready to carry out their evil intent. This being
so contrary to our intent, the *maese de campo* had gone forward half a league with a dozen companions, without taking
any military precautions, to explore the land. When he
reached the point where the people were they failed to come
out with signs of peace, but on the run began to surround
him and his companions, with bows and arrows in their
hands; but he, like a good soldier, did not give them a chance
to do so, for, retreating in good order, he emerged from among
them with no more damage than the loss of a horse or a couple
of arrow wounds.

Seeing the treason and that it was necessary to pass where
they were, or very near to them, the governor ordered that
all the men should provide themselves with armored horses,
which they always had with them, and, the *maese de campo*
telling them what they should do, the whole camp marched
forward with express orders that all should enter in peace,
since they had not come to injure anybody; but although
they did all this, and entered with the signal which the Indians used, which was to raise their hands as a token of peace,
those who most desired war began it with very great fury,
presenting in their first stand more than fifteen hundred persons, who, placed in order in a semicircle, attacked with great
valor and force.

[1] Other sources show that the men made a written request to go back (see
Doc. Inéd., XVI. 225).
[2] This is important evidence regarding the route. The point where the
Canadian was left was midway of the journey.
[3] The houses of the Quiviras.

The governor, noting that they did not cease their attack, that the shower of arrows was great, and that they made no sign [of peace], gave the signal to his people to defend themselves; and, the battle thickening on both sides, it pleased God our Lord to take our part, for without this aid it would have been almost impossible, as their people were multiplying. The brave soldiers showed an excess of courage and spirit, and in a short while repelled the attack of the people, killing and wounding many of a group who were stationed at an *arroyo*, whereas only two of our soldiers were wounded. But the battle continued and the Indians became more furious than at the beginning, keeping it up for more than two hours with the greatest of courage, although at their own cost, for they proved the valor of the Spanish nation.[1] At the end of this time, the greater part of our men being wounded, though not dangerously in any case, the adelantado and governor, seeing the great barbarity of our enemies, and that many of them were dead, and that they were not to be frightened and would not turn their backs, ordered his men to retreat; and, freeing some women whom the soldiers had captured, he would not consent that they be further injured, although they took some boys upon the request of the religious, in order to instruct them in the matters of our holy Catholic faith, and an Indian who could furnish information of all this land.[2]

Thereupon we returned to the camp to sleep, and, the

[1] The "Memorial sobre el Descubrimiento," p. 199, states that "they had with them an obstinate struggle, from which most of the men came out wounded." Members of the expedition declared in Mexico that "they fought with the entire army from ten in the morning till night, thirty soldiers being wounded" (*Doc. Inéd.*, XVI. 225). By the time Father Zárate wrote the event had become a great victory for the Spaniards, in which nearly one thousand Escanjaques were slaughtered (Zárate, *Relacion*, par. 38, in *Land of Sunshine*, XII. 45).

[2] His name was Miguel. He was a captive, and according to his own statement a Tancoa. In Mexico he told much about gold, and he drew a map for the factor Vergara, a copy of which, from the original, I have in my possession. Father Zárate tells of a map drawn by him in the possession of the Duke of the Infantado, Spain. According to Zárate, his reports induced the king to order an expedition of one thousand men, one-half furnished by a private individual, to be sent to the north country. The viceroy, Count of Monterey, did not think much of Miguel's testimony (see *Doc. Inéd.*, XVI. 54–55, 199, 212; Zárate, *Relacion*, in *Land of Sunshine*, XII. 46).

wounded having recovered, on the following day we set out, travelling with our usual care, and in fifty-nine days we reached this camp of San Gabriel, having spent in the entire journey the time from the 23d of June until the 24th of November.

The carts went over the country to the settlements very nicely, and so far as the nature of the land was concerned they could have gone as far as the North Sea,[1] which could not have been very far, because some of the Indians wore shells from it on their foreheads.   May God our Lord be forever praised, and may He be pleased to hasten the salvation of so many souls, and may He have pity on this land, so that in it His holy gospel may be preached and many poor souls be saved, for, judging from what we have seen, it must in time become their place of refuge and bring wealth to many.

Auto.

In the pueblo of San Gabriel of New Mexico, Señor Don Juan de Oñate, governor, captain-general, and adelantado of this kingdom of New Mexico, said that whereas his Lordship had set out from this camp to make an expedition to the great settlement which lies towards the north, in which undertaking he spent five months in going and returning, that he might be able to give to the king our lord and to whom he might deem it proper an account of all that might be discovered or all that might happen, he entrusted the writing of the said account to a person of much fidelity and trustworthiness, who prepared it;[2] and that it might be examined and learned whether what it contains is the truth, or if there is anything to be taken from it or added to it, in order that his Majesty might be more truthfully informed, he ordered that it be read to all the persons who went with his Lordship on said journey, that they might declare under oath if it were true, and, that

---

[1] In Mexico the authorities concluded that the point reached must have been about three hundred leagues from the North Sea and the same distance from the South Sea, and in lat. 39° or 40°.   They were not so far wrong regarding the latitude.   On this Bancroft was in error.

[2] It has not been determined who wrote it.

done, to take the other necessary steps.   Thus he ordered and signed on the 14th day of December, 1601.

Don JUAN DE OÑATE.

Before me, JUAN GUTIERREZ BOCANEGRA, secretary.

Authentication.

On this said day the said Señor governor requested the Reverend Father Fray Francisco de Velasco, guardian of the monastery of the pueblo, and the commissary who went on the said journey, and Father Fray Pedro de Vergara, lay-brother who also went on the said journey, to make a declaration according to the above *auto*.   In compliance therewith, the said Fray Francisco de Valesco took oath, placing his hand upon his breast in *verbis sacerdotis*, as is the custom, and the said Fray Pedro de Vergara took oath in due form, in the name of God and with the sign of a cross.   They promised to tell the truth, and, having seen the above account of the governor, they testified that all it contains is the truth, and that which actually occurred, and what they saw on the journey which they had made with the Señor governor, and that it contains no exaggerations, as everything occurred as stated therein, and the said Reverend Father Fray Francisco de Velasco signed the same.   The said Fray Pedro de Vergara did not sign as he did not know how.   All this they said with permission from the Very Rev. Father Fray Juan Descalona, their commissary general, which he gave to them in my presence, to all of which I testify.

Fray FRANCISCO DE VELASCO.

Before me, JUAN GUTIERREZ BOCANEGRA, secretary.

On this said day, month, and year, the said governor having ordered that all the captains and soldiers who went with him on the said journey should assemble, and all being assembled, I, the present secretary, read to them the whole of the relation, word for word, and I asked them if it were true, because they would have to swear to it; and all together they stated that the said account, so far as pertains to the report of the many people living beyond,[1] was not sufficient, because

[1] That is, beyond the New Discovery.

all the Indians had represented the settlements as follows: their ranchería, containing more than five or six thousand souls, they represented by making a circle[1] with seventeen kernels of maize; and for many of the settlements beyond they placed in the circles many grains of maize; and for one in particular they placed seven hundred and twenty-seven kernels of maize, which, in the opinion of all or most of those who were present, meant two hundred thousand people and more, and this in but one of the many settlements which they indicated. This, they said, was lacking in the said relation, and that all of it and of this was the truth by the oath which they had taken in due form; and that on the rivers where these many people were there was a great quantity of sumac, and other things which, if they were utilized, would be of great benefit. All who were able to do so signed it, and for those who could not write a witness signed, the witnesses to all the above being Captain Bartolome Romero, Captain Antonio Gomez Montelirios, and Alonso Naranjo, and I the said secretary, who testifies to the same.—Vicente de Çaldivar Mendoza, Juan de Vitoria Carbajal, Juan de Moreno de la Rua, Gaspar Lopez de Tabora, Juan Martinez de Montoya, Bartolome Gonzalez de Almocer, Don Pedro de Trugillo Gallegos, Francisco Garcia, Juan Munoz, Diego Martin de Guebara, Juan de Mallea, Francisco Vido, Don Cristobal de Oñate, Pedro Barela, Juan de la Cruz, Simon de la Paz, Juan Rodriguez, Rodrigo Zapata, Miguel de Villaviciosa, Miguel Montero de Castro, Juan Belarde, Alonso Nuñez Inojosa, Alonso Robledo, Juan Ranjel, Francisco Rascon, Juan de Leon. Witnesses, Alonso Gomez Montesinos, Baltasar Martinez Coxedor, Alonso Sanchez, Isidro Juarez de Figueroa. Before me, JUAN GUTIERREZ BOCANEGRA, secretary.

And I, the said Juan Gutierrez Bocanegra, secretary and captain of this kingdom, was present at all this, and have signed it by order of the governor, who here signed his name. I made this copy from the original, which remains in the government archives. It is a true copy, in witness whereof I here sign. Don JUAN DE OÑATE. JUAN GUTIERREZ BOCANEGRA, secretary.

[1] On the map made by the Indian Miguel settlements were likewise represented by circles.

JOURNEY OF OÑATE TO CALIFORNIA BY LAND, [ZÁRATE, 1626]

Journey of Don Juan de Oñate to California by Land.[1]

44. IN the year 1604, on the 7th of the month of October, Don Juan de Oñate set out from the villa of San Gabriel to discover the South Sea. He took in his company Father Fray Francisco de Escobar, who was then commissary of those provinces, and a lay-brother called Fray Juan de Buenaventura, apostolic men; and the Father Commissary was a very learned man and had a gift for languages, as he learned them all with great facility. He took on this journey thirty soldiers,[2] most of them raw recruits, and they did not carry more than fourteen pairs of horse armor. After having travelled towards the west sixty leagues, they arrived at the province of Çuñi, which is in some plains more inhabited by hares and rabbits than by Indians. There are six pueblos; in all of them there are no more than three hundred terraced houses of many stories, like those of New Mexico. The largest pueblo and head of all is the pueblo of Cíbola, which in their language is called Havico.[3] It has one hundred and ten houses. The food, like that general in all the land, is maize, beans, gourds, and wild game. They dress in *mantas* of *iztli*[4] woven of twisted cord. These Indians have no cotton. They set out from this pueblo, and having travelled twenty leagues[5] between northwest and west they arrived at the province of Mooqui. There are five pueblos and in all four hundred and fifty houses—the same kind[6] of houses and *mantas* of cotton.

---

[1] Zárate Salmerón, *Relaciones de . . . Nuevo Mexico*, paragraphs 44–57, in *Doc. Hist. Mex.*, tercera série, III., 30–38 (Mexico, 1856).

[2] *Soldodos*, a corruption of *soldados* in the text.

[3] Hawikuh. See Hodge, *Handbook*, I. 539.   [4] See note 7, p. 235, above.

[5] Oñate gave the distance as twenty-two leagues to the first pueblo and thirty-two to the last.

[6] It is quite certain that there is a corruption here. The sense is better satisfied by "manner" (*manera*) in place of "number" (*número*).

45. In the province of Zuñi are deposits of silver of so fine a blue that they use it for paint and carry it to sell to the settlements of New Mexico. I brought some stones to show, and the painters told me it was the best blue in the world, and that in this city[1] each pound of it was worth twelve *pesos*, and that there was not a pound to be had. Likewise the green of New Mexico, in particular that of Homex,[2] is extremely fine in the leaf; and of these two sorts whole cargoes could be gathered to bring here.

46. They set out from Mooqui and at ten leagues toward the west they arrived at the Colorado River.[3] They called it thus because the water is nearly red; the river runs from southeast to northwest, afterwards turning to the west, and they say it enters California. From here to where it empties into the sea there are more than a hundred leagues of pine forests. From this river they travelled toward the west, crossing a mountain range of pine forest which was eight leagues across, on whose southern slope runs the San Antonio River, seventeen leagues distant from San Jose,[4] which is the Colorado; it runs from north to south through rough mountains and very high cliffs. It carries little water, but has many good fish. From this river forward the land has a temperate climate. Five leagues farther on toward the west is the Sacramento River.[5] It has as much water as the San Antonio, and as many and as good fish. It rises eleven leagues towards the west, and runs from northwest to southeast, along the skirts of some very high mountains where the Spaniards took out very good ores;[6] and there are many mineral deposits. Until they arrived at this place the Spaniards had not found anything that satisfied them. The place is very well suited for the dwelling of the Spaniards; it is a place where reduction

---

[1] The City of Mexico.   [2] Xémez.

[3] The Little Colorado; the Río de la Alameda of Farfán. Farfán gave the distance, perhaps from a different pueblo, as nine leagues.

[4] Farfán gave the distance from the Little Colorado to the Agua del Valle as thirteen and one-half leagues. It is probable that the San Antonio River is the same. From the course described, it is clearly the western branch of the Rio Verde.

[5] Farfán reached "a very good river" at six leagues from the Agua del Valle.

[6] From this it is inferred that prospecting was done in a region farther east than that in which Farfán did most of his.

works can be erected; there are good lands for crops, beautiful fields and pasture for stock, and plentiful water. In this
mountain range the Cruzados Indians[1] have their homes.
They live in scattered dwellings,[2] the houses being of straw;
they plant no crops; they live on the game which they kill,
deer and mountain sheep, of which there are many. With
the skins both the men and women cover their loins; all go
shod, little and big. They also use for food *mescali*, which is
a preserve of the root of maguey.

47. They call these Indians Cruzados on account of some
crosses which all, little and big, suspend from the lock of hair
that falls over the forehead; and this they do when they see
the Spaniards. The origin of this custom was not known at
that time; subsequently it has been learned that many years
ago there travelled through that land a religious of my father
San Francisco who told them that if at any time they should
see men bearded and white, in order that they might not molest
or injure them they should put on those crosses, which is a
thing esteemed by them. They remembered it so well that
they have not forgotten it. The men are well-featured and
noble; the women are handsome, with beautiful eyes, and
they are affectionate.[3] These Indians said that the sea was
distant from there twenty days' journey, of those which they
travel, which are calculated at about five leagues. It is to
be noticed that none of these nations was caught in a lie.
They also said that two days' journey from there was a river
of little water,[4] by which they went to another very large one[5]
which enters into the sea, and on whose banks there was a
nation called Amacava,[6] and, a short distance beyond, many
nations who plant and gather maize, beans, and gourds.

They left the Sacramento River, travelling between west
and southwest fifteen leagues, finding at every step good water-
ing-places. They arrived at the river of little water; it is

---

[1] The Yavapai. See note to the Farfán documents, p. 242, above, note 2.
Farfán encountered the Cruzados two leagues beyond the Agua del Valle. This
confirms the conclusion that the latter was identical with the San Antonio River.

[2] "Son rancheros." A *rancho* usually meant a separate house; a *ranchería*,
a group of houses. To say that they are ranchers conveys an entirely erroneous
idea.

[3] The Yavapai women are still noted for their good looks.

[4] Bill Williams Fork.   [5] The Colorado.   [6] Mohave.

called San Andrés.[1] *From here the country has a hot climate.
There were many *pitayas*[2] and different kinds of trees. They
travelled along it twenty-four leagues, and arrived at the large
river, which they sought because of the report which the Indians had given. It is called Buena Esperanza River,[3] and
at the sea it is called Tizon River. It carries as much water
as the Duero, and is as quiet as the Guadalquivir. It runs
from northwest to southeast and soon forms a narrow channel
between high mountains which cross it; and after passing
these narrows it flows from northwest [*sic*] to southwest, having on both sides very high mountains[4] which run in the same
direction, forming on the banks a wide river bottom.*[5]

48. The next day after having arrived, the adelantado sent
Captain Gerónimo Márquez with four soldiers up the river to
discover this nation of the Amacavas Indians. In a short
time he brought two Indians, whom the adelantado regaled
and sent to call the rest. They said that they would do it
and that they would bring something to eat. On the day
following, as the adelantado saw that the Indians were making loads, he ordered that twelve soldiers should prepare to
go to the settlement for provisions; but before the soldiers
went, there arrived more than forty Indians loaded with
maize, beans, and gourds. Then arose an Indian who was
called Curraca, which in their language means Lord, and made
a long speech, giving to understand, as was supposed, that he
was pleased to have seen the Spaniards and that he desired
their friendship.

49. Here was heard the first news of the Lake of Copalla,[6]
whence they suppose the Mexicans set out who settled this
New Spain. They described this lake and land and all its

---

[1] The main stream of Bill Williams Fork. The name San Andrés was given
to one of the richest mines discovered by the Farfán party.

[2] *Pitahaya*, the *cereus giganteus*, whose fruit was much used as food by the
tribes of the Southwest.

[3] The Colorado River. It is about fifty miles from the junction of Big
Sandy and Santa Maria rivers to the Colorado.

[4] The Chocolate Mountains run parallel with the river, on both sides, for a
long distance.

[5] The lines between the * * are omitted from the translation in the *Land
of Sunshine.* See vol. XII., p. 48.

[6] The country sought by Ibarra in 1563 was called Copala.

banks as densely populated. An Indian said Copalla very plainly, and Captain Gerónimo Márquez told me that, hearing those Indians talk to a Mexican Indian, servant of a soldier, one of them asked, "Whence comes this man? Is he perhaps from Copalla? because those from there talk thus." And those Indians also said that those of that language wore bracelets of gold, on the wrists and on the fleshy part of the arms and in their ears, and that from there they were fourteen days' journey, of those which they travelled. They pointed to this language between west and northwest. The Indians also said that the Spaniards could travel by this river bottom all the way to the sea, and that it was ten days' journey, of those which they travel, and that it was all populated. This river can be navigated.

They set out from here and travelled five leagues without seeing Indians, because the mountain was very rough and the road narrow and steep; but beyond this narrow pass there is a wide river bottom, very thickly settled. Here as many Indians came out with food to receive the Spaniards as in the last ranchería. They are of the same nation. Being asked about the sea they said that down the river it was nine days' journey, but if they crossed the river it was only four. This river they kept on the north and they travelled toward the northwest. It did not seem proper to the adelantado to leave off following the river down stream, so he continued, travelling through its bottom lands, seeing always many Indians, asking all of them about the sea, which they now knew was called "acilla," and all answered pointing to the west, northwest, north, northeast, and east, saying that thus the sea curved, and was rather near, for they said that from the other side of the river it was only four days' journey, and that that Gulf of California is not closed,[1] but is an arm of the sea which corresponds to the North Sea and coast of Florida. All the Indians of this river are comely and good-featured; and the women are handsome, and whiter than those of New Spain, being people of whom the men go naked and the women[2] in skins, having the

---

[1] Father Zárate was writing at a time when it was generally believed that California was an island, which was not the case when Oñate made his journey. See the relation by Father Ascensión.

[2] *Ellos* for *ellas*.

loins covered. Always when these Indians travel they carry
a lighted firebrand in the hand, for which I think it should
be called Tizon River. Thus declared a soldier of this journey
who had gone with Sebastian Vizcaino to California; he said
that he went in search of the Tizon River, and I believe that
had he reached it he would not have returned, as he did, for
lack of food, because there is much here.

50. Having passed this nation of Amacabos, of which, as
of the others, they saw only what was along the road, they arrived at the nation of Bahacechas.[1] The language is almost
the same, they are friends, and they communicate with each
other. The dwellings of all those of this river are low, of wood,
and covered with earth. The chief of this nation is called
Cohota. He came out with a great following to the road to
receive the Spaniards and to beg them not to pass on that
day, but to remain over night in his pueblo; and this was
done to please him. This Indian and his people told of many
things and secrets of the land. They asked them about the
lake of Copalla and he said the same as has been told; and on
showing them a gold toothpick, he put it to his wrist as if
putting it around, giving to understand that the Indians of
that lake wore bracelets of that material. The adelantado
showed them a coral, and being asked where there was some
of that, they pointed toward the south. They said that the
Indians of the coast took them out of the sea, and that the sea
when it is rough casts many ashore, and that the Indians dig
in the sand and take it out to sell. This about the coral was
said by all the Indians where they passed, and it was seen to
be the truth, as much was found in the possession of the Indian women.

51. After having passed this place, and while resting in
the pueblo of Captain Otata, of the same nation, they asked
him and his people some questions and showed them some
silver buttons; and they declared, in the presence of many
soldiers, that near there, pointing toward the west, there was
much of that substance, and that it was called ñañe querro.
They showed them a silver spoon, and as soon as they saw it
they said that the bowls and pots from which they ate were

---

[1] Bandelier thought this tribe to be either a branch of the Mohave or of the
Huallapais. Arch. Inst. of Am. *Papers*, III. 110.

of the same substance, and they indicated that they were very big and deep. They rolled a plate of silver so that it would make a noise, giving to understand that the others sound the same when they fall on the ground, and that they do not break; and putting a silver plate on the fire with water in it they said that in the place they told about they boiled meat in those articles; but that the others, although they were of the same material, were large. And this performance was of their own accord, without anyone's suggesting it to them. And striking the plate several times with a knife and letting it fall upon it with violence, so that it would make more noise, they said that the others sounded the same, and that they were no farther than five days' journey from there, drawing on the ground the sea, and in the middle of it an island, which they call Ziñogaba, which is the name of the nation that inhabits it. To this island one goes by sea in canoes or boats, and since from the coast there it is only one day's sail, they set out in the morning and are there before sunset. They showed on the ground the size of the boat, drawing a line on the ground; he commenced to measure, and the boat was seventy feet long and twenty wide. On asking them if the boat carried a sail in the middle, the Indian took a stick and put it in the middle of the boat which he had drawn, with an Indian at the stern, making as if he managed the rudder. He then took a cloth and, stretching out his arms on the stick that he had set up, started to run as fast as he could, saying that thus the others ran through the water, and much faster. It is certain that if the Indians had not seen it they would not know how to draw it so perfectly. They said also that the inhabitants of that island all wear around the neck and in the ears pearl shells, which they call "xicullo." They also told of an instrument with which they make the sound when they dance. It is a long stick from which are pendant many pieces of that metal of which they make dishes from which they eat; and, making a great noise, they dance in pairs to the sound.

52. With all these reports, the adelantado did not wish to leave off going in search of a port, as it was so easy to see, with the advantage of guides, for they volunteered for that purpose. Having passed this nation of Bahacecha they ar-

rived at the nation of Ozaras[1] Indians, a difficult tongue; the Indians are ill-featured, less affable, and from them little satisfaction and less security can be had. These Indians are settled along a large river, although not of as much water as that of Buena Esperanza. It is called Nombre de Jesus River;[2] it runs between bare mountains, and flows into the Buena Esperanza from southeast to northwest, twenty leagues before reaching the sea. It was learned that all the river is inhabited by this nation, and that the people are numerous. They drew on the ground twenty rancherías or pueblos of this nation. They make *mantas* of cotton; the dress and hair are different from the rest; the hair is long and they wear it braided, and then covered with a cloth or deer skin. The river makes many basins[3] in this meadow. Here they saw some good and sweet oak acorns, which the Indians said were from the other side of the river, and that there were many of them. On asking about the source of the Buena Esperanza River, the Indians said that it is near the sea, toward the northwest, and that from its source to where it enters the sea it is one hundred and sixty leagues, all populated, and that at its source range buffaloes and deer of the kind as big as horses, from which it is seen that it is good level country and well watered.

From this river of Nombre de Jesus to the sea it is very thickly settled with more people than had been seen hitherto; but the language is like that of Bahacecha,[4] and if it is not the same, they differ very little. The dress, the manner of living, and the houses are the same, and they are well-featured and comely. All came out to receive the Spaniards, and offered them their food. Among these Indians were found many white pearl-shells and other shells, very large and shining, which they make into squares[5] and drills, which are very sightly. These Indians said that on the coast toward the west there were many of those shells, and they indicated that the sea ran behind a very large mountain, on the skirts of which the Buena Esperanza River enters the sea. From these Indians they again informed themselves anew of all the things

---

[1] Supposed by Bandelier to be the Maricopa. Arch. Inst. of Am. *Papers*, III. 110.

[2] "Name of Jesus"; the Gila.

[3] *Orteros*.   [4] The Yuman.   [5] Translation uncertain.

that Captain Otata had told of,[1] and they did not differ in anything. And showing them a pearl, they gave it a name and said there were many and very large. And one Indian, coming up to the Father Commissary and taking a rosary of large beads that he wore on his neck, said that there were pearls as large and thick as the beads of that rosary; and in regard to the island of Ziñogaba, they said that the mistress or chieftainess of it was a giantess, and that she was called Ciñacacohola, which means chieftainess or mistress. They pictured her as the height of a man-and-a-half of those of the coast, and like them very corpulent, very broad, and with big feet; and that she was old, and that she had a sister, also a giantess, and that there was no man of her kind, and that she did not mingle with anyone of the island. The mystery of her reigning on that island could not be solved, whether it was by inheritance, or tyranny by force of arms. And they said that all on the island were bald, having no hair on the head.

53. The first nation after passing the Nombre de Jesus River is the Halchedoma.[2] There are eight pueblos: the first has one hundred and sixty houses, and was judged to have about two thousand persons. I have already said that they saw only what lay along the road. Next is the nation of Cohuana.[3] There are nine pueblos. A great many of these went along with the Spaniards. There must have been more than six hundred men and women. They camped for the night with the Spaniards. Next is the nation Haglli.[4] There are one hundred pueblos. Next the Tlalliquamallas,[5] six pueblos. Here more than two thousand persons assembled when they brought the maize. Next the Cocapas;[6] there are nine pueblos. This is the last nation seen, and they reached to the last place where one can drink fresh water, which is five leagues from the sea, because the salt comes up

[1] *Hecho* for *dicho.*

[2] Alchedoma, a Yuman tribe. See Hodge, *Handbook*, I. 36.

[3] Bandelier identified this tribe with the Yuma proper or Cuchan. Arch. Inst. of Am. *Papers*, III. 110. See also Hodge, *Handbook*, I. 520, II. 1046.

[4] Regarded as part of the Halliquamayas, or Quigyumas (Hodge, *Handbook*, I. 520; Bandelier, Arch. Inst. Am. *Papers*, III. 110).

[5] Halliquamaya, or Quigyuma (Hodge, *Handbook*, II. 340, 1059).

[6] Still so called. See Hodge, *Handbook*, I. 319. They are noted for the great size of the men.

stream that far. In the space between the Nombre de Jesus River and the arrival at the sea they saw more than twenty thousand persons on that side of the river alone. They said that on the other side they were innumerable, but only the smokes were seen. The Indians said that they did not cross to the other side because the others were their enemies, although of the same nation, and that they came and killed them and did great harm to them, by which it can be seen that the others are numerous.

They arrived on San Ildefonso's day[1] at the last stopping place, nearest to the sea, and the last where water can be drunk. Then, the day of the conversion of San Pablo,[2] having sung mass, the adelantado and religious, with nine soldiers, set out and arrived at a wonderful port, which port and bay are made by the Buena Esperanza River when it enters the sea. We call it Port of the Conversion of San Pablo. So large is this port that more than a thousand vessels can anchor in it without hindrance to one another. The river enters the sea by a mouth four leagues wide. It forms in the middle of the mouth a small, low island, not of sand, as is all the coast, but of mud, the whole island, which must be about two leagues long from northwest to southeast.[3]

From what could be seen, it forms a great shelter[4] to the bay; the island enters it by that river, southeast-by-east, dividing it into two mouths, one to the east and one to the southeast, each being more than a league and a half wide. The port is guarded and protected from the south and west by a mountain range,[5] between whose bases the river enters the sea, which there trends nearly north and south, or northwest and southeast; and a point of the range runs more than six leagues into the sea.[6] On the east this port or bay has another mountain range,[7] which runs seaward from northeast to southwest. It is seen seven leagues distant from the bay; it ends and terminates at the sea in seven or eight small hills or buttes, with low points. Beyond these, on the edge

---

[1] January 23.   [2] January 25.

[3] Montague Island answers this description.

[4] Or barrier; the word is *reparo*.   [5] Sierra Gigantia (?)

[6] This might be Shell Point, or Point Diggs farther south.

[7] Sierra Sonóyta.

of the land, it forms a point, higher than the rest, in which the range ends.   On the west side, which is the one next to the bay, it ends in three small hills or round points, somewhat more elevated than those of the other range, and the last of these is higher than the other two.   Beyond these, toward the edge of the land, it forms a more elevated point, whence the range forms a sharp ridge which runs inland more than twenty leagues south-southeast and north-northwest.   The gulf, on this coast where they were, trends east and west, and doubling the point of this mountain range on the west side, which as I have already said enters the sea more than six leagues, it runs behind this mountain northward,[1] according to what all the Indians said, both those of the coast and those of the river, for they declared that it turns to the north, northeast, and east.

54. The adelantado, Don Juan de Oñate, took possession of this port in the name of his Majesty, and gave possession in his Majesty's name to the Father Commissary, Fray Francisco de Escobar, in order that our sacred religion may settle and people that land and the others next it and round about, and that we may occupy ourselves in the conversion of the natives in the place and places most suited to our mode of life.

55. We took this possession on the 25th of the month of January, day of the conversion of the Apostle St. Paul, patron of those provinces and of the Custodia of New Mexico, in the year of our Lord 1605, for the glory and honor of God our Lord.

56. This done, the adelantado and those who had gone with him returned to the camp, in order that the rest of the soldiers might go and certify to the sea.   They did so, the space of four days being spent therein.   Some soldiers stated that they had seen tunny-fish, and that they knew them because they were men from Spain.   Having seen this,[2] they came back by the same way they had gone, being as well received by the Indians and with the same hospitality as when going.

Having arrived among the Ozaras Indians, as they had

---

[1] This interpretation of what the Indians said agreed with the theory current when Zárate wrote, that California was an island.

[2] He refers now to the return of the whole party to New Mexico.

already inquired of the other nations, and all had said that this nation is very extensive and runs along the coast, and that these are the ones who get from the sea the coral which they call *quacame*, they made inquiry and found a few. They said that since they were a long distance from the coast they did not have many; but further up the Buena Esperanza River, among Indians of this same nation, a few more were found, and in the province of Zuñi still more were found and bartered for. They[1] said the Indians of the valleys of Señora[2] brought them there to sell; and that they are no more than seven days' journey from there,[3] and that they get them out of the sea, and are not far from there; and that this nation extends to that place. This sea they pointed out toward the south and southwest. Father Fray Francisco de Escobar found that from the province of New Mexico to the sea, on the road alone, there were ten different languages.[4] This priest was so able and had so fine a memory that wherever he went he promptly learned the tongue, and so on the return journey he talked with all the nations and they all understood him.

They arrived at the Bahacechas where, on going, Chief Otata and the others had given so many reports of the country, of the lake of Copalla and of the gold, and of the island of gold and silver. On examining them again, they made the same statement as on the journey going, without varying it in any respect. They went through the same performance with the plate of silver as on the outward journey, as has been said; only they added that this silver was taken out of the top of a hill which was on the further side of the island, behind which the sun hides when it sets; and they said that they cut it out with a hard instrument. Being asked if it was of the same they said no, and gave to understand that it was something dark-yellow; and being shown a small sheet of brass, they said it was not of that material. Seeing that they were not understood, one of them rose and went to the adelantado's kitchen and took hold of a copper kettle and said that the instrument with which was cut the metal of which they made their bowls and pots was like that.

---

[1] The Zuñis.   [2] Sonora.   [3] Zuñi.
[4] *Leguas,* a misprint for *lenguas* (Lummis).

The Spaniards set out from here, and Chief Otata came forth to the road to receive them, with a great following and a tumult of ceremonies, as is their custom, flinging their bows and arrows to earth.   He gave the governor a string of white beads which he wore on his neck, and the Father Commissary another, which among them is a great gift.   These he had sent to the island of Ziñogova to purchase with some cotton *mantas*, which on going the governor had given him for that purpose.   It is plainly to be seen that the island is near since he had gone and returned in so short a time.   They again examined them about everything and in nothing did they contradict themselves.

57. They told of many prodigies of nature which God has created between the Buena Esperanza River and the sea, and which have caused incredulity in the hearers.   When we see them we will affirm them under oath; but in the meantime I refrain from mentioning them, and pass them by in silence. And to put an end to this journey, I will say that after having endured much hardship and hunger (even coming to eat their horses) which, lest I be too long, I do not recount, they reached the villa of San Gabriel on their return, all sound and well, and not a man missing, on the 25th of April of the year 1605. There they rested, and were as well received as they had been anxiously awaited.

III. EXPLORATION AND SETTLEMENT IN TEXAS, 1675-1690

1. THE BOSQUE-LARIOS EXPEDITION, 1675

INTRODUCTION

In the course of the sixteenth and seventeenth centuries the frontiers of New Spain had expanded northeastward as well as northward and northwestward. In the sixteenth century the three columns of advancing outposts had kept a nearly equal pace. In 1522 Cortés founded Pánuco, and by 1565 the advance up the central plateau had resulted in conquests as far to the northeast as Saltillo and perhaps as far as Monterey. Advance was now made again along the Gulf plain when in 1579 Luis de Carabajal was authorized to found the new Kingdom of Nuevo León. This province was to extend two hundred leagues north from Pánuco, thus embracing much territory now within the state of Texas. In (or by) 1583 Carabajal took a colony inland, opened the mines of San Gregorio, and founded the capital city of León, now Cerralvo, a few miles south of the Rio Grande. Within the next few years several points were settled between Cerralvo and Monterey, and in 1590 Carabajal founded the Villa de Almadén, where Monclova now stands. While there he was arrested by order of the Inquisition and taken to Mexico, leaving Castaño de Sosa in charge. But Sosa, as has been stated elsewhere, promptly deserted the place and led his colony to New Mexico. In 1603 and again in 1644 efforts were made to open the mines at Almadén, but without success, and Cerralvo remained the northeastern outpost.

Attention was drawn beyond this frontier, however, by various interests. There was frequent talk of establishing communication with Florida by land. To discover a rumored Silver Hill (Cerro de la Plata) somewhere to the north, several attempts were made before 1650 from both Nuevo León and Nueva Vizcaya, but were frustrated by Indian hostilities. Soon after that date the pursuit of Indians led the frontier soldiery across the lower Rio Grande. In 1655, after long continued troubles, a troop of one hundred and three soldiers, supported by more than three hundred Indian allies, was led by Fernández de Azcué against the Cacaxtles. Going north from Monterey, at a place twenty-four leagues beyond the Rio Grande they encountered the enemy, slew a hundred warriors, and took seventy prisoners. This expedition made by Azcué is the first to cross the lower Rio Grande northward of which we have explicit information. And it was nearly twenty years more before another was made of which we have record.

Thus by 1670 the Spaniards had barely broken over the Rio Grande below the Pecos. Now, however, another forward step was taken, the frontier of settlement pushed northeastward, Coahuila founded, and missionary work extended beyond the Rio Grande. The pioneers in this advance were the missionaries; their leader was Father Juan Larios, a Franciscan friar of the province of Santiago de Jalisco, whose headquarters were at Guadalajara.

The principal factor in bringing this movement about was the Indian situation. The needs of the frontier settlements demanded that the Indians of the Coahuila be pacified. Not only the settlements of Nuevo León, but also those of Nueva Vizcaya, and even of Nueva Galicia, were greatly troubled by the tribes of the Coahuila district and of the region beyond the Rio Grande. The roads between the frontier outposts were unsafe for travellers, while mines and ranches were being abandoned. On the other hand, it is clear that for several years some of the Indians of Coahuila and even from beyond the Rio Grande had been asking for missionaries, and, under what influences we do not know, had sent messengers to Saltillo, Parral, Guadalajara, and Mexico City to seek them.

While on one of these journeys to Guadalajara they came into contact with Father Larios, whom they begged to go to aid them.

In response to this call Father Larios went in 1670 to the troubled Coahuila frontier, where he seems to have remained alone for some three years. Returning to Guadalajara for help, in 1673 he went again to Coahuila, accompanied by Father Dionysio de Peñasco and Fray Manuel de la Cruz, a lay brother. Aided by soldiers from Saltillo under Captain Elisondo, early in 1674 they founded of the roving tribes two Indian settlements, one on the Sabinas River and one to the northward of that stream. On one of his missionary trips made at this time Fray Manuel is known to have crossed the Rio Grande, where he came into contact with the Yrbipiames, Gueiquesales, and Boboles.

Thus far the conquest had been only "en lo espiritual." But in May, 1674, Don Antonio Balcárcel Riva de Neira Sotomayor was made *alcalde mayor* of the province of Coahuila, or Nueva Estremadura, and charged with its conquest and settlement. At the same time the missionary field was more completely organized. In November Balcárcel set out from Saltillo with settlers, stock, implements, and provisions, and a following of Coahuila Indians. Balcárcel's lieutenant was Fernando del Bosque, who had been with Elisondo. Father Larios, who now had the title of *comisario* of the missions, met Balcárcel a few leagues out. Fray Manuel was also with the party, as well as Father Dionysio de San Buenaventura, a new missionary. Father Peñasco does not appear in the records till the following April; he may have remained in the missionary field while Father Larios made preparations for larger work.

Beginning at a point twenty leagues from Saltillo, which point was regarded as the border of Coahuila, Balcárcel ceremoniously took possession of all the important watering places on the way, till on the 23d he reached the site of thrice deserted Nuevo Almadén. This place he selected as the head of his jurisdiction, and the site of a city called Nuestra Señora de Guadalupe, province of Nueva Estremadura. Municipal officers were elected, crops planted, ditches opened, a church begun, and by February 25 the outlines of a civil settlement were complete.

Meanwhile Father Larios and Fray Manuel were sent out to assemble the northern Indians with a view to establishing them in pueblos. In the course of the next five months they brought in the chiefs, sometimes with followers, of band after band, who made submission, received pardon for past wrongs, and were promised aid. By the end of April an Indian settlement, called Pueblo de la Luna, had been founded near Guadalupe. It was designed in the first place for the Bobole following, but as other bands arrived they were temporarily added to it, until the host was found to be too great and composed of too many hostile elements to be cared for on one spot.[1]

By this time, moreover, because of the declarations of the chiefs concerning the great number of Indians beyond the Rio Grande, especially near Sierra Dacate, of the petitions which they brought from their bands, and of the aversion of the different groups toward settling together, it was decided before proceeding further to send an expedition across the Rio Grande, to learn the facts of the Indian situation.

Being in ill health himself, Balcárcel entrusted the mission to Fernando del Bosque. Besides Fathers Larios and San

---

[1] For a sketch of the expansion of the northeastern frontier of New Spain in the sixteenth and seventeenth centuries, see Bolton, "The Spanish Occupation of Texas, 1519–1690," in the *Southwestern Historical Quarterly*, XVI. 11–17. See also Alonso DeLeón, *Historia de Nuevo León* (Mexico, 1909); Estéban L. Portillo, *Apuntes para la Historia Antigua de Coahuila y Texas* (Saltillo, 1888); E. J. González, *Lecciones Orales de Historia de Nuevo León* (Monterey, 1887); E. J. González, *Colección de Noticias y Documentos para la Historia del Estado de Nuevo León* (Monterey, 1885); Alejandro Prieto, *Historia, Geografía y Estadística del Estado de Tamaulipas* (Mexico, 1873).

Buenaventura, who went to take ecclesiastical possession of the country, Bosque was ordered to take ten Spaniards, Lázaro Agustín, governor of the Pueblo de la Luna and interpreter, the Bobole chief, Juan de la Cruz, accompanied by twenty-one of his men, and one hundred Gueiquesale warriors, these to be recruited beyond the Nadadores. He was to go as far as the Sierra Dacate (Sacatsol) or farther, if necessary, to take royal possession, see the Indians, aid the missionaries, and bring back a full report.

On the same day that he received his instructions Bosque set out northward, which direction, according to his diary, he continued to follow to the end of his journey. His return was by a more westward route. Of each of the stopping places on the way he took possession, giving it a name, while the missionaries set up a portable altar which they carried, said mass, and instructed the Indians whom they encountered.

In regard to the names and numbers of Indians no details are given before the crossing of the Rio Grande, Bosque's objective point being the country beyond. The distances given in the diary are thirty leagues to the Sabinas, thirty-one from that stream to the Rio Grande, nineteen to Sierra Dacate, and twenty-three leagues beyond that point to San Pablo, the last place reached. From the statements regarding directions and relative distances to the Sabinas and the Rio Grande, it is inferred that the route was northeast, toward Eagle Pass or above. The Ona River, crossed eleven leagues beyond the Rio Grande, was in all probability a branch of the Nueces, and it seems not improbable that the Sierra Dacate was the present Anacacho Mountain, and that San Pablo, the limit of the journey, was in Edwards County.[1]

North of the Rio Grande, Bosque and Larios encountered Indians of the Yorica, Jeapa, Bibit, Pinanaca, Xaeser, Teni-

[1] From other data we know that Sierra Sacatsol was between San Juan Bautista and the Pecos.

mama, Cocoma, Xoman, Teroodan, Teaname, Teimamar, Gueiquesale, and Geniocane tribes, some of whom lived on the other side but had crossed over to hunt buffalo. Among the Gueiquesales he rescued a Spanish boy who had lived among the Indians so long that he had forgotten his own language.

Returning to Guadalupe in June, Bosque reported that the country, so far as he had seen it, comprised three chains of settlements. That extending northward from Guadalupe on the left hand was of the following of Chief Estéban, Gueiquesale; the middle one comprised the followers of the Bobole chief, Juan de la Cruz; that on the right, or to the northeast, was of the Catujane following. Other reports added a fourth group lying to the northwest, under the leadership of the Salineros, but included by Bosque in the Gueiquesale following. In view of their great numbers, of their racial differences, and of their hostility toward each other, Bosque recommended three principal settlements, independent and separate, served by twelve missionaries, and kept in order by a *presidio* of not less than seventy soldiers.

The Bosque-Larios expedition across the Rio Grande, though not great in size or extent, was important in its bearings. Taken with the preliminary reconnaissance of Fray Manuel de la Cruz a few months before, it is the earliest well-authenticated missionary expedition on record to cross the Rio Grande from the south at any point below the Pecos. Bosque's report on the Indian situation is one of the most valuable extant for the region and period. As a result of the reports and recommendations of Bosque and Father Larios, four missions were soon established in the Coahuila district, to serve Indians living to the north as well as to the south of the Rio Grande. And now the Tejas, Indians living far on the Louisiana border, rose above the Coahuila horizon. In 1676 the Bishop of Guadalajara visited Monclova, and one of the reasons which he gave for favoring the adoption of the measures urged by Bosque was the opportunity it would afford to reach and convert the more important Tejas, beyond.

The principal source of information for the Bosque-Larios expedition is a manuscript in the archives of Saltillo, Coahuila, entitled: "Autos de la conquista de la Prov^a de Coahuila hecha en este año por D. Antonio Balcarcel, Alc^e Mayor de ella: gente que condujo: asiento y fundacion de la ciudad de N. Sra. de Guadalupe Prov^a de la Nva. Extremadura a 8 de Dbre de dho año (hoy Monclova): Religiosos que lo acompañaron en esta empresa: conversiones de las naciones barbaras que encontraron: Expedicion de Fernando del Bosque, Ten^te de Alc^e Mayor a la parte del Norte: descubrim^to de la tierra y nombres que puso á los diversos parajes en que estubo, hasta la otra banda del Rio g^e del Norte. Ereccion de las primeras miciones y naciones de que compusieron. Tiene este Quad^no 64 foxas sin 19 que le faltan al principio, y quedan en 45 utiles" (Archivo de la Secretaría de Gobierno del Estado de Coahuila, legajo no. 1, Años 1688 á 1736).

This document consists of the original records (*autos*) of the preparation of the Balcárcel expedition, the march to the site of abandoned Nuevo Almadén, the founding there of the City of Guadalupe and of Pueblo de la Luna, the Bosque-Larios expedition, and some subsequent events. These *autos* are followed by copies of the original records of the preparation of Father Larios at Guadalajara and Saltillo for his expedition in 1673, and of his expedition with Elisondo to Coahuila in 1673–1674. They contain also a report by Balcárcel dated July 6, 1675, to the audiencia of Guadalajara. In 1888 these documents were printed, with essential completeness, but with numerous minor inaccuracies, in Esteban L. Portillo's *Apuntes para la Historia Antigua de Coahuila y Texas*, pp. 44–181. In 1903 an abstract of the *autos* of the Bosque expedition across the Rio Grande was printed in the *National Geographic Magazine* (XIV. 339–348), as "Translated from an Old Unpublished

Spanish Manuscript by Betty B. Brewster." Presumably the translator used the manuscript in the archives at Saltillo, since it is evident that she had not seen the printed version which had appeared in the same city fifteen years before. The introduction preceding that translation gives a brief abstract of a part of the earlier documents, but besides containing grave inaccuracies it conveys no idea of the bearing of the expedition. The translation is likewise unsatisfactory. It is very much abbreviated, especially in the difficult places. While it gives most of the essentials with general accuracy, it is exceedingly free and inexact in matters of detail. A new translation, therefore, has been made.

DIARY OF FERNANDO DEL BOSQUE, 1675[1]

In the province of Nueba Estremadura de Quaguila, on the 30th day of April, 1675, I, Fernando de el Bosque, lieutenant *alcalde mayor*[2] of the province, its settlements and conquest, and its royal ensign, acting as notary public, according to orders, there being no public or royal notary within more than one hundred leagues, set out this day from the city of Nuestra Señora de Guadalupe, of said province, in fulfillment of the orders of Captain Don Antonio de Balcarcel Riba de Neira Sotomaior, *alcalde mayor* of said province, which appear in an *auto*[3] which he drew this day (and which is filed in the original *autos* of settlement and conquest) arising from the petition of Pablo, Indian chief of the nation of Manosprietas, and the other nations from the Rio del Norte and its vicinity,[4] and the rest contained in the *auto* to which I refer.

And having set out with the Spaniards and governor, captain, ensign, and the Indians of the pueblo of San Miguel de Luna, of said city, and in company with the fathers, the commissary missionary,[5] Fray Juan Larios, and Fray Dionisio de San Buena Ventura, chaplain of said conquest, of the order of the Seraphic San Francisco; and having travelled down the river[6] from said city toward the north, I arrived at a place which they said was called Pajarito, on said river, about six leagues from said city. Finding it unoccupied and uninhabited, and with no sign of having formerly been inhabited, I took royal possession in the name of the King, our Lord Carlos II., God preserve him. I took said possession in legal form,

[1] "Autos de la conquista de la Prov.ª de Coahuila" (manuscript in the Archivo de la Secretaría de Gobierno del Estado de Coahuila, legajo no. 1, Años 1688 á 1736).

[2] *Teniente de alcalde mayor.* "Lieutenant" is a rather free translation for *teniente*, and yet in this case it conveys the essential meaning.

[3] An *auto* is a judicial act, such as a decree, writ, or legalized record. In the following pages the meaning is usually conveyed by "legal record."

[4] They had asked to be settled in missions.   [5] *Comisario misionero.*

[6] Río de Monclova, which runs through Monclova.

made a legal record,[1] ordered a high wooden cross erected, and walked over the place and along the bank of the river, in which I saw many fish, some of which they caught, to which I certify.   And I named the place San Felipe de Jesus; and in order that it may always be known I set it down in a legal record, which I signed with the assisting witnesses, namely Ambrosio de Berlanga and Diego Luis Sanches; and the said fathers, the commissary missionary and the chaplain, being witnesses, also signed it.   FERNANDO DE EL BOSQUE (rubric); Ambrosio Berlanga (rubric), witness; Diego Luis Sanches (rubric), witness; Fray JUAN LARIOS (rubric); Fray DIONYSIO DE SAN BUENA VENTURA (rubric).

In said province, on the 2d day of the month of May of said year, I, said lieutenant *alcalde mayor* of said conquest and its settlements, having already left the post of San Felipe de Jesus on the first day of this month, and always travelling toward the north and down the river, in company with the said fathers, the commissary missionary Fray Juan Larios, and Chaplain Fray Dionisio de San Buena Ventura, the Spaniards, the governor, and Indians, arrived and saw at about four leagues, apparently, that this river joined another.   And travelling along it toward the north, having on the right hand and toward the sunrise some large hills with sharp peaks of rock, like sugar loaves, and passing beyond them, I arrived at the ford of a river called Nadadores.[2]   Finding it unpossessed and uninhabited I took formal possession of all of it in the king's name.   I walked over the ground and made a legal record; this day Christian instruction was given to the Indians; they caught fish from the river, which carries much water.   It has cottonwoods and many mesquite trees on its banks.   It is distant from San Felipe about ten leagues.   I had a high wooden cross erected on the bank of the river, and named the ford and post San Francisco del Paso.   I certify that I saw taken from the river large catfish, bream, *mojarros*, tortoises, mud-turtles, *bobos*, and eels, and had them in my hands.[3]

---

[1] *Hise auto.*   [2] Still so called.

[3] In this and the following entries the formal statements about signing have been omitted to save space, since they are practically identical with that in the foregoing entry.

In said province, on the 4th of the said month and year, I, said lieutenant *alcalde mayor*, set out from San Francisco del Paso de Nadadores in the company of the fathers commissary missionary and chaplain, and of the Spaniards, the governor, and Indians; and having crossed said river, and journeying north, keeping always on the left a high, long mountain range which forms what resembles a chain, and runs from south to north,[1] and having travelled apparently about four leagues, I arrived at an arroyo near a long hill, which flows apparently from west to east and has running water, for which reason, the Indians said, it was called in their language Toporica.[2] I took possession of it in the royal name for said settlement and conquest, in witness whereof I had a high wooden cross erected, made a legal record, and named it Santa Crus.

In said province, on said day, month, and year, I the said lieutenant *alcalde mayor*, having set out from the post of Santa Crus in said company, and having journeyed toward the north about four leagues, with the mountains on the same hand as before, arrived at an arroyo which is at the foot of a hill and in front of a little peak like a nipple.[3] In it I found running water and a growth of tule. I took possession of it in the royal name for said settlement and conquest, and named it Santa Catalina Martir.[4] As evidence of possession I had a high wooden cross erected, made a legal record, and performed other necessary legal acts. Instruction was given to the Indians. I found this post and the former uninhabited.

In said province, on the 5th day of the said month and year, I, said lieutenant *alcalde mayor*, left the post and watering place of Santa Catalina Martir in company with the fathers commissary missionary and chaplain, the Spaniards, governor, and Indians, and, having journeyed apparently about six leagues toward the north, keeping the mountain range on the

---

[1] Probably the Sierra de Obayas, which lies between Río Nadadores and Río Aura, and trends from northwest to southeast. Between Río Aura and Río de Sabinas the mountains are called Sierra de Santa Rosa.

[2] Evidently Río Aura.

[3] At about this point there is a branch of the Río Nadadores flowing from Sierra de Santa Rosa.

[4] St. Catharine the Martyr.

same hand, I arrived at a large river, very beautiful with many groves of very large cedars, cottonwoods, and mesquite brush, and with great plains of land which are very pleasing with green grass. I found it unoccupied and uninhabited. The Indians said it was called Rio de las Savinas,[1] and in their language Muero. Of it I took possession in the royal name, for said settlement and conquest, and named it San Antonio. And as evidence of possession I made a legal record, and ordered erected a high wooden cross. In this river are fish of all kinds in abundance. They caught *piltontes*, bream, and catfish ; and the Christian doctrine was taught to the Indians by the commissary.

In said province, on the 7th day of said month and year I, said lieutenant *alcalde mayor*, having set out in company with the fathers commissary missionary and chaplain, the Spaniards, governor, and Indians, and having travelled northward apparently about twelve leagues from San Antonio de las Sabinas, arrived at a post and watering place which the Indians said was called San Ylefonso.[2] Finding it unoccupied and uninhabited, with only some ruins of two grass huts, already almost rotten,[3] I took royal possession of it in the name of his Majesty, for said settlement and conquest, in witness whereof I made a legal record, and ordered a high wooden cross erected.

In said province, on the 8th day of said month and year,[4] I, said lieutenant *alcalde mayor*, set out in company with the fathers commissary missionary and chaplain, the Spaniards, governor, and Indians, from said post of San Ylefonso, and having travelled northward apparently about seven leagues, I arrived at a watering place where there was plentiful water, with wide plains, in the middle of which was much mesquite, and which I found unoccupied and uninhabited. The said Indians said that in their language it was called Cocomarque Jojona. I took possession of it in the name of his Majesty

---

[1] Río de Sabinas, called Salado lower down.

[2] San Yldefonso.

[3] Perhaps the remains of the mission settlement established in the previous year by Father Larios.

[4] In the Brewster translation the entry for May 8 is omitted, but a part of it is run into that for May 7. In this way one day's march is lost.

for said settlement and conquest, and named it San Juan
Evanjelista;[1] and as evidence of possession I made a legal
record, and ordered a high wooden cross erected. Christian
instruction was given to the Indians by said father commissary.

In said province, on the 9th day of said month and year,
I, said lieutenant *alcalde mayor*, set out in company with said
fathers commissary missionary and chaplain, the Spaniards,
governor, and Indians, from the post of San Juan Evangelista,
and having travelled northward apparently about six leagues,
through some plains with mesquite groves, I arrived at a
watering place consisting of a marsh with a growth of tule,
among some low hills having oak trees. Finding it unoccupied and uninhabited, I took possession of it in the name of
his Majesty for said settlement and conquest and named it
San Reymundo de Peña Forte de Fuertes Aires; and in evidence of possession I made a legal record and ordered a high
wooden cross erected. Religious instruction was given to
the Indians by Father Fray Dionisio de San Buenabentura.

In said province, on the 10th day of said month and year,
I, said lieutenant *alcalde mayor*, set out from said post of San
Reymundo in company with said fathers commissary missionary and chaplain, the Spaniards, governor, and Indians, and
having journeyed northward apparently about three leagues,
I arrived at a river which runs from west to east, which the
Indians said was called El Agua Asul.[2] In it there are many
fish of all kinds. It is very pleasing to the sight, having many
cottonwoods, willows, mesquites and *guisaches*,[3] and wide plains
with very green grass. Finding it unoccupied and uninhabited,
I took possession of it in the name of his Majesty for said
settlement and conquest, and named it San Jocefe[4] River. As
evidence of possession I made a legal record and ordered a
high wooden cross erected; and religious instruction was given
to the Indians by the fathers.

In said province, on the 11th day of said month and year,
I, said lieutenant *alcalde mayor*, set out from the post and San
Jocefe River in company with the fathers commissary and
chaplain, the Spaniards, governor, and Indians, and having
travelled northward apparently about three leagues through

[1] St. John the Evangelist.
[2] The blue water.
[3] A small shrub.
[4] St. Joseph.

plains with much mesquite, and with fine pastures of green grass, I arrived at a very copious and very wide river, with a current more than four hundred *varas* across, which the Indians said was called Rio del Norte. I found it unoccupied and uninhabited, with only rancherías of Indians, consisting of dwellings of grass huts after their custom. Having passed up stream in search of a ford and not having found one, as it is very deep, the said Indians decided to take us across at a place where the river forms three branches.[1] It was necessary to make a raft of poles to cross the middle one, having forded the first, which is more than two hundred *varas* wide and a *vara* and a half deep, with the water above the stirrup and near the hind bow of the saddle, with a current the whole width, and with willow and osier brush on a little island which is in the middle. On its banks it is very pleasing, and it had many fish, such as catfish, *piltontes*, very large turtles, and eels, all of which kinds were caught in my presence, and which, I certify, I took in my hands. I took royal possession of the river and its territory in the name of his Majesty. It runs, apparently, from west to east. And for said settlement and conquest I named it San Buena Ventura River; and as evidence of possession I made a legal record and ordered a high wooden cross erected; and religious instruction was given to the Indians by the father chaplain.

In said province, on the 13th day of said month and year, I, said lieutenant *alcalde mayor*, set out from said Rio de San Buenabentura del Norte in company with said fathers commissary and chaplain, the Spaniards, governor, and Indians, and having travelled northward apparently about four leagues, I arrived at an arroyo between hills, where I found fifty-four adult heathen Indians of the Yorica and Jeapa nations, loaded with tierces of jerked buffalo meat. I had them examined through interpretation of Don Lasaro Augustin, the governor, who is versed in their language and in Castilian; and having asked many questions, they said that they came to kill buffaloes and get meat for sustenance for themselves and their families and rancherías, since they were obliged, through having no food in the places where they lived, to come to seek it

---

[1] Evidently a place where the river widened out and formed islands. The Rio Grande is notable for its shifting back and forth.

at a distance; that they were numerous, but could not say exactly how many; that they wished to be Christians and settled in a pueblo, and that the religious should give them Christian instruction; that through fear of other nations, their enemies, they have not come out to seek it, but wander at a distance; that the enemies had killed one of them, and that the ones who did it were of the Ocane, Pataguaque, and Yurbipame nations; and that as evidence that they were obedient to the King our lord, they would go with me to the place where the Indian nations of the Sierra Dacate y Yacasole[1] are, and would send to their rancherías to have them come out to a place where they might be given Christian instruction. Of this place I took royal possession in the name of his Majesty for said settlement and conquest, and in evidence of it I made a legal record, and ordered a high wooden cross erected. Christian instruction was given to all the Indians by said father chaplain, and I named said post San Gregorio Nasianseno.

In said province, on the 14th day of said month and year, I, said lieutenant *alcalde mayor*, having set out in company with the fathers commissary missionary and chaplain, the Spaniards, governor, and Indians, both those who came from the city of Guadalupe and the Yoricas and Jeapas mentioned in the preceding *auto*, and having travelled from the post of San Gregorio Nasianseno about three leagues toward the north, arrived at a watering place in a plain without any trees except mesquite groves. Finding it unoccupied and uninhabited I took royal possession of it in the name of his Majesty, and named it San Bisente Ferrer;[2] and Christian instruction was given to said Indians by said commissary missionary.

In said province and in said post of San Bisente Ferrer on

---

[1] It seems quite possible that the Sierra Dacate (Yacasol, Sacatsol, Yacatsol), was Anacacho Mountain. Early in the eighteenth century Captain Diego Ramón pursued Indians above San Juan Bautista, and having crossed the hills called "Yacatsol" he reached wide plains and beyond them the Pecos River. Thus the Sierra Yacasol was between San Juan Bautista and the Pecos ("Relación del P\ Hidalgo De la Quivira," MS.). Assuming the word Yacasol to have been accented on the penult, "Yacásol," it would approach Anacácho in sound. Father Massanet stated in 1690 that Sacatsol meant "stone nostrils" (see his letter, p. 356).

[2] San Vicente Ferrer.

said day, month, and year, I, said lieutenant *alcalde mayor*, certify and testify that in my presence there were killed by said Indians and Spaniards three buffalo bulls and two buffalo cows for the people to eat. The meat is very savory. The form of the buffalo is very ugly. Although large, they resemble cows and bulls. Their hair is shaggy. The withers are very high, making them appear humpbacked, and their necks are large. The head is short and very shaggy, so that the wool covers the eyes and prevents them from seeing well. The horns are small and thick, but like those of the bull. The hips and haunches are like those of a hog, and the tail is bare except at the end, where there are long bristles. The hoofs are cloven, and at the knees and from there up to the shoulder there is much bristle-like hair, like he-goats. The females are of the same sort and have four teats. They gaze at the people sidewise like wild hogs, with hair abristle. They are of the size of cattle.

In said post of San Bisente Ferrer, on said day, month, and year, before me, Fernando de el Bosque, lieutenant *alcalde mayor*, appeared Juan, an Indian of the Bibit nation, and chief of it, and said that he was a Christian, having been baptized at the Villa of Saltillo, and another Indian, a heathen, who said he was chief of the Jume nation. I examined them through interpretation of Don Lasaro Augustin, who speaks their language and Castilian. And having asked them various questions, they said that for a long time they had desired to be Christians, and that some of them, having gone to the Villa of Saltillo, had succeeded, but that to the rest it had been impossible, because of being distant and unable to take out their people, of whom many had died from smallpox without receiving the water of baptism; and that they requested this, and desired to settle in pueblos and be under instruction in the Christian doctrine; and that they have not gone to do this or been able to join with the rest of the people of their nation through fear of other barbarian tribes, who kill them. The people whom they brought numbered one hundred and five persons, large and small, including women and children. Present at all this were the father commissary missionary, Fray Juan Larios, and Chaplain Fray Dionisio de San Buenabentura, who signed with me and with the witnesses assisting me, who were Anbrosio de Berlanga and Diego Luis Sanches.

In said post of San Bisente Ferrer, on said day, month and year, before me, said Lieutenant, came and appeared six adult Indians who said they were heathen of the Pinanaca, Xaeser, Tenimama, and Cocoma nations, of the band of Don Esteban Gueiquesal. I had them examined through interpretation of Don Lasaro Augustin, who knows both Castilian and their language; and having asked them what they had come for, they said to see me in the name of their chiefs and to render obedience to his Majesty, thus ratifying that rendered by Don Esteban in their name; and to let it be known that they are waiting to be Christians and to live under instruction in the Christian doctrine, and to settle in a pueblo; and that all their people and others remain in the Sierra de Matoat.

In said province on the 15th day of said month and year I, said lieutenant *alcalde mayor*, having set out from said post of San Vicente Ferrer in company with said fathers commissary missionary and chaplain, the Spaniards, governor, and Indians, and having journeyed toward the north, and arrived at a river which is distant from the post of San Vicente apparently about four leagues, and which the Indians said was called in their language Ona, which in Spanish means salty, took royal possession in the name of his Majesty for said settlement and conquest, in witness whereof I had a high wooden cross erected, had a legal record made, and named the place San Ysidro Labrador. This place has many groves of oak and mesquite; there are many buffalo; the country has fine pastures; and there are many fish in the river, which I found unoccupied and uninhabited.

In said province, on said day, month, and year, in said post of San Ysidro, before me, said lieutenant *alcalde mayor*, appeared the chiefs Xoman, Teroodan, Teaname, and Teimamar, with their people. I had them examined through sworn interpreters who understand their language, Mexican,[1] and Castilian, namely Don Lasaro Augustin, governor of the pueblo of San Miguel de Luna of the city of Guadalupe of this province, and an Indian named Pasqual. Various questions having been asked of these chiefs, each one separately, they said

---

[1] Aztec is probably meant here.

unanimously and in agreement that they were heathen; that in their lives they [never][1] had seen Spaniards; and had lived as heathen without knowledge that there was a God, or who He was, and without knowledge of the true way to salvation, and in the dark regarding it; that they wished to be Christians and be baptized, with their children and wives, and to live as such in a pueblo or pueblos where they might place them, so that while they, being old, would not enjoy it, their children would enjoy it and be reared as Christians, but that they would continue in the same way;[2] and that at once they were rendering and did render obedience to his Majesty the King our lord Don Carlos the Second; and that they would be friends of the Spaniards. Thereupon they shouted "Viva, viva, viva,[3] the King our lord!"

Seeing this, and that they appeared to be eager and to give signs of sincerity, I received them in the King's name under the royal protection, and assured them in the name of his Majesty that peace should not be withheld from them, but that what had been promised on his part would be fulfilled. And I ordered them to live quiet and peaceful and to come to be taught the Christian doctrine in the place most convenient for that purpose, both because of the remoteness of their dwelling places, and because of some dissensions which the nations of Indians, as barbarous natives of this country, have with one another, and as a result of which they kill each other; and because they have nothing with which to sustain so many people, until his Majesty provides what may please him, in order to settle them in the most convenient place.

This being understood by the chiefs, they replied through the interpreters that they would comply. And at once their people approached, and both men and women devotedly kissed the sleeves of the habits of the fathers, the commissary missionary, Fray Juan Larios, and chaplain Fray Dionisio de San Buenabentura; and they asked permission to give them as alms something of what they possessed, as a mark of gratitude to God for having opened to them the way to the truth. And

[1] Both my transcript from the original and the Portillo version omit the negative, but I feel confident from the sense that it is intended.

[2] That is, the old people would remain heathen.

[3] "Long live the King our lord."

at once they began throwing things upon the ground, some a piece of tallow, others hides or skins of animals, of the kind with which they clothe themselves or cover themselves, and in which they sleep. To all of this I certify.

In said post and river of San Ysidro of said province, its settlement and conquest, on the 16th day of said month and year, I, said lieutenant *alcalde mayor*, certify that this day there was erected in said post a portable altar, and that it was prepared to say mass; and at a signal made with a small bell the people came to hear it. It was chanted by the father commissary missionary, Fray Juan Larios, and was attended by all the people. After it was concluded they asked the said father to baptize them; and when they were given to understand by him through an interpreter that he could not baptize them until they knew their prayers, to console them he baptized fifty-five infants, the Spaniards acting as their godfathers. They were instructed in the doctrine and counted, and the people of the four chiefs named in the preceding *auto* were found to comprise four hundred and twenty-five warriors[1] and seven hundred and forty-seven women, boys, and girls, of all ages, making in all eleven hundred and seventy-two persons.

In said post of San Ysidro, on said day, month, and year, I, said lieutenant *alcalde mayor*, put the father commissary, Fray Juan Larios, in possession of his office and of the administration in said post, in virtue of a royal provision and of licenses, as is stated and appears in them, and to which I refer. Of this legal record was made in his despatches, following the rest of the ecclesiastical despatches regarding this settlement.

On said day, month, and year, in said post, before me, said lieutenant *alcalde mayor*, a heathen Indian of the Gueiquesal nation, made a demonstration and brought to my presence a Spanish boy apparently about twelve years of age, with a black streak on his face running from the forehead to the nose, and two on the cheeks, one on each, like o's, and many rows of them on the left arm and one on the right. And having examined said Indian, through the interpretation of Don Lasaro Agustin, versed in their language and in Castilian, and through an Indian named Pasqual, likewise versed in it, and

---

[1] *De arco y flecha, i. e.*, carrying, or capable of carrying bow and arrow.

asking him where he had got him, he replied that his mother had raised him, he having been given by her to the Cavesas many years ago ; that they had told him that they had brought him with others from Yndee, near Parral ; and that although they loved him like a brother, and were keeping him in this place, they would give him to me as a sign of friendship for the Spaniards, and that he might be sent to his relatives. The boy was not examined for the present to learn what other Spaniards they have, because he cannot speak the Castilian language.   The Indian was asked if there were other Spanish boys among the Indians.   He replied that all he knew was that at the time when they brought the boy the Cavezas brought another boy and a Spanish girl; that they killed the boy with arrows, having made him stand up for the purpose; that when the boy saw this he took a cross in his hands and began to say his prayers, and was praying till he died ; that the Spanish girl they brought with them likewise, as a servant, and because during an expedition which the Cabesas made to rob and kill, they killed one of their companions, they[1] captured and shot her with arrows until she died, leaving her lying where she fell ; that two years later they passed by there and found her just as they had left her, the body being undecayed and the animals not having eaten it.[2]   In view of this they took it and carried it to a cave, where it now is ; and that it has long hair; that he knows no more, and that this is the truth.

In said province, on the 18th day of said month and year, I, said lieutenant *alcalde mayor*, having set out from the post of San Ysidro in company with the fathers commissary missionary and chaplain, the Spaniards, governor, and Indians, and having travelled about eight leagues northward, and having arrived at a post and small river which they said was called Dacate, and finding it unoccupied and uninhabited, took royal possession of it in the name of his Majesty, and named it San Bernardino, in testimony of which I made a legal record and ordered a high wooden cross erected.   This day there came before me Chief Geniocane, a heathen Indian, who said that

---

[1] It is not clear from the syntax who did the killing.

[2] Stories of miraculous happenings of this particular sort were common in New Spain.

he was awaiting the religious with his people at another place farther on, that they might give them Christian instruction and catechise them in it; that the reason why he and his people had not come out was the multitude of enemies on the way who would not let them pass to seek aid; and that over this matter they were killing each other. In view of this and of their petition to the religious, it was decided to give them the consolation of the spiritual nourishment of Christian instruction.

In said province, on the 20th day of said month and year, I, said lieutenant *alcalde mayor*, having set out from the post of San Bernardino in company with said fathers commissary missionary and chaplain, the Spaniards, governor and Indians, and having travelled about eight leagues northward, the Indians of the Geniocane nation having come out to meet us and the rest of the Indians on the way, I arrived at the ranchería, or camp, at an arroyo between some hills where there are many grapevines like wild grape stocks, many being like vineyards, the green fruit being large like that of Castile. In this place I took royal possession in the name of his Majesty, in testimony whereof and for said settlement and conquest I made a legal record and ordered a high wooden cross erected, Christian instruction being given the Indians by Father Fray Dionisio de San Buenabentura.

In the said province and in the place named above, which I called San Jorje, on the 21st day of said month and year, I, said lieutenant *alcalde mayor*, certify that this day the father commissary missionary ordered an altar erected, and at it Father Fray Dionisio de San Buenabentura said mass. It was attended by the Geniocane Indians and the rest, and after it was concluded they were taught the doctrine by the father commissary missionary. They were counted and there were found sixty-five adult Indians and one hundred and thirteen Indian women, boys, and girls, making a total of one hundred and seventy-eight persons of this nation of Geniocanes. They told the father commissary missionary that they wished to be Christians, and he consoled them by saying that they should learn to pray and he would baptize them. This day the father commissary missionary took official possession, of which I made a legal record in the original *autos* of his despatches.

In said post of San Jorje, on the 23d day of said month and year, I, said lieutenant *alcalde mayor*, having seen that there are many nations of Indians who are asking to be Christians and who wish to settle in pueblos, since their chiefs come to me every day to ask it; and being so far from the city of Guadalupe; and because some are hostile to others; and because all ask instruction in the Christian doctrine at the same time; and because when they come together over their barbarous discords they kill each other like barbarians; and since the country thus far seen is divided into three tiers of settlements, according to the custom of such people, the one extending from the city of Guadalupe northward on the left hand obeying and following Don Esteban Gueiquesal, the one in the middle being devoted to Juan de la Crus, chief of the Bobole nation, and the one on the right hand including the Catujanos, Tilijaes, Apes, Pachaques, and their chiefs, all being very numerous; and to obviate dissensions among these natives, since all desire religious and Spaniards; and there being only hostility among them in the district seen; and not having force to prevent their plans, I decided to return to the city of Guadalupe to report to the *alcalde mayor*, counting if possible on the way back the people of said Don Esteban which are lacking, in order that in view of the report he may provide what is best for the service of both Majesties. And I ordered said nation of Jeniocanes to await in the place which would be the most convenient to them for their conversion and quietude.

In said province, on the 25th day of the said month and year, I, said lieutenant *alcalde mayor*, having set out from the post of San Jorje in company with the father commissary missionary, the chaplain, Spaniards, governor, and Indians, and having travelled about fourteen leagues northward, arrived at a small arroyo with heavy timber, between some knolls and high hills like nipples, where I took possession in the name of his Majesty for said settlement and conquest, naming the place San Pablo Ermitaño.[1] In witness thereof I made a legal record, and ordered a high wooden cross erected, instruction being given to the people by Father Fray Dionissio de San Buenabentura. And I ordered the nations of Indians of the four chiefs mentioned in the record[2] of the post of San

[1] Saint Paul the Hermit.   [2] *Auto.*

Ysidro, of the faction of Don Esteban and his following, to remain quiet in their country and live good lives, without killing each other, and to join with the other followers of their great chief. On hearing this they said they could comply, and remained awaiting a religious who should go to instruct them until they should settle in a pueblo.

In said province, on the 29th of said month and year, I, said lieutenant *alcalde mayor*, having set out from the post of San Pablo Ermitaño to return to the city of Guadalupe in company with the governor and Indians, arrived at another place on the River of San Buenabentura del Norte,[1] where I found part of the Bobole Indians with their women and children. They were killing buffalo for food, and it was some time since they had gone out to their pueblo and settlement.[2] I ordered them to go to it, which in fact they did, joining their chief and the rest of their nation. They were taught the doctrine by said father commissary missionary, and I made a legal record of it, which I signed with said fathers and witnesses.

In said province, on the 1st day of June of said year, I, said lieutenant *alcalde mayor*, having already set out from the San Buenabentura River, in company with said fathers commissary and chaplain, Spaniards, and Indians, and having travelled about twenty leagues to the west, arrived at a river which they said was called the Nueses,[3] where I found chiefs Bacora and Pinanaca, at some springs formed at a river with many walnuts and other kinds of trees. Here I took royal possession in the name of his Majesty for said settlement and conquest. As evidence of it I made a legal record and ordered a high wooden cross erected, the doctrine being taught to the people by the father commissary missionary, who ordered an altar erected in a bower, and that Father Fray Dionisio de San Buenabentura should say mass. This concluded, at the sound of a little bell the people again said the creed. The people of Captain Bacora were counted and were found to

[1] Evidently higher up than the place where it was crossed before. It is clear that Bosque's march beyond the Rio Grande was northward instead of eastward.

[2] That is, Pueblo de Luna.

[3] This was evidently a stream flowing eastward into the Rio Grande. The stream now called San Diego on some maps fits the conditions fairly well; if it was higher up, La Zorra might answer.

comprise one hundred and fifty persons, sixty-two warriors and eighty-eight women and children. In this post possession was given him[1] of that which concerns his administration, and I made a legal record of it in the original *autos* of ecclesiastical possessions.

In said province, on the 5th day of said month and year, I, said lieutenant *alcalde mayor*, having already set out from the River of Santa Clara de las Nueses in company of said fathers missionary commissary and chaplain, Spaniards and Indians, and having journeyed about fourteen leagues to the south and toward the city of Guadalupe, arrived at a river where I found the Gueiquesal and Manosprietas people. I took royal possession in the name of his Majesty and named the place San Diego,[2] and mass was said by the father commissary. The people were counted and found to comprise three hundred and eighty-seven persons, one hundred and three warriors and two hundred and eighty-four women, boys and girls. They said that of the rest of the men some were killing buffalo and others were with their chief, Don Esteban, in the city of Guadalupe. This day ecclesiastical possession was given to the father commissary missionary, of which a legal record was made in the ecclesiastical *autos*.

In this province, on the 10th day of said month and year, I, said lieutenant *alcalde mayor*, having previously set out for the river and post of San Diego in company with said fathers commissary missionary and chaplain, and the Spaniards and Indians, and having travelled about twenty-two leagues, passing through the valley of the River of San Antonio de Sabinas, and entering an opening in some large mountains called Obayas,[3] I arrived at an arroyo with water. Finding it unoccupied and uninhabited, I took royal possession in name of his Majesty for said settlement and conquest, and named it San Anbrossio, in witness whereof I made a legal record and

[1] The *comisario misionero*.

[2] This seems to be further south than the stream now called San Diego, entering the Rio Grande about twenty-five miles above Eagle Pass. The stream may have been the San Fernando, which enters the Rio Grande at Piedras Negras.

[3] Bosque seems to have followed the route of the International Railroad here. The stream was evidently the Río Aura. It is just possible that he had been west of the Santa Rosa Mountains and followed the pass made by the Río Aura.

ordered a high wooden cross erected. Mass was said by the
father commissary missionary, and was attended by Don Bernabe, chief of the Contotore nation, with his people. Mass
ended, they were instructed by the said father commissary.
This nation was counted and there were found sixty-eight
warriors and one hundred and thirty women and children.

In said province, on the 12th day of June, 1675, I, said lieutenant *alcalde mayor*, having previously set out from the
post of San Anbrossio, and having travelled apparently about
fourteen leagues toward the city of Guadalupe and opposite it,
at the foot of a large mountain and toward the west of it, in
company with the fathers commissary and chaplain, and with
said Spaniards, arrived at a watering place which I found unoccupied and uninhabited; taking royal possession in the name
of his Majesty for said settlement and conquest, in testimony
whereof I made a legal record, I ordered a large wooden cross
erected and named the place San Bartolome. At this place
there came to me Chief Don Salbador, of the Babosarigame
nation, with some of his people, saying that he had sent for
the rest, who, for lack of food, were scattered about. He and
the people whom he brought were instructed in the doctrine
by the father commissary missionary. This ended, they were
counted and found to comprise forty-two warriors and sixty-
six women and children, including the Tetecores. I ordered
him to assemble the rest and to keep them in sight of chief
Don Bernabe and of Don Esteban.

In said province of Nueba Estremadura, on said day,
month, and year I, said lieutenant *alcalde mayor*, make known
to Captain Don Antonio de Balcarcel Riba de Neira Sotomaior,
alcalde mayor of this province, its settlements and conquest
for his Majesty, that, having gone at his orders to reconnoitre
the nations of Indians of the following of Don Esteban Gueiquesale, who live toward the Sierra Dacate and in its vicinity,
and the others of their district and neighborhood, they mani-
fested before his Majesty, through me and their messengers,
that they wish to settle in pueblos and be Christians, with
religious to catechise and instruct them. And having passed
through the length and breadth of the country which appears
in the records, and having seen it and its inhabitants, I have
learned that they are divided into three followings or bands,

each very numerous, since the least numerous, although wild and the most bellicose, is that of the following of Don Esteban Gueiquesal, which are the nations counted, excepting the Yoricas, Jumees, Vivit, and Jeniocanes, who belong with the Boboles, Catujanos, and Tilijaes, of the districts already stated; and of the great discord between them, from which they kill and eat each other and capture each other's children, for they say this, being now actually at war with each other, the band of Don Esteban with that of the Jeniocanes and their allies, and the Yoricas, Jumees, and Vivit with the Arames, Ocanes, and those of their following, and the Boboles with the Yurbipames. These tiers of people are very numerous and their limits or that of one with another is not known, for neither on the north nor on the east is there any report of their terminus.

For this reason these Indians begged me to go to see their rancherías and those of their allies; and they have said that they wished to be Christians, and that all wish it, and to settle in pueblos, and to ask for religious; and they wish that aid be given to each one separately and not together, for it happens that for very slight causes they kill each other, and conditions become bad. I decided, therefore, to return from said post of San Jorge, counting on the way the people of Don Esteban who might be on the road, to inform said *alcalde mayor*, which I now do, both of this as well as that unless for these three bands or followings of people three head settlements[1] be made, in which each shall be regarded as independent of the other— one in the valley of San Antonio and Sabinas River, which will accommodate many settlements, and another at Los Baluartes and San Francisco River, which is of the same sort, and the one which is already made at the city of Guadalupe—it will not be possible to maintain these nations under instruction in the Christian doctrine. For they are people, one extremely barbarous, and the others barbarous, who have shown bad conduct toward the Spaniards and other vassals of his Majesty in La Viscaia, the Kingdom of Leon, and in part of La Galicia, robbing and killing for more than twenty years.

Even less will it be possible for any officer of his Majesty to keep them in order and under instruction unless he has forces for it, although he may have to use much love and blandish-

[1] *Cabeseras.*

ment when having to correct them, for since they are vicious
people and not habituated to labor to sustain themselves, they
will return to their natural habits, and greater damages will
result.   And there will not be Spaniards who wish to settle
in the country, for it is known that those who entered it have
left with misgivings or fears which some have been spreading
abroad.

The most important post found in which to establish forces
is Santa Cruz, since it is fourteen leagues from the valley of
San Antonio, a little less from Los Baluartes, and twenty from
the city of Guadalupe,[1] and in the heart and centre of the
country.   These forces will not be sufficient if less than seventy
men, since it is very remote from settlements and aid, for that
of the Villa of Saltillo is more than sixty-eight leagues away,
and the Kingdom of Leon the same, these being the nearest.
Likewise, ministers of the gospel are necessary, since these nations ask for them; and they do not wish to have those of one
nation attend the others, because they are of different languages,
the people numerous, and their homes far apart.   There are
necessary for the present at least four religious for each group,
if his Majesty, God preserve him, is pleased to have it settled
and given seed grain, oxen, and some families of Tlaxcalteco
Indians.[2]

This report I make to said *alcalde mayor* on the basis of
what I have seen and observed, and of my experience of more
than twenty years with barbarian natives and others.   And
in order that it may be on record I set it down as an *auto*, which
I signed with the witnesses assisting me, who were Diego Luis
Sanches and Anbrosio de Verlanga.

FERNANDO DE EL BOSQUE (rubric).

Witness, AMBROSIO BERLANGA (rubric).

Witness, DIEGO LUIS SANCHES (rubric).

[1] This statement gives an important clue to the relation of the going and
return routes to each other.

[2] The Indians from Tlascala played an important part in the founding of
frontier settlements, they being used as teachers of the new converts. About
1590 a colony of them was established at Saltillo, with the name of San Esteban.
In subsequent times this colony was freely drawn upon in the establishment of
new Indian pueblos on the northern frontier.

TEXAS

2. THE MENDOZA-LÓPEZ EXPEDITION TO THE JUMANOS, 1683–1684

INTRODUCTION

Long before the Bosque-Larios expedition had crossed the lower Rio Grande, Spaniards from New Mexico had frequently made their way into western Texas. Interest in Gran Quivira and the Aijados, and in the country beyond—an interest which had inspired the long northeastward expedition of Oñate—continued to attract the frontier explorers and missionaries. Writing of these "kingdoms" in 1630, Father Benavides, who had just ceased to be custodian of the missions of New Mexico, described them as rich in gold, and in danger of being possessed by the English and the Flemings. As a means of securing, subduing, and converting them, and at the same time of establishing a shorter route from Havana to New Mexico, he proposed opening a port at the so-called Bay of Espíritu Santo, at the mouth of the Mississippi River. Four years later, it is said by Father Posadas, Alonso de Vaca led an expedition three hundred leagues eastward from New Mexico to a great river across which was Quivira. What his route and its terminus were is unknown.

Another interest, more tangible and immediate, led the New Mexicans frequently southeastward in the early seventeenth century into what is now western central Texas. This interest was the Jumano Indians. In 1629 Father Salas, accompanied by soldiers, went more than a hundred leagues eastward and worked for a time among this nation. In 1632 he made another expedition to the tribe, whom he found two hundred leagues southeast of Santa Fé, on a stream called the Nueces River. It was clearly a branch of the upper Colorado.

No other expedition to the Jumanos is recorded till 1650, when one was made by Captains Hernando Martín and Diego del Castillo, with a party of soldiers. While there they found pearls in the Nueces River. Before returning some of the party went fifty leagues beyond the Jumanos and reached the borders of the territory of a people called "Tejas," who were ruled by a king. These two new objects of interest—pearls and the kingdom of the Tejas—now became motives to further journeys to the east. Hearing of the pearls, the viceroy at once ordered another expedition, and in 1654 Diego de Guadalajara went with thirty soldiers to the same place. Passing beyond the Jumanos thirty leagues, they engaged in a battle with the Cuitaos, taking two hundred prisoners, and rich spoils in the way of peltry. No other specific expedition to the Jumanos is recorded till that of Juan Domínguez de Mendoza in 1683–1684. But in the interim, we are told, trade and friendship had been maintained with these Indians "with such security that the Spaniards, six, eight, and ten, went to their lands and villages every year to trade with these Indians."

Meanwhile there had occurred in New Mexico the great uprising of the Pueblo Indians in 1680, during which a part of the settlers were massacred, the rest fleeing from the upper Rio Grande and taking refuge at El Paso, where a settlement had existed since 1659. This catastrophe cut off communication with the Jumanos for a time, but relations were soon reestablished through the initiative of the Indians. In 1683 two delegations from the tribe visited Governor Otermín at El Paso, asking for aid against the Apaches, and that the Spaniards might return to trade with them. As Otermín's term had expired, they were referred to his successor, Domingo Gironza Petris de Cruzate.

Accordingly, on October 15 of the same year, a delegation of seven Indians, Jumanos and others, appeared before Governor Cruzate to repeat the request. The leader of the embassy was Juan Sabeata, a Jumano, who had been baptized at Parral and now lived at La Junta, as the Spaniards called the region about the junction of the Conchos with the Rio Grande. A part of his own tribe lived to the eastward of La Junta on the buffalo plains and near the Nueces River. They were clearly the Jumano whom the Spaniards had so often visited in former times. Sabeata had been at El Paso with one of the former delegations. He now returned as representative of the chiefs of his neighborhood, as well as of tribes to the east, including the Texas, to ask for missionaries and for help against the Apaches. Among thirty-odd tribes of which he spoke, he told particularly of the "great kingdom of the Texas," a populous realm situated some fifteen or twenty days eastward of La Junta, and ruled by a powerful king. As for the chief who had visited Diego del Castillo, who had been to the east many years before, he was not the king of the Texas, but merely the king's lieutenant. The Texas were a settled people, he said, and raised grain in such abundance that they even fed it to their horses. They were neighbors of Gran Quivira, so close, indeed, that the two peoples visited back and forth almost daily.[1]

Governor Cruzate forwarded to the viceroy Sabeata's declaration, saying that he would consider it a great triumph if, in the present viceroy's day, "another New World" should be discovered, and "two realms with two crowns" should be added to the king's dominions. Equally interested was Fray

[1] For a sketch of the Spanish approach to western Texas see Bolton, "The Spanish Occupation of Texas, 1519–1690," in the *Southwestern Historical Quarterly*, XVI. 4–11. See also Benavides, "Memorial," translation in *Land of Sunshine*, XIV. 139–140; Fr. Alonzo Posadas, "Informe á S. M. sobre las tierras de Nuevo Mejico, Quivira y Teguayo," in Fernández Duro, *Peñalosa*, pp. 53–67; Fr. Amando Niel, "Apuntamientos," in *Doc. Hist. Mex.*, tercera serie (Mexico, 1856), pp. 91–93; Bolton, "The Jumano Indians in Texas," in the Texas State Hist. Assoc. *Quarterly*, XV. 68–74; Anne Hughes, "The Beginnings of Spanish Settlement in the El Paso District," in *University of California Publications in History*, I. 295–301.

Nicolás López, custodian of the missions, who at once set about responding to the appeal by founding missions at La Junta. After some preliminaries he set out for that place on December 1, accompanied by Fray Juan Zavaleta and Fray Antonio Acevedo. Arriving at their destination at the end of thirteen days, they found things favorable, and soon seven or more tribes about La Junta had built churches and dwellings for the missionaries.

Meanwhile Governor Cruzate, without awaiting orders from the viceroy, prepared an expedition "for the new discovery of the Jumanas and all other nations who hold friendship with them." As leader he appointed Captain Juan Domínguez de Mendoza, who had gone with Guadalajara to the Jumanos thirty years before. At La Junta he was to be joined by Father López. He was instructed to examine carefully the Nueces River, bring back samples of pearls and other products, and learn everything possible about the Indians. He was especially required to impress the natives with the respect shown the missionaries. The venture had a commercial phase, and the instructions provided for the regulation of trade with the Indians.

On December 15 Mendoza set out, opening his diary at Real de San Lorenzo, a few leagues below El Paso, on the south bank of the Rio Grande. He kept close to that stream all the way to La Junta, passing on the way numerous rancherías of Suma Indians. Leaving Father Acevedo in charge at La Junta, Fathers López and Zavaleta joined the expedition to the plains. From the starting point the route was northward to the Salado (Pecos), which was reached after seventy leagues of travel. Following down the river nine leagues, they crossed to a village of Jediondos, apparently near Horsehead Crossing.

Leaving the Pecos, Mendoza now struck out eastward, across an unwatered plain, and at the end of forty leagues reached a river which flowed east and was remarkable for nuts and clam shells (*conchas*). It was evidently the Middle Concho. Following it eastward for twenty-one (or twenty-four) leagues, he reached its junction with the Nueces River, the stream which he had come to explore and on which he had been with Guadalajara. He must have been where San Angelo now is. Nineteen leagues further eastward he reached the end of his journey at the San Clemente River, an east-flowing stream, apparently the Colorado near its junction with the main Concho.

At the San Clemente Mendoza's party remained six weeks, killed over four thousand head of buffalo, and received messengers from numerous eastern tribes. Mendoza built a combined stronghold and chapel, where numerous Indians were baptized, and before leaving the commander and the missionaries promised to come again within a year.

On his return to La Junta, Mendoza took possession of the north bank of the Rio Grande as a part of New Mexico and delivered rods of justice to four native chiefs. Leaving Fathers Acevedo and Zavaleta to continue missionary work, Mendoza and López returned to El Paso, going by way of the Conchos and the Sacramento, because the Sumas were in revolt and the Rio Grande high.

The expedition of 1684 now became the basis of an attempt to occupy the Jumano country with missionaries and soldiers. On their return to El Paso both Father López and Mendoza went to the city of Mexico, where they prepared memorials, in 1685 and 1686, urging such a step, and it is not at all improbable that if danger from the French on the Gulf coast had not just then arisen, the recommendations would have been put into effect.

The principal sources of information regarding the Mendoza-López expedition hitherto printed are: "Memorial de Fr. Nicolás Lopez acerca de la repoblación de Nuevo Mejico y ventajas que ofrece el reino de Quivira," and "Memorial del

Maestre de Campo Juan Dominguez de Mendoza, informando acerca de las Naciones de Oriente." These documents are printed in Cesáreo Fernández Duro, *Don Diego de Peñalosa y su Descubrimiento del Reino de Quivira* (Madrid, 1882), pp. 67–74, 74–77. The López memorial was used by Barcía, in his *Ensayo Cronológico*, p. 266. A brief contemporary account is contained in Fray Alonso de Posadas's "Informe á S. M. sobre las tierras de Nuevo Mejico, Quivira y Teguayo." This also is printed in Fernández Duro's *Peñalosa*, pp. 53–67.

Of much greater importance is the *expediente* of unpublished manuscripts entitled "Viage Que a solicitud de los Naturales de la Prov.ª de Texas, y otras Naciones circunvecinas, y de orden del Governador del Nuevo Mexico D. Domingo Gironza Petris de Cruzati, Hizo el Maestre de Campo Juan Dominguez de Mendoza, en fines del año de 1683, y principios de 1684, Copiado Del Original que existe en el oficio mas antiguo del Virreynato de Nueva España, en los Autos sobre la sublevacion del Nuevo Mexico, Quaderno 1°," Archivo General y Público, Mexico, Sección de Historia, vol. 298.

This lengthy *expediente* contains, besides the Itinerario hereinafter printed, reports of governor Cruzate to the viceroy; the declaration of Juan Sabeata, made at El Paso, October 20, 1683; *certificaciones* made by Mendoza at La Junta on the way back from the Jumanos; reports sent by the missionaries at El Paso to Mexico by Father López; *representaciones* made by Father López in Mexico in 1685 and 1686; and proceedings of the central government. As is indicated above, the *expediente* is a compilation from the *autos* of the Pueblo Revolt, and most of the originals of the documents copied in the *expediente* are still preserved in the archives of Mexico. This is true of the Itinerario, which is here translated from the original in *expediente* no. 4 of a manuscript volume entitled "Alsamiento Gral. de los Indios de Nuevo Mexico en 1680," which constitutes vol. 37 of the Archivo General y Público, Sección de Provincias Internas. There are few essential differences between the two versions. In the copy dates and distances have been added. An official copy of Mendoza's instructions is in the Bancroft Library.

ITINERARY OF JUAN DOMINGUEZ DE MENDOZA, 1684 [1]

MAESTRE DE CAMPO Juan Dominguez de Mendoza, commander and chief of this detachment of soldiers which is going to the discovery of the East and the kingdom of the Texas at the petition of Don Juan Sebeata, an Indian of the Jumana nation, who, with the other chiefs of that nation, went to petition before the Señor Captain Don Domingo Jironsa Petris de Cruzate, governor and captain-general of these provinces of New Mexico, and before the most Reverend Father Fray Nicolas Lopes, procurator, custodian, and ordinary ecclesiastical judge [2] of the said provinces, in order that they might be protected from both directions, by both the spiritual and temporal care. At this petition the said governor and captain-general, supporting what was for the best service of both Majesties, considered it well to issue to me an order for the execution of the aforesaid journey; and in order that it may be in the form which is required and which the case demands, and in conformity with the aforesaid order and instruction, I have considered it well that all should appear in this itinerary, as follows:

We set out from the Real de San Lorenzo, [3] which is apparently about twelve leagues distant from the mission [4] of Nuestra Señora de Guadalupe of the Mansos and Passo del Rio del Norte. From the aforesaid Real de San Lorenzo to this place in which we now are, it is about five leagues, this place being an adobe house where Maestre de Campo Thome

---

[1] "Alsamiento Gral. de los Indios de Nuevo Mexico en 1680" (manuscript in the Archivo General y Público, Mexico, Provincias Internas, vol. 37).

[2] *Juez ordinario eclesiástico.*

[3] The principal Spanish settlement established by the refugees at El Paso after the retreat of 1680. See Hughes, *The Beginnings of Spanish Settlements in the El Paso District*, pp. 315–333.

[4] *Conversión.*

Domingues de Mendosa[1] lived. It was given the name San
Bartolome. It has a very good watering place; its plain is
supplied with very good pasturage and an abundance of
wood. A holy cross was erected. In order that it may be
better attested, I signed it with my name, with my assisting
witnesses, who here signed it in my presence, as captain, commander and chief. Done on the 15th day of the month of
December, 1683. JUAN DOMINGUES DE MENDOSA. DIEGO
LUCERO DE GODOI. BALTASAR DOMINGUEZ DE MENDOSA.
HERNANDO MARTIN SERANO.

On the 16th day of the said month and year we arrived
at this place, which was given the name of Santisima Trenidad, and which is distant from the aforesaid house about
seven leagues. It is on the top of a hill where there was a
ranchería of Indians of the Suma nation. A holy cross was
erected facing toward the north. Opposite it is a thick-
trunked cottonwood,[2] where the Rio del Norte passes. Below
this cottonwood is found the watering place for the horse herd,
there being no other, because the river has such high and
steep banks. I crossed it with difficulty[3] on the said day,
month, and year.[4]

In this place, which was given the name Nuestra Señora
del Pilar de Saragosa, and which is distant from that of La
Santissima Trenidad about eight leagues. On the 17th day
of the said month and year we arrived at this place where
we found a populous ranchería, besides others which we passed,
all of the Suma nation, poor people who live chiefly on *mescal*,
which is baked palms.[5] All these rancherías asked of me
aid and help against the common enemy, the Hapaches nation, alleging generally that most of them were already disposed to becoming Christians. In fact a considerable portion of them were already reducing themselves to settlements

[1] Father of Juan Domínguez de Mendoza. He had left New Mexico with
the other refugees, settled here, and subsequently moved farther toward the
interior, as had numerous other New Mexicans.

[2] *Alamo*, literally poplar, but in the Southwest the term is commonly applied
to the cottonwood.

[3] *Por diligencia*. This may mean with legal formalities.

[4] Hereafter, in order to save space, the formalities concerning the signing
are omitted at the end of each entry except the last.

[5] See Espejo's narrative, p. 170, above, note 5.

and alleging that the Apaches did not allow them in their lands. Seeing that, in their way, they asked justice, I have promised them all help and protection on the return journey. On the top of a hill I had a cross erected.

On the 18th day of the said month and year we arrived at the place which was named Nuestra Señora de la Limpia Consepcion. It has as a landmark a deep arroyo which forms a stony beach where it empties into the Rio del Norte. This is the watering place. It is distant from Nuestra Señora del Pilar about eight leagues. It forms a nook with good pasturage and wood. On the top of a hill I had a cross erected.

On the 19th day of the said month and year we arrived at this place which was given the name Nuestra Señora de la Soledad. It is about three leagues west of the Rio del Norte, where there is a mountain from which issues an arroyo of good water, in sufficient quantity for any army. This arroyo flows toward the Rio del Norte, and has a very good grove of cottonwoods. It is distant from Nuestra Señora de la Limpia Concepcion about eight leagues. It has very good pastures and wood. I had a holy cross placed on the top of a hill. Between the two places there are three rancherías of the Suma nation.

On the 20th day of the said month and year we arrived at this place, which was given the name Nuestra Señora del Transito, and which is on the Rio del Norte. Its range of hills forms a pasture. Its bottom lands are well supplied with pasturage and wood. It is distant from Nuestra Señora de la Soledad about eight leagues, over country rough in parts. Between, there is a hot spring, which forms the said river. The land is intractable, and is settled by some rancherías. The watering place is good. On the top of a hill I had a holy cross placed.

On the 21st day of the said month and year we arrived at this place, which was named Nuestra Señora del Buen Suseso. It is distant from Nuestra Señora del Transito about four leagues. It has very good land, pasturage, and wood, which is near by in the canyon formed by the Rio del Norte, where the trail leaves it and turns toward the west, and then immediately turns to the east. It is necessary to stop here because on the next day's march there occurs rough land overgrown with mesquite and cat's-claw, although it is pass-able; and soon afterwards there occurs a high steep hill, and toward the east it is precipitous[1] and well overgrown with *lechuguilla*,[2] almost to the Rio del Norte, so that it was not possible to travel by night. It is here described with full specifications. I ordered a cross placed on the top of a hill. In this district were three inhabited rancherías of Sumas.

On the 22d day of the said month and year we arrived at this place, which was named Nuestra Señora del Rosario. It is distant from Nuestra Señora del Buen Suceso about eight leagues. It is like the rough land already described above. We arrived at Rio del Norte, where we found some rancherías of the same Sumas nation. It has very good meadows, pastures, wood, and a watering place. I caused a holy cross to be placed on the top of a hill.

On the 23d day of the said month and year we set out from this place, which was named Nuestra Señora de Regla, and which is distant from Nuestra Señora del Rosario about eight leagues. It has as a landmark a beautiful meadow. The hill is very near to the mountain. Toward the north is a grove of cottonwoods; then comes the river; it forms a long valley on the other bank. Then follows the Rio del Norte. The watering place is good. For further identifica-tion I ordered a holy cross placed on the top of this hill, which looks to the north.

On the 24th day of the said month and year we set out from this place, which was named Nuestra Señora de Belen[3] because of a narrow pass which is found on the top of a steep mountain, which is about a half-league from the said place. This pass is something like a window. The place has for marks the chain of hills and a grove in the form of an O. The watering place is good. It has in the middle a piece of meadow sufficient for the river. It is distant from the last place eight leagues. I ordered a holy cross placed on the top of a hill which faces north.

On the 25th of the said month and year we set out from

---

[1] *Ocinada, cf. hocino.*

[2] The maguey plant. See Espejo's narrative, p. 170. Literally, small lettuce.

[3] Our Lady of Bethlehem. It was Christmas Eve.

this place, which was named Nuestra Señora del Populo. It has for marks a large rock separated from the mountain, with buttresses on the sides, and the length to the north; in appearance it resembles a church. It is on the other side of the Rio del Norte; and on this side where we are, which is on the New Mexico side,[1] is the part which faces the south. Behind it there is a plentiful grove of cottonwoods and other trees. Toward the south the same river forks, and between the branches is a meadow supplied with pasturage. Here, on the top of a hill, I had a holy cross placed. From Nuestra Señora de Belen to this place it is about eight leagues.

On the 26th day of the said month and year we set out from this place which was named Nuestra Señora de Atocha. It has these marks: it is closed in by a chain of hills; it is elevated, and has on the west the mountain; on the south there is a little pass through which the Rio del Norte runs; the chain of hills is thickly covered with cactus, which appears to bear good fruit. Most of this river has watering places of stone. It is about three leagues distant from Nuestra Señora del Populo, for, because of the accident of having lost some horses, it was not possible to go farther. The pastures are good and the hills have plenty of wood and whatever is necessary.

On the 27th day of the said month and year we set out from this place, which was named Nuestra Señora de los Remedios. It has for marks on the north a high mountain. It is at the foot of a hill where the road descends, and before reaching the place there is a dry arroyo. The Rio del Norte flows toward the east. The meadows are the same on both sides of the river; they have an abundance of pastures and wood, and there is a good watering place. I ordered a holy cross placed on the top of a hill. From the place of Nuestra Señora de Atocha it is about seven leagues.

On the 28th day of the said month and year we set out from this place, which was named Nuestra Señora de Guadalupe. To the foregoing place of Nuestra Señora de los Remedios it is about seven leagues. It has for marks two moun-

[1] *I. e.*, he regarded the south bank as a part of New Mexico, but not the north. See Hughes, *The Beginnings of Spanish Settlement in the El Paso District*, chapter VIII.

tains. The one which is toward the north must be three leagues away, and the one which is in front of the Rio del Norte a quarter of a league. On opposite sides of the river are two groves of cottonwood, with dense canebrakes. There is a good watering place. I ordered a holy cross placed on the top of the hill, close to the road.

On the 29th day of the said month and year, we arrived at this place, which was named La Nabidad en las Cruces,[1] because of the crosses possessed by the rancherías which were settled on both sides of the Rio del Norte. These rancherías are of people of the Julimes nation; they are versed in the Mexican language, and all sow maize and wheat. Here we overtook the reverend fathers preachers, Fray Nicolas Lopes, custodian and ordinary judge of the provinces of New Mexico, Fray Juan de Sabaleta, commissary of the Holy Office,[2] and Fray Antonio de Asebedo. Generally all these Indians asked for the water of baptism, and more than one hundred persons were baptized. All the meadows of the river are very spacious, and have good lands, good climate, and abundant pasturage and wood.[3]

In this place, which was named El Apostol Santiago,[4] and from which we set out today, New Year's day, January 1, 1684, and where our very reverend father custodian and ordinary judge, Fray Nicolas Lopes, and Father Fray Juan de Sabaleta, commissary of the Holy Office, celebrated mass, I had a holy cross placed on the top of a hill. It is about seven leagues distant from La Nabedad, which is the settlement where Father Fray Antonio de Assevedo remains in charge. This district is very stony in parts, although I travelled over it. The aforesaid place of Señor Santiago has for marks an

[1] When Sabeata and his companions went to El Paso to ask for missionaries, they told a tale of the miraculous appearance of a cross in the sky near La Junta. The place where the apparition was said to occur was called by the Spaniards La Navidad en las Cruces. Sabeata later confessed that the story was a pure fabrication intended to stir the Spaniards to action. [2] Inquisition.

[3] The diary gives the distance from Guadalupe to La Navidad as one hundred and nine leagues plus the last day's march (for which no distance is given) or about one hundred and fifteen leagues. The air-line distance is about one hundred and ninety miles, but by the windings of the river it must be two hundred and fifty miles.

[4] The Apostle Saint James.

arroyo which flows from north to south.   It has very abundant pasturage, partly green and partly dry.[1]

On January 2, 1684, we set out from this place, which was named Nuestro Padre San Francisco.   It has the following marks: a spring of hot water which flows toward the southeast.   Its source is on a height.   The water and the pasturage are good.   The land is level and has little wood.   A cross was not erected for lack of timber.   It is distant from Señor Santiago about seven leagues.

On the 3d day of the aforesaid month we set out from this place, which was named San Nicolas.   It is distant from Nuestro Padre San Francisco about seven leagues.   It has the following marks: It is at the extremity of a mesa which extends to the north.   It is a watering place consisting of a beautiful reservoir which is supplied by the rains.   The passage[2] through the rocks forms two steep crags on the sides; on one of them I had a holy cross placed.   There are in the environs of the reservoir some ash trees and other kinds of timber; and in the cavities made by the rocks adjoining the reservoir there is a great quantity of maidenhair fern and most beautiful grape-vines.   Toward the west is a beautiful plain, with plentiful pasturage of couch grass.[3]   The direction which we were following was toward the north.

On the 4th day of the month and year we set out from this place which was named Nuestro Padre San Antonio.   It is in the midst of some hills, where there is a reservoir sufficient for any herd of horses.   It is surrounded by bare, denuded rock.[4]   Its inlet is an arroyo which runs toward the west. It is covered with oaks, and on the heights with cedars.   It is distant from San Nicolas about seven leagues.   Midway there are some little pools of brackish water.   All the land is level. In the neighborhood of the little pools there is a great quantity of white and yellow mesquites.   In the midst of so much evil there is a little spring of fresh and kindly water, and, as

---

[1] The party apparently went down the Rio Grande seven leagues before turning north.   The arroyo flowing south seems to have been the Alamito.

[2] *Esladeros.*   I cannot find this word in any dictionary.   *Cf. aisladero,* or *ailadero,* which is frequently used in the De León diaries in the sense of "passage way."   See p. 410, below, note 3.

[3] *Grama.*   [4] *Peña viva.*

an exquisite thing, I had it noted with particular care. On
the top of some rocks near this little spring I had a holy cross
placed.

On the 5th day of the said month and year, we set out
from this place, which is distant from San Antonio about four
leagues; in both places mass was celebrated. This district
consists in parts of rocks and knolls, and in parts of plain
without rocks. It is at the foot of a hill which is toward the
east. On the south rises a little arroyo which flows toward
the north.[1] There is water sufficient for any herd of horses.
The pastures are good, but there is little wood and that which
there is at a distance is oak. It was named San Lorenso
because of the fire which threatened to burn us by night, but
the damage which might have occurred was prevented by the
circle[2] which was made round about. The cross was not
erected because there was no timber of which to make it.

On the 6th day of the said month and year, the day of Los
Santos Reyes,[3] we set out from this place, where two masses
were celebrated. It was named the place of Los Reyes. It
is on the left hand, as we come from San Lorenso, turning aside
from the path about a half league for a valley apart with good
pasturage and with mountains on both sides. In the valley
is a dry arroyo with some pecans;[4] continuing up stream one
finds good water; it is toward the north; it is distant from
San Lorenso about five leagues. I had a holy cross erected.

On the 7th day of the said month and year we remained
in this place, which was named San Pedro de Alcantara. It
is distant from the place of Los Reyes about six leagues. This
detention was at the general request of the Indians of the
Jumana nation and the others who came with them, who were
constrained by the necessity which they suffered because of
not having any food to eat; for this reason they arranged to
surround the deer and other kinds of animals, in order to relieve the necessity which we all shared. This place has a

---

[1] The party were evidently in the neighborhood of Alpine.

[2] *Cerco*, perhaps a circle made by back firing. The allusion to San Lorenzo
refers to his death by burning.

[3] Day of the Holy Kings (Epiphany).

[4] The trees called *nogales* in the diary are in all probability pecans, which
are abundant in many parts of Texas.

beautiful plain which extends eastward, and toward the north are some hills without any trees. From the slope of a hill issues a beautiful spring, round about which there is fine black land. The place has little wood. The holy cross was not erected for lack of timber.

On the 8th day of the said month and year we set out from this place of San Pedro de Alcantara, whose marks are already given. We camped for the night without water and wood. All the road is level.

On the 9th day of the said month and year we set out from this place, which was named San Bernardino de Sena, which is distant from San Pedro de Alcantara about eight leagues. It is in a plain without water, and the watering place is apparently about three leagues away.

On the 10th day of the said month and year, we set out from this place, which was named San Francisco Xaviel.[1] It is distant from San Bernardino de Sena about four leagues. It has as marks three small hills standing toward the west; and toward the north a cliff[2] from which issues a spring of alkaline[3] but pleasant water. The pastures are good, and there is an abundance of mesquite wood. The tracks of buffalo began to appear, but, although search was made, none were found. The holy cross was not erected for lack of suitable timber.

On the 11th of the said month and year we set out from this place, which was given the name San Juan del Rio. It is in a beautiful plain. In its environs there are four high mesas; from the small one toward the north flows a spring; within three arquebus shots, apparently, there issue five other springs,[4] all beautiful; and within the distance of half a league a most beautiful river is formed, although without any kind of tree, it having only camalote[5] patches. The water is very clear, although a little alkaline; it is well supplied with fish. Mass was celebrated. It is distant from San Francisco Xaviel four leagues, rather more than less. The holy cross

---

[1] St. Francis Xavier.   [2] *Sexa, cf. ceja.*   [3] *Gordo.*

[4] The doubt here is between Barrilla Springs and those at Fort Stockton, but the distance from the Salado points to the latter.

[5] The camalote is an aquatic plant of the family *pontederiaceæ* (*Diccionario Salvat*).

was not erected for lack of suitable timber, although there is abundance of mesquite wood. Three bulls were killed in this place, and with them came relief to the great need which all the camp suffered.

On the 12th day of the month and year we set out from the above named place of Señor San Juan, and camped for the night about five leagues from it without water. Half way we found a very beautiful spring which flows toward the north; toward the east runs a chain of mesas, on the right hand as we came. All the road is level, without stones, covered with much pasturage and with mesquite and other kinds of wood. It was named San Anselmo. The holy cross was not erected for lack of suitable timber. Mass was celebrated.

On the 13th day of the said month and year we set out from San Anselmo, and arrived at this place on the Salado River, which comes from New Mexico; its course is southeast.[1] Apparently it carries as much water as the Rio del Norte. The water is muddy and somewhat alkaline, although pleasant. It has no trees, but it is very well supplied with mesquite and good pasturage. Mass was celebrated, but the holy cross was not erected for lack of suitable timber.

On the 14th day of the said month and year we were detained on the Salado River. The place was named San Christoval. It is distant from San Anselmo about six leagues. In front there is a little mesa separate from the others. The delay was for providing meat.

On the 15th day of the said month and year we set out from this place of San Christoval, where mass was celebrated. The day before, when we stopped, six buffalo bulls were killed, with which the camp was supplied. A great saline was discovered, without water, but abundantly supplied with salt in white and good grains. It is about a league on the other side of the Salado River, between a high hill and a mesa which

---

[1] Literally, from north to east. The distance from La Navidad en las Cruces is estimated at seventy leagues, or sixty-three from Santiago, which, it is inferred, was on the Rio Grande. It is clear that the direction was generally northward, and that the Salado (Pecos) was reached some distance above Horsehead Crossing. The air-line distance from the mouth of the Conchos to Horsehead Crossing is about one hundred and sixty miles, but by the trails it must be nearly two hundred miles.

is beyond.[1] All the foregoing are toward the east. In this part where we are there is a small mesa separated from the others already mentioned; in front of the small mesa is the saline.

On the 16th day of the said month and year we set out from this place, where two masses were celebrated. It is on the same Salado River, and is distant from San Christobal about three leagues. The water in the river became better. Toward the west it has a great mesa, from which a range of hills extends toward the east. On the other side of the river, toward the east, about four leagues apparently, there is a little range of mountains; from it extends a small mesa; above this rises another little mesa which commands a wide prospect. The holy cross was not erected for lack of suitable timber. The place was given the name of Santo Domingo Soriano de la Nocha Buena,[2] because we were free from cold. About the middle of the night it commenced to rain as if it were summer, but the glorious saint was pleased that it should not continue, for all the companions came without tents.

On the 17th day of the said month and year we set out from this place, which was given the name of San Juan de Dios. Mass was celebrated in it. It is distant from Santo Domingo about six leagues. All the district is a plain, particularly along the banks of the said Salado River. The pastures are apparently good, although we found them burned, and because of this we halted, a league, apparently, from the ranchería of the people whom they called the Jediondos. Their chiefs and other people came out to receive us with much rejoicing, most of them on foot, others on horseback, carrying a holy cross very well made, which apparently must be two and a half *varas* long, of somewhat heavy timber, painted red and yellow, and fastened with a nail which they call *taxamanil*. The holy cross showed that they had made it some time before. They also brought forth a banner of white taffeta, a little less than a *vara* long; in the middle of the banner were two successive crosses of blue taffeta, very well made. At the

---

[1] There is such a saline north of the Rio Grande in Crane County, a few miles above Horsehead Crossing.

[2] St. Dominic of Sora, of the Fortunate Night. Noche Buena is also the name applied to Christmas Eve.

time of meeting us they fired several shots, Don Juan Sabeata firing with a fuse an arquebus barrel without a lock; and I ordered the salute returned on our part with two volleys. As soon as we met I ordered that no soldier should dismount, but only the reverend fathers preachers, Fray Nicolas Lopes, custodian and ordinary ecclesiastical judge, and Father Fray Juan de Sabaleta, commissary of the Holy Office. Kneeling with much devotion, they kissed the holy cross. I did the same, being on horseback, with the other comrades; and the Indians kissed the garments of their reverences.

Together we arrived at the ranchería, to the middle of which we crossed the Salado River, without any shelter. When we approached the ranchería, all the women and children came shouting in token of the great pleasure which they felt at seeing us. All the women and children kissed the holy habit of the reverend fathers. All of the chiefs and other people wished to give us lodging and entertainment in their own ranchería in some huts of tule, which they had made for us, but I did not consent to it, because of the evil results which might follow, excusing myself with good reasons. I pitched the camp on a hill, according to the usage of war, separated from the said ranchería, which is at the foot of a great rock that serves it as protection against the hostile Apaches. It was given the name San Ygnacio de Loyola. Here I remained awaiting news of a great ambuscade which the enemy are coming to make on them in order to carry off many horses.

On the 19th of the aforesaid month and year, in the place of San Ygnacio, where I am detained at the request of all the Jumanos and the other nations, and being occupied with providing the soldiers with supplies of arms and other implements of war, on the said day all the chiefs, with the governor Don Juan de Sabeata, assembled, saying that they wished to speak to me, the said governor speaking for himself and all the chiefs and different nations. For this purpose, I on my part ordered all the chiefs of squad and soldiers of rank to assemble, in order that they might be present. This being done, I commanded Governor Don Juan Sabeata and all their chiefs to say what it was they wished; and all, in one voice, asked that for the love of God I should make war on the hostile Apaches, who were enemies of theirs and of the Spaniards. Because this was true, and because the said governor and the chiefs protested that it was not wise to leave them behind, on account of the many dangers which might follow, and seeing that they petitioned forcibly, I granted that war should be made upon them, with which the governor and other chiefs were pleased.

On the 20th day of the said month and year, in the said place of San Ygnacio, the governor, Don Juan Sabeata, appeared before me saying that, in order that some men might be armed, he was bringing me seventeen deerskins, which he did bring, and they were divided among those who were most needy. He promised that as soon as the others which were lacking could be cured, he would bring them.[1] These deerskins were divided among the following persons: Captain Hernando Martin Serano, three; Nicolas Lucero, two; Miguel Luxan, two; Melchor de Archuleta, two; Felipe Montolla, two; Captain Felipe Romero, one; Captain Ygnacio Baca, another; Ensign Antonio Solis, another; Sargento Baltasar Domingues, another; Juan Domingues, the younger, another; Antonio Gomes, another.

On the 24th day of the said month and year we set out from this place of San Ygnacio de Loyola, where we had been detained seven days. On the 8th we set out from the said place, in which mass was celebrated every day. On Saturday it was sung in honor of the Most Holy and Perfect Virgin and with all solemnity another prayer was celebrated. The following Sunday two other masses were celebrated. The place is distant from San Juan de Dios about a league. During the seven days all the camp killed twenty-seven beeves.

From this place, which was given the name La Conversion de San Pablo,[2] whose day occurred while we were here, we set out on the 25th of the said month and year. On arrival here meat was killed, and in the place two masses were celebrated. On the night which we camped there without water, Juan Sabeata told us that the spies had informed him that they had followed the tracks of the horseherd which the hostile Apaches had driven off. This place is distant from San Ygnacio about five leagues. It is in a plain, but because the

---

[1] Perhaps they were for shields or bucklers.

[2] The conversion of St. Paul is celebrated on January 25.

country was burned we stopped on a hill which was well supplied with pasturage.

In this place, which was given the name San Honofre.
It is distant from La Conversion de San Pablo about five
leagues. It is level country with wood, although without
pasturage because of its being burned. By the time of our
arrival at this place of San Honofre five beeves had been killed
on the way as we journeyed. Here God our Lord was pleased
to let us find an abundance of cattle and pasturage and sufficient wood. The place is in a plain. In a flat it has a spring
of clear and good water. We arrived here on the 25th and
remained two days in order that the horses might recuperate.
We set out from the place on the 28th. Mass was celebrated
every day. Thirty-four beeves were killed. A cross was not
erected for lack of suitable timber. In this place there joined
us the people whom they call the Arcos Tuertos;[1] their wearing apparel and all the rest is after the fashion of the Suma
nation.

On the 29th day of said month and year we set out from
this place, which was given the name San Marcos, because
upon arriving at it a bull was killed within the camp. It is
distant from the place of San Honofre about ten leagues.
The location is good, and has abundant pasturage and wood.
The watering-place runs from a hill where a holy cross was
placed, for there was suitable timber. Mass was celebrated.

On the said 29th day we did not set out from San Marcos,
through the accident of some horses having been lost. Including the first beef animal, thirty-two were killed in this
place. A holy cross was erected, two masses were celebrated,
and we set out on the 30th of the said month and year.

On the last day of the said month we arrived at this place,
which was given the name San Joseph. It is in a gorge which
has a pool of good water, much wood, and pasturage. It is
distant from San Marcos four leagues, rather more than less.
Mass was celebrated and a holy cross erected. We remained
to take advantage of the good pasturage one day, which was
the 1st of February.

On the 2d day of February of the said year we set out from
this place, which was given the name Nuestra Señora de la

---

[1] Twisted Bows.

Candelaria, because we spent that day there; our arrival was on the 21st,[1] I having decided to remain that day here. The day of the Most Holy Virgin[2] was celebrated, our reverend preacher custodian, Fray Nicolas Lopes, singing mass in her honor; the reverend preacher Fray Juan de Sabaleta said prayer. It is distant from the aforesaid place of San Joseph about six leagues and is at the point where the Nueces River is reached.[3] Here we ate some catfish. The source of the river is in some springs. It flows toward the east. The place is pleasant, having much wood, pasturage, and fish. A holy cross was erected.

On the 5th day of the month of February, 1684, we set out from this place, which was given the name El Arcanjel San Migel, and where we remained two and a half days pasturing the horses because of their being worn and thin. It is distant from Nuestra Señora de la Candelaria about three leagues. There is in the said place a river bearing much water, the source of which is not known because it comes from beneath the earth and issues through some rocks. A holy cross was erected above the orifice from which the river emerges. This place is very aptly named Where-the-Dogs-Live, because there come out from the water many dogs of all colors, of the same size as the other dogs, and of the same species, although bred in the water. They say that they are more savage. They tear the people in pieces, and do the same with the buffalo bulls and cows that come to drink at the orifice. We saw the skeletons of the cows and the bulls, and likewise the excrement and tracks of the dogs.[4]

The river flows toward the east. The water is clear and good. In this place were the first pecan trees that we saw, for its bottoms have many groves of them; many nuts were gathered, with which all the people of the camp were provided,

---

[1] Clearly an error for the 31st of January. It is in both transcripts.

[2] Feast of the Purification, or Candlemas, February 2.

[3] The distance from the village of the Hediondos to this point totals thirty leagues, and from the place where the Pecos was first struck, about forty leagues. The stream which he calls the Nueces is clearly the Middle Concho. The only other possibility is that it was the fork of the Colorado which runs through Midland County, but there are several considerations which exclude that stream.

[4] This report is perhaps partly fanciful. It may be that the animals described were wolves or coyotes.

for we had been subsisting on flesh only.   The river flows to
join that of the pearls.   It also has shells, a variety of fish,
and very lofty live oaks, so large that carts and other very
bulky things can be made of them.   There is a great variety
of plants and of wild hens which make noise at dawn.   The
river bottoms are very extensive and fertile; in its groves are
many grape vines and springs, and many prickly-pear patches;
and all of the foregoing are on both sides of the river.   The
watering places for the buffalo are so near to the roads that it
is not possible to round them up.   During this stop we had
always threatening us a rain storm, but God was pleased not
to let it descend except on the last night, which was stormy and
windy.

The hostile Apaches stole nine animals, seven from the
Jumana Indians, and the others, a horse and a mule, from the
chief and Ensign Diego de Luna, respectively.   Because of
carelessness, these animals joined those of the Indians.   It
was not possible to follow them because of the great advantage
which they had.

On the 11th day of the said month and year we set out
from this place, which was given the name San Diego.   It is
distant from San Migel about six leagues.   We remained here
four days because we were awaiting some spies, who brought
us news, saying that they had discovered a ranchería of hostile Apaches, wherefore it was necessary to dispatch new
spies in order to learn the truth of the matter.   The first news
proved to be false, though not altogether, because the tracks
which they saw were old.   Mass was celebrated every day.

There were killed at Señor San Diego forty-three beeves;
and while we were travelling to it there were killed by the
Spaniards and the Indians together sixty beeves, rather more
than less, by means of surrounding the cattle.   The place is
in a plaza which has several great groves of very tall pecan
and live-oak trees.   There are a great number of wild hens
and other kinds of game.   The watering place is a beautiful
river which flows toward the east.

On the 19th day of the said month and year we set out
from this place, which was given the name El Angel de Guarda.[1]
It is distant from Señor San Diego about four leagues.

---

[1] The Guardian Angel.

Through the accident of the bad weather a stop was made half way, where a heavy and tempestuous rain storm descended upon us, and through the information of the spies who many times brought us supposititious news that the hostile Apache were near and that it was best to stop. This craft and this deceitful procedure was all moved by Juan de Sabeata, who in nothing had told us the truth. The aforesaid places are on the banks of a river which flows to join with the principal, which they call Rio de las Perlas. The water is good. The country is well supplied with nuts and other food products, such as wild turkeys, sweet potatoes, buffalo, and many other kinds of animals. The river is supplied with many fish: catfish, *boquinete*, and *matalote*; and with shells; and with a variety of very agreeable song-birds. Mass has been celebrated every day. Eighty beeves have been killed, rather more than less. From this place, under this date, I dispatched the Jumana spies with the said Sabeata, because of the frauds in which he had been caught. There went in his company two Piros Indians.

On the 22d day of the said month and year we set out from this place, which was given the name San Bissente Ferrer. It is distant from El Angel de la Guarda about three leagues. Our delay was incurred to pasture the horses. Mass was celebrated every day. It is on the same river. On both sides are great bottoms; there is a great luxuriance of plants, nut, and other kinds of trees, and wild grapes, good pasturage, a variety of birds, and wild hens. The river has great abundance of fish. Eleven beeves were killed for the sustenance of the camp.

On the 24th day of the said month and year we set out from this place, which was given the name El Rio de Señor San Pedro, which is the principal branch of the river which they call Rio de las Perlas or, by another name, Nuesses River, although all have nuts. This river is the one named in the order which I bring from Governor and Captain-general Don Domingo Xironsa Petris de Crusate, which order is now executed.[1] This place is about eight leagues further down the said river

---

[1] Mendoza was now twenty-one (or twenty-four) leagues from the place where he had struck the Nueces River, which he had followed to its junction with the Río de las Perlas, or Río de San Pedro. Mendoza was apparently near San Angelo.

than the place where Don Diego de Guadalaxara arrived.[1] It is distant from San Bissente Ferrer about five leagues. It is very luxuriant with plants, as are the others, although with greater abundance of water, because the rivers are united. In it were killed seven beeves.

On the 27th day of the said month and year we set out from this place, which was given the name San Pablo. It is without permanent water, and that which we found was rain water. It is distant from the River of Señor San Pedro about six leagues. Mass has been celebrated every day, and twice on holidays. There were killed about twenty beeves.

On the 15th day of the month of March, 1684, we set out from the place which was given the name San Isidro Labrador. It is at the source of a beautiful river. At its headwaters it has many pecan trees. It is enclosed in a valley on both sides of which are rocky mesas. It is distant from the River of Señor San Pablo about eight leagues. The road is level, with much pasturage and woods, and many hens. Mass has been celebrated every day. The beeves that were killed by the whole camp were two hundred, rather more than less.

On the River of the Glorious San Clemente. On the 1st day of the month of May of the year 1684, we set out from this place with the advice of the reverend fathers preachers, Fray Nicolas Lopes, custodian and ordinary ecclesiastical judge of the provinces of New Mexico, and Father Fray Juan de Sabaleta, commissary of the Holy Office; and likewise with the advice of all the persons of rank—as are Sargento Mayor Diego Lucero de Godoi, chief of squad; Captain Hernando Martin Serrano, whom I have named as interpreter of the Jumana language; and other chiefs of squad, namely, Ensign Diego de Luna and Diego Barela—and of other soldiers, conforming to this advice because it seemed to me to be best for the service of both Majesties and the credit of the camp, because of my not being able to sustain the great war which, from the north, the common enemies, the Apache nation, have made upon us. They have attacked us three times by night and by day, and the last night they wounded a soldier,

[1] See the Introduction, p. 314. This statement, made by one who was on both the expedition of 1654 and that of 1684, is of great importance in establishing the identity of the points reached by both.

inflicting upon him three arrow wounds, besides other injuries which the Apaches have caused.

From the west the bandit Indians of the kingdom of La Bizcaia, whom they call the Salineros, with great boldness made by night three attacks upon the aforesaid camp, and killed in the field two friendly Indians who had gone out to hunt, because they were asleep; the latter Indians were of the Jediondos nation. And being without forces, and with only few munitions, I considered it best to return, in order to give an account to Captain Don Domingo Xironsa Petris de Crusate, governor and captain-general of the province of New Mexico and its presidio, that his lordship may do in the case what he may consider best for the service of both Majesties.

We arrived at the said place of San Clemente on the 16th of the month of March. It is distant from the place of San Isidro about five leagues. The San Clemente River flows toward the east.[1] In this place there are no shells whatever; but I learned that six days' journey below the place on the same road there was a great quantity of large shells, and that most of them had pearls. The bottom lands of the river are luxuriant with plants bearing nuts, grapes, mulberries, and many groves of plums; with much game, wild hens, and a variety of animals, such as bear, deer, and antelopes, though few, but the number of buffalo is so great that only the divine Majesty, as owner of all, is able to count them. The stay in this place was to await forty-eight nations—not counting those who were present with us, who were sixteen—besides many others whom, through their ambassadors, I was awaiting. Afterwards they will be set down with their names, although curious.

We were in said place, as already stated, from the 16th of March to the 1st of May. Every day the holy sacrifice of the mass was celebrated, for which purpose I built a bastion with two rooms; the one below served as a chapel where they celebrated mass, and they celebrated all the service of Holy Week, singing it, many Christian Indians who were among so many barbarous nations assisting in everything. All those present

---

[1] The distance from San Vicente, the junction of the two branches of the Nueces, totals nineteen leagues. San Clemente would seem to have been a point on the Colorado River not far from Ballinger.

in our company asked to become Christians.   The other room
of the bastion served as a safeguard against the aforesaid
enemies, because it was on a hill, where it served as great
security both for all the camp and for the horses.

There occurred in this place a noteworthy event. A
water-snake bit Diego Barela on the little finger, a deadly
poisonous thing.   In the time of four *credos* the poison went
down to the stomach causing such vehement pain that we all
thought that he would die at once.   But God our Lord was
pleased that our reverend father custodian should have with
him an antidote for every kind of poison, and his reverence,
caring with his own hands for the bitten part, and giving him
the said herb to drink, caused him to emit at once a great
quantity of what looked like carbon, and our Lord has been
pleased to spare his life.

By the whole camp of Spaniards and Indians there were
killed in the aforesaid place of Señor San Clementi four thousand and thirty beeves.[1]   These are only the large beeves
which were brought into the camp and do not include those
which they left lost in the fields, only removing the pelts from
them, nor the little calves which they brought to the camp, and
which were many.

In order that they may go with all specification, by their
names the aforesaid nations will be given.   First, the Jumana
nation; the Ororosos,[2] the Beitonijures, the Achubales, the Cu-
jalos, the Toremes, the Gediondos,[3] the Siacuchas, the Suajos,
the Isuchos, the Cujacos, the Caulas, the Hinehis, the Ylames,
the Cunquebacos, the Quitacas, the Quicuchabes, Los que
asen Arcos,[4] the Hanasines.   These nations are those who are
accompanying us.

Those for whom we are waiting are the following: People
of the Rio de los Tejas, who had sent me a message that
they would come, the Huicasique, the Aielis, the Aguidas,
the Flechas Chiquitas,[5] the Echancotes, the Anchimos, the
Bobidas, the Injames, the Dijus, the Colabrotes, the Unojitas,
the Juanas, the Yoyehis, the Acanis, the Humez, the Bibis,

---

[1] This is an indication of the size of the throng of Indians which gathered
at San Clemente, and also suggests the interest of the party in buffalo hunting.
[2] The Horrible Ones.   [3] The Stinking Ones.
[4] The Bow Makers.   [5] The Little Arrows.

the Conchumuchas,[1] the Teandas, the Hinsas, the Pojues, the Quisabas, the Paiabunas, the Papanes, the Puchas, the Puguahianes, the Isconis,[2] the Tojumas, the Pagaiames, the Abas, the Bajuneros, the Nobraches, the Pylchas, the Detobitis, the Puchames, the Abau, the Oranchos. The foregoing nations could not be awaited for the aforesaid reasons, but they remain friendly toward us. And an agreement was made with the messengers of the nations who were not present that a return would be made at their appointment, the time set being the aforesaid year of twenty-five.[3]   Separating ourselves, some nations departed toward their land with the Indian who governed them, who is a Christian and is proficient in the Mexican language and in Castilian.[4]

We provided meat and, with the other nations who were with us, took a different route from that which we first followed. There remained with us only some families. Juan Sabeata, fearful of his bad work, fled, for he had plotted with some nations to kill us, and then found out that we had learned it already from the same nations, who dealt with the Spaniards with great fidelity. His conduct having been so bad, he was perhaps afraid they would kill him, for he remained in bad repute with all those nations.

On the 2d day of the month of May of the said year we set out from this place, which was given the name San Atanacio, because it was his day. It is on the same river, and has the same plants, a quantity of fish, and the same animals. It is distant from San Clemente about four leagues.

In this place, which was given the name of Santa Cruz, we stopped to celebrate its day, which was the third, when its holy day was celebrated.[5]   Mass was sung in its honor. Another prayer was celebrated the night before, eve of its day, when we were all expecting to see the enemies come to attack us; but God was greatly pleased that they should not do so. Thirty beeves were killed. The place is distant from

---

[1] The People of Many Shells.

[2] This name is nearly identical with that of the Iscanis, a Wichita tribe.

[3] An error for "eighty-five."

[4] This might be taken as an indication that these tribes had come from the south.

[5] The Finding of the Holy Cross is celebrated on May 3.

San Atanasio about three leagues. We set out from the said place on the 4th of May.

In this place which was given the name of San Agustin, because it is in a valley with many pines. It is on a river which flows toward the west. It has many mulberries and plums and pond ferns. It is distant from Santa Cruz about six leagues. Mass was celebrated every day. One hundred and twenty beeves were killed. We set out from the said place today, the 7th of May of the said year.

In the place of La Hasencion del Señor, on the 11th of the month of May, which was the aforesaid day,[1] where our reverend father custodian sang the mass, and another prayer was said. It is on a river beautiful with pecan trees, grapes,[2] and mulberries. It flows toward the east. We remained here four days, awaiting some spies who had gone to explore the country. Two hundred and fifty-five beeves were killed. We set out from this place on the 11th of the said month.

On the 13th day of the said month and year we set out from this place, which was given the name San Lazaro, and where we remained one day. Half way between the two places is the source of the said River of La Hasencion. It is all rough land with much timber, although traversable. Its watering place is composed of rain water. Mass was celebrated. Thirteen beeves were killed.

On the 19th day of the month of May we set out from this place, which was given the name Nuestra Señora de la Piedad.[3] It is distant from San Lasaro about fourteen leagues. In that distance four stops were made because a young man named Francisco de Harchuleta, who had gone out to kill meat, got lost. We travelled six days in search of him, but although efforts were made to find him in every direction, it was impossible to find him, and at the date of this writing he has not yet appeared. Our reverend father custodian sang mass in his behalf to the glorious San Antonio, in order that he might favor him and bring him to this camp; may he be pleased to do so if it should be best. It was given the name Nuestra Señora de la Piedad, in order that she may have pity on this poor young man, taking him to a place where he may not lose

---

[1] Ascension Day fell on May 8 in 1684; May 11 was Sunday.
[2] *Abas,* perhaps a misprint for *Ubas.*   [3] Our Lady of Mercy.

his life.   Mass was celebrated every day; and during all these stops there have been killed one hundred and fifty beeves, rather more than less.   All the watering places have been formed of rain water, all the country is timbered and has very good pastures, and all the land is pleasant.

On the 21st day of the said month and year, the first day of the feast of Espiritu Santo,[1] we set out from this place which was given the name El Hespiritu Santo.   It is distant from Nuestra Señora de la Piedad about eight leagues.   Its watering place is not stable, it being rain water.   All this land is plain and traversable.   Our reverend father custodian sang the mass, and our reverend Father Fray Juan de Sabaleta the prayers.   Twenty beeves were killed.   It is worthy of note that from the place of San Clemente to this place in which we are we came by a different road from the one which we took on going, turning now on the way back to the right, and we are going almost straight west,[2] the luxuriance of the plants already having become less, as the fields are clothed only with good pasturage and some chaparral.   There is an abundance of wild grapes in the dry arroyos.

On the 22d day of the said month and year we set out from this place, which was given the name San Geronimo.   It is distant from Hespiritu Santo about seven leagues.   Its watering place is of rain water.   The country and vegetation are the same as the preceding.   Mass was celebrated.   Six beeves were killed.

On the said 22d day of the said month and year we arrived at sunset at this place on the Salado River, where God our Lord was pleased that we should come upon the track of the aforesaid Francisco de Harchuleta, who was lost at Nuestra Señora de la Piedad.   Mass was celebrated.   The Indians of the Xediondos nation withdrew without asking permission or telling us.   Three beeves were killed.   It is worthy of note that the place where we arrived at the Salado River is much below that where we left it in going, which was at San Ygnacio.

On the 23d day of the said month and year we set out from the Salado River, which was given the name San Pantaleon. We arrived at a beautiful river with good water.   The bottom

[1] Whitsunday came on May 18 in 1684.
[2] This statement gives us an important clue to the route.

lands are very luxuriant with pasturage, which looks like bar-
ley. Our reverend father sang the mass of the Most Holy
Sacrament,[1] in order that His Divine Majesty might be pleased
that it should rain; and His Divine Majesty, having pity
upon us, was pleased. To this river was given [the name of
Corpus Christi. From] San Pantaleon it is distant about
five leagues. Two bulls were killed.

On the 25th day of the said month and year we set out
from the said place of Corpus Christi and again struck the
Salado River, at a place to which was given the name Santo
Thomas de Villanueva, distant from Corpus Christi about ten
leagues. Here we crossed the Salado River and struck the
road which we followed on going, at San Juan de Dios, from
where we again followed our former route. Mass was celebrated. Only one bull was killed.

In order that it may be attested, I signed it with my assisting witnesses in my presence, on the said day, month, and
year. JUAN DOMINGUES DE MENDOSA. DIEGO LUSERO DE
GODOI. HERNANDO MARTIN SERANO.

[1] Corpus Christi.

TEXAS

3. THE DE LEÓN–MASSANET EXPEDITIONS AND THE FOUNDING OF TEXAS, 1689–1690

INTRODUCTION

BEFORE the Mendoza expedition was made, the King of Spain had already begun to consider the occupation of the country at the mouth of the Mississippi River. In 1678 news was received at the Spanish court that Peñalosa, a discredited ex-governor of New Mexico, had proposed at the court of France an expedition against northern New Spain. Incident to the investigation of the report the royal secretaries brought forth the Benavides memorial of 1630, and noted its recommendation that the Bay of Espíritu Santo, at the mouth of the Mississippi, be occupied as a base of operations in New Mexico and Quivira and as a defence against encroaching foreigners. Thereupon the king asked the viceroy for a report on the geography of the country east of New Mexico, and on the feasibility of Benavides's plan—"what advantages would come from Christianizing the kingdoms of Quivira and Tagago; what means would be needed to effect it; whether it could be done better by way of Florida than through the Bay of Espíritu Santo; and whether any danger was to be feared from the proposals of Peñalosa."

In the succeeding years there were numerous raids by French corsairs on the Florida coasts, and in 1685 Martín de Echegaray, *piloto mayor* in Florida, was commissioned to explore the Bay of Espíritu Santo with a view to its occupation. At the same time the king repeated his order of 1678 requiring from the viceroy a report on Quivira and Tagago. Matters were now brought to a focus by the La Salle expedition.

In 1684 La Salle left France with his colony destined for the mouth of the Mississippi, but by accident it was landed

347

on Matagorda Bay. News of La Salle's enterprise soon reached Spain and Mexico, and there began a series of expeditions, four by sea and five by land, in search for the French and the Bay of Espíritu Santo. In January, 1686, Juan Enríquez Barroto, sent by the viceroy from Vera Cruz, explored west from Apalache and returned to Vera Cruz, reporting that the Gulf was free from pirates. In 1687 the new viceroy sent out two brigs under Rivas and Yriarte, with Barroto as pilot, and two frigates under Pez and Gamarra. The brigs coasted west from Apalache to Matagorda Bay, where they found the wrecks of two of La Salle's vessels, and concluded that the French party had perished. Shortly afterward the frigates, coasting north, also saw the wrecks, and continued to Apalache. In the following year Pez explored from Mobile Bay past the mouth of the Mississippi, in another search for La Salle.

The five land expeditions were all made by Alonso de León, a soldier of Nuevo León, and son of a conspicuous pioneer of the same name. In 1686 he led a company from Monterey to the Río Grande, followed the right bank of that stream to the Gulf, and explored south along the coast to Río de las Palmas. Making another expedition in 1687, he succeeded in crossing the Río Grande, but was turned back by a river called Salado or Solo. In this same year he was made governor of Coahuila and captain of the new presidio of Monclova. Being informed early in 1688 that a Frenchman was living among the Indians across the Río Grande, in May De León crossed the river, captured Juan Jarri, as the Frenchman was called, and sent him to Mexico. In the following year, 1689, accompanied by Father Massanet, De León again crossed the Río Grande, went to Matagorda Bay and found the remains of La Salle's settlement, and on the Guadalupe River held a conference with the chief of the Nabedache, one of the Tejas tribes.

The report taken back by De León that there were Frenchmen living to the northeastward was a cause for further un-
easiness; and Father Massanet was eager to work among the
long-talked-of Tejas; consequently, in the following year,
1690, De León made a fifth expedition, in which he assisted
Massanet in founding two missions near the Neches River.
They were located among the Nabedache, the westernmost
division of the Tejas, or Asinai (Hasinai) Confederacy. This
was the beginning of Spanish settlement in the region then
called Texas.

In the same year Francisco de Llanos and Gregorio de
Salinas were sent from Vera Cruz in charge of an expedition
to explore Matagorda Bay with a view to finding a navigable
river leading thence to the Tejas country. The records of
this expedition have but recently come to light, and have en-
abled us to determine the exact location of La Salle's colony.
In the following year an expedition led by Domingo de Terán
penetrated to the Cadodacho country in the Red River Valley
and made explorations on the coast. But in 1693 various circumstances caused the Tejas country to be abandoned, and
it was more than two decades before it was reoccupied.[1]

The principal sources of the De León expeditions thus far
published are the following: (1) *Historia de Nuevo León con
Noticias sobre Coahuila, Tejas y Nuevo México, Por el Capitán
Alonso de León, un Autor Anónimo, y el General Fernando Sánchez de Zamora* (Mexico, 1909, in García, *Documentos Inéditos
ó muy Raros para la Historia de México*, tomo XXV.). The

---

[1] For account of the De León and Terán expeditions see G. P. Garrison,
Texas, pp. 20–33; R. C. Clark, *The Beginnings of Texas*, pp. 7–42; "Un
Autor Anónimo," in Alonso De León, *Historia de Nuevo León* (Mexico, 1909,
edited by Genaro García), pp. 296–390, *passim*. On the location of La Salle's
colony, see H. E. Bolton, in the *Austin American*, July 19, 1914, and his article
on "The Location of La Salle's Colony on the Gulf of Mexico," in the *Mississippi Valley Historical Review* for September, 1915, II. 165–182. On the Hasinai
Indians, see H. E. Bolton, "The Native Tribes about the East Texas Missions,"
in the Texas State Historical Association *Quarterly*, XI. 249–276.

first part of this work is by Alonso de León, one of the founders
of Nuevo León and father of Alonso de León, *conquistador* of
Texas. It is of great value for knowledge of the De León
family and of the early career of Alonso de León, the younger.
The second part of the work contains a continuation of De
León's *Relación*, by an anonymous author, from 1650 to 1690,
inclusive, and toward the end broadens in scope to embrace
the history of Coahuila and Texas. It is dated at the end,
September 7, 1690, just after the last De León expedition into
Texas, in which the author took part. The writer had access
to De León's papers, and the work is clearly intended as a
biography of the explorer. It is of highest importance, for,
besides throwing additional light on De León's early career,
it contains a diary of the expedition of 1686, and accounts of
the four remaining journeys of De León into Texas in 1687,
1688, 1689, and 1690. (For a description of this work, see the
American Historical Review, XV. 640–642.)

(2) "Carta de Don Damián Manzanet á Don Carlos de
Sigüenza Sobre el Descubrimiento de la Bahía del Espíritu
Santo." Father Damián Massanet, author of this document,
was a member of the College of the Holy Cross of Querétaro,
who went to the Coahuila frontier as missionary about 1687.
He accompanied De León to Matagorda Bay in 1689, and was
made *comisario* of the new missions which were immediately
thereafter planned for eastern Texas. He returned to Texas
with De León in 1690, and supervised the founding of the
missions on the Neches. In 1691 he again returned to Texas,
with the Terán expedition, of which he wrote a most important diary. Shortly afterward the Texas missions were abandoned, and Father Massanet disappears from history, so far
as available records show. He was a man of great personal
force, and his writings are among our most important sources
of information regarding the beginnings of Texas.

The *Carta* was published in 1899, in facsimile, in the

Texas State Historical Association *Quarterly*, II. 253–312, together with a translation by Miss Lilia M. Casís, professor of Spanish in the University of Texas. The facsimile is from a signed manuscript belonging to the Agricultural and Mechanical College of Texas, and formerly belonging to Ramírez, Maximilian's Secretary of State. The title under which the manuscript was published is that given it in Quaritch's catalogue. When vol. II. of the *Quarterly* was reprinted in 1911, the translation was revised somewhat. The version printed hereinafter is that of Professor Casís as revised.

(3) "Derrotero de la Jornada que hizo el General Alonzo de Leon para el descubrimiento de la Bahia del Espiritu Santo, y poblacion de Franceses: Año de 1689." This itinerary, by De León, is contained in the manuscript collection known as "Memorias de Nueva España," vol. XXVII., ff. 1–16. A translation of this version, reproduced here, was published in 1905 by Miss Elizabeth Howard West in the Texas State Historical Association *Quarterly*, VIII. 199–224. With it is published a map of the route, made by Sigüenza. Other manuscripts of this document are noted in Bolton, *Guide to the Archives of Mexico* (Washington, Carnegie Institution, 1913).

(4) "Alonso de Leon, Carta en que se da noticia de un viaje hecho a la bahia de Espíritu Santo, y de la poblacion que tenian ahi los Franceses," Coahuila, May 18, 1689 (printed in Buckingham Smith's *Colección de Varios Documentos para la Historia de la Florida y Tierras Adyacentes*, tomo I., London, 1857, pp. 25–28, and in French, *Historical Collections of Louisiana and Florida*, second series, New York, 1875, pp. 293–295). This is a brief report to the viceroy by De León immediately after he returned to Monclova. It contains interesting details not given in the diary or in Massanet's account regarding the conference with the "governor of the Tejas."

Besides these published documents there are numerous unpublished manuscripts in the archives of Mexico and Spain.

Of these the only one reproduced here is De León's Itinerary of the 1690 expedition. Of this the editor possesses three different transcripts: (A) one from the Archivo General y Público of Mexico, lacking the first few entries; (B) one from the Archivo General de Indias at Seville; and (C) one from a manuscript in the collection of Genaro García, the noted Mexican editor. This collection has recently been purchased by Yale University. B bears the title, "Diario, Derrotero y Demarcación de la tierra de la jornada que . . . hizo el General Alonso de León . . . al reconocimiento de los Franceses que hubiere[n] en la Bahía del Espíritu Santo y Provincia de las Texas." A and B, which represent the official report sent by De León from the Rio Grande on his return, are practically identical, with minor differences in spelling. The translation here presented is based on A, excepting the entries preceding April 9, which are lacking in A. These are supplied from B and C. C is the version included by the Autor Anónimo in the *Historia de Nuevo León*. Between C and the other two manuscripts there are many minor differences, and some essential ones. In general C is the fullest of the three, but not uniformly. Some of the more important differences are noted by the editor in foot-notes.

LETTER OF FRAY DAMIÁN MASSANET TO DON CARLOS DE SIGÜENZA, 1690[1]

Letter of Don Damian Manzanet to Don Carlos de Siguenza relative to the Discovery of the Bay of Espiritu Santo.

My dear Don Carlos de Siguenza y Góngora:
The following is the narrative for which you ask me, of the discovery of the bay of Espiritu Santo[2] and the Rio de los Tejas:[3]

In the year 1685–1686, His Excellency the Viceroy, who at that time was Conde de Paredes, Marqués de la Laguna, gave orders to the Marqués de S. Miguel de Aguayo, who was then governor of the Nuevo Reyno de Leon, to send out a company of horse soldiers along the sea-coast[4] lying north beyond Tampico, towards the Rio Bravo and the Magdalena.[5] And the said governor sent out fifty men, headed by Captain Alonso de Leon. With his soldiers, the said commander reached the sea-coast, and following along the coast, they passed the Rio Bravo[6] with considerable difficulty. This river is the same found at the passage[7] into New Mexico, and the Indians give it various names, for it is called by different persons Rio Bravo,

[1] Translation by Professor Lilia M. Casís, in Texas State Historical Association *Quarterly*, II. 253–312.

[2] Up to this time the name Bahía del Espíritu Santo was applied to the mouth of the Mississippi, but the accident of La Salle's landing at Matagorda Bay, when he was reported to the Spaniards to have sailed for Bahía del Espíritu Santo, caused it to be transferred to that point. The error was remarked upon by officials at the time.

[3] The Neches River.

[4] The document says "Mar del Norte," or North Sea, the name applied to the Atlantic Ocean and its arms.

[5] See note on the Magdalena River, p. 224, above, note 4.

[6] The diary of the expedition shows that Father Massanet is mistaken in this statement. The expedition did not cross the Rio Grande, but, following its south bank to the coast, turned south to Río de las Palmas (Diary, in De León, *Historia de Nuevo León*, pp. 307–308).

[7] El Paso.

Rio Grande, Rio Turbio.   In New Mexico it was never known whence this river originated; all that was ever found out was that it issued from the Gran Quivira.   Thus said the Indians who came to New Mexico from the interior.

But let us turn our attention again to the route taken by Captain Alonso de Leon and his soldiers.   After crossing the Rio Bravo they reached another river, to which they gave the name of Rio Solo.[1]   This river, they say, forms at its mouth a lake which they were unable to pass, and they returned to the Nuevo Reyno de Leon without having had any news of the bay of Espiritu Santo, and still less of the French who were settled about this bay.

By order of His Excellency, the said governor sent a second time an expedition to discover the bay, and he sent two companies of horse soldiers led by Captain Alonso de Leon, and they arrived the second time at the Rio Solo, when, not able to proceed any further, they returned without bringing any information.   And since they had twice gone down to the seacoast, and on both occasions failed to learn anything, they considered the whole report as being unfounded.   So it came about that they paid no more attention to the matter and took no further steps concerning it.

At this time I was living at the Mission Caldera,[2] in the province of Coahuila, whither I had gone with the intention of seeing whether I could make investigations and obtain information about the interior of the country to the north and northeast, on account of facts gathered from a letter now in my possession, which had been given in Madrid to our Father Fray Antonio Linaz.[3]   This letter treats of what the blessed Mother Maria de Jesus de Agreda made known in her convent to the father custodian of New Mexico, Fray Alonso de Benavides.[4]   And the blessed Mother tells of having been fre-

---

[1] In the 1687 expedition De León crossed the Bravo and was impeded by a Río Salado.   It was evidently the same as the Río Solo which Father Massanet places here (De León, *Historia de Nuevo León*, p. 310).

[2] Caldera is situated east of Monclova, near the Nuevo León border.

[3] Father Llinaz was founder of the College of the Holy Cross of Querétaro. Massanet had come to America with him in 1683.   A full biography of Father Llinaz is contained in Espinosa's *Chrónica*, libros II. and III.

[4] For the foundation of the story of the miraculous conversion of the Jumano, see Benavides, "Memorial," in *Land of Sunshine*, XIV., and Vetancur, *Chrónica*

quently to New Mexico and to the Gran Quivira, adding that eastward from the Gran Quivira are situated the kingdoms of Ticlas, Theas, and Caburcol. She also says that these names are not the ones belonging to those kingdoms, but come close to the real names. Because of this information, brought by me from Spain, together with the fact of my call to the ministry for the conversion of the heathen, I had come over and dwelt in the missions of Coahuila, and learning that His Excellency was taking steps to open up the interior, to lead to the discovery of the bay of Espiritu Santo, and to find out whether any Frenchmen were there, I endeavored to learn from the Indians coming from the interior whether they knew where there dwelt men white like the Spaniards. And in time I learned that there were indeed some, and he who told me was an Indian whom I had with me, a man whom I had converted a little before, and in whom, though he had been a pagan, I had recognized a high degree of truthfulness. Thereupon I charged him very earnestly to ascertain in detail where and how far distant these settlers might be, and what manner of people they were, likewise whether the country to be traversed were passable.

Just at this time there arrived another Indian, of the Quems nation, and he told me that he had been even in the very houses of the French; there were many of them, he said, including women; they were well armed, and had some very large firearms (which were the pieces of ordnance). On my asking whether he were well acquainted with the country, he said that, if I wished, he would take me to the place without any risk, that there we should also find priests[1] like myself, and that already the people were sowing maize and other crops.

At this time Captain Alonso de Leon, the same who had gone out as commander of the companies from the Nuevo Reyno de Leon, became captain of the presidio of Coahuila,[2] and before going out to his presidio he came to the Mission

de la Provincia del Santo Evangelio (1697), p. 96. Secondary accounts are in Shea, The Catholic Church in America, I. 195–198, and Schmidt, "Ven. María Jesus de Agreda: a Correction," in the Texas State Historical Association Quarterly, I. 121–124.

[1] Relijiosos, including both priests and lay brothers.

[2] His commission as governor of Coahuila and captain of the presidio of Coahuila (Monclova) was dated July 13, 1687.

Caldera, where I was living, and I made known to him what had passed between the Indians and me concerning the discovery of the bay of Espiritu Santo, endeavoring to persuade him that we should set out thither. He asked whether there were some unmistakable signs which might be made known to His Excellency and which would make it evident to him that the report was true, so that he might undertake the expedition.

Then I called the Indian named Juan, captain of the Pacpul nation, and bade him say what he would dare undertake in order to ascertain and prove that there were in the interior men white like the Spaniards. He said that in a ranchería of heathen Indians, which must be some sixty leagues distant, there was a white man, one of those dwelling in the interior, and that, if I so wished, he would go and bring the other out of the ranchería. Thereupon I despatched him, and that he might the more readily execute his commission I gave him the clothing and the horses which I had with me, for him to give to the chiefs of the place where was the man of whom he spoke (whom from the description given, I inferred to be French).

This captain of the Pacpul nation, known as Juan, set out, and having come close to the sierra of Sacatsol[1] (which means "stone nostrils," and in the language of the Indians of that place is called Axatscan, with the same meaning) he found an assembly of many Indian nations composed of the following: Mescales, Yoricas, Chomenes, Machomenes, Sampanales, Paquachiams, Tilpayay, Apis. This sierra of Sacatsol is twenty leagues beyond the Rio Grande, which is the stream coming from the north, and is called also Rio del Norte; the distance from the Mission San Salvador[2] to the said sierra is sixty leagues, and from Coahuila the same.

The said Indian Juanillo found the said Frenchman, told him that I was asking for him, and took him out to another ranchería, leaving word with the Indians that they should not be afraid, and that I desired to visit them. Returning, he told me how he had left the Frenchman, and that we might without fear go after him. I notified Captain Alonso de Leon, who, with twelve men, went quite undisturbed, and

---

[1] See note on Sacatsol on p. 297, above. This place was the objective-point of the Bosque-Larios expedition.

[2] Massanet's mission at Caldera.

they brought the Frenchman, painted like the Indians, old and naked.[1] His name was Juan Francisco So-and-so, and he says that he is a native of Cheblie in New France. This Frenchman Captain Alonso de Leon placed in the hands of His Excellency the Conde de la Moncloba, and in all his testimony the said Frenchman always lied.

After the Conde de la Moncloba had determined on the expedition to discover the bay of Espiritu Santo, there arrived as viceroy in this kingdom His Excellency the Conde de Galbe, who put his whole heart into this cause. As soon as he came into power His Excellency ordered Captain Alonso de Leon to pursue the journey to the bay of Espiritu Santo, as his predecessor had ordained, and for the said expedition forty men went out from the presidios of Vizcaya, and from the Nuevo Reyno de Leon forty others. From all the men three companies were formed, having Captain Alonso de Leon as commander-in-chief and Nicolás de Medina as *sargento mayor*; the leader of one company was Tomás de la Garza, of the second Lorenzo de la Garza, and of the third Alonso de Leon, the royal *alférez*,[2] Captain Francisco Martinez, who was a discharged *sargento*, having just finished his term of service in Flanders.

We left Coahuila on the twenty-sixth[3] of March in the year 1689, and went as far as the Rio del Norte,[4] which, in

---

[1] This was in May, 1688. Strangely enough, in the sworn declarations made by De León regarding the expedition to find the Frenchman, he makes no mention of Father Massanet. De León states that he got his information regarding the Frenchman from Agustín de la Cruz, a Tlascalteco Indian who had been sent across the Río Grande to summon the friendly tribes to aid in a campaign ("Auto para la salida á buscar al frances," in Portillo, *Apuntes*, p. 224). The Autor Anónimo writes that the wife of a Quems Indian living near the Río Bravo was captured by his enemies. He set about finding her, and in the attempt wandered to the French village. On his return he went to Massanet's mission and told his story, and then went on to Saltillo. No attention was paid to the report until the time of the expedition, but as they approached the ranchería of the Quems Massanet recounted the story, whereupon the Quems Indian was sent for and made the guide (De León, *Historia de Nuevo León*, pp. 323–324).

[2] Ensign.   [3] The start was made on March 23 (see Itinerary, p. 388).

[4] Reached April 1, at a point not far from San Juan Bautista. The Sigüenza map shows the route from the crossing of the Rio Grande to Matagorda Bay to be considerably north of east, when, as a matter of fact, the general direction is nearly east.

the said province of Coahuila, is called the Rio Grande, our
guide still being the Indian Juanillo, and when we reached the
said river, I sent for the Indian who knew the country and
had been among the Frenchmen, whom I call Quems, because
he belonged to the Indian nation of that name.   We travelled
on towards the northeast and at times east-northeast, until
we reached the river of Our Lady of Guadalupe.[1]   And here
I asked this Indian whether the dwellings of the French were
still a long way off, thinking that when we should be distant
from them a day and night's journey, some of us might push
forward in order, unnoticed, to take a survey of the village.
The Indian replied that the village was about fifteen leagues
distant from that river.

On the morning of the next day Captain Alonso de Leon
asked me what we should do in order to ascertain the number
of Frenchmen and the condition of things in their village.
With regard to this there were various opinions, mine being
that, since we had with us the Quems Indian, who was well
acquainted with the country, we should all have a mass sung
in honor of the Blessed Virgin of Guadalupe that very morning, at the very place in which we were; also that when we
should succeed in reaching the dwellings of the Frenchmen
we should have another mass celebrated, in honor of Saint
Anthony of Padua.   All consented very readily to this, and,
soon, at about nine o'clock in the morning, the mass to the
Virgin was sung.

After that it was arranged that, the two Indians, Juanillo
the Papul and the Quems Indian, serving as guides, twenty-
five men[2] should travel on with us until we should come upon
the French village in the early morning, while the remaining
soldiers with the beasts of burden should come behind us and
camp when they reached a suitable spot.   This spot they
should then not leave until we returned, unless by the express
command of Captain Alonso de Leon.   When we started out,
the rear-guard received orders to proceed slowly, watching

[1] Reached April 14.   The details of the journey to this point are supplied
by the Itinerary and the map.   The Guadalupe was crossed near Victoria, perhaps a little below it.

[2] According to the Itinerary the Guadalupe was crossed on the 15th, and the
governor went ahead on the 16th with sixty men.

cautiously lest any Indian should appear; in case any did, they were to seize him without doing him the least harm, and notify us of the capture.

After travelling some four leagues, the rear-guard saw an Indian come out of a dense wood, and called to him, and he went towards them without any show of resistance. They sent us word, and we halted.[1] On the arrival of the Indian the two we had along asked him whether there were thereabouts any of the white people who dwelt further on. He said that, as to those living further, they used to inhabit houses which now no longer existed, for, two moons[2] previous, the Indians of the coast had killed all but a few boys, whom they had carried off; that he himself lived in the ranchería of the Emet and Lavas Indians, which was about two leagues out of the route which we were following towards the bay of Espiritu Santo. We went with this Indian to the ranchería of which he spoke, and reached it at about three in the afternoon. As soon as the Indians became aware of our presence, they made for the wood, leaving to us the ranchería, together with the laden dogs, which they had not been able to drive fast enough when they fled. The Indian who served as our guide himself entered the wood, and called to the others, declaring that we were friends, and that they should have no fear. Some of them—and among these was their captain—came out and embraced us, saying: "*Thechas! techas!*" which means "Friends! friends!" One of those who came out first was a big young fellow about twenty years old, who wore a Recollect friar's cloak, and when we saw that it was the cloak of a friar, we gave him a blanket, and I took the robe from him.

The said Indians told how, two days previous, two Frenchmen had passed by with the Tejas Indians. That very afternoon we started in pursuit of the said Frenchmen, and at sunset, we reached the ranchería of the Toxo and Toaa Indians, who told us that the said Frenchmen had passed by with the said Tejas, and had been unwilling to remain there with them. That night we slept near the ranchería, and at eight in the evening some Indians came to the place where we were, one of them dressed after the fashion of the French. And they brought some French books and a Holy Bible. The next

---

[1] This was on the 16th (Itinerary).   [2] The Itinerary says three moons.

morning[1] we set out in quest of the said Frenchmen, passing through some very dense woods; and at about two o'clock in the afternoon we came to some ranchitos of Emet Indians.[2] On our inquiring concerning the Frenchmen, these Indians pointed out to us an Indian who had just arrived and who had conducted them (the Frenchmen) as far as the San Marcos River,[3] and when we wished to cross they told us that we would not be able to cross the said river. We told the Indian who had led the Frenchmen that if he would take them a paper and bring an answer we would give him a horse, and that he should take the answer to the houses where the Frenchmen lived. Captain Francisco Martinez wrote the letter in the French language because he was master of it.

We returned where the camp was, five leagues beyond the Guadalupe River,[4] and we learned that three days previous the horses had stampeded, and a number having been recovered, fifty were still missing, and in pursuit a soldier had lost his way. This man remained missing four days, and in the meantime he met with some Indians who were skinning a buffalo, who took him home with them at nightfall to their ranchería, giving him to eat of the buffalo meat, and whatever else they themselves had. On the day after this, an Indian belonging to the same ranchería came there with a small bundle of tobacco. This Indian was the one who had been with us, and he made a long harangue to all the Indians who were in the ranchería. As to the soldier who was lost, when he met with the Indians who had the buffalo, they spoke to him by signs, and he understood them to tell him to make a fire. This he must have inferred from seeing the meat they had, or he was frightened at seeing himself lost among barbarian Indians; he spilled on his cloak the powder he was carrying in a flask, and on his striking the light a spark fell on the powder, and it burned his whole side from head to foot. When the Indians learned that we were in their territory they must have come to the conclusion that, since that man was lost, his comrades would be sure to look for him.

[1] On the 17th (Itinerary).

[2] According to the Itinerary this place was fifteen leagues north of the Guadalupe crossing. It must have been somewhere near Hallettsville.

[3] The Colorado was probably meant here.

[4] It had moved eastward in De León's absence.

The next day they brought him his horse, and, since he was so badly burned that he could not help himself, the Indians themselves saddled it for him, and assisted him to mount, telling him by signs to go with them. They brought him very near to the place where we were, just a couple of shots away. The Indians who brought him, not wishing to approach us, signified to him that he should go on, using signs to indicate to him where we were, at the foot of a hill which he saw there. At the foot of that hill, on the other side, they left him, and he reached us at nine in the morning, which was for all a source of great satisfaction. We felt very sorry when we saw how badly burnt he was.

On the following day[1] we left for the settlement of the Frenchmen, and when we were about three leagues from it there came out some twenty-five Indians. Now the old Frenchman who accompanied us took occasion to say that the settlement of the Frenchmen was not in the place to which the two Indian guides were taking us. On the way this French-man tried several times, by means of an Indian of the Cavas nation whom he had with him, to make our two Indians de-sert us, or say that it was very far, and that we should not be able to cross the rivers which were on the way. I resented so much that the Frenchman should be given occasion to speak that I grew angry, and Captain Alonso de Leon said to me: "Father, we are going wherever you wish." We continued following the two guides quite three leagues;[2] we arrived at a stream of very good drinking water, and the two Indians said to me: "Lower down on the bank of this stream are the houses of the French, which must be about three leagues off." Then the old Frenchman saw that there was no help, and that we were certain to come upon the village. He then said: "Sir, now I know very well, yea, very well, that the houses are on this little river."

We started the next morning, and three leagues off we found the village of the Frenchmen on the bank of the stream,[3] as

---

[1] The 21st (Itinerary).

[2] Going east-northeast eight leagues they struck a creek three leagues above the French settlement; it was the Garcitas.

[3] On the Garcitas, about five miles above its mouth. The site of La Salle's settlement was identified by the present writer on July 5, 1914. It is on the

I had been told by the two Indians, the Quems and Juanillo the Papul. We arrived at about eleven in the forenoon, and found six houses, not very large, built with poles plastered with mud, and roofed over with buffalo hides, another larger house where pigs were fattened, and a wooden fort made from the hulk of a wrecked vessel. The fort had one lower room which was used as a chapel for saying mass, and three other rooms below; above the three rooms was an upper story serving for a store-house, wherein we found some six loads of iron, not counting scattered pieces, and some steel, also eight small guns and three swivels made of iron, the largest pieces being for a charge of about six pounds of shot. The pieces and one swivel were buried, and Captain Alonso de Leon carried off two of the swivels. There was a great lot of shattered weapons, broken by the Indians—firelocks, carbines, cutlasses—but they had not left the cannon, only one being found. We found two unburied bodies, which I interred, setting up a cross over the grave. There were many torn-up books, and many dead pigs.

These Frenchmen had a piece of land fenced in with stakes, where they sowed just a little corn, and had an asparagus bed; we found also very good endive. This place affords no advantages as to situation, for good drinking-water is very far off, and timber still further. The water of the stream is very brackish, so much so that in five days during which the camp was pitched there all the horses sickened from the brackish water.

The next day[1] we went down to explore the bay of Espiritu Santo,[2] and coasted it until we succeeded in finding the mouth; in the middle of this there is a flat rock, and all along the shore of the bay there are many lagoons which it is very difficult to cross. Blackberries are abundant, large and fine, and there are a number of stocks which seem to be those of grape

ranch of Mr. Claude Keeran, in Victoria County. See an article by Bolton in the *Austin American*, July 19, 1914, and his article on "The Location of La Salle's Colony on the Gulf of Mexico," in the *Mississippi Valley Historical Review*, II. 165–182.

[1] Saturday, April 23 (Itinerary). They did not get back till the 25th. Father Massanet makes it appear that the journey was all made in one day.

[2] The Itinerary and the Sigüenza map show that De León first turned southwest and went round the head of Zorillo Creek, going thence to a place near Port Connor.

vines, but no trees, and no fresh water. The Indians dig wells for drinking water.

After exploring the bay we returned to the main body of our party, whom we had left in the village; we arrived there at noon, and remained there that afternoon, and the next day they bent the large iron bars, making them up into bundles, in order to carry them with ease. We found the Indian with the reply to the letter which we had written to the French-men;[1] they said that we should wait for them, that they would soon come, that another Frenchman was further on, and that they were waiting for him in order that they might come all together. The Indian received the horse, as we had ordered. As to the fort, Captain Alonso de Leon would not have it burnt down, and it remained as it was.

The next day[2] we set out on our return trip to the Guada-lupe River, and when we got halfway, since we saw that the Frenchmen did not come, Captain Alonso de Leon, with twenty-five men,[3] went to the ranchería where they were, and the main party went on as far as the Guadalupe River, where it remained waiting three days. The Frenchmen were in the ranchería of the Toaa Indians, with the Tejas; they came to the Guadalupe with Captain Alonso de Leon and arrived there on the 2d [4] of May, '89. Two Frenchmen came, naked except for an antelope's skin, and with their faces, breasts, and arms painted like the Indians, and with them came the governor of the Tejas and eight of his Indians. Through that day and night I tried my utmost to show all possible consideration to the said governor, giving him two horses, and the blanket in which I slept, for I had nothing else which I could give him. Speaking Spanish, and using as an interpreter one of the Frenchmen whom we had with us, I said to the governor that his people should become Christians, and bring into their

---

[1] The letter, which was written with red ochre, is reproduced by the Autor Anónimo (De León, *Historia de Nuevo León*, p. 334).

[2] The 26th.

[3] De León made an expedition to the Lavaca River at this time which Massanet does not mention. Crossing the Garcitas and going three leagues east, he reached the Lavaca (he called it the San Marcos) and followed it nearly to its mouth (Itinerary, pp. 401–402). When he started north in search of the Frenchmen, De León took thirty men (**Itinerary**).

[4] The Itinerary says May 1.

lands priests who should baptize them, since otherwise they could not save their souls, adding that if he wished, I would go to his lands.   Soon the afore-mentioned governor said he would very willingly take me there, and I promised him to go, and to take with me other priests like myself, repeating to him that I would be there in the following year, at the time of sowing corn.   The governor seemed well pleased, and I was still more so, seeing the harvest to be reaped among the many souls in those lands who know not God.

The next day was the day of the Holy Cross[1] —the 3d of May; after mass the governor of the Tejas left for his home and we for this place.   We arrived at Coahuila,[2] and Captain Alonso de Leon sent two Frenchmen—the one named Juan Archebepe,[3] of Bayonne, the other Santiago Grollette—from Coahuila to Mexico, with Captain Francisco Martinez, and His Excellency the Conde de Galbe had the Frenchmen provided with suitable clothes and dispatched to Spain on shipboard in the same year, '89.

All this news did not fail to create excitement and to give satisfaction not only to His Excellency but also to other men of note in Mexico, and there were several meetings held in order to consider measures not only for keeping the French from gaining control of those regions and settling in them, but also for the introduction of religious ministers.

At this time His Excellency deigned to send for me, asking the Reverend Father Luzuriaga to give orders for my coming. I was living at the mission of San Salvador, in the valley of Santiago, in the province of Coahuila.   I went to Querétaro, arriving at my College of the Holy Cross on the 24th of October, in the year '89, and left for Mexico on All Souls' Day. On the 5th of November I came to the convent of San Cosme, and the next day there entered Mexico the Very Reverend Father Fray Juan Capistrano, who came from Spain as commissary general of this province of New Spain.

It seemed that our Lord had ordained that it should not be Father Luzuriaga's good fortune that in his time priests[4] of the order of our Father Saint Francis should go among

---

[1] Feast of the Invention of the Holy Cross.
[2] On May 13 (Itinerary).   [3] L'Archevêque.
[4] *Relijiosos*, including both priests and laymen.

the Tejas, for he always objected to the idea that the brethren
of that holy order should undertake missions to the heathen,
their chief office being that of apostolic missionaries among
communities of both the faithful and infidels. For after the
reverend fathers, Fray Juan Bautista Lazaro and the Predicador[1] Fray Francisco Esteves,[2] came to Guasteca,[3] and
founded at Tamaulipas a mission for heathen Indians when
already the mission included more than three hundred families, without counting a large number who were in process of
joining, and the Indians were very much pleased and very
attentive to the Christian doctrine, the Reverend Luzuriaga
ordered the fathers to depart, and to leave the said mission
and the Indians, no ground or motive being stated except
that those regions belonged to the district of Tampico, and
that the priests[4] belonging to that district would look after
that settlement of Indians. The reverend fathers obeyed the
Reverend Luzuriaga's orders with heavy hearts, seeing that,
after the arduous labors by which they had gained that post,
those poor heathens would be lost. After those priests had
departed and left the Indians, the district fathers[5] never
again gave a thought to them or the posts. When the fathers
took leave of the Indians there was a pitiful scene, and what
the Indians said moved one to tears, for they asked why the
fathers, though priests and ministers of God, had deceived
them, since they had pledged their word to minister to them,
to teach them and baptize them, and now, if the unsettled
life they led, without rule or law, were an evil one, whereby
they should lose salvation, the fathers would be to blame,
for these were leaving them and had deceived them. With
these and many other expressions they parted, the fathers in
tears over the fold which was now without a shepherd, yet
on the other hand feeling compelled to obey. On another
occasion, when the superior of our holy order begged for
permission to enter New Mexico, the Very Reverend Luzuriaga refused and would not allow it. He ever remained ad-

---

[1] Preacher.
[2] A biography of Father Estévez is contained in Arricivita's *Crónica*, lib. II.,
caps. I.–VI.
[3] Huasteca, the coast country about Tampico.   [4] *Ministros.*
[5] *Los padres de aquella custodia* (the fathers of that *custodia*).

verse to the introduction of priests among the heathen. However, when there came out of the land of the Tejas tidings of
discoveries which were noised abroad, he thought of many
possible measures, and of sending priests[1] out of the provinces, but our Lord God ordained that when I reached Mexico
another commissary general, as I have already said, was
ruling.

I reached the said city and saw the very reverend father
and we spoke of the Tejas. I told him how I had been called
by His Excellency and by the Very Reverend Luzuriaga, and
he said to me: "See His Excellency, and then we shall con-
fer." I had an interview with His Excellency, and spoke at
great length of the bay of Espiritu Santo and of the Tejas,
and immediately he replied that he would foster the cause
with might and main.

Besides the news which we had brought with us on returning from the bay of Espiritu Santo, Captain Alonso de Leon
had brought the information that an Indian who had come
from there at a more recent date than ourselves said that
among the Tejas there were eighteen Frenchmen, and that
houses had been built; that they had flocks of goats and
sheep, and that some of the Frenchmen had gone to their
country for women and for more men.[2] I do not know what
Captain Alonso de Leon had in view in giving this account
to His Excellency, for I had seen the Indian and spoken to
him before he saw Captain Leon, and he told _me_ that he came
from the interior, and had been told that six Frenchmen,
who seemed to have lost their way, were wandering among
the Tejas. He had also heard of the coming of some Tejas
Indians, and that on their advancing further on this side of
the Rio Hondo other Indians had come out to attack them,
that they had killed two of them, and that the rest had returned to their homes. It seems to me that they must have
made the old Frenchman who lived in Coahuila say this,
because in tracing the report to its source they said, "Juan
says so"; and since the said Juan lied in all his accounts,

[1] _Relijiosos._

[2] Detailed information relative to proceedings after De León returned to
Monclova is contained in Archivo General de Indias, Sevilla, _estante_ 61, _cajón_ 6,
legajo 21. Transcripts of these documents are possessed by the editor.

he certainly lied that time also, for the Indians themselves were ignorant of such an occurrence, and when we went among the Tejas they knew nothing about the reported murders.

But to return to our subject. When I was in Mexico and had spoken to His Excellency at different times concerning a second expedition to the bay of Espiritu Santo and a visit to the Tejas His Excellency resolved to call a general meeting[1] in order to decide what should be done. Taking for granted the information given by Captain Alonso de Leon about a settlement of Frenchmen among the Tejas, and concerning the death of those who had settled on the bay of Espiritu Santo, it was uncertain whether some French vessel might have come afterwards with settlers for the bay; besides, there were other grounds for action in the fact that the Tejas were asking for priests for their country. All these grounds being taken into account in the general meeting, there were various opinions, and finally His Excellency decided that a second expedition should be undertaken to the bay of Espiritu Santo. Previously Captain Alonso de Leon had already made known to His Excellency all that was necessary for that journey in case it should be undertaken. His Excellency ordained that Captain Alonso de Leon should go as commander, taking with him a hundred and ten soldiers—twenty from the presidios of Viscaya, those nearest Coahuila, forty who enlisted in Sombrerete[2] and Zacatecas, the rest from Saltillo and the Nuevo de Leon—one hundred and fifty loads of flour, two hundred cows, four hundred horses, fifty long firelocks, twelve hundred weight of powder, and three hundred weight of shot. They were to inspect the bay of Espiritu Santo and to ascertain whether there were any Frenchmen left of those who used to live there, or whether others had recently arrived; the wooden fort built by the French was to be burnt down, and Captain Alonso de Leon was to communicate with the governor of the Tejas from the bay of Espiritu Santo as to whether he would be willing to have the ministers of the Holy Gospel enter into his territory, as he had promised Father Fray Damian Manzanet a year

[1] *Junta general.* One was held July 5, 1689, and others later.
[2] A city north of Zacatecas, founded in the middle of the sixteenth century.

previous. If the governor consented, then they should escort the priests, proceeding with every precaution, and should dispatch an order requesting and charging the Very Reverend Father Commissary General to send with Father Fray Damian Manzanet those of the brethren of the Holy College of the Cross who should prove suitable, the said father to decide how many priests would be needed at first. At the same time he was to be provided with all the necessaries for the journey. And I, being present at this general meeting, remarked that I would take along three priests for the Tejas, myself being the fourth, besides two for the mission of San Salvador, which is on the way, making a total of six priests to be sent by the college; and in the event of the Tejas receiving the faith, then the college should send whatever other priests would be required. This was resolved by the general meeting.

Afterwards His Excellency bade me make a note of what I needed to take along, whereupon I replied that for the moment I only wanted wine for the masses, a wafer-box, and wax; as to other necessaries, such as vestments and other things, I should procure them myself. It was determined that the journey should take place after Christmas, so when the Christmas feast was over His Excellency dispatched Captain Francisco Martinez with twenty mules laden with wine, wax, and so on, also clothing for distribution among the Indians and six loads of tobacco; and at the College of the Holy Cross at Queretaro, with the priests who were to accompany me, I awaited him. These priests were the Father Predicador Fray Miguel Fontecuberta,[1] the Father Predicador Fray Francisco de Jesus María, the Father Predicador Fray Antonio Perea, the Father Predicador Fray Francisco Hidalgo, the Father Predicador Fray Antonio Bordoy. Those who remained in the Mission San Salvador were the fathers Fray Antonio Perea and Fray Francisco Hidalgo.

We left Coahuila[2] for the Tejas on the third day of the Easter feast, March 28, '90. When we left, the twenty sol-

[1] There is a biography of Father Fontcuberta in Espinosa's *Chrónica*, lib. IV., cap. II.; one of Father Casañas, *ibid.*, caps. II.–IX.; of Father Perea, *ibid.*, cap. XV.; of Father Hidalgo, in Arricivita, *Crónica*, lib. II., caps. X.–XII.

[2] Monclova. The baggage left Monclova on the 26th. On the 27th the soldiers set out (Itinerary).

diers from Vizcaya had not yet arrived. The forty from Zacatecas were for the most part tailors, shoemakers, masons, miners—in short, none of them could catch the horses on which they were to ride that day, for when they had once let them go they could manage them no longer. Besides, we had saddles that could not be worse.

Thus we went on travelling by the route described in the journal which was kept of this expedition.[1] What I noticed was that on our first trip we had found many Indians along the rivers and everywhere else, while this time we went to inspect the bay of Espiritu Santo and returned to the Guadalupe River without having found a single Indian in all the country. Twenty of us reached the fort built by the Frenchmen, the rest remained with the horses by the Guadalupe River. We saw no trace of Frenchmen having been there during our absence, all being as we had left it the year before, except that certainly there were signs that the Indians had dwelt there. I myself set fire to the fort, and as there was a high wind—the wood, by the way, was from the sloop brought by the Frenchmen, which had sunk on entering the bay—in half an hour the fort was in ashes. This was at the hour of noon; afterwards we went down to the coast of the bay, all along the banks of the arroyo by which the Frenchmen passed in and out of the bay with their barges and canoes. And after we had arrived, some of the soldiers of Reyno de Leon said that they wished to bathe, in order to be able to tell that they had bathed in the sea, this being esteemed so remarkable a thing that they carried away flasks of sea-water which later, in their own country of Monterey, it was held a great favor to try and to taste, because it was sea-water.

On our first journey there was a soldier in Coahuila who was a Creole from Pablillo. His father's name was So-and-so de Escobelo, and when he learned that an expedition to the

---

[1] Printed hereinafter. The party was met at the junction of the Nadadores with the Sabinas by the soldiers from Nuevo León and the missionaries on the 30th. On the 4th of April the Río Grande was reached; on the 9th the Nueces; on the 11th the Hondo; on the 19th the Medina; on the 23d the Guadalupe. On the 25th De León left the camp on the Guadalupe and set out with twenty men to reconnoitre the French settlement, arriving there next day; from there he went down to the Bay (see the Itinerary, pp. 405–409).

bay of Espiritu Santo was being planned, he wrote a letter to Captain Alonso de Leon, which letter ran as follows: "*Compadre*, I entreat you to do me the favor of taking my son Antonio among your troops, that when he is old, he may have a tale to tell."

While the soldiers were bathing, we saw in the bay two dark and bulky objects, looking like buoys, and though there was some discussion as to whether they might be buoys, no special investigation was made, such as Captain Alonso de Leon and Captain D. Gregorio Salinas made later in order to give information to His Excellency. The said buoys must have been distant from the land about two gunshots, and they were not in the mouth of the San Marcos River,[1] as they reported, nor is the mouth of the San Marcos River half a league wide, as they said, for whoever said so did not see it, and I, who saw it on the feast of San Marcos (that is why it is called the San Marcos River), I say that the mouth of the river is about a gunshot wide.

We returned to the main body of the army,[2] which awaited us by the Guadalupe River; arriving there we found nothing new. The next morning we left for the country of the Tejas,[3] and journeyed some six leagues. On the next day there was no travelling done. Some soldiers went out to reconnoitre, and to see whether there appeared any Indians from whom they might gather information. They found none, and no smoke was seen, nor was there ever any answer to that which daily we allowed to rise. The next morning while I was saying mass two gunshots were heard far away in the thicket towards the Guadalupe River. Some one went to see who it was, and it proved to be three[4] of the soldiers who belonged to the garrisons of Vizcaya. They came up, and we asked them about their journey, and they told us of hardships as follows:

On the second day of the Easter feast they had arrived at Saltillo, namely, twenty soldiers of the two presidios of Vizcaya

---

[1] The Lavaca.   [2] On April 27 (Itinerary).
[3] According to the Itinerary, on the 28th De León went up the Guadalupe six leagues and returned, and on the 29th set out for the Tejas, going six leagues that day.
[4] On the 30th the Itinerary mentions the same incident but gives the number of soldiers as two.

which are nearest Coahuila, *i. e.*, Cuencame and El Gallo. And the *sargento mayor* of Vizcaya, Juan Bautista Escorza, appointed a mulatto named Martincho So-and-so leader of the ten men he sent. The captain of the presidio El Gallo, a native of Vizcaya whose name was Ogalde, sent as leader of his ten soldiers Joseph de Salcedo, a Spaniard. While they were in Saltillo, a town inhabited by Spaniards, one of Martincho's men had words with Captain Anchiondo, and the *alcalde mayor*, Don Alonso Ramos, nephew to the president of Guadalajara, tried to seize him, but could not, because the said soldier and his companion decamped and went off where their camp was stationed on the hacienda of Captain Nicolás de Guajardo. Thither the said *alcalde mayor* followed them. He arrived close behind them, and spoke very politely to the leader of the said soldiers, and the said Martincho agreed to take along the soldier next day in order that he might make it up with Captain Anchiondo. They went next day, and on the arrival of the said leader with the soldier at the government houses, it happened that the *alcalde mayor* received word concerning a christening to which he was invited. He said to the soldiers, "Wait for me a while, I shall be back"; and so on his return the difference existing between the two men was settled, and they made friends. But next day a talebearer—they are numerous in the town of Saltillo—did not fail to tell Martincho that the *alcalde mayor* said that he would find means to punish the Vizcayan soldiers, and that when he was away at the christening he had left them as prisoners in the government houses. At this Mantincho took offense, questioning whether the *alcalde mayor* had jurisdiction over military cases, and he made a complaint. He called four of his soldiers, whom he took with him, saying to them that if they were not men, and intended to flee, they should not accompany him. Finally they went to the government houses, and Martincho left the four soldiers at the door, and, without giving warning, he entered the hall, and gained access to the room where the *alcalde mayor* was with a priest from Coahuila. On entering he drew his sword and dealt the *alcalde mayor* a stroke, taking off a considerable piece from his head, and cutting off one of his arms, so as to leave him crippled, and to a mulatto who sought to help his master he gave a back-handed

blow which split his head.   The priest took away Martincho's
sword, and just then the inhabitants of the place came crowd-
ing up to the door to assist the *alcalde mayor*.   The soldiers
who were keeping guard would not allow them to enter, but the
crowd afterwards came in through the corral.   It was then
about ten o'clock in the morning.   Martincho departed, he
and his companions getting upon their horses and returning
to the camp which he had established at the house of Guajardo.
All the men of the town followed with weapons in pursuit,
and after much dispute, Martincho having offered resistance
in the said house, he allowed himself to be seized because the
holder of the warrant, Gerónimo Montés de Oca by name, assured him that his life was safe.   This occurred on the Thursday after Easter; that night the *alcalde mayor* himself passed
sentence on him, and he received the notification in bed.   The
sentence was that he should be shot according to military
usage, and on the next day, Friday, March 21, in the year '90,
Martincho was shot on the plaza at Saltillo.[1]

This news the Vizcayan soldiers brought us as their excuse
for not having arrived in time to set out from Coahuila with us.

These soldiers of whom I have spoken as arriving on that
day were three that came along on the same trail while the
others were following slowly, driving their horses, which were in
a very bad condition.   So six soldiers were sent with a load of
flour to meet them, and Captain Alonso de Leon and myself
with fifteen men set out[2] in a northerly direction for the San
Marcos River,[3] in order to try to find some Indians, burning
fires day and night to see whether they should be answered
by others.   We spent six days in this sea-region without being
able to find a single Indian.   We crossed the San Marcos
River on the feast of the Cross, May 3.   The next day, as we
were still travelling north, it being already late, about five
o'clock in the afternoon, all of us weary now with the seven
days' journey,[4] we saw some buffaloes, and the soldiers went

[1] The Itinerary omits the foregoing story entirely.   [2] On the 30th.
[3] The Colorado. Seeing this stream higher up, they thought it the same
as the Lavaca, which they had seen at the mouth, where it was called the San
Marcos.
[4] The Itinerary puts this incident on the 3d, and the fifth day after setting
out. It would be only the fifth according to Massanet, likewise.

out to kill something for supper that evening. I remained
with a son of Captain Leon, and as we were walking directly
forward, at the report of a gun an Indian woman came out
of the thicket, and looking by chance to the left, I saw an object in the distance; it was impossible to tell whether it was
an Indian or a tree, but on watching closely to see whether it
was moving I saw another and a smaller object issue forth,
from which it was evident that they were both Indians. Leon's
son and I set out towards them, and when we had come closer
I waved my hat to them, whereupon they fled, making for
the thicket. Just then Captain Leon arrived with some soldiers, and we went up to the thicket and could not see or find
any Indian; we did find some buffalo hides set close to a tree
so as to make a shade, also a great quantity of buffalo meat,
dried as well as fresh, three wild turkeys that were roasting,
and buffalo tongues and udders very fine, like hams. Nothing
was taken away from them, nay, more, we left them a bunch
of tobacco, some small knives, and some ribbons, and went
away. We slept that night on a little hill a couple of gunshots away from that place, the soldiers keeping a careful
watch. At about nine that night, I noticed that the fire of
the Indians grew brighter, and then I said to Captain Alonso
de Leon: "Either these Indians are numerous, and therefore
they fear us not, or those that are here, seeing that we have
taken nothing from them, but, rather, left them more, are
good people and desire to be at peace."

In the morning before sunrise I called the Quems Indian,
and told him that we would try to ascertain whether those
Indians were few or many, whether they were willing or not
to be friendly, and to what nation they belonged. The Quems
replied, as usual, "Father, what you desire me to do shall be
done." Then I gave a soldier the order to take off the armor
he had on, bidding the Quems Indian wear it, and I had a
good horse given to the Indian, and said to him: "See here!
if the soldiers go to visit the Indians, perchance these will be
afraid, and flee; it will be better for you alone to go to reconnoitre. If one of them comes out peaceably to meet you, tell
him to come forward, for we are not here to take away from
them what they possess, or to hurt them; on the contrary,
we wish to be their friends, and help them to our utmost."

As the said Indians came forth Captain Leon and his soldiers
mounted their horses to be ready to assist our Indian in case
the others should be numerous and should try to kill him.
The Quems Indian came near the place where we had seen
the Indians, and soon one of them came out towards him.
The Quems waited for him, and they spoke at great length.
And our Indian told him by signs—this being the most usual
language—not to be afraid, and that he might safely come to
us, for we were good people, and the Indian, seeing the Quems
painted like himself, believed all that he told him, and the two
came on together.   After we had talked by signs a long time
to the aforesaid Indian, he led us to his *ranchito*[1] and we
found his wife and boy about ten, and there were no other
people.   These were of the Tejas nation, and had come to
hunt buffaloes and carry the meat to their village.   Soon we
arranged for the transportation of the meat they had, and
charged the man to take word to their governor, telling him
that we were waiting for him at the spot where we had found
them.[2]   At noon we sent them forward, and returned for the
night to the spot already referred to, where we had found these
Indians.   This place is at a distance of thirty leagues, rather
more than less, from the village of Tejas.

The next morning four soldiers were sent out to the main
body of the army to take a message, giving them the order to
come and join us, as we were waiting for them at that place.
By this time the provisions were consumed, and we were living
simply on roasted meat.   The next day at about five in the
afternoon the Indian whom we had sent out appeared with
his wife and the boy, in the same place, and on our asking him
how it was that he had not gone on to his settlement he told
us that his horse had run away from him that night,[3] that he
had left the meat hanging on a tree, and that he had come
near to us to try to catch the horse.   They slept with us that
night, and the next morning we held a consultation as to
whether it might not be that other Indians had come with
him, and he was acting as a spy; with this in view it was resolved that four soldiers should examine the country around
for about three leagues and see whether there were Indians or

---

[1] Hut.   [2] According to the Itinerary this occurred on May 4.
[3] The Itinerary recounts this incident as occurring on the 5th.

tracks of any kind. About three leagues away they found an
Indian, a very tall youth on an excellent bay horse; the Indian was hunting buffalo, and though he was by himself he
began to raise a hue and cry as soon as he saw the four soldiers, riding around as if he had no fear. The soldiers drew
near him without exposing their guns or making any show
of fight, and they made signs to him that he should come with
them. And they brought him, and we gave him of what we
had, and told him that if he would go with a message to the
governor of the Tejas we would give him a horse. As soon
as the other Indian whom we had first sent saw that another
man was going with the message, he asked for a good horse,
and said he would go, and leave his wife and boy for us to
take care of until he returned with the governor. So we sent
him, telling him to light fires along the road by which they
should come, and that we would answer by the same signal.

After four days, our company reached the San Marcos
River,[1] and came upon the Indians of the ranchería Emat,
Too, Toaa, and others, and these Indians said that further
along there were other Indians, and with them two Frenchmen. Leon, remaining with a few soldiers, sent for them and
they came.[2] The one was named Pedro Muñi, a Creole, from
the city of Paris, the other Pedro Talo, a Creole, from New
France; these had firelocks, a sack of powder, and shot, more
than twenty reales of the lowest value, in silver, Spanish
money, and eighty gold eight-dollar doubloons, French money.
After the doubloons had been passed from hand to hand, there
were only thirty-nine left. One of the two Frenchmen mentioned, P. Muñi, must have been about twenty years old; the
other, Pedro Talo, eleven or twelve.[3]

The main body of the soldiers reached the place where we
were, and the day after they came Captain Leon arrived with
the two Frenchmen.[4] There came also to that spot an In-

[1] The Colorado. It was crossed on the 9th (Itinerary).
[2] De León went after Talon himself, accompanied by eight soldiers, travelling twenty-six leagues (Itinerary).
[3] Pierre Meunier and Pierre Talon. See the latter's deposition in Margry,
Découvertes et Établissements des Français, III. 610–621. The real was then, as
now, equivalent to about twelve and one-half cents.
[4] De León returned with Talon, and took a part of the camp across the San
Marcos (Colorado) on the 11th; on the 12th three Indians brought Muñi (Itinerary).

dian who was thoroughly acquainted with the road into the country of the Tejas, and he showed us the way until we met with the governor of the Tejas,[1] together with fourteen or fifteen of his Indians, and the Indian whom we had sent to him with our message. It was about ten o'clock in the morning when we came upon them by an arroyo in which they were bathing, and, on account of the thick woods, they did not see us until we were very close to them. As soon as the governor saw me he came forward to embrace me; we sat down to talk by signs—this being the most usual mode of communication in those regions; and he produced a small sack of powdered tobacco, of the kind which they grow, and another small sack of *pinole*, white, and of very good quality. After talking we left the place, and went to rest a while. That night it was arranged to provide the governor with garments, in order that he might enter his village clothed, so that his people might see how highly we thought of him.

Three days later, on Monday, May 22, 1690, we entered the village.[2] It was raining heavily on our arrival. That year it had, up to that time, rained but little, and already the corn was suffering from the drought, but every day of the eleven that we spent in the village it rained very hard.

At evening on the day of our arrival, the governor being in the tent with us, an old Indian woman brought him for his meal a large earthenware vessel full of cooked *frijoles*,[3] with ground-nuts and tamales. That evening the governor said that he would spend that night with us in the tent, and take us to his house next day, but afterwards, it being already late, Captain Leon insisted that they should go at once, as he had some skirts and other articles of clothing which he wanted to take to the governor's wife. The governor replied that he did not want to go then, but would go next day; however, in spite of all, he was obliged against his will to take Leon to his house.

[1] This was on the 18th, after six days march from the Colorado. Meantime they had crossed the Colorado or Espíritu Santo (Brazos). The governor was met less than nine and a half leagues west of the Trinity River (Itinerary).

[2] On San Pedro Creek, just northwest of Weches and some six or eight miles west of the Neches River. See Bolton, "Native Tribes about the East Texas Missions," in the Texas State Historical Association *Quarterly*, XI. 249–276; also Bolton, in Hodge, *Handbook of American Indians*, II., under "Nabedache."

[3] Kidney-beans.

On the next day the governor said that he wished to take us home with him, and that we might live in his house, in which, he said, there was room for all. After dinner we, the priests, discussed what should be our conduct on visiting the governor's, and whether it would be advisable to stay there. My opinion was that we four priests should go on foot, carrying our staffs, which bore a holy crucifix, and singing the Litany of Our Lady, and that a lay-brother who was with us should carry in front a picture on linen of the Blessed Virgin, bearing it high on his lance, after the fashion of a banner.

We set out in this manner for the governor's house from the place where we had stopped, and this pious conduct proved so blessed that, although it had rained heavily, and the water stood high all along the road where we had to pass, so high, indeed, that for the greater part of the way it came nearly to our knees, yet our fervor was such that we paid no attention to the water. Following the example given, some of the soldiers who were walking through the water became animated with such zeal and ardor that they could not keep back tears of joy and gladness. Among these who thus especially exerted themselves, giving no heed to the water or to the mud, were Captain Francisco Martinez, Don Gregorio Salinas, and others. The rest, some twenty soldiers, were on horseback, and Captain Alonso de Leon was with them; we who walked were in their midst.

We came to the governor's house, where we found a number of Indians—men, women, and children. Kneeling, we concluded the Litany, and we blessed the house. Soon the governor and the other Indians came up to kiss my robe, and the former bade us enter, in order to look at his house. The house is built of stakes thatched over with grass, it is about twenty *varas* high, is round, and has no windows, daylight entering through the door only; this door is like a room-door such as we have here.[1] In the middle of the house is the fire, which is never extinguished by day or by night, and over the door on the inner side there is a little superstructure of rafters very prettily arranged. Ranged around one-half of the house, inside, are ten beds, which consist of a rug made of reeds, laid

[1] For a description of Hasinai house-building, see Espinosa, *Chrónica*, pp. 420–421.

on four forked sticks.   Over the rug they spread buffalo skins, on which they sleep.   At the head and foot of the bed is attached another carpet forming a sort of arch, which, lined with a very brilliantly colored piece of reed matting, makes what bears some resemblance to a very pretty alcove.   In the other half of the house, where there are no beds, there are some shelves about two *varas* high, and on them are ranged large round baskets made of reeds (in which they keep their corn, nuts, acorns, beans, etc.), a row of very large earthen pots like our water jars, these pots being used only to make the *atole* when there is a large crowd on the occasion of some ceremony, and six wooden mortars for pounding the corn in rainy weather (for, when it is fair, they grind it in the courtyard).

After a little while they brought out to each of us in the patio[1] a small wooden bench very skilfully fashioned, and after we had been through the house we sat down there, for the patio was bright and cool.   Then they brought us a lunch consisting of the tamales they make, with nuts, *pinole* of corn, very well prepared, a large crock full of corn cooked with *frijoles*, and ground-nuts.   Soon I noticed, outside the patio, opposite the door of the governor's house, another long building, and no one lived in it.   I asked who dwelt therein or what purpose it served, and was told that the captains were lodged in that house when the governor called them to a meeting. On the other side I saw yet another and smaller vacant house, and upon my inquiring about this one they answered that in the smallest house the pages of the captains were lodged, for the law provides that each captain shall bring his page when the governor assembles the captains, according to the custom which they observe.   As soon as they arrive they are lodged in that house, and for each one is laid a large, brightly colored reed mat, on which they sleep, with a bolster made of painted reeds at the head; and when they return home each one carries with him his mat and pillow.   While they attend the meeting the governor provides them with food, until he sends them home.

The following are the domestic arrangements in the governor's house: each week ten Indian women undertake the

---

[1] *Patio,* an open quadrangle round which the rooms of a house are ranged.

house-work; each day at sunrise these women come laden with firewood, sweep out the patio and the house, carry water from the arroyo at some distance—(for this water is very good, and though the river is close by, its water is not as good as that of the arroyo)—and grind corn for the *atole*, *tamales*, and *pinole*. Each one of the women goes home for the night, returning next morning. In the governor's house I saw a little wooden bench in front of the fire, and the Indians admonished me not to sit upon it, lest I should die. I was curious to learn what mystery there was connected with it, and they told me that no one but their lord, the governor, might sit upon that stool.

As to whether the priests should live in the governor's house, it seemed to me unadvisable that they should do so, on account of the number of Indians, men and women, who went in and out at all times. Using the Frenchman as an interpreter I told the governor with many kind expressions that his house was very fine, and that I heartily appreciated his desire to have the priests in his household, but that since we had to build a house for the celebration of masses, it might be well to build likewise a dwelling for the priests, because they must needs live near the church. Thereupon the governor said that we should build the house in the most suitable place, that he would show us the village, and that I might choose the spot. We agreed to visit the village on the following day in order to look for a favorable location for the church and the priests' dwelling; accordingly next day we went with the governor, who took us to the place the French had selected for their settlement, pleasantly and favorably situated on the riverbanks.[1] We did not locate the convent there because it was so far out of the way of the Indians. Just at that spot they showed us two dead bodies of Frenchmen who had shot each other with carbines. All this day we were unable to find a place which suited me.

The next morning I went out with Captain Alonso de Leon a little way, and found a delightful spot close to the

---

[1] According to the Itinerary, on May 24 a temporary chapel was built; on the 25th possession taken, obedience rendered, and ecclesiastical possession given to Massanet; on the 26th De León and the missionaries looked for a permanent site, reaching the Neches River.

brook, fine woods, with plum trees like those in Spain. And
soon afterwards, on the same day, they began to fell trees and
cart the wood, and within three days we had a roomy dwelling
and a church wherein to say mass with all propriety. We
set in front of the church a very high cross of carved wood.[1]

On the feast of Corpus Christi mass was sung, and before
mass we had a procession with the holy sacrament exposed,
a large concourse of Indians being assembled, for we had notified them the day before. The soldiers had been given leave
to fire as many salutes as they could during the procession,
at the elevation, and at the close of mass, and by the will of
the Divine Majesty we celebrated in that solitude a memora-
ble feast, which was rendered a source of great consolation
by our being able to carry the blessed sacrament exposed and
to walk in procession as Christian Catholics are wont to do.
After mass we hoisted in the name of His Majesty the royal
standard bearing on one side the picture of Christ crucified,
and on the other that of the Virgin of Guadalupe. A royal
salute was fired, and we sang the Te Deum Laudamus in
thanksgiving.

These Tejas Indians have always had among them an
old Indian who was their minister, and presented their offer-
ings to God. They observed the custom never to taste any
eatable without first taking a portion of it to their minister
for sacrifice ; they did this with the products of their lands—
as corn, beans, watermelons, and squashes—as well as with
the buffalo meat they obtained by hunting. This minister
had a house reserved for the sacrifices, and they entered
therein very reverentially, particularly during a sacrifice.
They never sacrificed to idols, but only to Him of whom they
said that He has all power and that from Him come all things,
who is recognized as first cause.

The captains as well as the governor himself all treat this
minister with much consideration, and in order to induce him
to visit us, as well as to avoid hurting his feelings, the governor
sent out the captains with orders to do honor to the Indian
priest and bring him with them. They went, and during the
three days and nights they entertained him with songs and

---

[1] It was located in the middle of the village. From the 27th to the 31st
was spent in building the church and the dwelling (Itinerary).

dances, as is their custom, and then they returned home, bringing him.[1] They arrived at noon, just as we were about to have dinner. Since I was eager to see the ceremonies of these people, I suggested that we should wait for that priest of theirs and ask him to eat at our table. He came, advancing slowly, and bearing himself with much dignity, and with him was a crowd of Indians, men, women, and children. He appeared extremely serious and reserved, and as soon as he reached the place where we were the governor bade him kiss our robe. This he did, and when we sat down to dinner I asked the governor to let our visitor sit by his side.

When the Indian priest took his first mouthful, instead of asking a blessing, he made with the food, as he took it out of the dish, a sign like that of the cross, pointing, as it were, to the four winds, or cardinal points. After dinner we gave him clothing for himself and his wife, and he was well pleased.

Later we were told by an Indian who was then with the Tejas but came from the country beyond—from Coahuila— and who spoke Mexican, that the above-mentioned priest of the Tejas had told all the captains and other Tejas, "Now you will no longer heed me, for these priests who have come to you are the true priests of Ayimat Caddi"—which name signifies, in their language, "The Great Captain." This was the name he gave to God, for since the only rank or title they know is that of captain, they call "Great Captain" him whom they consider as great above all things. Similarly, in order to give the governor a distinguishing name other than that of captain, since there are other captains, they call him *desza*, which means "Great Lord and superior to all."

When the church and the dwelling intended for the priests had been finished they carried into these buildings all that was to be left for the priests, and on the morning of the first of June, the octave of the feast of Corpus Christi, we consecrated the church and celebrated mass, after which the Te Deum Laudamus was sung in thanksgiving, the soldiers firing a royal salute. The church and village were dedicated to our Holy Father St. Francis.

After dinner on the same day our company left the place,

---

[1] The "minister" was the Great Xinesi. His chief temple was on the Angelina River.

to return hither, but I remained until the next day.[1]   When I left the place I called the governor, bidding him remember that he must take care of the fathers who remained there and try to cause his people to respect them and to receive the Christian doctrine.   I told him the fathers would not take anything away from them, nor ask them for anything, but rather help them whenever they were able.   And the governor said, "I shall take care of the fathers, so that, when you return, they will have no complaint to bring against me; they are perfectly safe, and may remain."   I then told him that I should be gratified if his brother and some other one of his relatives would come with me to visit our country and bring back numerous presents for those who remained at home, and that our great captain the viceroy was anxious to see them and entertained very kindly feeling towards them.   The governor then replied that his brother with two other relatives and a nephew of his would accompany me, and he thus admonished me, "Do not permit anyone to demand service from these men whom you take with you, nor to make them work."   From these words of his it is evident that they have among them the idea of rank, and that they distinguished their nobles from the mass of the people.

From the time of our arrival at the Tejas village until we left I took note of some things and gained experience concerning some men whose conduct proved so different from what it had seemed to be when we were on the road, that I hardly knew them for the same persons after we were in the village. Evidently some of them thought that they were to be made rulers of the Tejas, and forgot His Excellency's express orders concerning the journey, which orders provided that Captain Alonso de Leon should go as commander of the expedition to find out whether there were any Frenchmen in that region, and that Leon and his men should escort thither the priests who accompanied Fray Damian Manzanet. If the Tejas asked for priests and desired baptism, the priests were to remain there.   And if the Tejas proved quite friendly and no danger was to be expected at their hands, no large garrison was to be left behind; if, on the other hand, they proved troublesome, as many soldiers should remain as seemed need-

---

[1] So also did Governor De León and six soldiers.

ful, according to the advice and with the consent of Fathei
Fray Damian Manzanet. It was at no time necessary for
the safety of the priests to leave soldiers among the Tejas,
for from the very first they welcomed us with so much affection and good will, that they could hardly do enough to
please us. Yet, in the face of all this, Captain Alonso de
Leon made arrangements to leave fifty men, under the command of Captain Nicolas Prietto, an incapable and undeserv-
ing old man.

When the time came, the captain told me of his purpose
in a private interview, and I replied: "You are under orders
from His Excellency, and if you mean to consult with me, the
consultation must not take place in private; call your captains
and in their presence and in that of the priests state what you
wish to offer for consideration." This reply deeply wounded
Leon, for his passions had blinded him. He called the captains, and I called the priests, and Captain Alonso de Leon
told us that he had planned to leave for the protection of the
priests forty or fifty soldiers under a leader, and that he was
holding this consultation because His Excellency had ordered
that, if the soldiers were to be left, it should be with my consent. To this I replied that there was no necessity at all to
leave a military force in the district, since the people were so
peaceable and so friendly. In case the priests should need
assistance, I requested that three soldiers whom I thought fit
for the position should stay there. If he chose to leave a
greater number, well and good; but with no consent of mine,
for I did not wish more than three to remain. Leon was much
taken aback on account of what he had planned and discussed
with his *compadre*[1] Captain Nicolas Prietto, who was to remain
as leader of the forty or fifty soldiers. However, in the end,
it was arranged that the three soldiers recommended by me
should remain there. They were willing to do so, and were
quite content. They belonged to the Zacatecas company.
Leon left for the soldiers nine of the king's horses, firelocks, a
barrel of powder and some shot, and for the priests he left
twenty-six loads of flour, twenty cows, two yoke of oxen,
ploughs with ploughshares, axes, spades, and other little
necessaries.

[1] Intimate friend, or a person related by the tie of godfather.

On the 2d of June we took our departure, and the priests walked with us a little way out of the village. Then we took leave of one another with many tears of joy and gladness, for these men did not sorrow at being left behind,[1] nay, rather, they gave thanks to God for having merited such a grace as to be called to save the souls of the heathen. We arrived at the Trinity on the 3d of June, and found this river very high. On this account we were kept for a week from crossing. Meanwhile the governor's brother was taken ill and went home. After a week they made a raft of logs, on which the packs, the clothing, and all other baggage were taken across, while the horses were driven through swimming, some few getting drowned.[2]

We followed the road by which we had come, until we reached the ranchería of the Emat, Toaa, Too, Cavas, and other Indians, and in this ranchería we heard that the Indians on the coast had captured some young Frenchmen. The captain of the ranchería told us that although they themselves were at feud with the Indians on the coast, yet there was among them an Indian who held intercourse with those others, and if some of us desired to go and find them, this Indian would take those who wished to go. Captain Leon decided to go with twenty men for the purpose of trying to rescue the said young Frenchmen. They reached the coast of the bay and found the Indians whom they sought.[3] These had just arrived from some other portion of the same coast, armed with lances, and soon our people began to treat with them, about delivering up the young Frenchmen. The Indians were promised horses and clothing if they would give up the boys, and their reply was that they would do so promptly, and very willingly. The soldiers then began to enter the *ranchitos*[4] of the Indians, peering with too much curiosity into their belongings, and committing other acts so that the Indians became resentful against the soldiers and distrustful of them when they found out who was guilty.[5] Later, all being gath-

---

[1] The missionaries are named on p. 368, above.

[2] The crossing was effected on the 11th.

[3] They were found far south of the Garcitas River, on the coast of Matagorda Bay. See Itinerary, p. 420, below.

[4] Huts.   [5] De León places all the blame on the Indians (Itinerary).

ered together after the French boys had been delivered over to our men, the Indians commenced to shoot arrows among the soldiers. Two arrows struck Captain Leon in the side, but as he wore mail, they did not penetrate; also, the horses were shot down under two other soldiers. There were four Indians killed and two wounded, and our men took the young Frenchmen and returned to the main body of the army, which was waiting by the Guadalupe River.[1]

We returned by the way we had come, and, arriving at the Rio del Norte,[2] found it so high that we were kept from crossing for 18[3] days, and when we did get across it was by swimming, at great peril to our lives. The river current carried off many articles of clothing as well as horses, and one soldier, who bore among his comrades the ill name of Judas, was drowned. This man had the reputation of being likely to appropriate what belonged to other people, and on the morning of the day he was drowned he returned to one of the mule drivers a boiler he had stolen, saying, "Forgive me, friend, for I stole this boiler from you." And when he entered the river to cross, he said, "Let us hurry in, for this is the last time." When he was in the middle of the river he disappeared —he, the horse, and all he was carrying, and he was never again seen. Just at the time when he disappeared there arose a high wind which terrified us, and the waters of the river grew so angry that they seemed about to leave their bed.

There were some points of which I took special note on this journey. First, in the preceding year we had everywhere found Indians, while in the year '90 we saw not a single one, until we inspected the bay of Espiritu Santo and entered the land of the Tejas.

Secondly, in the year before the soldiers all behaved in a peaceable, orderly manner, performing their duties faithfully, so that there was no disorder on the march, and no loss of horses. But in this year '90 there hardly passed a day without some one fighting or else the officers stabbing soldiers, so

---

[1] De León crossed the Guadalupe on the 24th (Itinerary).

[2] On July 4. The circumstances of the crossing are stated in note to the Itinerary of 1690, p. 423, below.

[3] Father Massanet is in error. See note to De León's Itinerary of 1690, p. 422.

that a lay-brother who had come with me was generally kept busy tending the wounded. He treated them with tepid wine, which is, they say, an excellent cure for stabs in the head.

Thirdly, I noted that there were so many horses and mules that the laden mules were not missed until some article contained in their pack was needed. As to the number of horses, it was never known to the officers.

Fourthly, Captain Leon had a *compadre* along, Captain So-and-So, so honorable that he never failed to play the talebearer and excite quarrels; so kind-hearted that only his friend Leon drank chocolate, and the others the lukewarm water; so considerate of others that he got up early in the morning to drink chocolate, and would afterward drink again with the rest; so vigilant that he would keep awake and go at midnight to steal the chocolate out of the boxes: perhaps this vigilance was the reason why, while, by order of His Excellency, Captain Leon should have left for the priests three hundredweight of chocolate and the same quantity of sugar, he left only one and one-half hundredweight of each.

This same *compadre* is so smooth-tongued that he told me once: "In truth, in truth, since the time of Cortes there has not been in the Indies another man who can be compared with my *compadre* General Alonso de Leon." This aforesaid *compadre* is so compassionate towards the Indians that because he saw how poor they were, and that their only clothing was the skins of antelopes and buffaloes, he endeavored to give them in secret the articles which His Excellency had sent for them—*e. g.*, blankets, flannel, cloth and knives—but the *compadre* so arranged the almsgiving, by first robbing the Indians of what they had, that his gifts were equal to about one-fourth of what he took.

Fifthly, when the Indians brought some complaints against the soldiers for entering their houses, Captain Leon never attempted to remedy things at all. In one particular case, when the brother of the governor of the Tejas came to us, complaining that a rape had been attempted on his wife, I asked Captain Leon how he could tolerate such misdeeds. I urged that conduct like this, which would not be tolerated even among the Moors or heretics, should be the more severely reproved because we had come among these heathen people in order to

give an example of right living.   Leon did not say a word—
perhaps because he feared exposure.

For lack of more time I shall now only add what is the
most noteworthy thing of all, namely this : While we were at
the Tejas village, after we had distributed clothing to the
Indians and to the governor of the Tejas, the said governor
asked me one evening for a piece of blue baize to make a shroud
in which to bury his mother when she died.   I told him that
cloth would be more suitable, and he answered that he did not
want any color other than blue.   I then asked him what mystery was attached to the blue color, and he said that they
were very fond of that color, particularly for burial clothes,
because in times past they had been visited frequently by a
very beautiful woman, who used to come down from the
heights, dressed in blue garments, and that they wished to be
like that woman.   On my asking whether that had been long
since, the governor said it had been before his time, but his
mother, who was aged, had seen that woman, as had also the
other old people.   From this it is easily to be seen that they
referred to the Madre Maria de Jesus de Agreda, who was
very frequently in those regions, as she herself acknowledged
to the father custodian of New Mexico, her last visit having
been made in 1631, this last fact being evident from her own
statement, made to the said father custodian of New Mexico.[1]

[1] See p. 354, note 4.

ITINERARY OF THE DE LEÓN EXPEDITION OF 1689[1]

Itinerary of the Expedition made by General Alonso De León for the Discovery of the Bahía del Espíritu Santo and the French Settlement. 1689.

March.

DATE.   LEAGUES.

Wednesday, March 23, it was arranged that the detachment of soldiers and camp-followers who were in Coahuila should set out. Accordingly, they marched one league down the river.   1.

Thursday, the 24th, the whole body set out. The detachment, being ordered to go down the river,[2] travelled down the other bank to its junction with the Nadadores. They travelled that day seven leagues toward the north.[3] All this country is uninhabitable.   7.

Friday, the 25th, we travelled down the Rio de Nadadores, along the south bank, between two ridges which they call Baluartes. On the bank of the river we passed a cottonwood tree,[4] the only one within a great distance. We travelled that day seven leagues, keeping the same northeast course. All the country is level and affords good pasturage.   7.

Saturday, the 26th, we travelled down the river as on the day before, to its junction with the Sabinas. We travelled east, halting a league from the junction. The country is level and affords good pasturage.[5]   [6].

[1] Translation by Miss Elizabeth Howard West, in Texas State Historical Association *Quarterly*, VIII. 199–224.

[2] They crossed to the south side, and followed the right bank to a point three leagues below the junction with the Sabinas (Miss West). See the Sigüenza map.

[3] The Sigüenza map gives the distance as seven leagues (Miss West).

[4] The Alamo became a well-known landmark and was regularly noted in later diaries.

[5] The Sigüenza map supplies the distance lacking in the *Memorias* transcript of the diary.

DATE.   LEAGUES.

Sunday, the 27th, we went down the river Sabinas and crossed it toward the north. Passing along the bank we sighted the soldiers who were coming from the Nuevo Reyno de Leon to join us here according to agreement.[1] As we came together a salute was fired on each side. After we had travelled three leagues to the east, a general review and individual count was made of all the soldiers, drivers, and other servants, and of the baggage as well.[2]   3.

Monday, the 28th, we travelled to the northeast, a distance of six leagues. After crossing some unwatered plains, we halted at a pool of rain-water.   6.

Tuesday, the 29th, we set out toward the northeast. Before daybreak the French prisoner sent out one of the Indians whom we were bringing because of their loyalty, to tell the Indians, his acquaintances, that we were going through their village. As a result, more than seventy Indians, some armed, others unarmed, came out to meet us a league before we arrived at the village, and accompanied us thither. They had a hut ready, covered with buffalo hides; there they put the Frenchman, toward whom they made many demonstrations of affection.[3] In front of the hut was driven a stake, four *varas* high, on which were fastened sixteen heads of Indians, their enemies, whom they had killed. They were five nations, joined together (according to the account the Frenchman gave), entitled Hapes, Jumenes, Xiabu, Mescale, and another. We counted eighty-five huts. We distributed among them some cotton garments, blankets, beads, rosaries, knives, and arms, with which they were very much pleased. Five cattle were killed for them, too, so that all persons of all ages might

---

[1] The party from Monterey went down the Caldera River (De León, *Historia de Nuevo León*, p. 319).

[2] The original list is printed in De León, *Historia de Nuevo León*, pp. 320–321. It shows eighty-eight soldiers and religious, the French prisoner, called Andrés, twelve muleteers, thirteen servants, seven hundred and twenty horses and mules, eighty-two pack-loads of flour, biscuits, and other provisions, and three pack-loads of presents for the Indians. See *ibid.*, p. 318, and Massanet's *Letter*, p. 353.

[3] The Indians at this point are referred to in the diary of 1690 as "the Indians of the Frenchman." In De León, *Historia de Nuevo León*, p. 322, the names are given as the Apes. Mescales, Jumanes, and Ijiaba.

DATE.   LEAGUES.

eat. There were four hundred and ninety of them. We
crossed a creek about the time of evening prayer.[1]   4.

Thursday, the 31st, it was necessary to halt at this point
because of the suffering of the horses occasioned by lack of
water.

April.

Friday, April 1st, we travelled down the river five leagues,
traversing some low hills. There was no lack of water-holes
along the way. The route during the most of these five
leagues was toward the north. We halted on this south bank
in front of the ford.[2] The river was forded, and found easy
to cross the next day. Now we had with us a faithful Indian
guide,[3] who assured us that he knew the country, and that
he would bring us where there were some men like ourselves,
in a settlement of six or seven houses; that they had wives
and children, and that they were about six days' journey
distant from the said Rio Bravo. This Indian can not speak
Castilian, but we got some light on what he was saying
through another Indian who acted as interpreter, albeit a
poor one.   5.

Saturday, the 2d, we crossed the river and went about
one league north, to avoid some ravines and low hills. Afterward we went mostly northeast, until we reached some pools,
five leagues away. We named these El Paraje de los Cuervos,
because more than three thousand crows appeared at nightfall. The way was level and untimbered.   5.

Palm Sunday, the 3d, we marched northeast three leagues,
through level country, and afterward two more through several thickets of mesquite. We crossed some little dry creeks;
and then we came upon one that had water in it, on the bank

[1] The Sigüenza map gives a journey of four leagues for March 30, which is
omitted entirely from the *Memorias* copy of the diary. From a comparison of
distances between the Sabinas and the Rio Grande with the diary and map of
1690, it seems probable that the map is correct. The 1689 map gives the distance
as twenty-three and the diary of 1690 as twenty-two leagues.

[2] Of the Río Bravo. See De León, *Historia de Nuevo León*, p. 324. The
crossing was not far from San Juan Bautista.

[3] The Quems.

of which we halted. Altogether we travelled that day five long leagues. We named this creek the Arroyo de Ramos,[1] because we found it on Palm Sunday. There we observed the altitude of the sun with an astrolabe, though a defective one, and found our latitude to be 26° 31'.[2] I must call attention to the fact that the tables on which this observation was based were made before the so-called Gregorian correction. This correction was made in the year 1582, in which the equinox was on the tenth of March. Following the *Ephemerides* of the Roman Andrea Argoli, which places the equinox this year (1582) on the 20th of March, we found by these tables that today, April 3, corresponds to the 24th of March of this year (1689), which is the first since the bissextile. These tables, the author says, he took from the *Arte de Navegar*, by the Maestro Medina.[3] It has been necessary to state these facts in explanation, in case it should appear that a mistake has been made because of our lack of modern tables.   5.

Holy Monday, the 4th, we marched northeast most of the day, east-by-north occasionally, a distance of 8 leagues. At first the land was level, then there was a little mesquite thicket; and after that we got into a larger one, three leagues long. We came upon a river, which, as we could see, even though it contained little water at the time, overflows its banks in time of rain more than half a league from the main channel. We called it the Rio de las Nueces,[4] because there were many pecan trees. It is somewhat rocky, and all its rocks are flint and very fine.   8.

Holy Tuesday, the 5th, we crossed the river. We had to go half a league down its bank, and then we went through a glade. Then came a very dense thicket. We had to cut a passage into it for almost a league with our cutlasses and axes,

---

[1] Evidently one of the branches of the Nueces River.

[2] As pointed out by Miss West, the calculations were a degree or more in error.

[3] Pedro Medina's *Arte de Navegar* was first published at Valladolid in 1545. The Italian astronomer Andrea Argoli's *Ephemerides* was first published at Rome in 1621.

[4] The present Nueces, and not that which figured in the Spanish expeditions to the Jumanos. The 1690 diary and map mention Arroyo de Caramanchel between Arroyo de Ramos and the Nueces River.

DATE.   LEAGUES.

because of the numerous prickly pears and mesquite which blocked up the way. Afterward we got into a mesquite thicket in which at intervals we had to make a clearing. We travelled about seven leagues. We came upon a river to which we gave the name Rio Sarco,[1] because its water was blue. We went, I repeat, seven leagues, with many turns.   7.

Holy Wednesday, the 6th, we travelled about three leagues to the northeast, and two to the east. The country we passed through was level, with fine pasturage, with very pleasant glades, and, occasionally, little motts of oak. We came to a river, which we named Rio Hondo. *Apropos* of this river, its descent on each side is about forty feet; near it, on both banks, are some insignificant hills, some of them timbered. The water was plentiful, so that the horses were easily supplied. As we went down toward the river we found some large white rocks, on some of which we saw some crosses cut, and other figures artificially made with great skill, apparently a long time before.   5.

Holy Thursday, the 7th, we went more than four leagues down the river without crossing it, sometimes east, sometimes southeast; we halted on the hither bank. The country is of the same sort here as at the last stopping-place; level, for the most part, though there is a little mesquite timber. Ever since the thirtieth of last month, when we passed the village of the Five Nations,[2] we have found along the line of march traces of Indians, made some time ago; but not a single Indian has appeared.

Holy Friday, the 8th, we crossed from the other bank of the Rio Hondo, and travelled east-northeast, most of the day near the river. We came upon two ravines near together. Here, it appears, the river rises in time of flood as much as six feet. After the ravines comes a little creek in a thicket. Here it was necessary to change our course for a while, to let the loaded mules cross, which they did with difficulty, some bogging up. After crossing this creek, we came to some very level land, and then to a large mesquite thicket. In the

---

[1] Elsewhere called the Rio Frio, with which Clark identifies it (*The Beginnings of Texas*, p. 17).

[2] See the entry for the 29th of March.

midst of the thicket were some pools of water, where we
halted. We travelled that day eight long leagues, to the east,
as has already been said.   8.

Holy Saturday, the 9th, we set out to the north, but on
account of some thickets that were in the way, it was necessary to make some turns, sometimes north-by-east, sometimes north-northeast. We travelled that day five leagues.
The land was very good. We crossed a dry creek that day,
but a league farther on we found one with good water, with
abundant pasturage and many oak-trees near by. We named
this creek Arroyo del Vino, because we opened a cask[1] that
day and divided its contents among the men. Under the trees
we found well-grown nuts, as large as those of Spain, but very
hard to open. We saw many wild grape-vines, whose fruit,
as we were told by the Indians we had brought with us, is in
its season very pleasantly flavored. Our horses stampeded
at this camp about nine o'clock at night, and they could not
be stopped, though fifteen soldiers were on guard. According to the count made the following day, one hundred and
two got away.   5.

Easter Sunday, the 10th, soldiers set out in different directions to look for the horses, which they found at various
points. This search detained them till evening prayer,[2]
therefore the camp was not moved that day. We made a
reckoning of our latitude which we found to be 27° 55′.

Monday after Easter, the 11th, we set out to the east.
We crossed two creeks of good water, and immediately after
came to a great wood of pecan and oak-trees, more than five
leagues in extent, all fertile and pleasant land. After having
to travel twelve leagues to get water, we came that day upon
a river, which was very large, though it had not much water,
and which had a good ford. We named it the Rio de Medina.
The descent to it is about fifty or sixty feet. All the rest of
the way there were oaks and pecans. The course that day
was east half the way, and northeast half the way.   12.

Tuesday after Easter, the 12th, we crossed the river, and
found the ford very easy. We travelled five leagues to the
east, over some low hills, without any timber; we crossed

[1] Of wine.   [2] Vespers, would be a better rendering.

some ravines of red and yellow earth; we entered a mesquite thicket, and found water in a creek. The creek was dry where we first struck it, and we were somewhat discomfited because we thought our guide had mistaken the direction; about a league farther, however, there was a very good stream. We named this creek the Arroyo del Leon,[1] because we found a dead lion near by, very much mutilated. The country was level, and furnished good pasturage.   5.

 Wednesday, the 13th, we advanced to the east, sometimes east-northeast, six leagues. About half a league from the camp we passed by the point of a little hill on which ends a clump of oaks, and which we left on the right hand. Among them were small piles of stones placed by hand. We followed some low hills; there were about two leagues of oak timber which had to be partly cleared away; but after this all the country was level till we reached a little creek.   6.

 Thursday, the 14th, we moved forward, east-northeast, in search of a great river which the guide told us we should find and which we reached at two in the afternoon. We travelled six leagues, the first three over some hills, and the rest of the way over some hills that were timbered and marked with ravines. It was necessary in some places to clear away the timber so as to pass through. The country was the most pleasant that we had traversed; the river is not very full and has a good ford; its banks are covered with timber. Six buffaloes—the first we had seen for a hundred leagues—were killed along the way. We gave this river the name of Our Lady of Guadalupe, whom we had brought from Coahuila as our protectress,[2] and whom we had painted on our royal standard.   6.

 Friday, the 15th, the day dawned very rainy. None the less, however, our whole party set out toward the ford of the river, which was about a league away. We crossed the river, but as the water prevented our forward movement, we halted

---

 [1] Apparently the present San Antonio River. The name Medina now applies to only the upper waters of the stream (see Clark, *The Beginnings of Texas*, p. 17).

 [2] That is, they carried her statue or picture. The river was crossed not far from Victoria, perhaps a little below it.

on a little creek. We travelled that day not more than two
leagues. As the guide said that we were near the settlement,
a council of war was held, at which it was decided that the
next day a reconnaissance should be made with sixty soldiers,
while the camp should stay in another place at some distance
away, with a sufficient guard.   2.

 Saturday, the 16th, after a mass to Our Lady of Guadalupe
had been chanted with all solemnity, the governor, in accor-
dance with the decision of the day before, set out with the
sixty soldiers, well equipped. The whole force set out at the
same time. After travelling about three leagues with the sixty
men, the rear-guard caught sight of an Indian in the timber. When he was taken to the governor and examined—
through a poor interpreter—he declared that his ranchería was
near by, and that four Frenchmen were there. We quickened our pace, under the guidance of our Indian, after we had
sent word to the main body to stay in the place whence they
had sent the Indian. Before we came to the ranchería all
the people left. We sighted them, however, as they were
entering some motts; and after them came eight or ten dogs
loaded with buffalo hides. We sent the same Indian who
had guided us to call them, with the result that most of them
came. It was ascertained that the four Frenchmen were
not there, but that they had gone on to the Tejas four days
before. In this ranchería we found two Indians who told
us that we should find them in a ranchería two days' journey further. We gave these Indians some tobacco, knives,
and other things, to get them to guide us, which they did.
We turned and moved northward till sunset. Then we found
in a thicket a village of more than two hundred and fifty persons, where we tried to find the Frenchmen, our French guide
always serving as interpreter. They replied that the Frenchmen had gone to the Texas Indians four days before, and that
the rest who had settled on the little sea (which is the bay) had
all died at the hands of the coast Indians; that the Frenchmen had six houses; and that the event had occurred three
moons, that is, three months, before; that previous to this
there had been an epidemic of smallpox, of which most of them
had died. The main body travelled east that day, and halted

DATE.   LEAGUES.

at the place appointed by the governor, who went eight
leagues northward with the sixty men.   8.

Sunday, the 17th, after sleeping close by the Indian village,
we again set out to the north. After travelling five leagues
we found some ranchos[1] of Indians known to our French
prisoner. We found out from them by minute inquiry the
route of the four Frenchmen who were going to the Texas;
we found out, moreover, that they had passed on horseback
four days before. Here a consultation was held as to what
decision should be reached, with the result that it was determined, as the main force was far away and the country unknown, to write a letter to the Frenchmen and send it to them
by an Indian. Accordingly, the letter was written in French
by the royal *alférez*, Francisco Martinez. Its contents, in
substance, were as follows: that we had been informed of
their escape when some Christians on the coast had been killed
by the Indians of that vicinity; that they might come with
us; that we would wait for them three or four days in the
houses of the village from which they had set out. This letter
was signed by the governor and by our chaplain, Padre Fray
Damian Manzanet, religious of our patron San Francisco.
The letter added as a postscript some lines of Latin, in case
any one of the four should be a religious, exhorting them to
come. Putting in paper for a reply, we dispatched this letter
by an Indian carrier who assured us that he would overtake
them. About evening prayer[2] an Indian came from the North
to see the Frenchmen, of whom he must have had news.
When we asked him through the Frenchman whether it was
far from here to the Texas, he replied that it was not many
days' journey and said that it had been three days since the
four Frenchmen had gone on from his rancheria.

Monday, the 18th, in view of the harm the camp might
have suffered, even though we had left it well guarded, we
set out in search of it. On the way thither the governor received a letter stating that the drove of horses had stampeded
the night before, and that a hundred-odd had been lost; that
some had been found, but thirty-six were still missing. At
this we quickened our pace to the camp. There we heard

---

[1] Houses or huts.   [2] Vespers.

DATE.   LEAGUES.

also that a soldier[1] had been lost in the search for the horses. At this news sundry squadrons of soldiers were sent in search of him, but he did not appear that day.

Tuesday, the 19th, since neither the soldier nor the horses had appeared, two squadrons of soldiers set out in different directions to look for them; the governor went in person; but despite their diligent efforts the lost were not found. [The search-party], therefore, slept in the open, to continue the search. Indians from different rancherías came to the camp that day; we gave them tobacco and other things, and charged them to scour the country in search of the soldier and the horses that were missing, promising them due return for the service.

Wednesday, the 20th, the party did not set out, because neither soldier nor horses had appeared. The efforts of the day before were repeated with new squadrons of soldiers. Just after they had left the lost man came, guided by several Indians. He said that that night [after he had been lost] he had come to an Indian ranchería where he spent the night; that he had been undecided whether to stay there, because of his suspicion that they were going to kill him, but that he had been treated with great kindness. It was no little good fortune that he escaped from danger at the hands of so barbarous a race. Though the astrolabe was broken, we righted it that day as best we could and made an observation of the sun, and found ourselves in latitude 28° 41' north.[2]

Thursday, the 21st, our party advanced sometimes east, sometimes east-by-north, sometimes northeast-by-north. Our line of march lay through some wide plains which for long stretches were treeless. At the end of eight leagues we came to a creek of good water. Here the Indian guide told us that the settlement was on the bank of this creek[3] and in its vicinity. The land was all very pleasing; and we came across many buffalo.

Friday, the 22d, as we were near the settlement, our party

---

[1] His name was Juan de Charles (De León, *Historia de Nuevo León*, p. 327).

[2] The Autor Anónimo gives the latitude as 28° 4' (*Historia de Nuevo León, ibid.*).

[3] Garcitas River. See Massanet's Carta, p. 361, above, notes 2, 3.

set out though the day dawned rainy. Three leagues down the creek we found it. Having halted with the forces about an arquebus-shot away, we went to see it, and found all the houses sacked, all the chests, bottle-cases, and all the rest of the settlers' furniture broken ; apparently more than two hundred books, torn apart and with the rotten leaves scattered through the patios—all in French. We noted that the perpetrators of this massacre had pulled everything [the colonists] had out of their chests, and divided the booty among themselves ; and that what they had not cared for they had torn to pieces, making a frightful sack of all the French possessed ; for besides the evidence involved in our finding everything in this condition, further proof was found in the fact that in the rancherías through which we had passed before our arrival at the settlement, we had found in the possession of the Indians some French books in very good condition, with other articles of very little value. These books were recovered and their titles committed to memory. The Indians had done this damage not only to the furnishings, but also to the arms, for we found more than a hundred stocks of flintlock arquebuses, without locks or barrels. They must have carried these off, as was proved by an [arquebus] barrel found at some distance from the houses. We found three dead bodies scattered over the plain. One of these, from the dress that still clung to the bones, appeared to be that of a woman. We took the bodies up, chanted mass with the bodies present, and buried them. We looked for the other dead bodies but could not find them ; whence we supposed that they had been thrown into the creek and had been eaten by alligators, of which there were many. The principal house of this settlement is in the form of a fort, made of ship's timber, with a second story, also made of ship's timber, and with a slope to turn off water. Next to it, without any partition, is another apartment, not so strong, which must have served as a chapel where mass was said. The other five houses are of stakes, covered with mud inside and out ; their roofs are covered with buffalo-hides. All are quite useless for any defence. In and about the fort and the houses were eight pieces of artillery, iron, of medium bore,—four or five-pounders,—and three very old swivels whose chambers were lacking. Some iron bars were also found, and some ship's nails, estimated as altogether about five hundredweight. Some of the guns were scattered over the ground and some were on their broken carriages. There were some casks with their heads knocked in and their contents spilled out, so that nothing was worth anything. Around the building was also some tackle, much the worse for wear. The settlement was on a beautiful, level site, so as to be capable of defence in any event. On the frame of the principal door of the fort was inscribed the date of the settlement, which was 1684.[1] There are other details which are noted in the separate description of the post.[2] The party travelled that day three leagues to the east. It appears, therefore, that the total distance from the Presidio of Coahuila to this settlement is one hundred and thirty-six leagues.[3]

Discovery of Espíritu Santo Bay and its Harbor.

Saturday, the 23d, we set out with thirty men to reconnoitre the bay to the south, trying to follow the creek below the settlement. We took the French prisoner for a guide, because he had told us he knew the bay and had been all over it in a bark. In view of this assurance we let him guide us. He did not guide us down the creek, because he said it had no crossing. We went [instead] five leagues to the southwest; then, after going around the head-waters of two creeks, we went three leagues farther, to the east, when we came upon the shore of the bay. Here we slept, as we arrived at twilight.

Sunday, the 24th, very early in the morning, we set out along the shore of the bay, which at that season was at low water. There are many lagoons of salt water around it whose marshes prevented us at some places from crossing on horseback. For long stretches, therefore, we went on foot, leading

---

[1] See a drawing of the fort and of the inscription in De León, *Historia de Nuevo León*, pp. 330–331. Additional details are given there. See also De León's letter of May 18.

[2] From this it is inferred that a special description of the French settlement was contained in the *autos* drawn up by De León.

[3] The distances given by the map total one hundred and thirty-seven leagues; those of the Itinerary one hundred and nineteen, some being omitted. (Miss West.)

the horses.   The arm of the sea which appeared to us the long-
est runs in toward the north, another smaller one to the south,
and the other, the smallest, toward the settlement mentioned
in this diary.

We went eight long leagues along the shore, till it pleased
God that we should discover the mouth, through which one
enters the bay.   This was probably about two leagues from
the place we could reach on horseback.   We were greatly rejoiced at this discovery, in token of which we fired a salute
with our arquebuses.   The Frenchman affirmed that this was
the mouth of the harbor, through which he had entered when
he came into these parts with Monsieur Felipe So-and-So.
The mouth of the harbor, so far as we could judge, is about
two short leagues across.   There is a bar of low land across
it which is closer to the mainland on the side toward Vera
Cruz than toward Florida.   The Frenchman says that ships
enter through the narrowest passage.   On the south the river
which we named Nuestra Señora de Guadalupe falls into the
bay.   We did not actually see its mouth, because it was impossible to reach that point; but we came to that conclusion
because when we crossed it we saw that it was near the bay,
and also because the Frenchman made a statement to that
effect.[1]   The arm of the sea which extends inland on the
north of the bay is so wide that we could not see land on the
other shore.[2]   On the shore of the bay, which we ran for about
eight leagues, we saw a topmast of a large ship; another—a
small top-gallant mast, a capstan, some barrel-staves, and
other timbers, which must have belonged to some ship that
was lost in the bay or along the coast whose harbor we had
sighted.[3]   After seeing and exploring the mouth of the bay,
we went back the same way we had come, and we camped for
the night on the bank of a creek near a little mott.   Here
had been an Indian village, but it had been abandoned for
some time.   We found in the village a book in the French
language, a broken bottle-case, and other things which gave

[1] As a matter of fact, the Guadalupe River does not flow into Matagorda
Bay.

[2] The reference is to the main body of Matagorda Bay.

[3] These things were the wreckage of *L'Aimable* and *La Belle*, two of La
Salle's vessels.

us indications that the Indians of the village had taken part in the massacre of the French. In this creek, whose water was somewhat brackish, we found two canoes.[1]

On the 25th of April we set out from there and went to the camp. There we found[2] an answer to the letter that had been written to the Frenchmen who had gone to the Texas. The letter, read by the *alférez*, contained in substance that within two days they would come to where we were, for by that time they were tired of being among barbarians. There was only one signature—that of Juan Larchieverque[3] of Bayonne. It was written with red ochre. The distance traversed, in going to reconnoitre the bay and in returning, was fifty-two leagues. On that day, Monday, the 25th, the main camp remained stationary.

Discovery of the San Marcos River.

Tuesday, the 26th, it was decided that the main body should set out by the same route we had traversed, because the water of the creek is brackish, as has been stated, and the horses that drank it became sick. Accordingly, we moved three leagues up the creek, and halted in the same place where we had stopped in our advance; and then we went on with twenty men.

There was a very large river which the French prisoner said was toward the north and flowed into the bay. We found it at a distance of about three leagues,[4] and followed its bank to where some lagoons form an impediment. It is a very large river; larger, it seemed to us, than the Rio Bravo; so large that a small vessel can navigate it. We determined to see its discharge into the bay, even though it should be a

---

[1] Next year a place in this vicinity was called "Arroyo de las Canoas," probably referring to these canoes. (Itinerary of 1690, entry for June 20.)

[2] See Massanet's letter, p. 363, note 1.

[3] Jean L'Archevêque. See p. 364, note 3.

[4] The Autor Anónimo says six leagues (*Historia de Nuevo León*, p. 335). The stream was the Lavaca, but has been wrongly identified by some writers as the Colorado, a stream fifty miles or more distant. The stream called the San Marcos further inland was the Colorado.

DATE.   LEAGUES.

matter of difficulty. Finally we accomplished our purpose, looking from a little hill, which is about three quarters of a league distant from the mouth of the river. It appeared to us that it was about a league and a half from the mouth of the San Marcos to the mouth of the creek on which the Frenchmen had lived,[1] and the same distance from the mouth of the creek to the settlement. We travelled that day fifteen leagues. We took an observation on the shore of the creek, and found ourselves, allowing for mistakes on account of the defect in the astrolabe, in latitude 26° 3′ more or less.[2] We named this river San Marcos, because we discovered it the day after that saint's feast day.

The Diary of the Return, continued, with the New Entrada made toward the North in search of the French.

Wednesday, the 27th, our party moved forward and halted on some pools, near a little mott which borders on the trail.

Thursday, the 28th, we set out on our way, and the governor set out the same time with thirty companions toward the north bank, to look for the Frenchmen who had written. The main body halted on the River Nuestra Señora de Guadalupe, on the other bank.

Friday, the 29th, the main body halted.

Saturday, the 30th, the main body again halted.

May.

Sunday, May 1st, about evening prayer,[3] the governor arrived with his companions, bringing two Frenchmen, streaked with paint after the Indian fashion. He had found them twenty-five leagues and more from where we had set out with the main body.[4] One of them, the one who had written the letter, was named Juan; the other, a native of Rochelle, was

---

[1] The Garcitas.

[2] The Autor Anónimo says 29° 3′. The figures of the diary are evidently a misprint. The actual latitude of La Salle's fort was not far from 28° 40′.

[3] Vespers.   [4] He had found them near the Colorado River.

named Jacome.[1] They gave an account of the death of their
people, the first saying that an epidemic of smallpox had killed
more than a hundred persons; that the rest had been on
friendly terms with the Indians of all that region, and had no
suspicion of them; that a little more than a month before five
Indians had come to their settlement under pretext of telling
them something and had stopped at the most remote house in
the settlement; that the Frenchmen, having no suspicions, all
went to the house unarmed to see them; that after they were
inside other Indians kept coming and embracing them; that
another party of Indians came in from the creek at the same
time, and killed them all, including two religious and a priest,
with daggers and sticks, and sacked all the houses; that they
were not there at the time, having gone to the Texas; but that
when they heard the news of this occurrence, [the] four of
them came, and, finding their companions dead, they buried
the fourteen they found; that they exploded nearly a hundred
barrels of powder, so that the Indians could not carry it off;
and that the settlement had been well provided with all sorts
of firearms, swords, broadswords, three chalices, and a large
collection of books, with very rare bindings.   The two Frenchmen were streaked with paint after the fashion of the Indians,
and covered with antelope and buffalo hides.   We found them
in a ranchería of the chief of the Texas,[2] who were giving them
sustenance and keeping them with great care.   We took him
[the chief] to the camp and treated him with great kindness.
Although unable to speak Castilian he was an Indian in whom
was recognized capacity.   He had a shrine with several images.
The governor gave him and the other Indians who had come
with him generously of what was left of the cotton garments,
knives, blankets, beads, and other goods.   He was very much
pleased and promised to come with some Indians of his nation
to the province of Cohaguila.   The governor made a separate
report of all that was expedient or important in the declarations of the two Frenchmen, to send it to His Excellency.
We continued our march to the Nueces River.   On Tuesday,

---

[1] Called Santiago Grolette in Massanet's letter, p. 364, above.

[2] The Autor Anónimo, who was in the expedition, writes: "This captain
of the Tejas was not in his own country there, but a long distance from it."
(De León, *Historia de Nuevo León*, p. 339.)   See also De León's letter of May 18.

May 10, the governor went ahead[1] with some companions to send a dispatch to His Excellency, giving an account of this discovery. We arrived at the presidio of Cohaguila today, May 13th, at nightfall. Here ends the diary. To insure its authenticity, it is signed by the governor,

ALONSO DE LEON.

[1] *Adelantó.* He went ahead with fifteen men, the two Frenchmen, and Martínez. On the 18th Martínez was sent to Mexico with the Frenchmen and the despatches.   (De León, *Historia de Nuevo León*, p. 342.)

ITINERARY OF THE DE LEÓN EXPEDITION
OF 1690[1]

Diary, Itinerary, and Description of the Country of the Expedition which, by order of the Most excellent Señor Conde de Galve, Viceroy and Captain-general of Nueva España, was made by General Alonso de Leon, Governor of the province of Coahuila, and Captain of the Presidio which, on the Account of his Majesty, is established there, and Commander-in-chief of the Soldiers who went on the Expedition to Reconnoitre the French who might be in the Bay of Espiritu Santo and the Province of the Texas.[2] It is as follows:

DATE.   LEAGUES.

Sunday, the 26th day of the month of March, 1690, the pack-animals and the baggage left the Villa of Santiago de la Monclova, stopping a league outside the Indian pueblo and a league and a half from the Villa, toward the north.   1½.

Monday, the 27th, camp was broken, and we set out, marching eight[3] leagues northeast-by-east and halting below Las Lomitas on the bank of the Cuaguila River.   8.

Tuesday, the 28th, we left the said place and valleys, going down stream towards the northeast, and, leaving the river, entered the Pass of Baluartes. From this pass we made a detour of a league in order to halt on the bank of the river, where the company camped, having marched this day eight leagues.   8.

Wednesday, the 29th, the company proceeded down stream east-by-northeast, and passing El Alamo,[4] halted on the bank

---

[1] Manuscript in the Archivo General y Público, Mexico, Provincias Internas, vol. 182. See p. 352 for the different texts.

[2] The title and all the entries before April 9 are from B, excepting the entry for March 28, which is omitted from B, and is taken from C.

[3] C reads three leagues, instead of eight. It is evidently correct, as is shown by the map, and by comparison of distances with the 1689 journey.

[4] C reads "a little more than a league beyond El Alamo."

DATE.   LEAGUES.

of the river, having marched five leagues this day. All the
land is level, although there is some chaparral and lechu-
gilla.   5.

    Thursday, the 30th, we set out east-by-northeast, down
stream, going to the junction of the Savinas River, having
marched this day four and one-half leagues. That night the
company from the Kingdom of Leon and the missionary
fathers with it joined us.[1]   4½.

    Friday, the 31st, we marched down stream and, traversing
a hill towards the east, we crossed the Savinas River, on whose
banks the company halted. We travelled two leagues.   2.

    Saturday, April 1st, we marched towards the northeast and
halted at a pool of rain-water. The company travelled this
day six leagues.   6.

    Sunday, the 2d of April, after mass we set out northeast-
by-north and arrived at some pools of rain-water, where the
company halted, having marched this day five leagues. All
the country is level although there is some chaparral.   5.

    Monday, the 3d, we set out towards the north over level
land and went to the bank of an arroyo where we found the
Indians of the Frenchman, to whom we gave tobacco and
clothing. We travelled this day four leagues.   4.

    Tuesday, the 4th, we set out towards the north for the Rio
Grande.[2] The company camped on its bank, and some buffalo were found. They marched this day five leagues.   5.

    Wednesday, the 5th, we remained in camp, in order that
all might be confessed and fulfill their duties to the Church
before crossing the river.

    Thursday, the 6th, we crossed the river and marched north-
by-northeast and camped on the bank of a dry arroyo, having
marched eight leagues. We camped for the night without
water.   8.

    Friday, the 7th, we set out towards the northeast over
level land, and camped on Arroyo de Ramos, having marched
this day three leagues.   3.

    Saturday, the 8th, the company set out northeast-by-north
over level land, bearing in places much mesquite brush, and ar-

---

[1] C states that they camped on the bank of the river.

[2] C adds "over level land with some mesquite, and having found the ford."

DATE.   LEAGUES.

rived at an arroyo which we named Caramanchel.[1] On account of the poor ford, most of the day was spent in getting the pack-animals across. We marched this day three leagues.   3.

Sunday, the 9th, after mass we set out northeast-by-north over level land and, crossing two wooded valleys, entered a mesquite grove and found the ford of the Nuezes River. Here we camped in a meadow on the bank of the river, having marched this day five leagues.   5.

Monday, the 10th, having crossed the river on a passage-way of trees,[2] we set out towards the east, and travelled two leagues. Then we marched towards the north another two leagues and, making a detour[3] to the east over level land, but with some mesquite brush, crossed the Sarco River. The company camped here, having marched this day seven leagues.   7.

Tuesday, the 11th, we set out towards the north over some plains, crossing some knolls. We camped by the Rio Hondo, having marched six leagues.   6.

Wednesday, the 12th, we were delayed with the company, to search for two comrades who were lost in a severe rain-storm the preceding day. We marched   0.

Thursday, the 13th, at noon, the two comrades arrived, and at the same time we learned from some Indians that six leagues from this place there was a gathering of Indians where a Frenchman had come. With twenty soldiers I set out this day towards the west along the northern bank of the river.[4] At about five leagues I camped for the night.   5.

Friday, the 14th, at dawn, I continued my march and, making a detour towards the north over a plain, arrived at the bank of a river where the Indian encampment was. A great number of them, both large and small, came out to see us and, upon giving them tobacco and biscuits, they informed us that two Frenchmen were on the other bank of the Guada-lupe River. One Indian had a French musket. Having heard

[1] This stream is not mentioned in the 1689 expedition.

[2] "Por un ailadero de arboles," omitted from C.

[3] The same detour is mentioned in the 1689 diary and map, under date of April 5.

[4] C adds that Captain Don Gregorio Salinas Varona was among the twenty.

this news, we returned to the camp, a large number of Indians accompanying us. At the camp we presented them with clothing, flour, tobacco, and other trifles. We had marched seven leagues.   7.

Saturday, the 15th, the company set out towards the east, going down stream until the ford was reached. They marched six leagues.   6.

Sunday, the 16th, after mass, we crossed the river, going east-by-north over level land, and reached the Chapa River, where we made a bridge in order to cross it, advancing until some pools were found on whose banks the company halted, having marched eight leagues.   8.

Monday, the 17th, we set out towards the northeast through some woods which were encountered, making several detours to the north-northeast and east until we arrived at the Arroyo de los Robalos,[1] where the company halted, having marched this day five leagues.   5.

Tuesday, the 18th, we set out in different directions to search for one hundred and twenty-six horses which had stampeded. The company set out, but at a short distance the guide lost his way and it was necessary for us to continue towards the north in search of the Medina River. As it was already late, the company camped on a knoll to which we gave the name of El Real del Rosario. Although there was little water, it sufficed for the company. We marched this day four leagues.   4.

Wednesday, the 19th, we set out towards the north. Having arrived at the Medina River above the ford, we crossed at a shoal, having marched seven leagues.   7.

Thursday, the 20th, we set out towards the east and, at a distance of two leagues, reached the ford of the river, where the company halted, as it was necessary to arrange for fording it.   2.

Friday, the 21st, we marched towards the east and arrived at Arroyo del Leon. We marched this day five leagues.   5.

Saturday, the 22d, we marched towards the east and at times towards the northeast. We camped by a stream of brackish water, having marched six leagues.   6.

[1] Apparently the stream called Arroyo de Vino in 1689.   (Itinerary, April 9.)

DATE.
LEAGUES.

Sunday, the 23d, after mass the company set out east by northeast through some live-oak groves and camped near the Guadalupe River, where there is an arroyo close to the river. We marched five leagues. 5.

Monday, the 24th, the company set out down stream and, having crossed the river with much difficulty,[1] because there was so much water, we camped on the other bank, having marched two leagues. 2.

Tuesday, the 25th, I set out with twenty soldiers,[2] leaving the company in the aforesaid place, and went towards the east to reconnoitre the Bay of Espiritu Santo. This day we marched fourteen leagues and camped on the banks of some small pools of water. 14.

Wednesday, the 26th, we arrived at the French settlement, which we saw last year.[3] Having ascertained from its form that it was as before, and having learned where the artillery was buried, we burned the wooden fort; and, going two leagues further, we recognized in the bay what were apparently two buoys, one at the mouth of the San Marcos River and the other at one side, indicating the same channel. The sun was not observed as the day was cloudy. From there we returned up the arroyo of the French settlement, to see if we might meet some Indians from whom to obtain information, but, not having met any, we camped on the bank of the arroyo,[4] having marched this day, in going and coming, fourteen leagues. 14.

Thursday, the 27th, we returned to the camp, having marched up the arroyo of the French in search of some Indians of whom to obtain news. After making some detours we reached the camp. We marched this day twenty leagues. 20.

[1] The crossing was at the same place, or not far from the same place, as that of the 1689 expedition. In 1689 the distance from the Guadalupe to the French settlement was given as seventeen leagues east-northeast. In 1690 the settlement was reached by going nineteen leagues eastwardly, the difference being probably one of estimating.

[2] C adds that Salinas Varona went also.

[3] C adds that the journey to the French settlement was about five leagues to the east.

[4] Called a river in C.

LEAGUES.

DATE.

Friday, the 28th, I set out with eight soldiers up the Guadalupe River,[1] sending up several smokes to see if I might meet some Indians, of whom to obtain news. Having gone six leagues, we returned to the camp, having marched this day, in going and coming, twelve leagues.   12.

Saturday, the 29th, the company set out towards the east about three leagues and then we turned towards the northeast another three leagues, over level land, arriving at some pools of rain-water, which we named San Pedro Martir. We marched this day six leagues.   6.

Sunday, the 30th, after mass, there arrived two soldiers from the presidios of La Viscaya,[2] who informed us that their comrades were coming behind to overtake me and to join this expedition by order of the Most Excellent Señor Conde de Galve, viceroy and captain-general of New Spain. I sent to meet them with clothing and supplies. I left the company there to await them, and set out with sixteen soldiers to cut passageways[3] and to seek some Indians who could guide us and inform us whether there were any Frenchmen in these regions. I passed this night by some pools of rain-water, having marched nine leagues.   9.

Monday, May 1st, I continued on my journey, passing various arroyos[4] and deserted rancherías without meeting an Indian. We slept on a small hill, having marched twelve leagues.   12.

Tuesday, the 2d, I set out and arrived at a pasture near the San Marcos River, where we slept,[5] having marched this day fourteen leagues because of several detours.   14.

Wednesday, the 3d, after placing a cross in a tree, I reached the San Marcos River and, having crossed it,[6] I advanced and, at about five leagues, on the edge of a small wood, we

---

[1] This journey is not shown on the map.

[2] C reads "Presidios del Parral."

[3] A and B read "a que desmontasen unos ailaderos." C reads "a desmontar algunos pedazos de monte."

[4] He was crossing the upper waters of the Lavaca in the neighborhood of Hallettsville.

[5] C adds, "since it is a deep river I could not cross it."

[6] The Colorado. C states that De León went up-stream and found a good ford.

saw an Indian woman and a boy. Upon signalling them with
a handkerchief they did not wish to emerge, but instead took
refuge in the wood. We camped this night on a hill, level as
a villa, leaving for them in their settlement a handkerchief,
biscuit, tobacco, razors, and knives. We marched this day
seven leagues.   7.

Thursday, the 4th, an Indian came to see us and, having
spoken with him by signs, he told us that he was of the Texas,
that this day we would arrive at a ranchería, and that he,
with his wife and a young brother-in-law of his who lived
there, would guide us. I gave him a horse upon which he
might load his belongings, but at a distance of three leagues
we decided to send him on, and, returning to the place where
we had slept, we told him we would wait there for him to go
to summon the governor of the Texas, among whom were
some Frenchmen. We marched this day six leagues.[1]   6.

Friday, the 5th, in the morning I sent Captain Francisco
de Venavides with three soldiers to the camp in order that it
should come on. About five in the afternoon, the Indian
whom I had sent to the captain of the Texas returned to inform me that his horse had run away from him.

Saturday, the 6th, I sent four soldiers over the trail to
ascertain whether he had joined any Indians and, having met
another Indian, they brought him to camp. We offered him
clothing if he would go to the Texas to tell the governor to
come to see us. Thereupon, the Indian, greedy for the gift,
told me that if I would give him another horse he would go
to summon the governor of the Texas and that he would leave
his wife and a brother-in-law of his to guide us. So I sent
him on this day.

Sunday, the 7th, Monday, the 8th, we halted where the
Indian told us to await him and, also, to see if we could dis-
cern any smoke, in order to go to meet the company, for that
was the signal we gave them.[2]

[1] C adds that on this day the twenty soldiers of the presidios of Parral
(Nueva Vizcaya) reached the camp of San Pedro Martir.

[2] C states that the camp set out from San Pedro Martir on this day, going
three leagues northeast through heavy timber, crossing two dry arroyos then
going west and north through heavy timber, crossing four dry arroyos, and

DATE.   LEAGUES.

Tuesday,[1] the 9th, having discerned smoke, I set out with four soldiers to meet the company. Having crossed the San Marcos River, about noon I met two Indians, and, at a little distance, Captain Francisco de Benavides and three soldiers, with an Indian who spoke the Mexican language. From him we learned that a French boy was in a ranchería about two days' march to the westward and another in another ranchería to the east. I sent the said Captain Benavides with two soldiers to the place where I had left the comrades awaiting me and went on to the company, which I found in an arroyo where it had just halted. Giving them orders to march next day and to await me where their comrades were, and, having chosen three horses, eight soldiers, and supplies, the Indian interpreter guiding us, we advanced twelve leagues by evening.[2]   12.

Wednesday, the 10th, continuing to the west about nine leagues, we marched through a forest of oaks and grape-vines another five leagues, and upon the edge of the wood met some Indians and a French boy named Pedro Talon.[3] As he told us that there was no other in that vicinity, we returned to sleep near the camp of the night before, having marched that day in going and coming twenty-seven leagues.[4]   27.

stopping on one called San Miguel Arcangel. The entry omits entirely the data printed here. De León evidently reached the Colorado near La Grange   The map shows above the network of arroyos crossed on May 1 a stream corresponding to the upper Navidad, and just before reaching the Colorado a small stream flowing into the Colorado from the west. Such a stream enters at La Grange.

[1] Both A and B lack entries for the 8th, but C states that the camp left San Miguel Arcangel, moved north, passed eight dry arroyos, travelled nine leagues, and camped at San Gregorio Nazianzeno.

[2] C states that on the 9th the camp moved from San Gregorio north seven leagues, to a hill named Jesus María y Joseph de Buenavista; that De León reached the camp in the afternoon, and set out with eight men, including Salinas Varona, to seek a French boy who was in the ranchería toward the southwest, going twelve leagues.

[3] Talon must have been found in the region of Gonzales, probably to the northward of that place.

[4] C states that they set out before morning, went southwest nine leagues to a high hill, before entering the forest, then five leagues through a forest on the edge of which they met Pedro Talon coming with a ranchería of Indians, returning that day almost to the hill of Jesus María y Joseph. It adds that Captain

Thursday, the 11th, we continued our journey towards the northeast about twelve leagues, to a high hill which had a clump of very high trees, where we found some Indians camped, who informed us of another Frenchman who was near there in a ranchería.   I sent an Indian to summon him and another Indian afterwards told us that other Frenchmen had arrived at the entrance to the Bay of Espíritu Santo.   At the same time I sent two soldiers to the camp in order that four should come with supplies and a relay of horses, so that, if the Frenchman should not come, we might go in search of him.   We crossed the San Marcos River this afternoon in order that, since it had rained heavily, it might not rise and keep some of us on one side and some on the other.   We marched this day sixteen leagues.[1]   16.

Friday, the 12th, in the morning the French boy arrived with three Indians and said his name was Pedro Muni; at the same time came the soldiers whom I sent to summon from the camp.   We therefore advanced towards the northeast until we reached it.   We marched this day six leagues.[2]   6.

Saturday, the 13th, the company set out from San Joseph towards the east about three leagues, and another three towards the northeast, crossing some valleys and arroyos with little water.   Stopping upon the bank of an arroyo, we gave it the name of San Francisco de Asis.[3]   We marched six leagues.   6.

Sunday, the 14th, the company set out for the Colorado River, crossing some valleys towards the northeast and, halting on its banks, we gave it the name of Espíritu Santo River,[4] having marched six leagues.   6.

Monday, the 15th, the company set out down stream and at a distance of half [5] a league crossed the river.   Passing

Francisco Martínez continued north with the camp, crossing the San Marcos, and proceeded to the place where De León had left his companions, at San Ildefonso, having travelled eight leagues.

[1] C adds that the camp moved this day to a better site, called San Joseph, three leagues northeast.

[2] C adds that they found the camp, which awaited them, six leagues from the river, towards the north.

[3] Evidently the Yegua River.   [4] The Brazos River.

[5] C states that the camp moved east three leagues, crossed the river, then one league northeast, then north one league to San Juan, going the same distance

DATE.   LEAGUES.

through a very thick wood towards the northeast, and making several detours to the north, we halted at an arroyo to which we gave the name of San Juan. We marched this day five leagues.   5.

Tuesday, the 16th, the company set out towards the northeast for about two leagues, crossing two arroyos in the same direction, and camped in a hollow, having marched four leagues. We gave it the name of Beatto Salvador de Hortta.   4.

Wednesday, the 17th, the company set out towards the northeast-by-north and camped at an arroyo to which we gave the name of San Diego de Alcalá.[1] We marched this day six leagues.   6.

Thursday, the 18th, the company set out northeast-by-east, crossing several arroyos at one of which we met the Indian whom we had sent, with the governor of the Texas, accompanied by fourteen of the principal Indians among them. I gave them clothing and other goods from those we were carrying, the said governor and his people manifesting much joy at having seen us and making known that all his people were awaiting us with much pleasure.

Returning to a very pleasant valley, the company halted there at an arroyo and gave it the name of Valle de Santa Elvira. We marched this day eight leagues.   8.

Friday, the 19th, we marched north-by-northeast and at a little distance we entered another very large and pleasant valley to which we gave the name of La Santissima Trinidad,[2] and although the passage was arranged, we spent most of the day in getting the supplies across, and, having crossed the river, found another very pleasant valley which was given the name of Monclova. We marched this day one and one half leagues.   1½.

Saturday, the 20th, we marched northeast-by-east through

of five leagues. The crossing of the Brazos was above the mouth of the Navasota River, to which the name of San Juan was given.

[1] Evidently a branch of the Bidais.

[2] There is an ellipsis here. C states that they reached a large valley named Galve, *beyond which* they came to the Rio Trinidad. C adds that the camp east of the river was called San Sebastián, although it mentions a valley of San Sebastián next day. The Trinity was apparently reached near the mouth of Boggy Creek.

some groves of live-oak and some arroyos for a distance of four leagues. Upon emerging from the wood we found a large valley which was named San Sebastian and at one side of said valley we found four ranches of Indians who had planted maize and *frijoles,* and had very clean houses and high beds in which to sleep. We bestowed gifts upon them and continued towards the northeast through groves of live-oak and arroyos to some pools of rain-water to which we gave the name of San Bernardino, having marched seven leagues.[1]	7.

Sunday, the 21st, after mass we set out northeast-by-east, through some groves of live-oak and of pine, crossing the dry beds of four arroyos. Having arrived at an arroyo with water the company halted in a small plaza to which we gave the name of San Carlos, having marched six leagues.	6.

Monday, the 22d, we set out northeast-by-east through some groves of live-oak, crossing five dry arroyos and some small hills where there are veins of black and red stone, and continued until we reached a valley thickly settled with the houses of the Texas Indians. About them were fields of maize, beans, pumpkins and watermelons, and we gave the valley the name of San Francisco Xavier. Making a detour to the north by a hill clad with live-oak, at about a quarter of a league we found another valley of Texas Indians and their houses; and their governor telling us that his house was very near, the company halted upon the bank of an arroyo, having marched this day five leagues.[2] To this settlement we gave the name of San Francisco de los Texas. This afternoon I went with the governor of the said Texas to leave him at his house, where his mother, his wife, a daughter of his, and many people who were expecting him came out to receive me, bringing out a bench upon which to seat me and giving me a luncheon of corn tamales and *atole,* all very cleanly.

Tuesday, the 23d, I set out with the reverend missionary fathers over the half-league intervening between the camp and the house of the governor, in a procession with the officers and soldiers, who were followed by a large number of Indians with the said Indian governor. Having reached his house, the

[1] They were now near Crockett, Houston County.
[2] C omits all the rest of this entry.

DATE.   LEAGUES.

missionaries sang the Te Deum Laudamus.[1] After remaining a while at his house seated upon benches which the said governor ordered brought, they served us, in jars and crocks, a luncheon of boiled beans, *atole*, and *pinole*, which the said fathers and soldiers ate. We then returned to camp.

Wednesday, the 24th, a chapel[2] was prepared in which to celebrate the feast of Corpus Cristi, having this day bestowed upon the Indians clothing and the other commodities. This day I notified the governor to summon all his people to come to the feast of Corpus Cristi.

Thursday, the 25th, the feast of the Most Holy Sacrament[3] was celebrated with all solemnity and a procession, all the officers and soldiers, the Indian governor, and many of his people accompanying the procession and witnessing the high mass.[4] Mass having been completed, the ceremony was enacted of raising the flag in the name of his Majesty (whom God protect), and I, the said General Alonso de Leon, as the superior officer of all the companies which, by order of his Excellency, the Señor Conde de Galve, viceroy of this New Spain, had come on this journey in the name of his Majesty, accepted the obedience which they rendered to his Majesty, and in his royal name promised to befriend and aid them. I delivered to the governor a staff with a cross, giving him the title of governor of all his people, in order that he might rule and govern them, giving him to understand by means of an interpreter that which he should observe and do, and the respect and obedience which he and all his people ought to have for the priests, and that he should make all his families attend Christian teaching, in order that they might be instructed in the affairs of our holy Catholic faith so that later they might be baptized and become Christians. He accepted the staff with much pleasure, promising to do all that was desired of him, and the company fired three salutes. Likewise, the Reverend Father Commissary of these conversions in this mission, Fray Damian Masanet, was given possession, in order

---

[1] C omits most of the rest of this entry. The settlement was in the valley of San Pedro Creek. See Massanet's letter, p. 376, above, note 2.

[2] The preparation of the chapel is not mentioned in C.

[3] *I. e.*, Corpus Christi.   [4] *La missa cantata.*

DATE.   LEAGUES.

that he might instruct them in the mysteries of our holy
Catholic faith. The governor and his people having begged
us to leave them religious to teach them the Christian doctrine, as a pledge of friendship we asked the said governor to
give us three of the principal Indians of this province, among
them being a brother, a nephew, and a cousin of the governor,
who with much pleasure promised to go with us to see the
most Excellent Señor Conde de Galve, viceroy and captain-
general of New Spain. This day the sun was observed and
we found ourselves in 34° 7'.[1]

Friday, the 26th, I set out with the missionary fathers,
some soldiers and officers, and the said Indian governor,
towards the northeast, to find the most suitable place to put
the mission, and after having seen three small valleys,[2] we
came to where they told us two Frenchmen had died, where they
had wished to make a settlement, and where we saw the
graves. We placed a cross in a tree for them and went to a
river which we found could be crossed only by means of a
tree which the Indians have athwart it, and a rope of which
they take hold. We named the river San Miguel Arcangel,[3]
and from there we returned to camp, having travelled six
leagues.   6.

Saturday, the 27th; Sunday, the 28th; Monday, the 29th;
Tuesday, the 30th, and Wednesday, the 31st,[4] they labored
to build the church and the dwelling of the apostolic fathers,
in the midst of the principal settlement of the Texas.

Thursday, June 1st, I gave possession of the said mission,
the reverend father commissary, Fray Damian Masanet, having sung mass in the said church, the said Indian governor
and his people attending mass and the blessing of the church.
This afternoon I sent the company to begin the return march
to the province of Coahuila, over the same road by which we

---

[1] The entry for the 25th is much less complete in C.

[2] C says they went about three leagues before reaching the three small
valleys.

[3] C adds that this crossing was used by most of the Indians of this province,
and that the valley at the river was named San Gaspár. The other three valleys
they named San Antonio de Padua, Santa Margarita, and San Carlos.

[4] C adds that on the 31st possession was taken of the house and church, an
event which is assigned to June 1 by the other diaries.

DATE.   LEAGUES.

came. They halted this night at the camp of San Carlos, having marched five leagues.   5.

Friday, the 2d, with the reverend father commissary, Fray Damian Masanet, and six soldiers,[1] I set out from the pueblo of San Francisco de los Texas to follow the company, there being with us a brother of the governor, a nephew, and a cousin of his, and another Indian of the said pueblo. Having joined the company we advanced to the Real de San Bernardino, a little over half a league. The company marched this day a little over six and one-half leagues.   6½.

Saturday, the 3d, we continued our march, crossing the valley of San Sebastian and that of Monclova. We reached the Santisima Trinidad River and, as it was so swollen that we could not cross, we camped near the river,[2] having marched this day six and one-half leagues.   6½.

Sunday, the 4th; Monday, the 5th; Tuesday, the 6th; Wednesday, the 7th; Thursday, the 8th; Friday, the 9th; Saturday, the 10th; this day a raft was built and the crossing of the river was begun.

Sunday, the 11th, the crossing of the river was completed, and at about two in the afternoon the company set out through the Valle de Galbe, until that of Santa Elbira was reached, where they camped by some pools of rain-water, having marched three leagues.   3.

Monday, the 12th, the company set out from the said camp and, passing through that of San Diego de Alcala about two leagues, camped by some pools of rain-water, having marched nine leagues.   9.

Tuesday, the 13th, the company set out from the said place and, passing through El Beato Salvador de Horta, we reached the Arroyo de San Juan, having marched this day eight leagues.   8.

Wednesday, the 14th, the company set out from the said place and, crossing the Espiritu Santo River, we reached a range of low hills where there was an arroyo with water, by

[1] C says Salinas Varona, Martínez and four soldiers. It omits to mention the four Indians who accompanied them.

[2] C states that they camped in the Valle de Monclova. It gives the distance for the second as six leagues and for the third as seven leagues.

DATE.   LEAGUES.

which the company halted, having marched this day eight
leagues.   8.

Thursday, the 15th, the company set out from the said
place, and passing by the Real de San Francisco de Asis, we
reached some arroyos of water whence I had dispatched the
Indian to summon the governor of the Texas,[1] having marched
this day seven leagues.   7.

Friday, the 16th, the company set out from the said place
and, passing by the Real de San Joseph,[2] we reached an
arroyo with water, where the company halted, having marched
this day six leagues.   6.

Saturday, the 17th, the company set out from the said
place, and, crossing the San Marcos River, we reached an
arroyo with water, where the company halted, having marched
this day five leagues. It was given the name of Jesus, Maria
y Joseph de Buena Vista.[3]   5.

Sunday, the 18th, the company continued their journey
and I, General Alonso de Leon, with sixteen soldiers,[4] set out
towards the northeast in search of two French boys and a
French girl, of whom some Indians, who were camped in the
said place,[5] gave me information. We travelled over some
plains for about four leagues, until we reached a small wood,
through which we went, and afterward marched towards the
east about three leagues over another plain, where we found a
small wood and a ranchería[6] of the Indians. We continued
from there over some very large plains[7] where there were a
great number of buffalo, to the edge of a small river, near which
was a large clump of trees, where we halted, as it was already
very dark, having marched this day seventeen leagues. 17.

Monday, the 19th, we continued our journey along the
banks of said stream, which has timber on both sides and,

[1] C omits the item regarding the sending for the governor of the Texas.
[2] C calls it Real de San Joseph y San Ildefonso.
[3] It was given the name on the way northeast.
[4] C says Salinas Varona and sixteen soldiers.
[5] C adds "In this camp there were many nations of Indians, such as the
Cantoná, the Thoagá, the Chaná, and the Cabas."
[6] C says they were called the Tho ó.
[7] C adds that they were going southeast, and gives the distance for the day
as sixteen leagues.

DATE.   LEAGUES.

having crossed it and marched about two leagues, we found a
ranchería of Indians,[1] to whom I gave presents and who remained friendly towards us.   From there we continued towards
the south over some plains, and after going about one league
we found another ranchería[2] of Indians to whom I also gave
presents.   From there we continued over the said plains in
the same direction for about four leagues until we entered a
small wood.   We went through this and continued towards the
west and, crossing a large arroyo in a wood, we found a very
large nation of Indians,[3] to whom I gave presents and who
remained friendly towards us, and gave us Indians to guide us
to another ranchería.   From there we set out over some
plains and, as it was now night, we halted on the bank of an
arroyo, having travelled this day fifteen leagues.   15.

Tuesday, the 20th, we continued our journey towards the
east where we found a ranchería of Indians,[4] to whom I gave
presents and who gave us four Indians to guide us to where
the French children were.   From there we set out in the same
direction over some plains which were covered with buffalo,
to cross the arroyo of the French, and having crossed it, we
continued to the old settlement, and from there continued
towards the south until we reached the arroyo which the Indians call "de Las Canoas,"[5] and having crossed it we came
to another small arroyo where we halted, having marched this
day fourteen leagues.   14.

Wednesday, the 21st, we set out towards the south[6] and
after about one league we met two Indians who were coming,
on horseback, from the nation which had the French children.[7]
They took us to their ranchería which was on the headland
of a small bay.   Here were Roberto and Magdalena Talon.
I discussed their ransom, and having given them presents and
paid the ransom which they asked, they came with us with a
thousand impertinencies, begging of us all the horses, and

---

[1] Called the Có oé (C).   [2] Called the Tho ó (C).
[3] C states that it contained more than three thousand persons and was
called the Na aman.
[4] Called Caisquetebana (C).   [5] See Itinerary of 1689.
[6] C says southeast.
[7] Called Cascossi, often written Caocosi (C).

DATE.   LEAGUES.

even the clothing which we wore upon our backs.   Meanwhile they went to get the other French boy, who was two leagues from there in the same nation.   Having brought him, they proceeded further with their impertinence, carrying bows and arrows, a large number of the Indians coming with shields, begging exorbitant things, and saying that if we did not give them to them they would have to shoot and kill us all.   Their saying this and beginning to shoot were simultaneous, where-upon we attacked them, and, having killed four and wounded others,[1] they retreated, having wounded two of our horses. We departed in an orderly manner to camp for the night at a distance of about four leagues, where we had slept the night before, having travelled this day twelve leagues.[2]   12.

Thursday, the 22d, at dawn we set out in the same northerly direction over some very large plains to the bank of the Guadalupe River, and about ten o'clock at night we halted near a small wood, having marched this day fourteen leagues.   14.

Friday, the 23d, we set out towards the north for about two leagues, where we found the track of the company which had gone by, and after about three leagues we came up with them at the ford of the Guadalupe River, where we halted, having marched five leagues.   5.

Saturday, the 24th, St. John's day, the company set out from the said place, and, crossing the Guadalupe River, we continued our march to an arroyo which is before the Real de Agua Salada, where we camped, having marched this day seven leagues.   7.

Sunday, the 25th, the company set out from the said place, and passing by the Real de la Salada, we reached the Arroyo del Leon, where the company halted, having marched this day seven leagues.   7.

Monday, the 26th, the company set out from the said place, and we reached the Medina River,[3] where the company halted, having marched this day five leagues.   5.

Tuesday, the 27th, the company set out from the said

---

[1] C says four were killed and two wounded.
[2] C says twelve leagues north.
[3] C says they crossed the Medina and gives the distance as six leagues.

DATE.   LEAGUES.

place, and arrived at an arroyo with water, where the company
halted, having marched this day eight leagues.[1]   8.

Wednesday, the 28th, the company set out from the said
place, and, the guide having lost the way, we camped at an
arroyo with water above the ford of the Robalos River, having
marched this day five leagues.[2]   5.

Thursday, the 29th, the company set out from said place,
and passing the Real del Aire, we reached some pools of water,
where the company camped, having marched five leagues.[3] 5.

Friday, the 30th, the company set out from the said place,
and crossing the Rio Hondo we reached Las Cruzes, about three
leagues above the ford of the Jondo River, having marched
this day eight leagues.   8.

Saturday, July 1st, the company set out from the said
place, and we arrived at the Sarco[4] River, having marched
this day five leagues.   5.

Sunday, the 2d, the company set out from the said place
and, crossing the Nueses River, we reached some pools of
water, where the company camped, having marched this day
eight leagues.[5]   8.

Monday, the 3d, the company set out from the said place,
and crossing the Arroyo de Ramos,[6] we reached some pools
of water, where the company halted, having marched this day
ten leagues.   10.

Tuesday, the 4th, the company set out from the said place,
and we arrived at the Rio Grande but, as it was very much
swollen, it could not be crossed, and the company halted
there, having marched this day eight leagues.   8.

Wednesday, the 5th; Thursday, the 6th; Friday, the 7th;
Saturday, the 8th; Sunday, the 9th; Monday, the 10th, and
Tuesday, the 11th, we remained in camp upon the bank of the
said Rio Grande, through being unable to cross, as it was still

---

[1] C gives the distance as seven leagues.

[2] C says nothing about the guide losing his way, but states that they went
west four leagues, and south one league to a ranchería of Tho oé Indians.

[3] C states that on this day the horse herd of two hundred and seven head
and twenty-five men were left behind to come more slowly, being worn out.

[4] Called Rio Frio in C.   [5] C says seven leagues.

[6] C calls it Arroyo de Caramanchel, and gives the distance as eight leagues.

DATE.   LEAGUES.

very much swollen.[1] From there I dispatched a courier to
his Excellency sending him a Frenchman named Pedro Muni,
the autos, map, and this itinerary, giving an account to his
Excellency of the entire expedition.—ALONSO DE LEON.

[1] C states that on the afternoon of the 12th De León swam his horse across,
followed by Father Massanet, four soldiers, and Pedro Moñe. C continues the
journey to Monclova. On the 13th they went to Los Charcos de Agua Verde,
fourteen leagues; on the 14th to the Sabinas, above the junction, seventeen
leagues; and on the 15th to Monclova, twelve leagues.

IV. ARIZONA

THE JESUITS IN PIMERÍA ALTA (SOUTHERN ARIZONA AND NORTHERN SONORA) 1687–1710

INTRODUCTION

WHILE the frontier was being pushed northeastward into Texas, it was at the same time being extended northwestward into Arizona. Little was accomplished before the end of the seventeenth century toward colonizing California, but steady advance had been made up the Pacific slope into Sinaloa and Sonora. By the middle of the seventeenth century large herds of cattle were grazing in the valleys of the Mayo, Yaqui, and Sonora Rivers. Mining outdistanced stockraising, and in advance of both went the border military posts.

But the most notable factor in pushing northward the frontier on the Pacific slope was the work of the Jesuit missionaries. Beginning their labors there about 1590, by 1600 five Jesuit missionaries had founded eight substantial churches near the Sinaloa River. Ten years later Fuerte de Montesclaros was built on the Río del Fuerte, and in the same year a notable treaty was made with the Yaquis. Thus encouraged, the Jesuits advanced to the Mayo River in 1613, when they built what is regarded as the first mission in modern Sonora. According to Father Pérez de Ribas, in 1644 there were thirty-five missions in Sinaloa and Sonora, each serving from one to four Indian pueblos, and the records showed a total of over 300,000 baptisms to that date. By the end of the third quarter of the century missions, followed or preceded by mining camps and ranches, had ascended the valley of the Sonora River, on the eastern and western branches respectively, as far as Arispe and Cucurpe. Meanwhile, since Vizcaino's time, pearl fishing in the Gulf of California had been intermittently carried on, and several unsuccessful attempts had been made to colonize the Peninsula.[1]

The next forward step on the mainland was taken when Father Eusebio Kino and his companions entered Pimería Alta, in 1687. Pimería Alta, the home of the Upper Pimas, extended from the valley of the Altar River to that of the Gila, and thus included that part of Arizona which was later contained in the Gadsden Purchase. The region had been entered by Friar Marcos de Niza, in 1539. It had been crossed on its eastern and western edges by different divisions of the Coronado party, and in 1604 Oñate had descended Bill Williams Fork and the Colorado. Between that time and the Pueblo Revolt of 1680 the colonists of New Mexico opened a trade with the Pimas of the San Pedro River valley. But no record has come to us of Spaniards having entered what is now Arizona from the south, after 1542, until the advent there of Father Kino, and when he arrived in northern Sonora in 1687 all the region beyond the Altar River valley was practically unknown.

Father Kino (Kühn) was born in Trent, on the border between Germany and Italy, in 1644. He was educated in the universities of Freiburg and Ingolstadt, where he distinguished himself in mathematics. At the age of twenty-five he decided, during a severe illness, to become a missionary to heathen lands. He hoped to go to the Far East, to follow in the footsteps of Saint Francis Xavier, but instead he was sent to Mexico, where he arrived in 1681. There he at once came into prominence by entering into a controversy with the learned Jesuit Sigüenza y Góngora, concerning the comet of that year. Two years later, in the capacity of royal cosmographer and superior of the missionaries, he joined the expedi-

[1] Bancroft, *North Mexican States and Texas*, I. 235–236; Pérez de Ribas, *Historia de los Triumphos de Nuestra Fé entre Gentes las mas Bárbaras y Fieras del Nuevo Orbe* (Madrid, 1645); Venegas (Burriel), *Noticia de la California* (Madrid, 1757); Alegre, *Historia de la Compañia de Jesus* (Mexico, 1841); Ortega, *Apostólicos Afanes de la Compañia de Jesus* (Barcelona, 1757).

tion sent under Atondo y Atillón to attempt anew the conquest and conversion of California. This enterprise failing,
he returned to Mexico and secured permission to work on the
mainland opposite the Peninsula, which he had visited while
in California. His request was that he might work among the
Guaymas and Seris, but he was sent to Pimería Alta instead.

Arriving at his destination in 1687, he at once established
the mission of Nuestra Señora de los Dolores, in the valley of
the San Miguel River, something over a hundred miles south
of Tucson. This mission was his headquarters for twenty-
four years of exploration, missionary work, and writing.
Operating from this base, he established a number of missions south of the present United States in the valleys of the
Magdalena and the Altar; crossed the line into Arizona and
founded the missions of San Xavier del Bac, Guevavi, and
Tumacácori; several times explored the Gila River; and in an
attempt to answer the old question whether California was
an island or a peninsula, twice descended the Colorado below
the mouth of the Gila, once crossing into California and once
reaching the Gulf. This inquiry was one of the chief interests
of the last eleven years of his life, and, as a result of his explorations, he answered it to his own satisfaction in a treatise, as
yet unpublished, I believe, which he called "Cosmographical
Demonstration that California is not an Island but a Peninsula, and that it is continuous with this New Spain, the Gulf
of California ending in latitude thirty-five degrees."[1]

In his day Father Kino was the principal personage in his
field. It was he who created Pimería Alta as a Spanish prov-

[1] These paragraphs follow closely Bolton, "Father Kino's Lost History, its
Discovery, and its Value," in *Papers* of the Bibliographical Society of America,
VI. 10–13. See references cited therein and also Sommervogel, *Bibliothèque de la
Compagnie de Jésus*, première partie, IV. 1044; Kino, "Favores Celestiales"
(MS.), *passim*; Bancroft, *North Mexican States*, I. 186–187, 250–251; Alegre,
Hist. de la Compañia de Jesus, III. 42; Beristáin, *Biblioteca Hispano-Americana
Septentrional*; Clavigero, *Historia de la Antigua ó Baja California* (Mexico,
1852); Ortega, *Apostólicos Afanes*, p. 284.

ince and inspired the occupation of Lower California. Had life and strength been spared him to push with his wonted zeal and skill his projects for conversion and conquest in Alta California, six decades would not have elapsed, perhaps, before his dreams were realized, and then by the Franciscans, after his own order had been expelled from Spanish America. He not only created Pimería Alta, but he first made known its geography. His map is the earliest extant showing the Gila, the Colorado, and southern Arizona, on the basis of actual exploration. His letters, diaries, and map, and his recently rediscovered History are indispensable sources for knowledge of the development of geographical ideas concerning California and for the early history of the region south of the Gila on both sides of the Gulf.[1]

Hitherto our knowledge of the work of Kino and his companions has come mainly from Ortega's *Apostólicos Afanes de la Compañia de Jesus* (Barcelona, 1754; Mexico, 1887); Venegas (Burriel), *Noticia de la California* (Madrid, 1757); Alegre, *Historia de la Compañia de Jesus* (Mexico, 1841); Manje, *Lúz de Tierra Incógnita*, libro II. (printed in *Doc. Hist. Mex.*, cuarta série, tomo I., Mexico, 1856), and some of Kino's own writings. Of these the following is a list of those which have been known and available to modern scholars, eliminating all duplications, all titles of doubtful authenticity, and all unpublished manuscripts whose whereabouts have not been ascertained:

1. *Exposicion Astronomica de el Cometa* (Mexico, 1681).

2. "Tercera Entrada en 21 de Diciembre de 1683" (printed in *Documentos para la Historia de Mexico*, cuarta sér., I. 405–468; original manuscript in the archives of Mexico).

3. A letter of May 13, 1687, "an einen unbenannten

---

[1] For a fuller statement concerning Kino bibliography, see Bolton, as above, and references cited therein. The following statement is taken mainly from that paper.

Priester" (quoted in "Brief Patris Adami Gilg," in Stöcklein, *Neue Welt Bott*, 1726).

4. "Relacion del estado de la Pimeria que remitte el Pᵉ Visitador Horacio Polici: y es copia de Carta que le escribe el Capitan Dⁿ Christoval Martin Bernal," December 3 and 4, 1697 (printed in *Doc. Hist. Mex.*, tercera sér., IV. 797–809; original manuscript in the archives of Mexico).

5. "Colocasion de nuestra Sᵃ de los Remedios en su nueva capilla De su nuevo pueblo de las Nuevas Conversiones de la Pimeria En 15 de Setiembre de 98 aˢ," Nuestra Señora de los Dolores, September 16, 1698 (printed under a wrong title in *Doc. Hist. Mex.*, tercera sér., IV. 814–816; the title given above is that of the original manuscript in the archives of Mexico).

6. "Carta Del padre Eusebio Kino, al padre visitador Horacio Polici, acerca de una entrada al Noroeste y mar de la California, en Compañia del Capitan Diego Carrasco, actual teniente de esta dilatada Pimeria, que fue de ida y vuelta mas de trescientas leguas, a 22 de setiembre de 1698," signed at Nuestra Señora de los Dolores, October 18, 1698 (printed in *Doc. Hist. Mex.*, tercera sér., IV. 817–819. The above title is that of the original manuscript in the archives of Mexico).

7. "Relacion Diaria de la entrada al nortueste que fue de Yda y Buelta mas de 300 leguas desde 21 de setiembre hasta 18 de otubre de 1698. Descubrimiento del desemboque del rio grande hala Mar de la California y del Puerto de Sᵃ Clara. Reduction de mas de 4000 almas de las Costas Bautismos de mas de 400 Parbulos 1698. Con Enseñanzas y Experienzias." (Unprinted. The above title is from the original in the archives of Mexico. Known hitherto only in the form of a manuscript copy at the end of libro I. of *Lúz de Tierra Incógnita* in the Biblioteca Nacional).

8. "Breve relacion de la insigne victoria que los Pimas Sobaipuris en 30 de Marzo del Año de 1698 han conseguido

contra los enemigos de la Provincia de Sonora," May 3, 1698, postdated October 25 (printed in *Doc. Hist. Mex.*, tercera sér., IV. 810–813. The above title is from the original manuscript in the archives of Mexico).

9. *Paso por tierra a la California y sus Confinantes Nuebas Naciones*, etc., 1701. (This is Kino's famous map of Pimería Alta, which has been printed in many editions.)

10. Une lettre. (So cited by Sommervogel, as printed in Scherer's *Geographia Hierarchica*, Munich, 1702. As a matter of fact, the extract is not a single letter, "but a gathering of several letters" of Kino.)

11. "Favores Celestiales de Jesus y de María SS^{ma} y del Gloriosissimo Apostol de las Yndias," etc. (manuscript in the Archivo General y Público, Mexico, Sección de Misiones, vol. 27). This manuscript is a history by Father Kino of his entire work and that of his companions in Pimería Alta between 1687 and 1710, with considerable attention to California affairs. It was used by the early Jesuit historians, especially Ortega, and is the principal source of all they wrote about Kino and his companions. It has been unknown to modern scholars until recently discovered by the present writer, and its existence actually denied. Part V. of this work is an "Ynforme y Relasion de los nuevos Comversiones de esta America Septentrional" (printed below), written in 1710. It is a general summary of all of Kino's work, with a statement of possibilities for future development. The entire work has been translated and edited for publication by the present writer, and, it is hoped, will soon appear in print.

REPORT AND RELATION OF THE NEW CON-VERSIONS, BY EUSEBIO FRANCISCO KINO, 1710

Dedication[1]

To his royal Majesty, Philip V., God preserve him for many years:

YOUR royal Majesty has ordered in your very Catholic *cédula* of July 17, 1701, which my Father Provincial of this New Spain as well as the Father Visitor of these missions of Sonora had sent me in printed form (in it being printed my name, though I do not deserve it, and the name of Father Juan María de Salvatierra), that report be made to your royal Majesty of the location and state of the heathen of this province of Sonora; therefore, with this report unknown North America places itself at the sacred feet of your royal Majesty, for by means of the more than two hundred leagues of new conquests and new conversions, which have a compass or circumference of more than six hundred leagues and contain very fertile lands and new nations already very friendly, discovered in these last twenty-three years by the fathers of the Company of Jesus in more than fifty expeditions or missions which on different occasions they have made to the north, northeast, northwest, and west, some of which have been of fifty, seventy, ninety, one hundred, one hundred and fifty, two hundred and more leagues, there now remain very well reduced all these many nations. And they ask for fathers and holy baptism, and it would seem that they know very well what our Holy Mother, the Church, says to them on the first feast day in May, day of San Felipe and Santiago,[2] namely, that the Gentiles, desiring to see the Saviour of the world, came to Philip (*Gentiles Salvatorem videre cupientes ad Philippum accesserunt*). And if in those times there was an apostolic Philip

---

[1] "Favores Celestiales de Jesus y de María SS^ma y del Gloriosissimo Apostol de las Yndias," parte V. (Archivo General y Público, Mexico, Misiones, vol. 27).

[2] St. Philip and St. James.

to whom the Gentiles drew near, it is very notorious that to-
day also we have (and we of this unknown North America
know it) our very grand and Catholic monarch Philip to whom
these innumerable Gentiles come.

May the sovereign Lord of the heavens preserve the life
of your royal Majesty many happy years.   Mission of Nuestra
Señora de los Dolores, February 2, 1710.

The sacred feet of your royal Majesty are kissed by your
humble chaplain,

EUSEBIO FRANCISCO KINO.

Report and relation of the new conversions of this North America[1]
*which comprise more than two hundred leagues of fertile
country, and extend to the recently discovered land route*[2] *to
California, which is not an island but a peninsula, and is
very populous, and to the very large Río Colorado, which is
the true Río del Norte of the ancients; with new maps of
these nations and of this North America, which hitherto has
been regarded as unknown. Likewise, of the very great advantage to both Majesties which even at small cost to the royal
treasury can be secured by sending father laborers in the royal
service to these new conversions, in which, in the opinion of
prudent persons, can be formed a new kingdom, which can
be called Kingdom of New Navarre.*

*By Father Eusevio Francisco Kino, of the Company of Jesus,
missionary for more than twenty-five years in the missions of
California and these new missions and conversions of this
province of Sonora.*

BOOK I.

Of the Motives for writing this Report and Relation.[3]

FOR days and years many persons have asked of me maps,
reports, and accounts of these new conversions, and although
on various occasions I have given reports, at present they are

---

[1] That is, this part of North America.

[2] He refers to his own explorations between 1699 and 1706.

[3] In the manuscript the books are divided into chapters, with headings, in
some cases nearly as long as the text.   To save space the chapter headings
have been omitted.   Book I. is divided into five chapters.

pressing me more urgently, some of them alleging first the royal *cédula* of his Majesty, God preserve him, of July 17, 1701, which orders that report be made to him of the state of California (which has been very well done by the printed report of Father Francisco Picolo),[1] and of the "state and location of these heathen Indians of these provinces of Sonora."

In different letters our Father-General, Thyrzo Gonzalez,[2] with other superiors, has asked of me reports of all edifying incidents that might happen, and of the celestial favors of our Lord which we might experience in these new conversions, since they are always a source of comfort to our people, in Europe especially, and of edification to those in foreign lands.

Fray Manuel de la Oyuela,[3] of the Sacred Order of the Seraphic Father San Francisco, having a little more than a year ago come from his holy convent of Guadalaxara to these provinces of Sonora and to these new conversions, to ask alms, went with me on an expedition far enough to plainly sight the land route to California from the very high hill of Santa Clara,[4] which is north of the head of the Sea of California, traversing in going and returning more than two hundred and fifty leagues of these fertile lands, among Indians so friendly, affable, and industrious that his Reverence said that in these new conquests and extensive new conversions a new kingdom could and should be founded. To this I replied that if this should come to pass I should rejoice if it were called New Navarre, in honor of the blessed land of the most glorious apostle of the Indies, San Francisco Xavier, my great patron, as other kingdoms are named New Viscaia, New Galicia, etc. Afterward, while on the way to Guadalaxara, within the last few months, his Reverence wrote me that if I did not make report of the ripeness of so great a harvest of souls an account of them would be required of me in the tribunal of God.

[1] Missionary in California, who took Kino's place there. He wrote a well-known report on the missions of Lower California in 1702, published in *Lettres Édifiantes*.

[2] Father Tirso González, general of the Jesuits from 1687 to 1705.

[3] Father Oyuela accompanied Kino on the expedition of 1706. "Favores Celestiales," part IV., bk. IV.

[4] A mountain range west of Sonóita and near the head of the Gulf, reached by Kino several times.

Two months ago Father Juan de Hurtassen, rector of the College of Vera Cruz, wrote me the following: "My Father Eusevio Francisco Kino, from Spain persons, to whom I cannot excuse myself, are writing me, asking an exact account of the provinces which your Reverence has discovered, to what degrees of latitude and longitude they extend, the disposition of the nations, what rivers and land they comprise, especially those which slope to California from south to north, and whether California is an island or a peninsula, or which view is more probable; what reports there are of the kingdom of La Quivira, in what latitude it is found, how far it is to the land of Jesso in that region, whether any rivers run into the Sea of the North, or all empty into the Sea of California, and, in fine, everything touching this matter; for they write me that upon this matter there is now much controversy in Madrid, with a variety of opinions. If everything can be shown on a map, so much the better. I have no doubt your Reverence will take this trouble; and, as I conjecture, perhaps it will contribute to the glory of God."[1] Some three weeks ago I received a very courteous and long letter from my Father Provincial of this New Spain, Juan de Estrada, in which his Reverence, among other things, writes me the following: "In regard to your Reverence's coming to Mexico to print the map, you will be needed in that Pimería and new Christendom and catechumenical heathendom. We see that they print relations and maps of less consequence in France; and your Reverence may judge whether a map of more consequence and novelty, accompanied by some brief relation, with arguments and documents showing that the Californias are only peninsulas, will move more the eagerness of the printers of France to make the map and print the written relation. I have found out that the Father Rector, Juan de Hurtassum, asks your Reverence for those maps that they may be printed in France, whence they are asking for them and for reports of new conversions and lands, to put it all into print." Thus far the letter of my Father Provincial and the reasons for writing this brief report.

[1] This letter illustrates the lively interest taken in Kino's explorations.

Book II.

Beginnings and Progress of the New Conquests and New Conversions of the Heathendoms of this extensive Pimería and of the other neighboring New Nations.[1]

It is well known that during almost two whole centuries the royal Catholic crown of Spain has spent more than two millions and a half for new conquests and new conversions and for the extension of the Holy Evangel, and for the eternal salvation of the souls of the Californias; but it appears that, thanks be to His Divine Majesty, the blessed time is now coming when not only the conquest and conversion of the Californias is being accomplished, but also at the same time that of these other neighboring extensive lands and nations of this North America, most of which has hitherto been unknown, and when the Lord is adding to the rather poor lands of the Californias the necessary succor of these very extensive and rich lands, abundant champaigns, and fertile rivers and valleys.

The immense but very Catholic expenditures abovementioned, which the sovereign Lord always most liberally repays, have been those of the various navigations and expeditions following:

In the year 1533 Don Fernando Cortes, eleven years after having conquered Mexico, discovered California and entered into the port of Nuestra Señora de la Paz.[2]

In 1535 Don Anttonio Mendosa, first viceroy of this New Spain, sent to California General Francisco de Alarcon with twelve other high-decked ships, which, however, were all lost.[3]

In 1597 Sebastian Biscaino[4] went at his own expense to California with five religious of San Francisco.

In 1602 he went a second time at the expense of Philip the Third with three religious of Nuestra Señora del Carmen, the Count of Monte Rey being viceroy.

In 1606 there came to him a royal *cédula* that he should go

---

[1] Book II. is divided into nine chapters.

[2] Jiménez, sent out by Cortés, discovered California in 1533; Cortés attempted to found a colony on the Peninsula in 1535.

[3] Alarcón's voyage was made in 1540.   [4] Vizcaino.

to colonize at the port of Monte Rey, which, however, his death prevented.

In 1615 Captain Juan Yturbi went with one ship.

In the years 1632, 1633, and a little later, Captain Francisco de Ortega went to California a first, second, and third time.

About the year 1636 Captain Carboneli went.

In 1642 Captain Luis Cestin de Canas went, taking with him Father Jacinto Cortes, of the Company of Jesus.

In 1643 and 1644 Philip the Fourth sent Admiral Don Pedro Porter Casanate.

In 1648 and 1649 he went a second time, taking with him Father Jasinto Cortes and Father Andres Baes, of the Company of Jesus.

In 1664, at the expense of his royal Majesty, Philip the Fourth, Admiral Bernardo Bernal de Pinadero went the first time, and in 1667 he went the second time, with borrowed money.

In 1668 Captain Francisco Lusenilla went to California with two religious of San Francisco.[1]

In the years 1681, 1682, 1683, 1684, and 1685, at a cost to the royal treasury of more than half a million, by order of Don Carlos the Second, Admiral Don Ysidro de Atondo y Antillon, having built three ships, captain's ship, admiral's ship, and tender, in the Sinaloa River, went with the necessary soldiers and mariners to California; at the same time we, three missionary fathers of the Company of Jesus, went also, I going with the offices of rector of that mission and cosmographer of his Majesty. In pursuance of that enterprise[2] we were some months at the post and bay of Nuestra Señora de la Paz in latitude twenty-four degrees, and more than a year at the Real de San Bruno, in latitude twenty-six degrees, whence we went to the opposite coast and the Sea of the South, about fifty leagues' journey. We left about four hundred souls reduced. And we having come to the harbor of Matanchel, of Nueva Galicia, to supply ourselves with some things which

---

[1] For accounts of the foregoing voyages see Bancroft, *North Mexican States and Texas*, chs. VII., VIII., and authorities there cited; Venegas (Burriel), *Noticia de la California, passim.*

[2] *Empesa. i. e., empresa.*

we needed, the señor viceroy, Don Thomas, Marqués de la Laguna, sent us to meet and warn and rescue the China ship, since at the same time the Pichilingues pirates were waiting in the port of La Navidad for the ship to rob it. Meeting her within two days, thanks be to the Lord, and putting to sea with her, so that she should neither come to land nor be seen by the enemies who were in the port of La Navidad, we all arrived in safety at the port of Acapulco, leaving the pirates mocked, and our Lord having rescued four or five millions for the royal crown and his loyal vassals without loss, in reward of the very Catholic expenditures which the royal monarchy makes in honor of His Divine Majesty and for the good of countless souls.[1]

We have also seen and now see at this very same time, and in the very years and months of the expenditures for this above-mentioned enterprise of California, how God our Lord has granted the discovery of the very rich mines of the camps which they call Los Frailes, Los Álamos, and Guadalupe. These posts are opposite, near to, and on the same parallels of twenty-five and twenty-six degrees as California, which through those Catholic expenditures was intended to be conquered and is being conquered for our holy Catholic faith. The very richly laden China ship, or Philippine galleon, having unloaded, most of us went with the admiral from the port of Acapulco to the City of Mexico, where, within a few days, we having conferred in regard to the most suitable means for continuing the conquest and conversion of California, an appropriation of thirty thousand pesos[2] was assigned to us ; but the same week, when eighty thousand pesos had just come from Zacatecas, and they were about to give it to us and let us go, a ship came from Spain, which, with a most pressing order, asked five hundred thousand pesos, even though it should be borrowed, in order thereby to repay at once the damages done to a very richly laden French ship which a few years before had gone to the bottom in the Bay of Cadiz. Thereupon the conquest and conversion of California was suspended.

As soon as I knew that the conversion of coveted California

[1] Kino's own account of his experiences in California is contained in his Tercera Entrada, listed on p. 430. That document, however, is a fragment.
[2] Dollars.

was suspended, I asked and obtained from my superiors and his Excellency permission to come meanwhile to these heathen coasts nearest to and most in sight of California, to the Guaimas and Seris;[1] and I having arrived at the end of February, 1687, in this province of Sonora, and gone to Opossura to see the Father Visitor, Manuel Gonzales, his Reverence came with me to this post of heathen Pimas, as the father of Cucurpe, near by, Joseph de Aguilar, was asking of him a father for them.[2] We named the place Nuestra Señora de los Dolores. It is in thirty-two degrees and a half of latitude. We entered March 12,[3] 1687, accompanied by Father Joseph de Aguilar and his servants; and the Father Visitor returning the following day to observe Holy Week in his pueblos, I went inland two hours after his departure with said Father Joseph de Aguilar and some guides, going ten leagues beyond Nuestra Señora de los Dolores, toward the west, to the good post and valley which we named de San Ygnacio,[4] where we found even more people, although they were somewhat scattered. We returned by the north through the ranchería of Himeres,[5] which we named San Joseph, and through that of Doagibubig,[6] which we named Nuestra Señora de los Remedios, which rancherías immediately, thanks be to the Lord, we began reducing to new good pueblos, making a beginning of teaching them the Christian doctrine and prayers, by means of a good interpreter and a good native helper,[7] whom I procured from the old Pima mission of Los Ures,[8] and of the building of the churches and houses, of crops, etc.

Afterward I made other missions, or expeditions, to the north and farther to the west, and despatched friendly mes-

[1] He left Mexico City on November 20, 1686.

[2] This is the most specific explanation of the change of Father Kino's plans which I have seen.

[3] He elsewhere gives the date as the 13th. Dolores was situated on the San Miguel River, a few miles above Cupurpe. The ruins are on the hacienda of Dolores. They were visited by the editor in 1911.

[4] It still bears that name. It is over the mountains from Dolores, on the Southern Pacific Railroad. The Indian village where the mission was founded was called Caborica.

[5] Imuris, on the Southern Pacific Railroad a few miles north of San Ignacio.

[6] East of Imuris and north of Dolores.   [7] *Temastian.*

[8] On the Sonora River east of Hermosillo.

sages inviting all the heathen of these environs to receive our holy Catholic faith for their eternal salvation, in imitation of these Pimas, their relatives and countrymen. Soon many came from various parts to see me for this purpose, and we arranged for the beginning of other new missions and pueblos. There came to see and to visit us, with great comfort on our part and his, Father Manuel Gonzales. He asked and obtained, through the señor *alcalde mayor*, four additional alms from the royal chest, for four other new missions for this extensive Pimería; and four other missionary fathers came to it at the time when I dedicated this my first and capacious church of Nuestra Señora de los Dolores.[1]

Father Juan María de Salvatierra having entered in the year 1691 as visitor of these missions of Sinaloa and Sonora, his Reverence came in December from Chinipas to visit us; and, seeing in his holy visit to these new missions such fertile, abundant, and pleasant lands, valleys and rivers, he expressed the opinion that they were the richest he had seen in all the missions, to which I replied that it appeared to me also that these lands, so rich, might be the relief and support of the somewhat sterile and poor California, where we left so many souls scattered and lost and who were still asking us for holy baptism; and we planned to make every endeavor to effect the return with all possible haste to continue said conquests and conversions.[2] His Reverence, with his holy zeal, immediately, even before setting out from these Pima missions, made a very good report to his royal Majesty and his royal ministers; and, although in the beginning there were difficulties and delays, in the year 1697[3] said Father Juan María

---

[1] Father Luis Pinilla took charge of San Ignacio, Santa María Magdalena, and San Miguel del Tupo; Father Antonio Arras of San Pedro del Tubutama and San Antonio de Uquitoa; Father Pedro de Sandoval of San Lorenzo del Saric and San Antonio del Tucubabia; and Father Juan del Castillo of Cocóspera, San Lázaro, and Santa María. Most of these pueblos were farther north than Dolores. "Favores Celestiales," pt. I., bk. I., ch. 7.

[2] The most notable event of Salvatierra's visitation was his journey with Kino over the divide into the valley of the Santa Cruz River. This was the first recorded expedition into Arizona from the south since the time of Coronado. They went as far north as Tumacácori. "Favores Celestiales," pt. I., bk. II., chs. 1–2.

[3] In the meantime Kino had done great work in Pimería Alta, of which he says little in this report. In 1692 he again entered Arizona, going to the impor-

de Salvatierra, availing himself of the alms which he had secured among faithful, pious persons, obtained a license from the señor viceroy, Don Sarmiento de Valladares y Montesuma, permitting his Reverence and me to go to California. For this purpose his Reverence came from Mexico to the missions of Sinaloa and Hyaqui, provided with all that was necessary from Mocorito de Sinaloa. He informed me of his arrival, and of having accomplished the desired purpose that we two should go to California, sending me the very pleasing letter of the Father Provincial, Juan de Palacios, in regard to the matter. Thereupon I immediately reported to the Father Visitor, Horacio Polise, and set out to go to Hyaqui and our best beloved California. But, although I was going most gladly, they detained me over here as being necessary, as the Father Visitor, Horacio Polise, and the señor governor of arms and *alcalde mayor* of this province of Sonora, Don Domingo Xironsa Petriz de Cruzatt,[1] wrote me by messenger. Father Francisco María Picolo went in my place to California, and afterwards made a glorious report[2] of the good state of California, which, thanks be to our Lord, goes on being so happily conquered and converted that other better pens than mine consider and will consider it well to write of its apostolic missions.

Remaining, as I did, over here, with the sole relief and

tant village of Bac, where later he founded the mission of San Xavier, and visiting the San Pedro valley ("Favores Celestiales," pt. I., bk. II., ch. 3). In the same year he went down the Altar valley to the coast (*ibid.*, ch. 5). Next year, accompanied by Lieutenant Juan Matheo Manje, he again went to the coast and at Caborca began the building of a boat for navigating the Gulf. In the same year his church at Dolores was dedicated. In 1694 he made two or three journeys to Caborca, where he founded a mission in which he established Father Saeta. In November, 1694, he went north and discovered the Casa Grande, on the Gila River, of which he left an interesting description. By 1695 the missions had become important enough to be formed into the separate rectorate of Nuestra Señora de los Dolores, Father Marcos Antonio Kapus being first rector. In that year the Pimas revolted and destroyed the missions of the Altar valley, and Kino played an important part in quieting the Indians. As soon as this had been effected he went (1695) to Mexico City to get funds for the mainland and to urge the conversion of California. Father Salvatierra went at the same time, for the same purpose. Kino secured a promise of new missionaries, and as soon as he returned to Dolores, in May, 1696, he made new journeys northward to prepare for them.

[1] Governor of New Mexico from 1683 to 1686.   [2] See p. 435, note 1.

comfort of the hope that, availing myself of the licenses which
Father Juan Maria de Salvatierra had just brought me from
Mexico from the Father Provincial and from his Excellency, I
also was able from here to find and open a way to the same
California and to its reduction, in latitudes thirty, thirty-one,
thirty-two, thirty-three, thirty-four, thirty-five or more degrees. For this purpose I made various missions, or expeditions, to the west and to the coast of the Sea of California.
I undertook the building of a little vessel, in sections, part
here at Nuestra Señora de los Dolores and part at La Con-
cepsion de Nuestra Señora de Caborca, which is about fifteen
leagues distant from the Sea of California, and from whose
coasts flames and smokes in the Californias can be seen.
Afterwards, however, since by the divine grace, through different expeditions which I made, to the northwest in particular,
I discovered that in latitude thirty-four and one-half degrees
the Sea of California ended completely, I suspended the building of the vessel.

In general, in these twenty-one years, up to the present
time, I have made from the first pueblo of Nuestra Señora
de los Dolores more than forty expeditions to the north, west,
northwest, and southwest, of fifty, eighty, one hundred, two
hundred, and more leagues, sometimes accompanied by other
fathers, but most of the time with only my servants and with
the governors, captains, and caciques of different rancherías
or incipient pueblos from here and from the interior.

To the north and northeast I have travelled [1] on different
occasions more than one hundred and thirty leagues to Casa

---

[1] *He encontrado, i. e., entrado.* In December, 1696, and several times in
1697 Kino went to the valleys of the Santa Cruz and San Pedro and began the
founding of stock ranches to support future missions. In the fall of 1697 he went
with Captain Bernal and a guard of soldiers down the San Pedro to the Gila,
returning by San Xavier del Bac. In 1698 he went again to the Gila and returned
by way of Sonóita and Caborca. In 1699 he went northward by way of Sonóita
and along the Gila Range to the lower Gila, which he ascended to Casa Grande.
In the fall of 1699 a visit was made to San Xavier del Bac and Sonóita. In
April, 1700, he went to Bac and founded there the mission of San Xavier. In
the fall of the same year he reached the Yuma junction. In 1701 he made an
expedition with Salvatierra to the Santa Clara Mountain near the head of the
Gulf. In the fall of the same year he descended the Colorado to the Quiquimas
and crossed to the California side. In 1702 he again descended the Colorado
and reached the Gulf.

Grande, which is a building of the ancients of Montesuma, who set out from those lands when they went to found the City of Mexico, and to the Rio Grande, or Rio de Hila,[1] which issues from the confines of New Mexico through the Apachería, and comes to these our Pimas Sobaiporis, and afterwards flows more than one hundred leagues to the west by the Cocomaricopas and Yumas, until it unites with the most voluminous Colorado River, which is the true Río del Norte of the ancients. And I have penetrated to the borders and in plain sight of the Apachería, which intervenes between this extensive Pimería and the province of Moqui and Zuñi.

To the westward of New Mexico with different fathers, Father Agustín de Campo, Father Marcos Antonio Kappus, and Father Gerónimo Minutuli, I have penetrated the seventy leagues extending to the Sea of California, and far enough to get a very plain view of more than twenty-five leagues of continuous land of California.   And now they have their missions well founded: Father Agustín de Campos at San Ignacio, San Joseph de Himires, and Santa Maria Madalena; and Father Gerónimo Minutuli at San Pedro y San Pablo del Tubutama, Santa Tereza, and San Antonio del Uquitoa. Besides, there are good beginnings of baptisms, building of churches and houses, cattle, sheep and goats, horses, sowings and harvests of wheat, maize, beans, etc., in the new pueblo of Nuestro Señora de la Conzepzion del Caborca, at San Antonio de Busanic, and in other parts.

To the northwest I have travelled more than two hundred leagues, to the head of the Sea of California, where enters the very voluminous, populous, and fertile Colorado River, which is the true Río del Norte of the ancients, and the river which Francis Drake and his followers called del Coral, as he calls the other, the Hila River,[2] which issues through the borders of this Pimeria, the Tizon River.

It is true that on its banks and in its vicinity it has many fire-brands,[3] which the natives in cold weather carry in their hands, warming the pit of the stomach to relieve their nakedness.   At eight or nine in the morning, when the sun usually warms up a little, they throw them away, of which I have been an eye-witness.   But Drake is very much in error in

[1] Gila.   [2] Gila.   [3] *Tizones.*

his fabulous demarkation, in which he very wrongly depicts California as an island, saying that its sea extends up to the Sea of the North and the much talked of Strait of Anian, for in these ten years, in fourteen expeditions which I made for this purpose, we have plainly discovered that this Sea of California extends no farther than to thirty-four degrees and a half of latitude, where there is plainly a passage to California. By it there continually come to us many of those blue shells[1] which are produced only on the opposite coast of the above-mentioned California and South Sea, whereby every year the ship from China is accustomed to come.

On one of these journeys to the northwest Father Adamo Jilg went with me to the Huma[2] nation, by order of the Father Visitor Horasio Polise;[3] and Father Juan María de Salvatierra, who since has been most deservedly Father Provincial of this Province of New Spain, went to San Marcelo del Sonoydag, and far enough to catch a sight of the closing of these their lands at the head of the Sea of California.[4] Father Manuel Gonzales went with me to the very mouth of the large Colorado River;[5] and only a year and a half ago Fray Manuel de la Oyuela, of the Sacred Order of San Francisco, went with me to the very high hill of Santa Clara,[6] which is exactly north[7] of the head of the Sea of California, and from which it is seen most plainly that this sea ascends no higher up, and that California has a continental connection with this mainland of New Spain. Of the truth of this his Reverence, with Ensign Juan Mateo Ramires and Commander Juan Duran, gave me a sworn certificate.

From two other journeys which I made, one to the north and the other to the west, it came about that more than twenty governors and captains of this extensive Pimería came

[1] In 1699, while on the Gila above the Yuma junction, Kino was given a present of some blue shells, which became the inspiration for a new series of explorations. He reasoned that if these shells came from the Pacific Ocean, there must be land connection with California. With this conviction, he made his journeys of 1701 and 1702.

[2] Yuma.

[3] Father Gilg went on the expedition of February and March, 1699.

[4] In 1701. They went to the seacoast west of Sonóita.

[5] In 1702.   [6] In 1706.

[7] It is considerably south of east from the very head of the Gulf.

from fifty, seventy, ninety, and more than one hundred leagues'
journey to this pueblo of Nuestra Señora de los Dolores to
ask of me fathers and holy baptism for all the people of their
rancherías. And, I having suggested to them that those
fathers must be asked from the Father Visitor, who was
about one hundred leagues from here, they asked me to give
them guides to go with them, that they might go there to ask
the means for their salvation; so I had to go with them for
that purpose as far as Santa Maria de Baseraca,[1] ninety-six
leagues beyond, to see the Father Visitor, Horacio Police,
who, particularly since then, has always been most sym-
pathetic toward and fond of these new conversions. He consoled them as best he could, receiving them with all affection,
promising them that he would do his very best to secure for
them the necessary missionary fathers desired, and they asked
them from Mexico of the Father Provincial, Juan de Palacios.
In his new and large church of Santa Maria de Baseraca the
Father Visitor catechised and baptized one of the captains,
who was named Marcos, after his godfather, the governor of
Baseraca, and who aided us generously, particularly in all the
environs of his incipient pueblo of San Ambrosio del Busanic.

The Father Visitor, Horacio Polise, in thanksgiving for the
comfort which he felt in the coming of so many new people,
although it was in October, chanted a solemn mass to the
three holy kings, who were the first to see and recognize and
adore the Redeemer of the world;[2] for some of them came
more than two hundred leagues, and, with as many more
which they had to travel in return to their homes, the distance
was more than four hundred. His Reverence wrote to the
señor governor of the arms of this province that he also ought
to try to inform himself of the good state of this Pima nation,
since if it were promoted it would be very advantageous for
everything, and especially to restrain the enemies of this
province of Sonora, the Hocomes and Apaches. His Lordship therefore sent twenty-two soldiers to Quiburi,[3] whither
we went and found Captain Coro, who with his people was
dancing over the scalps of some hostile Hocomes whom he had
killed a little while before.[4]

---

[1] This was in 1697.   [2] *Primitiæ Gentium.*
[3] In 1697 under Captain Bernal.
[4] Quiburi was in the San Pedro valley near the present Mexican border.

On this occasion, when I made a mission, or journey, to the neighboring Pimas Sobaiporis, and met the twenty-two soldiers and their captain, Christoval Martin Bernal, since it was said that in the interior there were horses stolen from this province of Sonora, and since I knew the contrary to be the fact, and that not these Pimas but the Hocomes, Apaches, and Janos were the ones who were committing these injuries, stealing horses from this province and its frontiers, I took them with me, that they might become eye-witnesses to the very friendly and good state of all these Pimas Sobaiporis. Their principal cacique and captain, called Aumaric [Humaric],[1] had come with his two sons two years before to Nuestra Señora de los Dolores to be catechised and baptized, and he was named Francisco; and his elder son was named Francisco Xavier, and the other son Horasio Polise.

We entered together from Santa Ana de Quibori by the valley and river of San Joseph de Terrenate,[2] Captain Coro also accompanying us. We arrived by the same river at the very pleasant valley of the Pimas Sobaipuris, and at the Rio Grande de Hila, the above-mentioned Captain Francisco Humari coming more than thirty leagues to meet and receive us, with his two sons, one of whom was governor and the other alcalde of his great ranchería of San Fernando. In no place did we find the least trace of horses stolen from this province of Sonora. Everywhere they received us with crosses and with arches erected on the roads, and with various gifts, and with their many viands. By the Hila River we descended more than forty leagues farther to the west, to the Casa Grande and to La Encarnacion del Tusconimo,[3] where we were received with much joy on his part and on ours, with many crosses and with many arches placed on the roads, by the captain of that great ranchería, who was called Juan de Palasios, for we had given him this name of the actual Father Provincial at his baptism, he being one of those who two months before had gone to Santa Maria de Baseraca to see the Father Visitor Horacio Polise.

Afterwards we returned by the extensive valley of the other Pimas Sobaiporis to the west, namely, San Francisco Xavier del Baac of the Rio de Santa María;[4] and coming by

[1] From near the Gila River.
[2] The San Pedro.
[3] Villages on the Gila near Casa Grande.
[4] The Santa Cruz.

San Caietano, San Gabriel de Guebavi,[1] San Luiz de Bacoancos, and Santiago de Cocospera, to this pueblo of Nuestra Señora de los Dolores, we went also to the neighboring pueblos of Cucurpe and Toape, where was found Father Melchor Bartiromo.

Hearing that we had found those more than seven thousand Pima Sobaiporis so friendly, and disposed to receive our holy Catholic faith, and without the very least trace of hostilities, or of having stolen horses, and that in almost all places they received us with arches and with crosses placed on the roads, and with their many provisions, and that they had given us more than seventy little ones to baptize, and that we had given more than sixty staffs of office to justices, governors, captains, alcaldes, fiscales, constables,[2] etc., and that the principal captain of these natives, Humaric, had come more than thirty leagues to meet and receive us, said Father Melchor de Bartiromo chanted another solemn mass at Toape to Nuestra Señora de la Concepcion, in thanksgiving for so happy a result and for the great ripeness of that harvest of so many souls.

In all the more than forty journeys or missions which I made into the interior, through the teaching of the Christian doctrine and the love and fear of God, in order that the poor natives may arrive at eternal good fortune and escape from the eternal fires, and through the charitable, paternal, and good treatment which according to our holy institute we have attempted to give these poor Indians, they have always given me many little ones to baptize. In the first journey or mission, which, coming from the Rio Grande, from the north to the south, I made to these coasts of the Sea of California,[3] where they never had seen any white face or Spanish person in the eighty leagues of coast which I travelled, more than five thousand Indians being reduced, they gave me four hundred and thirty-five infants to baptize in the great rancheria alone which we named San Francisco.[4] On the 4th

---

[1] In the Santa Cruz valley, a few miles northeast of Nogales. The ruins of the mission founded by Kino were still visible in 1911, and were seen by the present writer. San Cayetano and San Luis de Bacoancos were both in the Santa Cruz valley, with Guebavi between them.

[2] *Topiles.*   [3] That of 1698.   [4] San Francisco del Adid.

of October, after mass, they gave me one hundred and two little ones to baptize; and in the afternoon, at the neighboring ranchería which followed it, and which we named San Serafin, they gave me sixty others. When two years afterwards the Father Visitor, Anttonio Leal,[1] in his holy and apostolic visit, penetrated, with Father Francisco Gonzalvo and me, more than eighty leagues northward and went as far as San Francisco Xavier del Baac of the Sobaiporis, and as far as San Augustín,[2] and returned by the westward, he arrived at San Serafin and San Francisco, solemnizing several baptisms in different places, greatly consoling and edifying all this extensive Pimería and its neighboring nations; and at San Serafin and San Francisco the little ones whom I had previously baptized received his Reverence with their little crosses in their hands, a great number of which were afterwards collected, some being given to the Father Visitor and others to me. Those which they gave me I took to Nuestra Señora de los Dolores. The Father Visitor, with his paternal holy zeal, was captivated by, and looked always with his very warm love and affection upon these new conversions and these holy new Pima missions; and having visited this one of Nuestra Señora de los Dolores, that of San Ygnacio, and that of San Pedro y San Pablo del Tubutama, he aided us to secure some fathers for the rest.[3]

With all these expeditions or missions which have been made to a distance of two hundred leagues in these new heathendoms in these twenty-one years, there have been brought to our friendship and to the desire of receiving our holy Catholic faith, between Pimas, Cocomaricopas, Yumas, Quiquimas,[4] etc., more than thirty thousand souls, there being sixteen thou-

---

[1] In 1699.

[2] San Agustin del Oyaut, north of where Tucson now stands. Across the river and farther south was San Cosme del Tucson.

[3] They came in 1701. Father Juan de San Martín took charge of the mission of Guebavi, with San Cayetano and San Luis as *visitas*; Father Francisco González took charge of San Xavier del Bac; Father Ygnacio de Yturmende went to Tubutama, and Father Gaspar de los Barrilas went to Caborca. "Favores Celestiales," pt. II., bk. II., ch. 13. Bancroft maintains that there were no resident missionaries in Arizona in Kino's day, but this shows that he was mistaken.

[4] The three tribes last named were all Yuman, living on the lower Colorado and the lower Gila rivers. See Hodge, *Handbook*, under the respective names.

sand of Pimas alone. I have solemnized more than four
thousand baptisms, and I could have baptized ten or twelve
thousand Indians more if the lack of father laborers had not
rendered it impossible for us to catechise them and instruct
them in advance.[1] But if our Lord sends, by means of his
royal Majesty and of the superiors, the necessary fathers for
so great and so ripe a harvest of souls, it will not be difficult,
God willing, to achieve the holy baptism of all these souls
and of very many others, on the very populous Colorado
River, as well as in California Alta, and at thirty-five degrees
latitude and thereabouts, for this very great Colorado River
has its origin at fifty-two degrees latitude.[2]

And here I answer the question asked of me in the letter
of the Father Rector Juan Hurtasum,[3] as to whether some
rivers run into the North Sea or all empty into the Sea of
California, by saying that as this Colorado River, which is the
Rio del Norte of the ancients, carries so much water, it must
be that it comes from a high and remote land, as is the case
with the other large-volumed rivers of all the world and
terraqueous globe; therefore the other rivers of the land of
fifty-two degrees latitude probably have their slope toward
the Sea of the North, where Husson[4] wintered. Some more
information can be drawn from the maps which I add to this
report; and in order not to violate the brevity which I promised herein, I will add only that in regard to the fourteen
journeys for two hundred leagues to the northwest, I have
written a little treatise of about twenty-five sheets which is
entitled "Cosmographical Proof that California is not an
Island but a Peninsula,"[5] etc.; and that of these new discoveries and new conversions in general, by order of our Father-
General, Thirso Gonzales, I am writing another and more
extensive treatise, with maps, of which more than one hundred sheets are already written. By suggestion of his Reverence it is entitled "Celestial Favors of Jesus Our Lord, and of
Mary Most Holy, and of the most Glorious Apostle of the

---

[1] Ortega, and others who follow him, state that Kino baptized more than
forty thousand Indians. This is the result of adding a cipher to Kino's own
figures, which he more than once gives as four thousand.

[2] In reality, about 43° 20′ N.   [3] See page 436.   [4] Hudson.

[5] So far as the editor knows, this is not extant.

Indies, San Francisco Xavier, experienced in the New Conversions of these New Nations of these New Heathendoms of
this North America." [1]

Book III.

*Of the very great Advantage to both Majesties which can be secured
by the Promotion of these New Conquests and Conversions,
on account of the many great Benefits and Utilities which they
promise.* [2]

For many years this province of Sonora has suffered very
much from its avowed enemies, the Hocomes, Janos, and
Apaches,[3] through continual thefts of horses and cattle, and
murders of Christian Indians and Spaniards, etc., injuries
which in many years not even the two expensive presidios,
that of Janos[4] and that of this province of Sonora, have been
able to remedy completely, for still these enemies continue to
infest, as always, all this province of Sonora, with their accustomed murders and robberies and their very notorious
and continual hostilities. They have already reached and
they now go as far as Acenoquipe, in the Valley of Sonora
itself; and as far as Tuape in the Valley of Opodepe;[5] and
as far as San Ygnacio and Santa María Magdalena in this
Pimería.

But, by founding very good missions for them in these
new conquests and conversions, particularly in the good
eastern valley of the great valley of Santa Ana de Hiburi,[6]
where Captain Coro is at present,[7] who already is a Christian
and is called Anttonio Leal, a great restraint can be placed
upon these enemies, who are accustomed to live in the neighboring sierras of Chiguicagui; and by fortifying for said Captain Coro his great ranchería for a new pueblo, as shortly,
God willing, we shall fortify him for the protection of Santa

---

[1] See the titles listed on page 432.
[2] Book III. is divided into twelve chapters.
[3] Tribes living in general to the northeast of Dolores.
[4] Janos is in northern Chihuahua.
[5] Tuape and Opodepe were in the San Miguel River valley, south of Dolores.
[6] Quiburi. The San Pedro valley in Arizona is meant.
[7] The principal Indian chieftain of that region.

María Baseraca, he will continue better his accustomed expeditions against these enemies; and he will be able to chastise them, as he is accustomed to do, winning very good victories, as always, and even much greater, for the total relief of this province of Sonora, just as when a few years ago[1] he killed at one blow more than two hundred of those enemies, and as four months ago, in the expedition which he made in pursuit of those who were carrying off cattle and horses from the Real de Bacanuche,[2] he killed fifteen adult enemies and carried off ten little prisoners. One of them I have here in my house. One of them, having baptized and catechised them, I named Joan Miguel, which are the names of our Father-General and of the Provincial; the other I named Phelipe, in honor of our very Catholic monarch, God save him.

The promotion of these new conversions will serve also for the advancement, good government, and good administration of the many more missions which can be founded farther on, for there are prudent and weighty persons, zealous for the service of the Majesties, who are of the opinion that in these more than two hundred leagues of new rich lands, inhabited by Indians industrious and newly conquered and reduced, a new kingdom can with ease be founded, which can be called New Navarre, as others are called New Viscaia, New Galisia, New Kingdom of Leon, etc.

By promoting the new conversions of this extensive Pimería, with the favor of Heaven we shall be able shortly to enter upon the reduction and conversion of the neighboring Apachería,[3] which lies to the north and northeast of us, and extends northwest to the very large Colorado River, or Rio del Norte, above the thirty-fifth, thirty-sixth, and thirty-seventh degrees of latitude and beyond, for we know that it flows from northeast to southwest and issues about ten leagues west of the province of Moqui;[4] for, we having sent messages to those natives up the Colorado River, already they invite us to enter to see them, and already they give us certain reports that soon, in imitation of the rest over here, they will

---

[1] In 1698. See list of Kino's writings, no. 8, on p. 431, above.

[2] A mining camp in the Sonora River valley east of Dolores, and north of Arispe.

[3] The whole body of Apaches.   [4] The Hopi, in northeastern Arizona.

become reduced to our friendship and to the desire of receiving our holy Catholic faith.

By way of the same Apachería, which is in thirty-two degrees latitude, we shall be able, with the divine grace, to enter to trade with New Mexico and with its nearest provinces, Moqui and Zuñi, for on an average it is not more than forty or fifty leagues, which is the distance at thirty-four degrees latitude, where live our already well-subdued and domestic Pimas Sobaiporis of San Fernando, the most remote, at the junction of the rivers Hila and San Joseph de Terrenate, or de Quiburi; at latitude thirty-six degrees, where are the provinces of Moqui and Zuñi; and as far as thirty-seven degrees, in which is found the Villa of Santa Fé of New Mexico; for we have also certain reports that before the revolt of New Mexico[1] the Spaniards of those provinces used to come by way of Apachería to these our most remote Pimas Sobaiporis to barter hatchets, cloth, sackcloth, blankets, *chomite*, knives, etc., for maize.

With the promotion of these new conversions not only will the Christian settlements already formed, new and old, have more protection, and be defended by them, as has been suggested, but at the same time a way will be opened to many other new conquests and new conversions, in many other more remote new lands and nations of this still somewhat unknown North America: as for example, to the northward, to the Gran Teguayo; to the northwest, to the Gran Quibira;[2] and to the west, to California Alta, of this our same latitude of thirty-four, thirty-five, thirty-six degrees, and farther, and to its opposite coast and the South Sea; and to its great Bay of the Eleven Thousand Virgins;[3] to the famous port of Monte Rey, which is in neighboring and fertile lands (and a royal *cédula* came to Sebastian Biscaino that he should go to colonize it), and to the very renowned Cape Mendozino.

[1] The Pueblo uprising in New Mexico in 1680.

[2] Gran Teguayo and Gran Quivira were two geographical names which persisted in Spanish-American geography until the nineteenth century. They were always assigned to regions northward of New Mexico, but were variously shifted about by different writers and map-makers. See indexes of Bancroft, *Arizona and New Mexico*; Bancroft, *History of the Northwest Coast*, II.; Bancroft, *North Mexican States and Texas*, II.

[3] Port San Quentín. See Vizcaino documents, pp. 73-76, above.

At the same time, after having entered to Moqui and New Mexico, to the northwest and the east, it will be possible to have communication with New France, and with the new conquests, conversions, and missions which at present they are making with their glorious and apostolic journeys from east to west. And if we enter to the north and northeast, and afterwards turn to the east, it will be possible to open a way to Europe from these new conquests and conversions of this North America where we are, only half as long as the road which we now have and are accustomed to travel, by way of the City of Mexico and the Port of Vera Cruz; for if the one road is much more than two thousand leagues, the other will be little more than a thousand.[1]

Just as to the northeast and east of this North America we shall be able to have a shorter road to Europe, in the same way we shall be able to have by the northwest and the west a convenient land route to Asia, and to Great Tartary and to Great China, since to the westward of Cape Mendocino and connected therewith follows the land of Jesso; afterwards comes the land which they call Tierra de la Compañia (may our Lord grant that some day it may be of the Company of Jesus and converted to our holy Catholic faith) and the land nearest to Japan; and afterward the narrow Strait of Anian, which is no more than ten or twelve leagues across, and has the convenience of an island in the middle by which to pass to Great Tartary, and from there to Great China. For lately the very learned author of the very curious New Geographic Mirror,[2] Don Pedro de Mendosa, gentleman of the Order of Calatrabe,[3] notes that a few years ago Father Grimaldi, of our Company, having gone from Great China to Great Tartary, near those places and countries, learned that the sea, where I know that the Strait of Anian enters, was no farther distant than forty days' journey. And it is patent that there is no other Strait of Anian than this which I here mention, for although Drake, in order to carry his point that California was an island, would feign another Strait of Anian with another much-talked-of Sea of the North over here above California,

---

[1] To open a northeastern route to Europe by way of the northern interior had long been contemplated.

[2] *Nuevo Espejo Geográfico.*   [3] Calatrava.

and that he had turned back from his navigation, yet it is all false.

Another great advantage of much value to both Majesties will be that these new conversions and this province of Sonora and all the kingdom of Nueva Biscaia, by way of the Rio Grande, or Hila, which is that of El Tison, and by the land route to California will be able to provide a port of call to the China ship,[1] and trade with her, and succor with fresh food persons sick with the very painful disease of scurvy which she is accustomed to bring with her, originating from their salt, dry, and stale food, and all with very great advantages and gains for all, obviating the very long and costly transportation of many of their goods from these latitudes above thirty degrees to the port of Acapulco and from Acapulco to Mexico, and to these provinces of Nueva Biscaya, etc. And this port of call, with all due deference to the navigators of the China ship, it appears, might be at the Bay of Todos Santos, or at the famous neighboring port of San Diego of the opposite coast, which are at about the same latitude (though a little below) as the passage by land to California, that is, at thirty-five degrees.

There are royal *cédulas* and royal provisions which charge us to report the new heathendoms, and happily we shall comply with them if we try to secure, as is so just, the promotion of these new conversions. The new royal *cédula* of our very Christian, very Catholic monarch, Philip the Fifth, God save him many happy years, of July 17, 1701, orders that report be made to him not only of the state of the new conversions of California, which already has been very well executed in the exact printed report by Father Francisco María Picolo, but "also of the location and state of the uncivilized heathen Indians of this province of Sonora."

And the royal *cédula* of his immediate predecessor, Don Carlos the Second, God rest his soul, charges the same, as given me by the royal Audiencia of Guadalaxara inserted in my royal provision when twenty-one years ago I came from California and from Mexico to these new conversions of this extensive Pimería. It is dated at Buen Retiro, May 4, 1686. With this royal *cédula* his royal Majesty relieves his conscience, and

[1] The Manila galleon.

that of the royal council, by charging the consciences of those of us who live over here near and bordering upon these heathen nations in order to seek the means for the eternal salvation of so many souls in this North America who live in such helplessness and even neglect, as the royal *cédula* expresses it, as hitherto has been unknown, in a matter so very essential, and by commanding that all the time possible be gained for him therein without sparing expense, since it is plainly recognized that our Lord always repays well known and very much augmented increase to the royal crown.   All these are words from the royal *cédula*.[1]

It is plain, moreover, that by the Catholic promotion of these new conquests and conversions, or the new kingdoms of this New Navarre, the Catholic empire of the Catholic royal crown and of our holy mother, the Roman Catholic Church, is happily extended, so that happily all the world may be one fold with one shepherd,[2] and this, by the divine grace, without great expenditure from the royal chests, and with only the accustomed alms for the missionary fathers, because the natives are so reduced and so domestic that they themselves, even without the expense of sustaining soldiers, are able to inflict and do inflict very exemplary punishment of whatever evil, crime, theft, adultery, or murder which may or is accustomed to happen.

At the same time we hope, God willing, that by means of our superiors over here in Mexico, and those in Madrid and Rome, we shall bring it about that his Holiness will grant to all the benefactors and promoters of these new conquests and new conversions some very favorable indulgences, and fullest rejoicing[3] in life and for the hour of death ; and that also his royal Majesty, God save him for many years, will be pleased to honor the benefactors and promoters with immunities, privileges, and exemptions, from his royal magnificence and magnanimous liberality.   And perhaps of these benefactors there

---

[1] This *cédula* is quoted in full in "Favores Celestiales," pt. I., bk. I., ch. 2. The date is given there as May 14, 1689.   Kino does not here quote exactly, but only in substance.

[2] *Utt (i. e.) ut fiat unum ovile et unus pastor.   Cf.* John x. 16.

[3] *Jubileos plenisimos.*

may be founded a pious congregation of Mary Most Holy and of the Twelve Disciples, as it is said there is one in Peru.

If we continue with the promotion and advancement of these new conversions, we shall be able to continue to make correct maps of this North America, the greater part of which has hitherto been unknown, or practically unknown, for some ancients blot the map with so many and such errors and with such unreal grandeurs and feigned riches as a crowned king whom they carry in chairs of gold, with walled cities, lakes of quicksilver, of gold, of amber, and of corals. With reason Father Mariana rebukes them for deceiving us with these riches which do not exist. They do not say a word about the principal riches that exist there, which are the innumerable souls redeemed by the most precious blood of our Redeemer, Jesus Christ, and these accompanied by the very abundant conveniences and temporal means, utilities, facilities, and opportunities which immediately and without any fiction I shall mention in this fourth part of this report.

Book IV.

Of the many Temporal Means, Facilities, and Opportunities, which Our Lord offers and gives in these new Conversions in order to be able to secure this great Advantage for both Majesties.[1]

The greater the means the greater our obligation to seek the salvation of so many souls in the very fertile and pleasant lands and valleys of these new conquests and conversions. There are already very rich and abundant fields, plantings and crops of wheat, maize, frijoles, chick-peas, beans, lentils, bastard chick-peas, etc. There are good gardens, and in them vineyards for wine for masses, with reed-brakes of sweet cane for syrup and *panocha*,[2] and, with the favor of Heaven, before long for sugar. There are many Castilian fruit trees, as fig-trees, quinces, oranges, pomegranates, peaches,

---

[1] Book IV. contains fifteen chapters.
[2] A sort of candy made by boiling cane sap.

apricots, pear-trees, apples, mulberries, pecans, prickly pears, etc., with all sorts of garden stuff, such as cabbages, melons, watermelons, white cabbage, lettuce, onions, leeks, garlic, anise, pepper, mustard, mint, Castilian roses, white lilies, etc., with very good timber for all kinds of building, such as pine, ash, cypress, walnut, china-trees, mesquite, alders, poplar, willow, tamarind, etc.

Another temporal means which our Lord gives us for the promotion of these new conquests are the plentiful ranches which are already stocked with cattle, sheep, and goats, many droves of mares, horses, sumpters, mules as well as horses, pack animals necessary for transportation and commerce,[1] with very rich and abundant pastures all the year to raise very fat sheep, producing much tallow, suet, and soap, which already is made in abundance.

The climate of most of these new lands and new conquests where the promotion of these new conversions is asked, is very good and pleasant, and somewhat similar to that of Mexico and to the best of Europe, with neither too great heat nor too great cold.

In these new nations and new lands there are many good veins and mineral lands bearing gold and silver; and in the neighborhood and even in sight of these new missions and new conversions some very good new mining camps of very rich silver ore are now being established.

The natives of these new conquests and new nations are industrious Indians, who are docile, affable, and very friendly, and at the same time warlike and valiant, able to defend themselves against their enemies and to fight against our adversaries the enemies of this province of Sonora, for these our Pimas defend themselves very well, better than any other nation whatsoever, against the warlike Apaches, and their allies, the Hocomes, Janos, etc.; and they continually win very good victories over them, even with notable relief to this province of Sonora, taking away from them at times their prisoners and stolen articles.

---

[1] In the last years of the seventeenth century Kino established several stock ranches in the Santa Cruz and San Pedro valleys to supply the missions projected. Farther south he and his associates established many more ranches.

These natives, particularly those of this extensive Pimería, have very good fabrics of cotton and of wool; also many nicely made baskets, like hampers, of different sizes, many colored macaw feathers, many deer and buffalo hides, and toward the sea coast much bezoar, and the efficacious *contrayerba*,[1] and in many parts the important medicinal fruit called the *jojoba*.[2]

On this coast of the Sea of California, or Californian Gulf, of these new conquests, we have very good salt beds, of white as well as rock salt; and there are inlets and posts very suitable for fishing for all sorts of very savory fish, shrimps, oysters, etc.

All these nations, not only those of this extensive Pimería, but also those of the neighboring Cocomaricopas, Yumas, Quiquimas, etc., all the year continually come to see me from fifty, seventy, one hundred, one hundred and fifty and more leagues from the interior. Others from even more remote parts have sent very friendly messages and gifts, among them blue shells[3] from the opposite coast and South Sea, and they ask me to go to see them and baptize them, and to secure for them missionary fathers who may go to minister to them.

Not only do these natives come so many leagues to this my pueblo of Nuestra Señora de los Dolores to ask of me the succor of the missionary fathers whom they need, but as I cannot give them and do not secure for them, many of the governors, captains and caciques, after having come from the north, northwest, west, etc., fifty, seventy, one hundred, and more leagues, go and have gone many times to see the father visitors and father rectors and *alcaldes mayores* and their deputies, to the valley of Sonora, to the Real de San Juan, and to Oposura.[4] Sometimes they have gone to the valley of Santa Maria de Baseraca, which is about one hundred leagues distant from here. Last year during the journey and visit of

---

[1] *Dorstenia contrayerba*, a medical plant.

[2] "American fruit, similar to judías [*phaseolus vulgaris*], small and of the color of a chestnut. The inside is white and bitter but pleasing to the taste. It is used as a digestive" (*Diccionario Salvat*).

[3] See p. 445, note 1.

[4] San Juan and Oposura are both on the upper water of the Yaqui River, southeast of the Arispe.

the Father Visitor, Francisco María Piccolo, to this Pimería, more than thirty governors, captains, alcaldes, fiscals, etc., came from the interior, all on horseback. As his Reverence had just set out from this Pimería, all went, and I with them, to overtake his Reverence as far as Cucurpe, where he promised them that the necessary fathers, for whom they very anxiously prayed, should come to them. Up to the present they have not arrived, perhaps because there has not been in Mexico, as has been written me, means with which to equip them ; but at present two pious persons offer to send from here the necessary equipment for two or three fathers. May our Lord bring them !

Another of the advantages and means which here facilitate the desired service of both Majesties, is the fact that this Pima language which we speak here extends more than two hundred leagues into the interior, even among the other and distinct nations of the Cocomaricopas, Yumas, and Quiquimas, for in all places are found intermingled some natives who speak both languages, that of the nation where they are and our Pima tongue, and therefore everywhere we have plenty of good interpreters, both men and women, for the reduction and teaching of all, and to explain to them promptly the Christian doctrine and the mysteries of our holy Catholic faith.

In all these new conquests and new people where we have travelled they have no particular idolatry or doctrine which it will be especially difficult to eradicate, nor polygamy, nor *ponios* as in Japan and in Great China, and although they greatly venerate the sun as a remarkable thing, with ease one preaches to them, and they comprehend the teaching that God Most High is the All-Powerful and He who created the sun, the moon, and the stars, and all men, and all the world, and all its creatures.

In these new conversions the natives have, even far in the interior, as is the case of Nuestra Señora de la Consepcion del Caborca, forty-six leagues to the westward, in San Ambrosio del Busanic, thirty-seven leagues to the northwest, and in San Francisco Xavier del Bac, sixty leagues to the north, pueblos or missions begun, with good beginnings of instruction in the Christian doctrine and in prayer.[1]   In these places there are *temastianes*, or teachers of the doctrine, and many infants and some adults have been baptized.   They have their cabildos of justices, governors, captains, alcaldes, fiscales, and their *topiles, alguaciles*, etc.   They have good beginnings of houses for the comfortable living of the fathers whom they hope to receive, and of churches, fields of wheat, maize and beans, cattle, sheep and goats, horses and mules, droves of mares and of horses, and beginnings of gardens, all of which the very domestic and loyal natives tend, as if the fathers whom they pray and beg for and hope and deserve to receive were already living there.

This first mission, or district, or pueblo, of Nuestra Señora de los Dolores, is actually arranging for and delivering a decent equipment for founding the new mission of Santa María de Bagota, which is twenty-two leagues from here toward the north, that is, new vestments with which to say mass, three hundred head of cattle for their ranch, one hundred head of sheep and goats, a drove of mares, a drove of horses, a house in which to live, the beginnings of a church, with provisions and the necessary furnishings for a house, and the beginnings of sowings and crops of wheat, maize, etc.   Almost as much was given, to the value of three thousand pesos, from the stock of Nuestra Señora de los Dolores, a few years ago, for the founding and equipment of the mission of San Ignacio ; and other like aid this and other missions of these new conquests and new conversions will be able to give in time.

The promotion of these new conversions and the service of both Majesties which is hoped for in them is greatly facilitated by the fact that different benefactors, missionary fathers of the old missions of the Company of Jesus, as well as secular gentlemen, promise very good aid in the form of cattle, sheep and goats, horses, clothing, fabrics or garments, provisions, and some silver, to aid the new missionary fathers who may come to these new conversions to found new missions, for their churches and houses, the value already amounting to more than twenty thousand pesos.   One person alone offers

---

[1] From this, as from other data, it is inferred that there was now no resident missionary at San Xavier.

five thousand in suitable goods, with some silver, for the
founding and for the church, house, and fortification of the
settlement or great mission of Santa Ana de Quibori, where
Captain Coro lives; because it is notorious that those his
natives will be able to continue to pursue the neighboring
avowed enemies, the Hocomes, Janos, and Apaches, for the
very great and total relief, or remedy, of all this province of
Sonora.

Now, in addition, at the very same time that this brief
report is asked of me and I am writing it, the Señor commissary
curate and vicar of the Real de San Juan, Don Anttonio de
Zalasar, writes me that his Illustriousness, the Most Pious
Prince of the church, the Señor Doctor Don Ygnacio Dias de
la Barrera, most meritorious Bishop of the city of Durango
and of all these provinces, has said to his Grace in the city of
Guadiana, Durango,[1] within the past few months, that he is
possessed of very Catholic and most zealous holy determina-
tion to seek, although it may be by alms, the necessary aid and
equipment for some few missionary fathers to live in and ad-
minister these new conquests and conversions. These, then,
are the opportune means which our Lord offers us to enable
us to accomplish a great service of both Majesties and the
eternal salvation of very many souls in all this most extensive
North America.

*Epilogue very suitable and so much the more because unlooked
for, in regard to the above-mentioned Means, as well as in regard to the Subject-Matter of all this Report or Relation, for
which prays the new Letter of our new Father-General,
Miguel Angel Tamburini, which has just arrived from Rome,
at these new Conversions.*[2]

More than three years ago, by order of our Father-General, Thirso Gonzales, God rest his soul, I sent to Rome a relation of the state of these new conversions, which was alto-

---

[1] Pimería Alta was under the jurisdiction of the diocese of Durango at this
time.

[2] This appears as chapter 16, book IV., in the manuscript. Father Michele
Angelo Tamburini was general of the Society of Jesus from 1706 to 1730.

gether very conformable to and uniform with a relation which the Father Visitor Orasio Polise had also made, and which the Father Rector Juan María de Salvatierra had seen, subscribed to, and approved. And now, in the most courteous, holy letter, which, having just written this present report, I have just received from our new Father-General, Miguel Angel Tamburini, his Reverence writes me, very much to our purpose, the following:

"I received with special comfort two letters from your Reverence, dated January 24 and June 30, 1704. With them comes what your Reverence calls a dedicatory for the treatise which is being perfected with the title of 'Celestial Favors Experienced in the New Conquests and New Conversions of North America.' In the letters as well as in the draft of the dedicatory, which contains the notices of the new discoveries and of their state, I find much wherein to praise the mercies of God, in those nations which are being discovered and brought to his knowledge; and our Company owes special thanks to His Divine Majesty, because He uses her sons as an instrument so greatly to His glory.

"Very much do I rejoice at the aid which your Reverence has sent and is arranging to send every year to the Californias, and at the two churches which you have built and dedicated, which have become among the best there are in the province, and that you are continuing your treatise on those missions with the title of 'Celestial Favors,' of which you have sent us hither the first part. I am hoping for the other two which your Reverence promises, and that they all may be approved in Mexico, that they may be published. All the notices which your Reverence gives me fill me with joy, and with a desire •to repay the anxieties and glorious travails of your Reverence and of your companions; but just as you have opposition there, we here regret that the war, lack of commerce, and perils of the seas keep our missionaries detained. But we all hope, with great confidence in the loving providence of God, that, since in these very contrary times He has willed to discover those new nations and to show us so many souls who wander scattered outside of His fold, it is not that we may see them perish, but to give us means and forces to bring them from their forests, and reduce them to pueblos and churches. Therefore, I pray His Divine Majesty to guard your Reverence many years, as I desire.

Your Reverence's servant in Christ,
"MIGUEL ANGEL TAMBURINI.
"Rome, Sept. 5, 1705.

INDEX

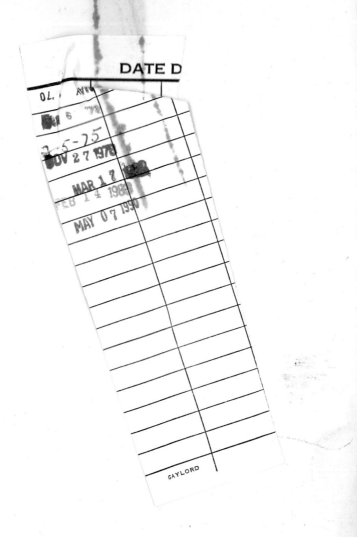